OXFORD CONSTITUTIONAL THEORY

Series Editors:
Martin Loughlin, John P. McCormick, and Neil Walker

Europe's Functional Constitution

OXFORD CONSTITUTIONAL THEORY

Series Editors:
Martin Loughlin, John P. McCormick, and Neil Walker

Oxford Constitutional Theory has rapidly established itself as the primary point of reference for theoretical reflections on the growing interest in constitutions and constitutional law in domestic, regional, and global contexts. The majority of the works published in the series are monographs that advance new understandings of their subject. But the series aims to provide a forum for further innovation in the field by also including well-conceived edited collections that bring a variety of perspectives and disciplinary approaches to bear on specific themes in constitutional thought and by publishing English translations of leading monographs in constitutional theory that have originally been written in languages other than English.

ALSO AVAILABLE IN THE SERIES

Post Sovereign Constitution Making Learning and Legitimacy
Andrew Arato

Popular Sovereignty in Early Modern Constitutional Thought
Daniel Lee

The Cultural Defense of Nations A Liberal Theory of Majority Rights
Liav Orgad

The Cosmopolitan Constitution
Alexander Somek

The Structure of Pluralism
Victor M. Muniz-Fraticelli

Constitutional Courts and Deliberative Democracy
Conrado Hübner Mendes

Fault Lines of Globalization Legal Order and the Politics of A-Legality
Hans Lindahl

The Cosmopolitan State
H. Patrick Glenn

After Public Law
Edited by Cormac Mac Amhlaigh, Claudio Michelon, and Neil Walker

The Three Branches A Comparative Model of Separation of Powers
Christoph Möllers

The Global Model of Constitutional Rights
Kai Möller

The Twilight of Constitutionalism?
Edited by Petra Dobner and Martin Loughlin

Beyond Constitutionalism The Pluralist Structure of Postnational Law
Nico Krisch

Constituting Economic and Social Rights
Katharine G. Young

Constitutional Referendums The Theory and Practice of Republican Deliberation
Stephen Tierney

Constitutional Fragments Societal Constitutionalism and Globalization
Gunther Teubner

Europe's Functional Constitution

A Theory of Constitutionalism beyond the State

Turkuler Isiksel

OXFORD
UNIVERSITY PRESS

OXFORD
UNIVERSITY PRESS

Great Clarendon Street, Oxford, OX2 6DP,
United Kingdom

Oxford University Press is a department of the University of Oxford.
It furthers the University's objective of excellence in research, scholarship,
and education by publishing worldwide. Oxford is a registered trade mark of
Oxford University Press in the UK and in certain other countries

First Edition published in 2016

Published in the United States of America by Oxford University Press
198 Madison Avenue, New York, NY 10016, United States of America

British Library Cataloguing in Publication Data
Data available

Library of Congress Control Number: 2016936899

ISBN 978–0–19–875907–2

To my family

Aileme

Preface

Speaking in early 2015, former European Commission president Jose Manuel Barroso chastised European Union (EU) scholars for wallowing in what he called the "intellectual glamour of pessimism."[1] Alas, this book's take on the EU is summed up by the glamorous pessimist intellectual who quips in the opening scene of *Annie Hall*: the food here is terrible, and the portions are too small. In the more dignified words of Claus Offe, the European project is ensnared by a contradiction: "what is urgently *needed* to be done ... is also extremely unpopular and therefore democratically, within member states as well as the EU, virtually *impossible* to carry out."[2]

The European Union is the most promising option its beleaguered member states have for tackling such pressing challenges as the ravages of global casino capitalism, the erosion of social welfare states, yawning inequality, intense economic competition, impending environmental catastrophe, and myriad threats to Europe's security. In many of these instances, however, the EU either lacks the power to respond effectively to the challenge in question, or exacerbates it due to the market-oriented and technocratic configuration of its institutions. Coordinated solutions to shared problems are more necessary than ever, but today's EU is ill-equipped to address them.

Barroso's frustration with snarky scholars who relentlessly scrutinize supranational institutions is understandable. However, critique need not be limited to criticism, and it need not be pessimistic. Appropriately calibrated, it represents scholarly engagement with and investment in the EU's effort to address the shifting challenges that confront it. The kvetchy ladies in *Annie Hall* may be caught in a comedic contradiction, but there is nothing contradictory about believing in a project and unflinchingly acknowledging its shortfalls. A vigilant desire for self-correction is preferable to a hubristic belief in the EU's infallibility.

In the former spirit, this book offers a critical reconstruction of the EU's existing legal structure, rather than a normative blueprint for what it could or should have been. To many, this will come as a disappointment: their fellow social scientists often expect political theorists to paint meticulously detailed, brightly colored utopias that they can gleefully wipe off with their hard-nosed empiricism. Utopian thought is essential to political theory, but it is not all that political theorists do.

[1] JMD Barroso, "The State of the European Union," public address delivered at Princeton University Woodrow Wilson School of Public and International Affairs, 8 April 2015. Text on file with the author.

[2] Claus Offe, *Europe Entrapped* (Polity 2015) 4. Emphasis original.

For its part, this book engages in interpretation, critique, and concept formation. Although these three modes of analysis are relevant to any social scientific inquiry, they are particularly urgent for understanding the ever-elusive EU and its present tribulations.

Like utopian thinking, critical interventions are invariably situated in a particular time and place. This book was written at a dour moment for the EU, when supranationalism is experienced less as an emancipatory project than as a hegemonic one. Having been designed to safeguard democracy, promote dialogue, and enhance solidarity both within and beyond the state, the EU seems as often to imperil those values. With any luck, by the time the reader picks up the book, the gray skies overhanging Brussels will have cleared up: the eurozone may be growing again at a respectable clip, unemployment may be declining precipitously, refugees may have stopped drowning on Europe's shores by their thousands, and Syria, Libya, and Ukraine may be at peace again. Or today's crises may have given way to bigger, as-yet unforeseeable ones. Whatever happens, however, the EU's legal system is likely to still be on the path it has trodden for decades: the path of *functional constitutionalism*. This book gives an interpretive account of the principles that frame the EU's powerful legal structure, and argues that they are inadequate—in fact, counterproductive—for sustaining a democratic union with vastly expanded responsibilities.

*

Doing slow, painstaking academic work on the EU is a Sisyphean task if there ever was one. Even harder than doing justice to the EU, however, is doing justice to the teachers, colleagues, interlocutors, and friends who have challenged, inspired, and encouraged me to write this book.

Knowing full well the futility of trying to count all the conversations from which the arguments presented in this book have benefited, I am particularly grateful for enriching exchanges with Jan Beyers, Hauke Brunkhorst, George Bustin, David Cameron, Samuel Dahan, Axel Domeyer, Michael Doyle, John Erik Fossum, Dieter Grimm, David Law, Jeffrey Lenowitz, Peter Lindseth, Jenny Mansbridge, Gary Marks, David Mayhew, Tom McCarthy, Dipali Mukhopadhyay, Andrea Pozas-Loyo, Rogers Smith, Peter Verovšek, Glyn Morgan, Jan-Werner Müller, Ira Katznelson, Andrew Moravcsik, Tonya Putnam, Jack Snyder, Thomas Streinz, Brian Taylor, and Jim Whitman.

Perhaps because this is my first book, it is difficult to distinguish between people who shaped the work and those who shaped its author. I will err in favor of the latter, and would like to express my deepest thanks to Cengiz Aktar, who commissioned a nerdy teenager to write a feature article on EU enlargement, and inexplicably published it; Elizabeth Bomberg, whose support and enthusiasm helped chart my path to graduate school; Emilios Christodoulidis, the profound questions of whose seminar gnawed at me for so long that I entitled one of this book's chapters after it; Bryan Garsten, whose generously dispensed professional advice could fill the curriculum of a school of practical wisdom; Christian Joerges, for the example of his scholarship and his long-standing encouragement of my own; the late, great Neil MacCormick, MEP, who was a walking refutation of the false choice between teaching and doing; Nicola McEwen, who wrangled an opportunity for me to work for McCormick during his stint at the Convention; John McCormick, who is not only a treasure trove of intellectual and professional guidance but to whose brilliant book on the EU the present work is at best a dim homage; Melissa Schwartzberg, whose insight steers me past many a rocky shoal; Sophie Meunier, for the precious opportunity to subject my claims to the rigors of the Princeton University EU workshop; Steven B Smith, for being an inspiring teacher, scholar, and reader of books; Alec Stone Sweet, for teaching me EU law, teaching me how to teach it, and inviting me to argue with him about it; Jim Tully and Antje Wiener for generously reading, critiquing, and encouraging successive iterations of the argument since its sketchy beginnings; Neil Walker, whose inexplicable faith in this book was reflected in his willingness to schlep over the Atlantic for just the few hours it took to attend my manuscript workshop.

Over the last few years, I have been extraordinarily fortunate for the intellectual company of my colleagues at the Columbia Political Science Department. I am particularly grateful to my fellow political theorists Jean Cohen, Jon Elster, David Johnston, Josh Simon, and Nadia Urbinati for numerous enriching conversations. In addition, the support of successive department chairs Page Fortna and John Huber allowed me to bring the draft out of the dusty recesses of my computer and to expose it to the cathartic light of a manuscript workshop.

In what is my most humbling professional moment to date, I was able to persuade a group of brilliant scholars and colleagues to participate in a discussion of the manuscript. Sheri Berman, Jean Cohen, Gráinne de Búrca, David Johnston, John McCormick, Michel Rosenfeld, Nadia Urbinati, and Neil Walker paid my work the wholly undeserved compliment of reading and critiquing it. Readers should be disappointed that what they got in the end is this book instead of a record of that splendid exchange.

In addition, I am very grateful to several institutions and programs for supporting and facilitating my research on this project from start to finish, including a Yale University Dissertation Fellowship, a John F. Enders Fellowship, and a junior faculty summer research grant from Columbia University. The drafting of the book was bookended by four incredibly stimulating scholarly sojourns. I began the process, appropriately enough, during my time as a Jean Monnet Fellow at the Robert Schuman Centre for Advanced Study at the European University Institute, a pedigree that has made me all the more anxious to "get the EU right" (if such a thing is possible). I am particularly fortunate to have had many illuminating conversations about the EU's legal system with Miguel Maduro, who hosted my stay at the EUI as a Global Governance Program fellow. I had the chance to further revise the manuscript during a year spent as a Perkins fellow at Princeton University's Law and Public Affairs Program (LAPA). For a law-engaged political theorist, LAPA might just be the happiest place on earth. I heartily thank its director, Kim Lane Scheppele, for giving me the opportunity to be a part of an invigorating intellectual environment that only she could have built. Several weeks spent at the Forschungskolleg Humanwissenschaften in Bad Homburg, together with vivifying interludes at the Freie Universität in Berlin and the Normative Orders project at Goethe Universität in Frankfurt, eased the agonizing task of finalizing the book's argument. I am grateful to Rainer Forst and Stefan Gosepath for inviting me to be a part of the Justitia Amplificata research group during this time. I put the last tortured period on the book during a semester spent as an Emile Noël fellow at the Jean Monnet Center for International and Regional Economic Law and Justice, whose director, Gráinne de Búrca, not only coached me through the hectic submission period but also celebrated the book's (near-) arrival with the kind of launch panel that I could otherwise only have dreamt of. I am grateful to the panel participants, Piet Eeckhout, Daniel Francis, Jan Klabbers, and Joseph Weiler, for giving the manuscript the stiff jousting it deserves and the lofty praise it likely does not.

Luise Papcke provided enthusiastic and marvelously detailed research assistance with musty treatises that could not possibly excite any but the most dedicated scholar. Kevin Elliott made the manuscript workshop happen, and kept a meticulous and witty record that made an otherwise arduous task *almost* entertaining. Nick Lombardi applied a law review editor's fine-toothed comb to the final draft, smoothing many snags in the process. I very much appreciate their invaluable help. I am also grateful to my editors at Oxford University Press, Elinor Shields and Alex Flatch, for fielding my innumerable queries and seeing the book through the production process.

Self-indulgent though it is to read into Hobbes's famous description of the state of nature the bleakness of graduate school, I am fortunate and grateful to have friends who break up the solitude of academic life, enrich its occasional poverty, and lighten up its brutish moments. Ana Arjona, Onur Bakıner, Sonali Chakravarti, Stephen Engel, Gülru Göker, Jennifer Green, Sinem Gürbey, Gaye Ilhan Demiryol, Stephen Kaplan, Alex Kirshner, Dominika Koter, Bahareh Lampert, Joe Lampert, Rob Person, Abbey Steele, Shatema Threadcraft, and Justin Zaremby have been steadfast friends and forgiving critics (and the other way around!). For years, Sophie Hardach inspired me with her prose, relentlessly cheered me on, tolerated my social science patois, and even helped me wrangle a sentence or two that no other novelist could forgive.

I consider myself extremely fortunate to have landed in Bruce Ackerman's classroom before I could spell "constitution." He has shepherded this project from prospectus to thesis to conclusion, made a literary genre out of marginalia, and has given me nearly enough discipline and willpower to avoid the word "governance" altogether.

It was an inexplicable piece of dumb luck and an immense privilege that I got to work on this project under the watchful eye of Seyla Benhabib. Her unfailing encouragement has made possible not only this book but also pretty much every other proud professional moment since I first walked into her office. I am ever grateful for her sage guidance.

In short, if the book fails utterly to persuade, it is due not to the scarcity of wise interlocutors but the doggedness of its author.

Finally, I am grateful to Sarper Işıksel for showing me, every day, what it means to be dedicated to what you do, and really good at it; to Nihal Başıbüyük for her ferocious *anne şevkati*, and for keeping her every promise; and to Mike O'Neil for his endless store of patience, humor ("give it to me, I'll finish it"), sweetness, and homemade pizza.

N. Turkuler Isiksel

Table of Contents

Table of Cases

EUROPEAN CASES (CHRONOLOGICAL)

EUROPEAN COMMISSION OF HUMAN RIGHTS

GERMANY

ITALY

UNITED KINGDOM

UNITED STATES

Table of International Legislation

RESOLUTIONS OF THE UNITED NATIONS SECURITY COUNCIL

Table of European Legislation

INTERNATIONAL TREATIES AND CONVENTIONS

EUROPEAN REGULATIONS

EUROPEAN DIRECTIVES

"The actual system of Government ... is so unexampled in its origin, so complex in its structure, and so peculiar in some of its features, that in describing it the political vocabulary does not furnish terms sufficiently distinctive and appropriate, without a detailed resort to the facts of the case. With that aid I have endeavored to sketch the system which I understand to constitute the people of the several States one people for certain purposes, with a Government competent to the effectuation of them."

James Madison, letter to Daniel Webster dated May 27, 1830

"Nothing in law springs entirely from a sense of convenience. There are always certain ideas existing antecedently on which the sense of convenience works, and of which it can do no more than form some new combination; and to find these ideas is exactly the problem."

Sir Henry Maine, *Ancient Law* (1888)

"Les traités ne prévoient aucun mécanisme d'aller et retour ... On a parfois parlé d'Europe à deux vitesses, mais jamais d'un droit communautarie à marche arrière."

Robert Lecourt, *L'Europe des Juges* (Bruylant 1976)

Introduction: Constitutionalism beyond the State? Assessing the Stakes

Is constitutionalism an idea whose relevance must remain confined to the sovereign state? Could it be adapted to other forms of political ordering, such as international organizations? Is it already possible to observe elements of constitutional rule in the international realm? These questions have become increasingly germane in view of the contemporary multiplication and expansion of international and supranational institutions. Bodies ranging from the United Nations (UN) to the World Trade Organization (WTO), the North American Free Trade Agreement (NAFTA), the International Monetary Fund (IMF), and the International Center for the Settlement of Investment Disputes (ICSID); human rights regimes including the European Convention on Human Rights (ECHR); juridical constructs such as *jus cogens* and transnational contract law; and treaties from the Vienna Convention on the Law of Treaties to the New York Convention on the Enforcement of Foreign Arbitral Awards have all been considered in constitutional terms at one point or another.[1] Is the house of constitutionalism great enough to accommodate all of these mansions?

[1] For a constitutional perspective on the UN, see Bardo Fassbender, "The United Nations Charter as Constitution of the International Community" (1998) 36 *Columbia Journal of Transnational Law* 529; Bardo Fassbender, "Rediscovering a Forgotten Constitution: Notes on the Place of the UN Charter in the International Legal Order" in Jeffrey L Dunoff and Joel P Trachtman (eds), *Ruling the World? Constitutionalism, International Law, and Global Governance* (Cambridge University Press 2009). Compare with Michael Doyle's more circumspect assessment of a purported UN "constitution": "The UN Charter—A Global Constitution?" in the same volume.

A prolific literature addresses the WTO in constitutional terms. See Ernst-Ulrich Petersmann, "Time for a United Nations 'Global Compact' for Integrating Human Rights into the Law of Worldwide Organizations: Lessons from European Integration" (2002) 13 *EJIL* 621; Robert Howse, "From Politics to Technocracy—and Back Again: The Fate of the Multilateral Trading Regime" (2002) 96 *AJIL* 94; Robert Howse and Kalypso Nicolaïdis, "Legitimacy through 'Higher Law'? Why Constitutionalizing the WTO is a Step too Far" in Thomas Cottier and Petros C Mavroidis (eds), *The Role of the Judge in International Trade Regulation: Experience and Lessons for the WTO* (University of Michigan Press 2003); Philip Alston, "Resisting the Merger and Acquisition of Human Rights by Trade Law: A Reply to Petersmann" (2002) 13 *EJIL* 815; Steve Peers, "Fundamental Right or Political Whim? WTO Law and the European Court of Justice" in Gráinne de Búrca and Joanne Scott, *The EU and WTO: Legal and Constitutional Issues* (Hart Publishing 2001). Also see Deborah Z Cass, *The Constitutionalization of the World Trade Organization. Legitimacy, Democracy,*

Simple though it may seem, this question raises a profound methodological issue. Most modern political concepts have matured within the context of the sovereign territorial state. Constitutionalism is one of them. The debate concerning the constitutional prospects and credentials of supra-, trans-, post-, or international institutions is symptomatic of a broader challenge of conceptual adaptation. It is far from obvious that what justice, democracy, or citizenship mean in the context of the modern state can readily be applied to other forms of political organization. The traditional normative and descriptive concepts that we use to interpret and evaluate the exercise of public power are often ill equipped to comprehend contemporary international institutions and the challenges to which they respond. To be sure, emphasizing the significance of new institutions of governance does not mean that settled notions of democracy, justice, or citizenship are irrelevant; much less that the sovereign state itself is withering away. Rather, it is to highlight the necessity of directing political theory's critical gaze towards new loci of political power, and of recalibrating its core concepts in order to do so.

Since the eighteenth-century revolutions waged under its banner, constitutionalism has become a byword for legitimate government. In addition to being a placeholder for political ideals, moreover, constitutionalism represents a particular legal and institutional configuration. Its dual status as a normative and empirical category makes constitutionalism a particularly challenging candidate for conceptual renovation, and raises the stakes of preserving its relevance in new institutional contexts. International institutions scramble the correspondence that domestic constitutional regimes establish between key principles of political legitimacy and the institutions through which political power is exercised. What could possibly be left of the constitutional ideal if the political system to which it is applied lacks

and Community in the International Trading System (Oxford University Press 2005); Peter Holmes, "The WTO and the EU: Some Constitutional Comparisons" in de Búrca and Scott, *The EU and the WTO: Legal and Constitutional Issues*.

On NAFTA's impending constitutional drift, see Ari Afilalo, "Constitutionalization through the Back Door: A European Perspective on NAFTA's Investment Chapter" (2001) 34 *NYU Journal of International Law and Politics* 1; David Schneiderman, "Constitution or Model Treaty? Struggling over the Interpretive Authority of NAFTA" in Sujit Choudhry (ed), *The Migration of Constitutional Ideas* (Cambridge University Press 2007).

On the IMF's "constitutional functions," see Ernst-Ulrich Petersmann, *Constitutional Functions and Constitutional Problems of International Economic Law* (University Press Fribourg Switzerland 1991) 64.

On the ECHR, see Alec Stone Sweet and Helen Keller, *Assessing the Impact of the ECHR on National Legal Systems* (Oxford University Press 2008).

For arguments about the constitutionalization of arbitration and transnational contract law, see the contributions in Pierre-Marie Dupuy, Ernst-Ulrich Petersmann, and Francesco Francioni (eds), *Human Rights in International Investment Law and Arbitration* (Oxford University Press, 2009); Alec Stone Sweet, "Investor-State Arbitration: Proportionality's New Frontier" (2010) 4 *Law and Ethics of Human Rights* 48, 58.

the attributes of territorial contiguity, civic commonality, and consolidated public authority that characterize states?

In fact, many contemporary international institutions have acquired familiar features of domestic constitutional systems, including legislative organs that produce binding norms, autonomous mechanisms of dispute resolution and norm interpretation, procedures by which individuals and civil society actors can participate in decision-making processes, and schedules of rights that they can often invoke against states. Furthermore, bodies such as the European Union (EU), the WTO, and NAFTA are in the process of reconfiguring constitutional practice *within* as well as *beyond* the state by mandating, second-guessing, and rearranging domestic policy structures and priorities. Constitutional theory has been slower to adapt to the circumstances of global governance than constitutional practice.

The European Union is the Galapagos of these transformations: its idiosyncrasy is a boon rather than a bar to theorizing the constitutional effects of heightened economic interdependence.[2] Europe's diverse political composition, the dense interconnectedness of its member states, and an abundance of acute crises have prompted remarkable institutional experimentation within the relatively rapid span of just over half a century. Though they are unquestionably the product of particular historical conditions, Europe's supranational institutions magnify the challenges of postnational constitutional adaptation, and are of critical importance for observing and assessing the prospects of constitutionalism beyond the state.

Starting in the 1960s, the institutions called into being in the previous decade by the Treaties of Paris and Rome acquired important constitutional features, including extensive legislative competences, a hierarchical normative structure, judicial review, and a schedule of individual rights guarantees. From the 1970s onwards, legal scholars began discussing the supranational legal order of the European Economic Community in constitutional terms.[3] With the founding of the European Union in the 1990s, these constitutional features were strengthened and expanded along with

[2] James Caporaso, Gary Marks, Andrew Moravcsik, and Mark Pollack, "Does the European Union Represent an *n* of 1?" (1997) X *ECSA Review* 1.

[3] In his classic 1972 treatise on EC law, German jurist Hans Peter Ipsen described the EC as a constitutional system while underscoring that it was qualitatively distinct from domestic constitutional systems, and that it need not follow a federal trajectory of development. Hans Peter Ipsen, *Europäisches Gemeinschaftsrecht* (JCB Mohr 1972). For other early appraisals of the EC legal order in constitutional terms, see Ami Barav, "The Judicial Power of the European Economic Community" (1980) 53 *Southern California Law Review* 461, 466; Eric Stein, "Lawyers, Judges, and the Making of a Transnational Constitution" (1981) 75 *AJIL* 1. For a retrospective on the application of a constitutional theory perspective to European integration, see JHH Weiler, "The House that Eric Built," in *The Constitution of Europe* (Cambridge University Press 1999).

the tasks, principles, and powers entrusted to supranational institutions. Despite having the strongest constitutional credentials among contemporary international institutions, however, the EU has yet to secure the kind of political legitimacy implied by that term. The dismal failure of its clumsily staged "constitutional moment" in the early 2000s stands as a warning against using this term casually.[4] Designed to generate civic engagement with the European integration project, the Constitutional Treaty scored a perverse victory: it mobilized citizens in two founding member states *against* further integration, and demonstrated the powerful political evocations of the term "constitution" as well as the public's sensitivity to them.

Although it has an aspirational ring, constitutional language does not provide a shortcut for discharging the burden of legitimation that international institutions face. Neither does replicating the machinery of constitutional rule automatically reproduce the values and virtues we associate with constitutionalism. In fact, constitutional terminology can be invoked in a way that elides and obfuscates the pressing questions of legitimacy associated with postnational governance, and can ultimately squander the credibility of constitutionalism as a desirable form of political ordering.[5] Clearly, then, the appropriation of constitutional mechanisms at the level of international institutions and the arrogation of constitutional terminology to characterize them occasion focused theoretical inquiry into the meaning of constitutionalism. This book contributes to that inquiry.

(I) CONSTITUTIONAL AUTHORITY AND THE EUROPEAN UNION

Typically, a modern constitution enshrines the basic commitments that a body politic resolves to respect in governing itself.[6] To the extent that these commitments guide and constrain ordinary political processes,

[4] The term "constitutional moment" is borrowed from Bruce Ackerman, *We the People. Foundations* (Belknap Press 1991). For critical engagements with the idea of constitutional moments in the EU context, see Neil Walker, "The Legacy of Europe's Constitutional Moment" (2004) 11 *Constellations* 368; András Sajó, "Constitution without the Constitutional Moment: A View from the New Member States" (2005) 3 *International Journal of Constitutional Law* 243.

[5] Howse and Nicolaïdis, "Legitimacy through 'Higher Law'?"

[6] Before tackling the definitional and methodological issues, I provisionally use the term "constitution" in a broad sense to denote the body of norms that govern the exercise of public power within a body politic, that is, as the laws of rule. Depending on the system, some of these norms are codified in the "large-C" constitutional document, while some proportion almost invariably derives from important statutes, landmark jurisprudence, the law of administrative institutions, political customs and usages. This more capacious range of basic norms that guide the exercise of public power is correspondingly referred to as the "small-c" constitution. For an overview of this distinction, see David S Law, "Constitutions" in Peter Kane and Herbert Kritzer (eds) *Oxford Handbook of Empirical Legal Research* (Oxford University Press 2010). Challenging a narrow understanding of constitutional norms as those contained in the eponymous

they occasion friction. Their extraordinary authority must be justified to citizens, groups, institutions, and officeholders who are enjoined to pursue their ends exclusively through constitutionally sanctioned means. In a constitutional system, those who seek to alter what they consider to be unjust, irrational, or disadvantageous features of the political order are bound to challenge these features with resort to constitutional argument. Consequently, the competing reasons we give in order to justify or to contest the extraordinary authority of the constitution can serve to establish or undermine the basis of political obligation.

The justificatory enterprise is prone to infinite regress: if all political authority derives from and is subordinate to the constitution, whence does the latter draw its authority? Modern constitutions appeal to a range of sources, from the sovereign will of the people to the inalienable rights of individuals, attachment to a repertoire of civic values, narratives of national destiny, divine sanction or revelation, founding myths, and ancient customs. Political theorists, too, have been centrally concerned with accounting for the authority of constitutional norms. In secular, diverse, post-traditional societies committed to reconciling public power with the autonomy of those governed by it, entrenched norms pose a particular challenge of justification. This book focuses on two principles that framed the eighteenth-century constitutional revolutions and continue to guide most scholarly discussions of constitutional authority, namely those of individual liberty and popular sovereignty. According to most democratic conceptions, the constitution draws its legitimacy from enabling and organizing the exercise of collective self-rule by the *demos*.[7] By contrast, liberal accounts tend to

document of 1787 as subsequently amended, American legal scholars have argued that the domain of US constitutional law comprises several bodies of fundamental norms that govern key areas of political power, including the "fiscal constitution" (Kenneth W Dam, "The American Fiscal Constitution" (1977) 44 *The University of Chicago Law Review* 271); the "administrative constitution" (William N Eskridge Jr. and John Ferejohn, *A Republic of Statutes. The New American Constitution* (Yale University Press 2010)); the "political constitution" (Arthur S Miller, "Toward a Definition of 'the' Constitution" (1983) 8 *University of Dayton Law Review* 633, 641); the "economic constitution" (Miller, "Toward a Definition of 'the' Constitution" 671) and more. On each of these accounts, legislative and administrative norms, in addition to the large-C Constitution, "create entrenched governance structures and norms" (Eskridge and Ferejohn, *A Republic of Statutes* 7). While this approach casts a wider net than the strict documentary definition, some versions of it risk over-inclusion and submerge the distinction between ordinary and constitutional law. For further discussion, see Chapter 2.

[7] Contributions that fit under the broad tent of republican constitutional theory are too numerous to list. Landmark studies include, Ackerman, *We the People*; Richard Bellamy, *Political Constitutionalism: A Republican Defense of the Constitutionality of Democracy* (Cambridge University Press 2007); John Hart Ely, *Democracy and Distrust. A Theory of Judicial Review* (Harvard University Press 1980); Jürgen Habermas, *Between Facts and Norms: Contributions to a Discourse Theory of Law and Democracy* (William Rehg tr, MIT Press 1996); Frank Michelman, "Law's Republic" (1989) 97 *Yale Law Journal* 1493; Philip Pettit, *Republicanism. A Theory of Freedom and Government* (Oxford University Press 1999), esp. ch 6; James Tully, *Strange Multiplicity: Constitutionalism in an Age of Diversity* (Cambridge University Press 1995).

construe the constitution's primary task as carving out a sacrosanct sphere of individual liberty and safeguarding it against encroachment by the majority or by the organs of the state.[8] Suitably blended, these arguments yield various models of how an emancipatory constitutional order ought to look.

While constitutional theory has reached its present level of sophistication in the context of the nation-state, international institutions face a daunting challenge of political legitimacy, not least because they shape the policy options available to sovereign states and the democratic publics that they represent. To the extent that they are attenuated from the control of citizens, their decisions are vulnerable to charges of heteronomy. The EU provides a case in point. The extensive legislative, executive, and judicial powers it exercises over mature democracies place it under a heavy burden of legitimation. As I will argue in the next two chapters, the EU acts as a supranational constitutional system that guides, constrains, and enables the domestic institutions of its member states. As such, it must be able to offer its subjects, which comprise both member states and citizens,[9] non-coercive reasons as to why they ought to abide by its decisions. Still, the EU's authority does not comfortably map onto either liberal or democratic conceptions of constitutional legitimacy. Because the EU operates at arm's length from traditional mechanisms of popular representation, it does satisfy traditional democratic criteria of political obligation. Similarly, its mandate for protecting individual rights and liberties is considerably narrower than what a liberal model of constitutional rule would require.

The EU's failure to meet the legitimacy conditions associated with liberal and democratic models of constitutional rule is sometimes interpreted as meaning that it should not be considered in constitutional terms. This book draws a different conclusion from the same observation. It argues that the EU has produced a qualitatively distinct form of constitutional practice, one whose authority is justified by a claim to govern effectively rather than with reference to traditional principles of popular sovereignty and individual liberty. Put differently, although the EU mobilizes the machinery of constitutional rule in the exercise of its powers, its authority rests on what I will call a functionalist legitimacy claim. In particular, the EU is widely conceived as "a means of addressing numerous transborder policy problems that [elude]

[8] See especially, Ronald Dworkin, *Taking Rights Seriously* (Harvard University Press 1977). See also, Cécile Fabre, "A Philosophical Argument for a Bill of Rights" (2000) 30 *British Journal of Political Science* 77.

[9] As the European Court of Justice observed in its landmark *Van Gend en Loos* judgment of 1963, "The European Economic Community constitutes a new legal order of international law for the benefit of which the states have limited their sovereign rights, albeit within limited fields, and the subjects of which comprise not only the member states but also their nationals." Case 26/62 *Van Gend en Loos v Nederlandse Administratie der Belastingen* [1963] ECR 1.

purely national solutions."[10] Chief among its tasks is that of "establishing [and] ensuring the functioning of the internal market"[11] "without internal frontiers in which the free movement of goods, persons, services and capital is ensured."[12] As subsequent chapters of this book will show, the EU's legislative mechanisms, its extensive regime of individual rights, citizenship provisions, and the doctrinal structure of its legal system are conditioned by and tailored to this purpose. Its constitutional features draw their authority from the functional imperatives of creating and maintaining an economic union, which is understood here in the broad sense of a policy space that encompasses a single market, monetary union, exhaustive fiscal coordination, and regulatory powers ranging from consumer protection to environmental standards. In this book, I develop the concept of *functional constitutionalism* to describe this teleological repurposing of constitutional rule.[13]

In contemporary social science, the terminology of functionalism is already overburdened. In the context of EU scholarship, it is most readily associated with the neofunctionalist research program, which typically explains the course of regional integration with reference to the interactions between supranational and domestic institutions and actors.[14] In this book, I repurpose the terminology of functionalism to convey the distinctive pattern of legitimacy embodied by the EU's supranational constitutional system. I neither presume nor challenge the empirical value of the neofunctionalist account of European integration. My approach is to examine the values that guide the EU's normative structure, rather than to isolate the causal factors that explain its existence. Put differently, my claims are interpretive and critical, rather than explanatory or predictive.

[10] Anand Menon and Stephen Weatherill, "Transnational Legitimacy in a Globalising World: How the European Union Rescues its States" (2008) 31 *West European Politics* 397, 402.

[11] Art 26(1) TFEU. [12] Art 26(2) TFEU.

[13] The idea of *functional constitutionalism* has been used by others, particularly in the German literature on European law. It derives principally from the work of Hans Peter Ipsen. See especially, Ipsen, *Europäisches Gemeinschaftsrecht*. For a more detailed discussion of the affinities between Ipsen's account and mine, see Chapter 2. Also see Hauke Brunkhorst, "The Legitimation Crisis of the European Union" (2006) 13 *Constellations* 165, 167; Udo di Fabio, "A European Charter: Towards a Constitution for the Union" (2001) 7 *Columbia Journal of European Law* 159, 164; Christian Joerges, *The Law in the Process of Constitutionalizing Europe* (EUI Working Paper 2002).

[14] Classic neofunctionalist accounts include Ernest B Haas, *The Uniting of Europe* (first published 1958, Stanford University Press 1968); Philippe C. Schmitter "Three Neo-Functional Hypotheses about International Integration" (1969) 23 *International Organization* 161; Anne-Marie Burley and Walter Mattli, "Europe Before the Court" (1993) 47 *International Organization* 41; Wayne Sandholtz and Alec Stone Sweet (eds), *European Integration and Supranational Governance* (Oxford University Press 1998); Alec Stone Sweet, Wayne Sandholtz, and Neil Fligstein (eds), *The Institutionalization of Europe* (Oxford University Press 2001); Alec Stone Sweet, *The Judicial Construction of Europe* (Oxford University Press 2004).

The use of constitutional mechanisms to augment the governing capacity of political institutions is not specific to the supranational domain, of course. Social scientists have long understood some early experiments in constitutional rule in terms of their role in enabling the sovereign to exercise its power more effectively.[15] Even the framers of the US Constitution understood their endeavor at least partly as one of investing the central government with more power and defended it on such grounds.[16] Far from being unique to the EU, effective government is a ubiquitous but underemphasized justification for constitutional mechanisms. However, the EU reinvigorates and prioritizes the functionalist logic of constitutional rule at the expense of the principles of democracy and individual liberty that typically underpin constitutional authority in the domestic context. Entrusting the power of adopting, monitoring, and enforcing certain policies to the EU helps member states secure a range of collective goods that would otherwise elude them.[17] Similarly, the EU's supranational legal system enables member states to commit themselves to shared objectives and ensure that their peers do the same. My claim is therefore not that traditional constitutional systems are unconcerned with the imperative of governing effectively, but rather that the EU is distinctive for the degree of its reliance on this particular justification of constitutional authority.

This thesis has important implications even for constitutional theorists who otherwise have little interest in issues of global governance. The EU's postnational constitutional experiment redirects the attention of constitutional theorists beyond the well-rehearsed tension between individual liberty and democratic self-rule.[18] The quest to reconcile, sublimate, or calibrate this tension has distracted our attention from an equally basic set of tensions between the principles of democracy and individual liberty, on the one hand,

[15] Hilton Root, "Tying the King's Hands" (1989) 1 *Rationality and Society* 240; Douglass C North, "Institutions and Credible Commitment" (1993) 149 *Journal of Institutional and Theoretical Economics* 11; Douglass C North and Barry R Weingast, "Constitutions and Commitment: The Evolution of Institutions Governing Public Choice in Seventeenth-century England" (1989) 49 *Journal of Economic History* 803; Stephen Holmes, *Passions and Constraint* (University of Chicago Press 1995).

[16] A substantive parallel between *The Federalist* and the reasons traditionally marshaled for the European integration project is that both unions were expected to produce peace and prosperity. As Russell Hardin writes, "Perhaps the most important very early effects of the US Constitution were to eliminate military insecurity between the states (Federalist no.9) and to increase the scale of the market in which entrepreneurs in the states could trade (*Federalist* nos.11, 23)." See Russell Hardin, "Why a Constitution?" in Bernard Grofman and Donald Wittman (eds), *The Federalist Papers and the New Institutionalism* (Agathon Press 1989) 106. I further discuss this parallel in Chapter 1.

[17] Peter L Lindseth, "The Contradictions of Supranationalism: Administrative Governance and Constitutionalization in European Integration since the 1950s" (2003) 37 *Loyola of Los Angeles Law Review* 363, 375–6.

[18] For a definitive account of this tension, see F Michelman, "Law's Republic" (1989) 97 *Yale Law Journal* 1493.

and the imperative of setting up an effective scheme of public power, on the other. The challenge of justifying constitutional authority is more accurately understood as a trilemma rather than a dilemma: A constitutional system must be assessed not only in terms of how well it protects individual autonomy and allows for collective self-rule, but also in terms of how well it can realize those commitments *and* enable effective government.

The constitutionalization of international institutions can upend the delicate balance domestic constitutional systems strike among these three commitments. For its part, the EU extracts competences from the nation-state's once-comprehensive palette of public policy prerogatives and relocates them within a partially autonomous institutional framework whose guiding commitment is to an effective economic union. In so doing, it changes the domestic distribution of powers and constraints, destabilizes domestic constitutional values, and limits the extent to which member states can realize those values. In each of these respects, the EU's system of functional constitutionalism has transformed domestic constitutional systems and reconfigured their priorities.

Framed in this way, the book responds to a twofold puzzle. The first is specific to European integration. It is to go beyond Jacques Delors's famous description of the EU as an *"objet politique non-identifié"* by systematically articulating its generic and distinctive features. The constitutional perspective helps to locate the normative anchors of European integration, and to chart the patterns of justification that guide its institutions.[19] The second puzzle is an extension of the first. Because there is no standard of constitutionalism readily applicable to legal systems beyond the state, the task of application leads us into the domain of constitutional theory proper. Put differently, reflecting on whether there can be such a thing as postnational constitutionalism requires revising our ideas of what it is that we expect constitutions to do. Many existing discussions of constitutionalism beyond the state have understated this challenge, and have treated constitutionalism as a fixed, quasi-natural category. This approach usually dead-ends in definitional disputes. By contrast, this book treats constitutionalism as a dynamic category that is shaped by institutional practice rather than some a priori blueprint in light of which institutions are designed. Viewed from this perspective, international institutions that cannot meet the conventional criteria of constitutional authority do not portend the obsolescence of constitutionalism, but its transformation. Such a transformation need not be salutary, of

[19] Works in constitutional theory that exemplify this approach include Ackerman, *We the People*; Akhil Amar, *America's Constitution: A Biography* (Random House 2006); Gary J Jacobsohn, *Apple of Gold* (Princeton University Press 1993); Ronald Dworkin, *Freedom's Law: The Moral Reading of the American Constitution* (Harvard University Press 1996).

course. Before we can make that normative assessment, however, we need to illuminate the effects of the functional disaggregation of public power on the capacity of political institutions to realize traditional constitutional principles of democratic autonomy and individual liberty. I treat the experience of European integration as an opportunity to reflect on the principles of political legitimacy that anchor the idea of constitutional rule, and on the extent to which supranational institutions can instantiate them.

Finally, although the book's main focus is on the EU, functional constitutionalism is a potentially helpful concept for understanding international legal regimes that have come to incorporate familiar mechanisms of constitutional rule to ensure cooperation among states. Insofar as bodies such as the EU, WTO, NAFTA, and investment treaties codify and expand the binding obligations of states, adjudicate disputes, and monitor compliance, they fundamentally shape domestic policy choices and constrain the autonomy of political communities. Broadening the domain of constitutional theory beyond the state allows us to gain a critical perspective on these developments. For better or worse, functional constitutionalism is part of constitutionalism's future.

(II) SUPRANATIONAL TECHNOCRACY AND THE DISPLACEMENT OF POLITICS

Some international institutions are dismissed as talking shops. The EU, by contrast, commands action verbs.[20] It decides, bargains, disciplines, legislates, judges, enforces, and sanctions; in short, it governs. Nonetheless, the EU's founding treaties and official documents conceal its enormous power behind a dense fog of linguistic obfuscation.[21] According to its own terminology, the EU has competences, not powers. It does not legislate; it issues directives and regulations. It does not tax; it draws contributions. It provides structural and cohesion funds to administrative regions rather than redistributing wealth from affluent nations to poorer ones. Wherever possible, it recommends, harmonizes, and benchmarks; it tabulates best practices rather than imposing standards. Its political structure is supranational, not federal.[22] It invokes the managerial language of convergence, coordination,

[20] The phrase "displacement of politics" is borrowed from Bonnie Honig, *Political Theory and the Displacement of Politics* (Cornell University Press 1993).

[21] There is an apparently un-ironically entitled book on the subject (Francois Godrand, *Eurospeak: The User's Guide. Dictionary of the Single Market* (Nicholas Brealy Publishing 1992)). For an ironic guide, see Charles Moore, "A Maastricht Phrasebook" *The Spectator* (London, November 23, 1991).

[22] As Ernst Haas, the founding father of European integration theory recorded, the term "supranationalism" was coined to dispel the sovereign reservations associated with the term "federalism." Haas, *The Uniting of Europe* 32.

and consensus to smooth over dissensus, incommensurability, bargaining, and power politics. To adapt the Saint-Simonian adage, the EU has replaced government not with administration but with *governance*, a cryptic term implying that political power has been sublimated, when in fact it has simply become more opaque. The EU does not only pursue "integration by stealth" in Majone's apt expression; it also *governs* by stealth.[23]

This obfuscatory discourse is symptomatic of the broader political philosophy of European integration. In a nutshell, this philosophy calls for emancipating the exercise of public power from democratic scrutiny, citizen participation, and majoritarian control by entrusting it to competent, stable, impartial, and rational actors and institutions. The integration project owes its current design to a postwar elite chastened by and deeply distrustful of democratic politics. As Jan-Werner Müller documents, the cataclysm of World War II clinched the inherent liberal apprehension towards the masses, and produced "a highly *constrained* form of democracy, deeply imprinted with a distrust of popular sovereignty—in fact, even distrust of traditional parliamentary sovereignty."[24] War-weary liberals of the 1940s, 1950s, and 1960s associated mass mobilization with a politics of passion that sacrificed utility, pragmatism, and mutual advantage at the altar of power and national grandeur.[25] "European integration was part and parcel of the new 'constitutionalist ethos', with its inbuilt distrust of popular sovereignty, and the delegation of bureaucratic tasks to agencies which remained under the close supervision of national governments."[26] The empowerment of institutions operating at arm's length from majoritarian influence was pursued in the domestic and supranational contexts alike as a strategy for bridling the destructive tendencies of popular power.[27] The functionalist configuration of supranational institutions dovetailed with the empowerment of administrative over democratic mechanisms in the domestic realm.[28] Seen from this perspective, the EU's so-called democratic deficit—the purported

[23] Giandomenico Majone, *Dilemmas of European Integration. The Ambiguities and Pitfalls of Integration by Stealth* (Oxford University Press 2005).

[24] Jan-Werner Müller, *Contesting Democracy: Political Ideas in Twentieth-Century Europe* (Yale University Press 2011), 128.

[25] ibid 128. [26] ibid 149.

[27] Peter L Lindseth, *Power and Legitimacy. Reconciling Europe and the Nation-State* (Oxford University Press 2010); Lindseth, "The Contradictions of Supranationalism".

[28] This point has been powerfully made from a number of perspectives, especially, Lindseth, *Power and Legitimacy*; Bruce Ackerman, "The New Separation of Powers" (2000) 113 *Harvard Law Review* 633; Nico Krisch and Benedict Kingsbury, "Global Governance and Global Administrative Law in the International Legal Order" (2006) 17 *EJIL* 1; Giandomenico Majone, *The European Community: An 'Independent Fourth Branch of Government'?* EUI Working Paper SPS No. 93/9 (European University Institute 1993); Giandomenico Majone, "Europe's 'Democratic Deficit': The Question of Standards" (1998) 4 *ELJ* 5.

dearth of democratic mechanisms of control, accountability, and responsiveness commensurate to its powers—is a systemic feature, not a bug.

The institutional design of European integration from its origins to its current form bears out its framers' aversion to mass participation in politics. The Treaties of Paris and Rome enshrined long-term commitments on the part of states,[29] narrowed the policy choices available to them, and effectively entrenched certain matters against electoral contestation. Writing in 1943 in Algiers as a member of the French Committee for National Liberation, French statesman Jean Monnet argued that popular pressure goaded nation-states to sacrifice the benefits of free trade to a "politics of prestige."[30] Protectionism further galvanized the masses and their leaders into belligerence. Nation-states were too narrow minded to break this vicious cycle. By contrast, commercial interdependence would ease the conflictual disposition of the nationalist mind. Inspired by interwar plans to place the Ruhr and Lorraine heavy industries under multinational control, the initiative of a European Coal and Steel Community (ECSC) bore the stamp of this mistrust towards populist mobilization and national sovereignty.[31] Attenuating states' ability to marshal core industries of warfare was part of an incremental strategy of sovereign commitment intended to tamp down nationalist passions. As Robert Schuman famously put it in the declaration announcing the inauguration of the ECSC, the "fusion of interests" would gradually build "a wider and deeper community between countries long opposed to one another by sanguinary divisions."[32]

If the ECSC was hardly inspiring to ordinary citizens, it was so by design. As Monnet conceded, "increased coal and steel production is not the basis of our civilization."[33] However, it provided a workable framework of supranational institutions whose legitimacy was based on their competence and pragmatism, not on popular support. The failure of a more ambitious agreement for a European Defense Community (EDC) in the French National Assembly reaffirmed the wisdom of keeping

[29] The Treaty of Rome specified that it was "concluded for an unlimited period." Ex-art 240 TEC (art 356 TFEU).

[30] Jean Monnet, *Note de Réflexion de 5 août 1943*. Translation adapted from http://www.cvce.eu/obj/note_de_reflexion_de_jean_monnet_alger_5_aout_1943-fr-b61a8924-57bf-4890-9e4b-73bf4d882549.html accessed October 5, 2015.

[31] William Diebold, "A Personal Note" in Klaus Schwabe (ed), *Die Anfänge des Schuman-Plans 1950/51* (Nomos 1988) 27.

[32] Robert Schuman, *Declaration of May 9th 1950*. Available at http://www.cvce.eu/obj/the_schuman_declaration_paris_9_may_1950-en-9cc6ac38-32f5-4c0a-a337- 9a8ae4d5740f.html accessed March 17, 2016.

[33] Jean Monnet, Speech to the Common Assembly of the ECSC, Strasbourg, January 12, 1953 in *United States of Europe Has Begun. The European Coal and Steel Community Speeches and Addresses 1952–1954* (University of Pittsburgh Archive of European Integration, microfiche, 1955) 17.

integration on a technocratic footing and attenuating it from democratic control as far as possible. Reporting on the negotiations for setting up the European Economic Community (EEC), Paul-Henri Spaak warned that "if, after having encountered failure in the military and political spheres, we were, by any misfortune, to fail in the economic sphere, there would never again be a European revival, and our destiny would be sealed."[34] For committed federalists like Spaak, the gambit was to take grand political questions off the table until such a time as when they would be resolved seamlessly thanks to the relentless logic of functional imperatives. Although Monnet initially spurned the idea of market integration, and resigned his leadership of the ECSC High Authority in 1954 "in disgust at the slow pace of integration,"[35] the ECSC nevertheless provided the institutional framework for the EEC. The 1957 Treaty of Rome Establishing the European Economic Community repurposed the supranational bodies created by the ECSC Treaty—most notably its High Authority (now Commission), Court of Justice, and parliamentary assembly—toward this new aim.

Most importantly, the EEC preserved the technocratic emphasis and democratic mistrust that had guided the ECSC. Whereas the latter had sought to remove some of the infrastructure of warfare from the purview of state control as one might take away a sharp object from a child, the EEC offered rewards to motivate cooperation. The prosperity generated by market integration would facilitate further concessions of sovereignty and eventually bring states under the canopy of a supranational legal order. Despite his lack of enthusiasm for the EEC, Monnet himself had written that "[t]he political and economic aspects" of integration "must not be artificially separated, since this distinction is contrary to the lessons of history and to the necessities of government," and that the project of integration would have "no chance of success unless it is pragmatic."[36] Integration would work with the grain of national ambition rather than against it, using material incentives to gradually envelop states in a web of obligations. Its *finalité politique* would be reached through a whole host of instrumental, interim consensuses, rather than through a major, principled decision to unite. As a 1955 publicity pamphlet stated, the ECSC's aims were not only to "raise the standard of living by encouraging an expanding economy

[34] Paul-Henri Spaak, Address to the ECSC Common Assembly, Strasbourg, March 13, 1956. Available at http://www.cvce.eu/content/publication/1999/1/1/3d626775-5b70-49b8-b0ca-c4c9c22cb02b/publishable_en.pdf accessed October 6, 2015.

[35] Anne Deighton, "Introduction" in Anne Deighton (ed), *Building Postwar Europe. National Decision-makers and European Institutions 1948–63* (St. Martin's Press 1995) xvi.

[36] Monnet, *Note de Réflexion de 5 août 1943*. Author's translation.

through competition on a wide market" but also "to take the first step towards a United States of Europe."[37]

Since the founding of the European Communities, then, the selling point of supranational institutions has been their purported impartiality, expertise, professionalism, and ability to harness the collective strength of member states towards shared policy priorities. Robert Marjolin, who was among the framers of the EEC and served as a member of the inaugural European Commission, predicted that "a Community conscience, a common enthusiasm for Europe" would not look like traditional forms of political allegiance based on identity and attachment. One ought to hope "not for any abstract idea of Europe," he wrote, "but for a Europe which can find its justification in the improvement of the living conditions of its inhabitants."[38]

More to the point, the technocratic gains were meant to make up for the loss of domestic democratic control over policy choices. In Müller's words:

> [T]he creators of the European Community followed an indirect way of gaining legitimacy for their project: rather than having the peoples of the initial member states vote for supranational arrangements, they relied on technocratic and administrative measures agreed among elites to yield what Monnet time and again called "concrete achievements"—which were eventually to persuade citizens that European integration was a good thing.[39]

As the predominantly economic priorities of the Treaty of Rome illustrate, supranational authority was initially premised on the imperatives of postwar industrial and economic recovery. In addition, member states like France, Belgium, and Italy were either in the process of losing the economic lifeline of their colonial possessions or had recently lost them.[40] As the 1956 Spaak Report openly lamented, "Europe, which once monopolized transformative industries and drew important resources from its overseas

[37] European Coal and Steel Community High Authority Information Service, *The European Community for Coal and Steel* (High Authority 1955) 3.

[38] Cited in Willem Maas, *Creating European Citizens* (Rowman & Littlefield Publishers 2007) 19–20.

[39] Müller, *Contesting Democracy*, 142.

[40] Hansen and Jonsson argue that European integration was initially conceived as a way of reasserting European control over Africa in a way that would be compatible with nominal self-determination for former colonial possessions. They claim in particular that France's desperation to hold onto its "overseas countries and territories" in Africa was one of the motors of European integration in the 1950s: "For the promoters of European integration, their community … extended far beyond the European continent and constituted a new geopolitical sphere of influence. Colloquially as well as officially, the EEC negotiations referred to this sphere as Eurafrica, and one of the main intentions of the advocates of European integration was precisely to bring this entity into being" and to "consolidate European interests in a world order where its range of opportunities rapidly dwindled." Peo Hanssen and Stefan Jonsson, *Eurafrica. The Untold History of European Integration and Colonialism* (Bloomsbury 2014) 7.

possessions, is now seeing its external position weaken, its influence decline, and its capacity for progress disappear amidst its divisions."[41] European states would have to compensate for these losses by forging economies of scale at home. In a passage that would be reproduced almost verbatim in the 1957 Treaty of Rome, the intergovernmental commission tasked with devising plans for a European Economic Community declared:

> The goal of a European common market must be to create a vast sphere of common economic policy that will constitute a powerful unit of production and allow for continuous expansion, greater stability, a rapid rise in living standards, and the development of harmonious relations between the states united by it. To attain these objectives, the fusion of separate markets is an absolute necessity.[42]

Tasked with assisting the process of economic recovery from the very start, the EEC took some of the credit for the *trente glorieuses* of rapid economic growth and rising living standards that followed. In the ensuing decades, the acceleration of global commercial and financial interdependence renewed the urgency of economic integration. The widespread economic reverberations of the US's abandonment of the gold standard in the 1970s and the subsequent oil price crisis underlined the need for European states to manage the effects of global interdependence through concerted action. Deregulatory policies of the 1980s increased domestic and transnational strains on national regulatory and social welfare institutions, raising expectations that European integration might be able to compensate for their erosion.[43]

From the 1990s onwards, the economic justification for supranational governance acquired a new lease on life. The completion of the single market emboldened member states to undertake the project of Economic and Monetary Union (EMU), which attempted to lock them into a uniform system of monetary policy complemented by domestic fiscal discipline. At best, this attempt has been only partially successful: in the initial decade, the convergence criteria of monetary union were flexibly applied and occasionally flouted,[44] and the eurozone remained a "non-optimal currency area" composed of states with "differing inflation dynamics driven by diverse sectoral structures, political-administrative institutions and practices

[41] Comité intergouvernemental créé par la Conférence de Messine, *Rapport des Chefs de Délégation aux Ministres des Affaires Etrangères* (Secrétariat 1956) 9.

[42] *Rapport des Chefs de Délégation*, 13. Author's translation.

[43] Christopher J Bickerton, *European Integration: From Nation-States to Member States* (Oxford University Press 2012).

[44] Wolfgang Streeck, *Buying Time. The Delayed Crisis of Democratic Capitalism* (P Camiller tr, Verso 2014) 106.

and, above all, by different wage-setting institutions."[45] The grave flaws in the design of EMU, most notably the transfer of monetary policy to the European Central Bank without commensurate supranational powers over fiscal policy, hampered the EU's ability to respond effectively to the global recession. Many member state economies have not yet fully recovered from the ensuing tailspin.

Although most observers have interpreted the euro crisis as a failure of institutional competence, it has only served to augment, rather than roll back, the EU's powers in the economic realm. Member states, together with the Commission and the European Central Bank, responded to the crisis with a range of pragmatic solutions intended to break the credit freeze, reassure markets, and ensure domestic structural reforms. The adoption of a Treaty on Stability, Coordination, and Governance (TSCG) and a new series of secondary legislation tightened existing constraints on domestic fiscal policy and mechanisms of monitoring and enforcement. The policy cycle known as the European Semester is set to intensify this trend toward close surveillance and supervision of member states' economic priorities, budgetary choices, and structural reforms. When member states exceed the deficit and public debt thresholds specified by the rules of the EMU, the excessive deficit procedure subjects them to a rigorous corrective diet. Memorandums of understanding between creditor institutions and debtor states codify the structural reforms member states must adopt in exchange for much-needed financial assistance. These measures have cumulatively shepherded member states into a protracted austerity zone, and acutely reduced their budgetary autonomy (particularly for member states that do not conform to the German economic model).[46] Most egregiously, the TSCG calls on member states to implement balanced budget rules "through provisions of binding force and permanent character, preferably constitutional,"[47] requiring them not only to tighten fiscal discipline but to inscribe that discipline into their constitutions.[48]

Despite the tribulations of its monetary union, however, the EU is still regarded as a shared vehicle for economic control, for containing the destructive force of global financial and economic fluctuations, and securing greater influence in international trade and investment.[49] In other words,

[45] Fritz W Scharpf, "No Exit from the Euro-Rescuing Trap?" MPIfG Discussion Paper No. 14/4 (Max-Planck-Institut für Gesellschaftsforschung 2014) 5; Martin Feldstein, "EMU and International Conflict" (1997) 76 *Foreign Affairs* 60.

[46] Streeck, *Buying Time*, 106–9.

[47] Treaty on Stability, Coordination, and Governance, art 3(2).

[48] Kenneth Armstrong, "The New Governance of EU Fiscal Discipline" (2013) 38 *European Law Review* 601.

[49] Menon and Weatherill, "Transnational Legitimacy in a Globalising World" 403.

the EU's value added is still understood in functionalist terms, even if supranational gains in effective government come at the expense of democratic control over policymaking. Other challenges associated with globalization have reinforced the EU's functionalist calling. The EU's agenda has expanded in response to imperatives of mass migration, climate change, transnational criminal networks, and armed conflicts in its neighborhood and beyond. The technocratic discourse that helped launch the supranational project continues to provide the central justificatory narrative of the EU's vastly expanded powers today.

The EU's reliance on this "output-oriented"[50] mode of legitimacy has had mixed success. On the one hand, paring down the purview of European institutions to technocratic tasks enabled the European Community to succeed where other, more ambitious political projects had foundered. On the other hand, this strategy owed its success to a widespread recognition by European citizens that market integration was framed by a broader political mission. During the founding decades, no European was in any danger of forgetting the grim legacy of the century's wars, against the background of which the integration project acquired a meaning well beyond material gain. Paradoxically, however, European institutions have been a victim of their own success insofar as they can be credited with "making war unthinkable" among member states.[51] The idea of peace has little mobilizing appeal for citizens who are several generations removed from the memory of Europe's wars and who therefore cannot but assess the European project on the basis of its economic benefits.

More importantly, it now seems mistaken to assume, as the founders of the integration project seem to have, that unification in the economic sphere could be a purely instrumental conduit for some greater political vision beyond itself. Put differently, the legal and institutional framework of market integration competes with, and has so far edged out, other normative visions of European unity. The cunning attempt to deploy economic integration as an instrumental means of political integration has itself fallen victim to the cunning of economics. Today, EU member states find themselves ruled by the logic of economic necessity that was set in train by their own deliberate decisions to create an internal market and an economic and monetary union. The exercise in constraining sovereign discretion through supranational institutions has proven, if anything, a little too successful.

[50] Fritz Scharpf, *Governing in Europe. Effective and Democratic?* (Oxford University Press 1999) ch 1; Fritz W Scharpf, "Problem Solving Effectiveness and Democratic Accountability in the EU" IHS Political Science Series No. 107 (Vienna Institute for Advanced Studies 2006).

[51] Liesbet Hooghe and Gary Marks, "The Making of a Polity: The Struggle over European Integration" (1997) 1 *European Integration Online Papers*, 2. Available at http://eiop.or.at/eiop/pdf/1997-004.pdf accessed October 6, 2015.

Even though market integration was never intended to be the terminus of European integration, therefore, it prevails over blurry and contested political visions of European unity. Lacking a compelling *finalité politique* beyond the vague promise of "ever closer union," the EU has come to be defined by a *finalité economique*. "This does not mean that the EU is not *more than* a market too; but it does suggest that the EU exists *primarily* to deliver a market, albeit a complex [one]."[52] Not only does the vast majority of the EU's activity pertain to the market and its externalities, but being associated in the public imagination with a common currency, commercial and capital mobility, market liberalization, and competition policy, its contribution to civic discourse has failed to move beyond a crude calculus of material affluence. Market integration has turned out to have its own immanent normativity that rivals and occasionally undercuts the political ends it was originally intended to serve. This book's task is to make that normativity explicit.

The following chapters document the ways in which the teleology of economic union continues to dominate the EU's legal and institutional structure and thwarts other normative aspirations associated with the integration project. Alas, this is an unpopular and largely outdated position to take. Since the 1990s, market integration has come to be seen as a historic achievement rather than a live, let alone predominant, constitutional force. With the internal market firmly in place, it is assumed that there is little more to be learned from the EU's unmysterious and rather uninspiring regime of commercial mobility. According to the prevailing view in the literature, "The Union has overcome its existence as a functionalist entity devoted to market integration ... it should be seen as an open-ended polity where highly sensitive social choices are made."[53] The watershed for this transformation is generally regarded as the 1993 Maastricht Treaty, which ensconced the European Community within the broader structure of the European Union, with the declared intention to "mark a new stage in the process of European integration."[54] This treaty vested the newly minted EU with impressive political tasks (though not necessarily the powers to carry them out) and broadened its political ambitions by establishing democratic institutions of citizenship and representation. Subsequent treaties, not least the Treaty of Lisbon, have built on these foundations. As a result, the EU is said to have transcended the original economic rationale of integration.

[52] Niamh Nic Shuibhne, "The Resilience of EU Market Citizenship" (2010) 47 *CMLR* 1597, 1608.

[53] Armin von Bogdandy, Matthias Kottmann, Carlino Antpöhler, Johanna Dickschen, Simon Hentrei, and Maja Smrkolj, "Reverse Solange—Protecting the Essence of Fundamental Rights against EU Member States" (2012) 49 *CMLR* 489, 495.

[54] Preamble to the Treaty on European Union.

This book contests that final conclusion. Although its sphere of activity has dramatically expanded, the EU still follows the blueprint of functional constitutionalism established by the 1957 Treaty of Rome. Although it has been endlessly amended, renumbered, and even renamed, the functional pattern of legitimacy established by that founding document is still the EU's operating system. Even the new name chosen by the member states to rechristen it—the Treaty on the Functioning of the European Union (TFEU)—reaffirms this pattern. Subsequent agreements, including (but not limited to) the Single European Act, the Treaty on European Union, the Amsterdam and Nice Treaties, and the Treaty of Lisbon, should be understood as modifications, buttresses, and annexes to this original blueprint. While I do not understate the significance of the respective changes effected by these agreements, I wish to underline the resilience of the legal structure on which they have built. While there have been many attempts to shift the paradigm of European integration, the most significant of which is the failed Constitutional Treaty, none has so far succeeded. In giving up on their ill-fated attempt to remodel the EU as a constitutional federation, the member states have renewed the vows of their economic union. This book redirects the discussion on the aims, promises, and limitations of supranationalism in Europe back to the project of economic integration, which frames the EU's universe of values notwithstanding its (or our own) broader political aspirations.

Without a doubt, the EU commands far greater resources and makes far more "highly sensitive social [and political] choices" compared to its institutional predecessors, most notably the EEC.[55] While most observers tend to see the expansion of the EU's tasks as evidence that it has grown beyond its economic origins, however, I contend that the reverse is true: the expansion of the EU's operations has engendered the colonization of ever greater swathes of public policy by institutions designed primarily to create and govern a supranational market. Policy issues that were once subject to democratic control at the domestic level have been shunted into the domain of technocratic decision-making. The EU's new normative powers in the areas of human rights, citizenship, migration policy, and non-discrimination are colored by the peculiar teleology of market integration. Public policy objectives such as sex equality or social inclusion enter into its remit as externalities of economic interdependence, and are administered by extrapolating rules initially tailored to the market sphere. The result is the refraction of key principles of political legitimacy such as democracy, equality, and solidarity, and of key institutions such as representation, citizenship, and constitutionalism through the prism of economic union.

[55] von Bogdandy and others, "Reverse Solange" 495.

With greater power comes a more formidable challenge of legitimacy. Could the EU one day live up to its bombastic billing as a postnational democracy or cosmopolitan federation? Perhaps it could, but clairvoyance is not among this book's ambitions. Instead, I will attempt to reconstruct the EU's existing system of ends, expose it to critical scrutiny, and marshal the experience of European integration to update some of the core insights of contemporary constitutional thought.

In the following section, I will situate the book's claims within the heated debate about the relevance of constitutional theory with respect to international institutions in general, and the EU in particular. I will argue, on the one hand, that constitutional theory supplies a key normative and conceptual vocabulary for assessing and reforming international institutions. On the other hand, I will caution against the inflationary and indiscriminate use of constitutional terminology, as it threatens to erode the concept of constitutionalism itself. To thread this needle, I will propose a methodology of "reflexive readjustment," which calls for revising constitutional theory in light of novel forms of constitutional practice. Reflexive readjustment enables us to retain the critical force of the constitutional ideal without losing its contemporary relevance. I will conclude with an overview of the individual chapters.

(III) CONSTITUTIONALISM AS A "CHECKLIST:" PARAMETERS OF A STALLED DEBATE

Constitutional theory has become a particularly crowded conceptual terrain for scholars mapping new configurations of political power beyond the state. Despite the abundance of reflections on the purported constitutional qualities of international public bodies such as the EU, the WTO, and the UN, however, much of the existing scholarship follows a strikingly uniform argumentative tack. Most observers posit what they consider to be the essential characteristics of a constitutional order and assess their subject on the basis of those characteristics. Jeffrey Dunoff and Joel Trachtman call this methodology the "checklist approach."[56] The checklist usually features a hierarchically organized normative structure, the authority to produce binding norms, quasi-judicial organs that interpret rules and settle disputes, individual rights guarantees, and mechanisms of democratic accountability. Regimes that approximate features typically associated with constitutional rule are accordingly considered in constitutional terms. As Alec

[56] Jeffrey L Dunoff and Joel P Trachtman, "A Functional Approach to International Constitutionalization" in Dunoff and Trachtman, *Ruling the World?* 9.

Stone Sweet colorfully concludes, "if it looks, walks, and quacks like a duck, then it is probably a duck."[57]

More often than not, scholars in this debate opt for minimalist criteria, which lead more readily to the conclusion that a given international regime is in the process of "constitutionalization" or that it is already constitutionalized. Because many international institutions create norms binding on states, settle disputes, and create individual rights, the checklist approach yields as many positive results ("yes, it is constitutionalized") as we are willing to allow. The more we relax the criteria, the more numerous the constitutionalized regimes we see.

Unfortunately, however, easy resort to constitutional terminology creates some problems for constitutional theory. For one thing, it can result in dignifying every legal and quasi-legal entity with the constitutional label. As a consequence, constitutionalism has been undergoing what Giovanni Sartori refers to as "concept stretching" in his celebrated essay on social science methodology.[58] The result of concept stretching, Sartori writes, is that "our gains in extensional coverage tend to be matched by losses in connotative precision."[59] Applying a favorite concept to an ever-greater set of phenomena comes at the expense of analytical exactness and clarity.

Given the aspirational significance of the idea of constitutional rule, a glut of poorly conceptualized academic work may turn out to be the least of our worries. The real danger of conceptual profligacy is the prospect of devaluing constitutionalism as a placeholder for contemporary ideas of political legitimacy. As Sartori pointed out, the revolutions of the late eighteenth and nineteenth centuries established constitutionalism as an authoritative normative ideal.[60] Insofar as constitutionalism is a repository of political values as well as a mode of political ordering, its analytical erosion through overuse can limit our ability to understand, assess, design, and redesign the institutions that govern us.

Should we counteract terminological laxity by adopting a more demanding standard of constitutional rule? This has been the preferred response of scholars who understand constitutionalism as a system of self-legislation willed into being by an autonomous political community,

[57] Alec Stone Sweet, "Constitutionalism, Legal Pluralism, and International Regimes" (2009) 16 *Indiana Journal of Global Legal Studies* 621, 642.

[58] Giovanni Sartori, "Concept Misformation in Comparative Politics" (1970) 64 *American Political Science Review* 1033.

[59] ibid 1035.

[60] Giovanni Sartori, "Constitutionalism: A Preliminary Discussion" (1962) 56 *American Political Science Review* 853. Also see Neil Walker, "Beyond the Holistic Constitution?" in Petra Dobner and Martin Loughlin (eds), *The Twilight of Constitutionalism* (Oxford University Press 2010) 307.

the *demos*. On this view, institutions founded through interstate agreements cannot be considered constitutional regimes in their own right, however constitution-like their formal features. An influential proponent of this approach is former German Federal Constitutional Court (GFCC) Justice Dieter Grimm, who has been a steadfast dissenter in the debate about whether the EU ought to be considered in constitutional terms.[61] Grimm insists that the EU's advanced legal structure does not have freestanding constitutional status because its authority does not proceed immediately from an assenting *demos*, but is rather mediated by the states that represent individual *demoi*. In his view, "it is inherent in a constitution in the full sense of the term that it goes back to an act taken by or at least attributed to the people,"[62] which can never be the case with a treaty system, no matter how constitution-like its formal characteristics.[63] Because Europe's democratic publics can only make their mark on the EU's founding treaties indirectly, that is to say, through their national executives and legislatures, the crucial element of democratic authorization that would allow us to call the EU a constitutional entity is absent.

Grimm is surely right to observe that something essential is lost when constitutional mechanisms are severed from the democratic processes of opinion- and will-formation that create and sustain them within the domestic context. However, insisting on a rigid distinction between constitutional and treaty-based regimes has a far-reaching implication: it greatly diminishes the possibility of adapting constitutionalism to political units other than the sovereign territorial state. Democratic representation at the level of international institutions is typically too weak to substitute for the act of collective self-rule that Grimm insists is the proper origin of constitutional authority. Similarly, yoking constitutionalism to sovereignty rules

[61] Dieter Grimm, "Does Europe Need a Constitution?" (1995) 1 *ELJ* 282. cf Jürgen Habermas, "Remarks on Dieter Grimm's 'Does Europe Need a Constitution?'" (1995) 1 *European Law Journal* 303.

[62] Dieter Grimm, "Treaty or Constitution? The Legal Basis of the European Union after Maastricht" in Erik Oddvar Eriksen, John Erik Fossum, and Augustin Jose Menendez (eds), *Developing a Constitution for Europe* (Routledge 2004) 75.

[63] Grimm's account dovetails with US Chief Justice Marshall's account of constitutional authority in the landmark decision of *McCulloch v Maryland* (1819): "The government proceeds directly from the people; is 'ordained and established,' in the name of the people; and is declared to be ordained, 'in order to form a more perfect union, establish justice, insure domestic tranquility, and secure the blessings of liberty to themselves and to their posterity.' The assent of the States in their sovereign capacity is implied in calling a [constitutional] convention, and thus submitting that instrument to the people. But the people were at perfect liberty to accept or reject it; and their act was final. It required not the affirmance, and could not be negatived, by the State governments." *M'Culloch v State of Maryland et al.* 17 US 316 (1819) 403–4.

out, almost by default, the possibility of applying it to entities with functionally limited competences.[64]

And yet, to deny that constitutionalism can have any purchase beyond the sovereign state is to throw the baby out with the bathwater. As Udo di Fabio, another former member of the GFCC, puts it in relation to the EU's constitutional debate, "those who insist only on [categories based upon the closed nation-state] squander the opportunity to anchor the *telos* of the Union more strongly than ever in the values of Western constitutional culture."[65] Few would be content with jettisoning the constitutional idea in the postnational context given its centrality to modern democratic rule.[66] More importantly, if constitutional mechanisms remain confined to the domestic context while governance functions migrate to international institutions, the constitutional mesh that restrains the arbitrary exercise of public power will gradually loosen.[67]

I address the relationship between constitutional authority and democratic authorization more extensively in the next two chapters. For now, it is sufficient to note that both more and less demanding uses of the checklist approach are unsatisfactory: they leave us with the choice either of tolerating the indefinite conceptual erosion of constitutionalism, or confining its applicability to the domestic context. Second, the stipulative nature of checklists encourages a definitional stalemate.[68] Third, the checklists in question are usually based on what constitutionalism is or does within the context of the state, which is not necessarily what it does (or should do) when it is applied to new institutional contexts. As Helfer cautions, "[t]he many and profound differences between domestic and international legal systems" should discourage "merely identifying successful domestic constitutional responses and transposing them *mutatis mutandis* to international governance structures."[69]

64 On the concept of "legalization," see Kenneth W Abbott, Robert O Keohane, Andrew Moravcsik, Anne-Marie Slaughter, and Duncan Snidal, "The Concept of Legalization" (2000) 54 *International Organization* 400.

65 di Fabio, "A European Charter" 159.

66 As Neil Walker writes, "It is precisely because the language of constitutionalism, considered as a normative technology, finds it ever more complex and difficult to address the problems of communal living it poses in and for a post-state world, that it becomes all the more important to retain the language of constitutionalism, considered as a symbolic legacy, as an insistent reminder of what and how much is at stake." Walker, "Beyond the Holistic Constitution?" 308.

67 Anne Peters, "Compensatory Constitutionalism: The Function and Potential of Fundamental International Norms and Structures" (2006) 19 *Leiden Journal of International Law* 579.

68 Sartori, "Constitutionalism: A Preliminary Discussion" 857–8.

69 Lawrence R Helfer, "Constitutional Analogies in the International Legal System" (2003) 37 *Loyola of Los Angeles Law Review* 193, 198.

Finally, using a statist standard of constitutionalism to argue about the possibility or desirability of constitutionalism beyond the state is to treat constitutionalism as a fixed category. Like other social science concepts, constitutionalism is historically conditioned and politically contingent. By evading the necessary work of rethinking the concept itself, the checklist approach obscures the distinctive and normatively salient aspects of post-national modes of political organization and fundamentally misconstrues the nature of social science concepts. As James Tully explains with regard to citizenship—whose meaning, like that of constitutionalism, is similarly called into question by globalization—the history of a concept "is not the endless repetition of the same formulae, stages of historical development towards a predictable end, an instrument controlled by the hegemonic class or the dialectical overcoming of antagonistic forces."[70] Understanding a concept is not the unilateral "application of a universal rule to particular cases," but requires engaging in a dialogue enriched by normative aspirations, informed by historical and institutional context, and conducted "within the weighty constraints of the inherited relations of use and meaning."[71]

(IV) OLD CONCEPTS MEET NEW INSTITUTIONS: A METHODOLOGY

The checklist approach leaves us in a methodological bind: on the one hand, it fails to tackle what Neil Walker has termed the challenge of "translation."[72] In borrowing standards from the nation-state, we neglect the pressing need to rethink constitutional theory in light of new instantiations. At the same time, however, the essential normative qualities that make constitutionalism worth preserving must not be lost in translation. The fact that some political power has to some degree "gone transnational" does not mean that it has become benign; rather, we must insist on applying demanding standards of political legitimacy to all claims of public authority. Since it is no longer obvious whether "states [are] still the main keepers of normative principles" and whether "they still carry the sole responsibility to protect (their) citizens' fundamental rights," it is necessary to focus on "who fills the gaps, and to what effect."[73]

[70] James Tully, *On Global Citizenship: James Tully in Dialogue* (Bloomsbury 2014) 6.

[71] ibid 4–5.

[72] Neil Walker, "Postnational Constitutionalism and the Problem of Translation" in Joseph Weiler and Marlene Wind (eds), *European Constitutionalism beyond the State* (Cambridge University Press 2003). Also, Michael Zürn, "Globalizing Interests: An Introduction" in Michael Zürn and Gregor Walter (eds), *Globalizing Interests. Pressure Groups and Denationalization* (SUNY Press 2005).

[73] Antje Wiener, Anthony F Lang Jr., James Tully, Miguel Poiares Maduro, and Mattias Kumm, "Global Constitutionalism: Human Rights, Democracy, and the Rule of Law" (2012) 1 *Global Constitutionalism* 1, 3.

In order to strike the appropriate balance between conceptual continuity and change, I propose to abandon the checklist approach in favor of a methodology I will call *reflexive readjustment*. Reflexive readjustment calls for updating a normative concept in light of new, practical instantiations of it, while using the concept to subject the practices themselves to critique. These two inquiries are concurrent, and neither theory nor practice is taken to be authoritative. The former provides the evaluative perspective that exposes the imperfections of the latter, which in turn helps to identify and update outdated assumptions of the former.

Following this approach, this book reinterprets the constitutional idea in a way that allows us to assess the political and legal possibilities opened up by institutions beyond the state. On the one hand, I hope to preserve constitutionalism's critical edge as a concept that couples key principles about political legitimacy with institutional mechanisms to realize them. To dispense altogether with these principles and to attempt to theorize the post-national condition from scratch would be to reinvent the proverbial wheel. On the other hand, clinging to a rigid notion of constitutionalism may foreclose the possibility of fashioning new institutions that approximate the principles associated with it. Critics have rightly argued that describing non-democratic entities in constitutional terms rewards them with a mantle of legitimacy that they do not at present deserve.[74] Conversely, however, the complex legitimation problems posed by the institutions in question do not disappear when we refuse to use constitutional terminology in relation to them. Describing the EU's authority in constitutional terms attributes to it a greater, not lesser burden of legitimation relative to describing it as an international organization or an administrative body. Constitutional theory brings a more demanding normative standard to the table compared to some other approaches, not least because it underlines the expansive scope of the EU's power. As Michel Rosenfeld writes, it is more advantageous "to note the constitutional defects" of governance in the EU "from a critical constitutional standpoint than from a perspective that stipulates that the ideals of constitutionalism are inapposite when considering the EU."[75] Not only do we risk more by shying away from constitutional terminology than by using it, but we also miss an important opportunity to think about how constitutionalism may look outside its statist cast. Handled with analytical

[74] Sartori, "Constitutionalism: A Preliminary Discussion" 859 (arguing that "it is a scientific requirement to discuss whether it is proper to use 'constitution' where, in order that the public (and even, at times, the expert) be not deceived, we should *not* use this term"). Also see Stefano Bartolini, "Taking 'Constitutionalism' and 'Legitimacy' Seriously" in Andrew Glencross and Alexander H Trechsel (eds), *EU Federalism and Constitutionalism: The Legacy of Altiero Spinelli* (Lexington Books 2010) 11–12; Howse and Nicolaïdis, "Legitimacy through 'Higher Law'?"

[75] Michel Rosenfeld, "Is Global Constitutionalism Meaningful or Desirable?" (2014) 25 *EJIL* 177, 198–9.

care, constitutional terminology is potentially more illuminating than it is obfuscating.

Certainly, the project of conceptual renovation I have outlined here is likely to bear fruit only through a cumulative effort by constitutional scholars, jurists, and citizens.[76] The idea of functional constitutionalism provides a partial response to this challenge by underlining a shift in the justificatory logic of constitutional mechanisms as a result of their appropriation by postnational institutions. Beyond offering a hermeneutic account of the EU's legal system, I use the idea of functional constitutionalism in a way that helps to identify and address the EU's normative shortcomings. As such, my first task is analytical and interpretive: I consider why we consider some modes of political rule to be constitutional, and how we construct the relationship between the idea of constitutionalism and the institutions that claim to instantiate it. My second task is critical: I submit that some constitutional systems fail to realize the principles for which we value constitutionalism, and I offer some ways of identifying such failure. This dual focus is intended to overcome a split in global governance scholarship between the twin tasks of mapping the postnational constellation and critically shaping it.[77]

Finally, the reflexive readjustment approach treats postnational constitutionalism not simply as the misshapen fruit of an eighteenth-century tree, but as an opportunity to continue the evolution and refinement of the constitutional idea. Although much recent commentary on the EU's constitutional attributes has been critical (a normative orientation this study shares), the European experience nevertheless illuminates the postnational horizons of constitutionalism. It is more valuable to scan these horizons than to look backwards in wistful longing for a false Eden of solipsistic states.

(V) OUTLINE OF THE BOOK

The conceptual groundwork of the book is laid in the two initial chapters. The first chapter provides an overview of alternative normative grounds of constitutional authority as a background against which to situate the EU. Although the attention of contemporary political theorists has been

[76] Such an effort is well under way. A reliable indication is the recent inauguration of several new academic journals devoted to investigating the global, international, or comparative dimensions of the constitutional idea, including *Global Constitutionalism, International Constitutional Law Journal, Indiana Journal of Global Legal Studies*. As the editors of *Global Constitutionalism* note in the inaugural issue, "the nature of constitutionalism as being at the intersection of law and politics makes a particularly strong argument for multi-disciplinary engagement." Wiener, Lang, Tully, Maduro, and Kumm, "Global Constitutionalism: Human rights, democracy, and the rule of law" 4.

[77] ibid 8.

absorbed by the challenge of reconciling the liberal and democratic impulses of constitutional rule, I contend that this represents only two horns of the trilemma of constitutional legitimacy. In addition to safeguarding individual liberty and facilitating democratic self-rule, constitutionalism has long been defended as a way of enhancing the capacity of public institutions to govern effectively. Although this is a generic basis of legitimacy for all political regimes, the EU's authority is premised primarily on a functionalist pattern of justification at the expense of the liberal and democratic principles that typically frame contemporary constitutional systems. Surrendering power over the adoption, monitoring, and enforcement of certain policies to EU institutions is intended to help member states secure a range of collective goods in the long run. The EU embodies a pragmatic mechanism of sovereign commitment rather than one designed to enable popular self-rule or safeguard individual liberty.

The second chapter develops the concept of functional constitutionalism to describe this system. Inevitably, I begin by reviewing the reasons why the EU has often been considered a constitutional order in its own right despite deriving its authority from a series of international agreements. This overview will be familiar to EU scholars. Nonetheless, I will argue, standard constitutional mechanisms acquire some distinguishing characteristics at the supranational level. First, unlike domestic constitutions, whose validity typically extends across the full range of public power within the body politic, the EU's legal order has a functionally delimited scope of validity. This generates an intricate, pluralist constitutional accommodation between the EU and its member states that differs from most domestic federations. Second, the EU's legal system is purposive in nature, and marshals the constitutional device of entrenchment to insulate the teleological agenda of economic union from democratic challenge and revision. This results in a body of constitutional norms that is far more detailed relative to constitutions that merely specify "the rules of the game." Third, its legitimacy hinges almost exclusively on the successful realization of these purposes; that is to say, the normative basis of the EU's authority is functionalist rather than based on individual or collective autonomy. The chapter concludes by noting the shortfalls and contradictions of a pattern of legitimation premised almost exclusively on technocratic competence.

Chapters 3–6 attend to the ways in which the EU has repurposed several familiar mechanisms of constitutional rule to reflect and advance the project of economic union. A book that emphasizes the EU's market teleology may be expected to focus on the legal architecture of the internal market and of EMU, but that would hardly be revealing. Rather, I aim to show that the purposive logic of economic union is prominent even in areas of policy where the EU is said to have *transcended* that rationale.

Rather than competition law, the single currency, customs union, or common commercial policy, therefore, I focus on the EU's basic rights regime, citizenship provisions, and equal treatment rules to show the enduring significance of market logic. With regard to each of these areas, my analysis reveals the distinctiveness of the EU's system of *functional constitutionalism* by contrasting it with more familiar models of constitutional authority, including those guided by democratic, liberal, and cosmopolitan principles.

Accordingly, Chapter 3 addresses the EU's regime of individual rights in light of the idiosyncratic distinction between *fundamental rights* and *fundamental freedoms* enshrined in the jurisprudence of the Court of Justice of the EU (CJEU). Although the EU constitutes an autonomous source of rights guarantees for individuals, the rights that have an exclusively supranational provenance protect cross-border economic activity rather than the traditional roster of basic human interests. In a telling discursive choice, the CJEU refers to the former category of rights as "fundamental freedoms." This linguistic appropriation is indicative of the way in which the EU has converted traditional mechanisms of constitutional rule into vehicles of market integration. Meanwhile, conventional human rights norms occupy an auxiliary, even strategic role within the EU's constitutional structure. This is not to say that the EU neglects—much less that it habitually violates—traditional civil, social, and political rights, but rather that they are incidental to its autochthonous system of values. When it comes to protecting human rights proper, the EU's mandate is largely limited to patrolling the actions of its own institutions.

Against the background of several decades of agonizing about the EU's so-called democratic deficit, Chapter 4 assesses the extent to which the EU relies on popular democratic autonomy as a legitimating principle, and whether its democratic mechanisms are commensurate with its vast scope of authority. Unlike most observers, I do not believe that the EU's primary democratic problem is the lack of adequate mechanisms for citizen participation in decision-making. More troubling, I argue, is the fact that the EU's most effective participatory mechanisms exemplify and reinforce its system of functional constitutionalism. Although the EU provides some innovative means for citizens to exercise political agency in its policy processes and constitutional development, these are mostly configured to advance the EU's substantive commitment to integration in the economic sphere. As such, these mechanisms are neither inclusive nor necessarily democracy enhancing. Rather, they amplify the voices of citizens and groups who favor further market liberalization, but leave large constituencies with few effective channels through which to contest the policy decisions that affect them. In other words, the EU encourages functionally differentiated forms of political agency, which contrasts with traditional democratic institutions that ensure equal participation.

Among the commercial mobility rights protected by the EU's constitutional system as fundamental freedoms, Chapter 5 focuses on the freedom of movement of persons and investigates its political significance. As a historical and legal matter, personal mobility rights, together with the right to equal treatment on the basis of nationality, constitute the nucleus of EU citizenship. This chapter cautions against the prevalent tendency to exaggerate the transformative potential of personal mobility either for creating a supranational form of citizenship *or* for aligning the EU with cosmopolitan principles. As long as it remains anchored in mobility, the civic content of supranational citizenship will remain modest. I illustrate this claim by showing that the EU has tended to rely on personal mobility as a market-based surrogate for social justice, encouraging jobless citizens to move to member states that offer greater employment opportunities instead of creating social benefits for non-mobile citizens in need. As long as its enjoyment remains tied to mobility, EU citizenship will be a "citizenship of aliens"[78] that lacks all-important elements of civic obligation and solidarity.

Chapter 6 traces the evolution of the principle of non-discrimination on the basis of nationality from a market-liberalizing norm into a market-regulating one. Like the personal right to free movement, the principle of non-discrimination enjoys a dual justification. Intended to eliminate protectionist policies that hamper the goal of economic union, it has expanded into a supranational constitutional principle of equality before the law. Not only does it mitigate the salience of national membership as the decisive precondition for legal protection, but the EU's non-discrimination mandate has also been marshaled to eliminate disadvantages arising from sex, racial and ethnic origin, religion and belief, disability, age, and sexual orientation. Perhaps more than any other aspect of the EU's constitutional system, therefore, the non-discrimination framework gestures towards a more comprehensively validated political project than market integration. At the same time, prohibiting discrimination does not necessarily engender universal inclusion or equal treatment; nor does it amount to a particularly generous framework of social protection. For instance, the functionally circumscribed scope of EU law allows practices of reverse discrimination against a member state's own citizens. Most importantly, the repurposing of the non-discrimination framework to govern other, more complex

[78] This term is borrowed from the work of Linda Bosniak, who describes alien citizenship as entailing "a demand for [the] fair treatment and social empowerment" of non-citizens, particularly those who reside within a political community without enjoying full recognition under its laws. Linda Bosniak, "The Citizenship of Aliens" (1998) 56 *Social Text* 29, 33.

social relations is indicative of the weak, voluntarist, and negative norm of equality the EU has chosen over richer conceptions including reciprocity, social justice, and fair equality of opportunity.

The conclusion takes stock of the EU's constitutional architectonic in view of the ongoing tribulations of its monetary union, and assesses the extent to which the EU can fulfill the constitutional desiderata that have been ascribed to it. Since the onset of the financial and sovereign debt crisis, the debate concerning the adequacy of the EU's mechanisms of democratic legitimation has been eclipsed by a crisis of technocratic competence in the economic sphere. Far from shielding member states from the rigors of global financial volatility and economic competition, the endless discipline of austerity demanded by the design of EMU has further strained threadbare domestic welfare systems. The fiscal straitjacket member states have had to wear as a consequence of this latest phase of "ever closer integration" has not only proven unsuited to addressing the disparate economic and financial pressures affecting them, but its returns have been too meager to make up for the democratic autonomy member states have surrendered. Monetary union is the latest and perhaps most troubling example of the way in which the rigid teleology of the EU's system of functional constitutionalism impedes the pursuit of other public values and interests, not least those of democratic autonomy and social justice.

The EU's functional constitutionalism flags a tension between alternate and occasionally conflicting conceptions of political legitimacy, which, far from being unique to the supranational context, affects all advanced capitalist democracies. It is unclear whether the complex governance tasks required to sustain Europe's high standard of economic security and prosperity in the face of global interdependence are compatible with the commitment to democratic self-rule. The transfer of an ever-widening array of decision-making powers to international institutions underlines the question of how far democratic autonomy can be traded off in favor of technocratic governance before democracies cease to be democratic in any but a ceremonial sense. The citizens of domestic and supranational polities alike face a fundamental choice: do we wish to collectively make the rules by which we are bound, regardless of the limits of our ability to understand and control the complex forces that affect us, or do we prefer to entrust such tasks to authorities who claim to have the relevant expertise, even if we cannot view their decisions as having been author(iz)ed by us? Or must we accept democratic and effective government as desiderata that are no longer concomitant or entirely compossible, and make our choices accordingly? Far from being *sui generis*, the EU's legitimation crisis reinvigorates one of the oldest challenges of political theory, namely, whether government *of* and *by* the people is also the most effective use of public power *for* the people.

1

The Trilemma of Constitutional Authority

What, exactly, is a constitution? What rides on whether a particular regime is or is not considered constitutional? If even golf clubs have constitutions, as former British foreign secretary Jack Straw quipped during the controversy surrounding the adoption of a constitution for the European Union (EU), have gallons of ink been wasted in scholarly arguments about whether the EU should be considered in those terms? Does the EU's lack of an eponymous constitutional document defeat any suggestion that it is constitutionalized? Or do *all* political systems have constitutions in the sense of Aristotle's *politeia*, namely, "the organization of offices in a state, [which] determines what is to be the governing body, and what is the end of each community"?[1] Surely, a political regime whose authority rests purely on coercion cannot properly be considered constitutional, but how much higher is the bar? According to the French Declaration of the Rights of Man and Citizen, "A society in which the guarantee of rights is not assured, nor the separation of powers defined, has no constitution at all." The guarantee of rights and the separation of powers are prominent motifs in the history of constitutional thought and practice, to which others can easily be added, not least the rule of law, constitutional supremacy, judicial independence, entrenched and hierarchically arranged rules, to mention a few. And in this way, the perfunctory definitional paragraph can easily balloon into a full chapter and take over the entire monograph.

The question of definition is more than just prefatory in a discussion about the possibility of adapting constitutionalism to international institutions. It contains a hidden methodological snare. As I intimated in the introduction, many observers treat constitutionalism like a yardstick one might pick off a shelf and use to measure existing institutions. Unlike a natural category or a mathematical constant, however, constitutionalism is a historically contingent and discursively molded concept. For this reason, it is not clear whether constitutional rule can have the same features or perform

[1] Aristotle, *Politics* (Carnes Lord tr and ed, The University of Chicago Press 1984) 1289a15.

the same tasks in the international context as the constitutional regimes cataloged by Aristotle, proclaimed by eighteenth-century revolutionaries, or established during post-communist transitions. Similarly, associating constitutionalism exclusively with any single feature, principle, or purpose might lead us to look past interesting new adaptations of constitutional ideas and mechanisms. As a social scientific category and a key term of public discourse, constitutionalism is deeply conditioned by the phenomena to which it is applied. As Giovanni Sartori, the *eminence grise* of social science methodology and concept formation writes:

> definitions are not private conventions of each speaker, but (whenever they have a historical referent) storehouses of past experience shaped by former practice. We bring them up to date, but their ultimate truth-value lies in the fact that they tell us how to behave *as experienced people* in matters regarding which each generation starts by having no experience.[2]

As with many core concepts of social science, but particularly when it comes to one so closely associated with normative judgments about legitimate government as constitutionalism, "the storehouse of past experience" is rich indeed. Heeding Sartori's advice, I deliberately refrain from approaching the EU with a stipulative definition of constitutionalism in hand. Instead, this chapter will extract from several distinct traditions of political thought several distinct models of constitutional authority. In particular, I will highlight three key principles of political legitimacy with which constitutional rule has come to be associated: collective self-rule, individual liberty, and effective government. As different articulations of the idea of autonomy, the first two bear an unmistakable family resemblance to one another. I will keep my discussion of them brief, since working out their tension-laden relationship has preoccupied much of contemporary constitutional theory. The third, however, is more puzzling: all regimes, constitutional or not, appeal to some extent to a claim to govern effectively. What makes this a principle on the basis of which one can justify constitutional authority?

One of the earliest and most enduring patterns in modern constitutional rule is the idea that certain constraints on public institutions and officeholders can enhance their capabilities in the long run. I will argue that this logic of enabling constraints—rather than the familiar principles of democracy or individual liberty—supplies the key justification for the EU's authority. The EU's constitutional features reflect and reinforce this rationale. To some extent, they also reflect the traditional commitments of democracy and individual rights, but what distinguishes the EU as a *functional* rather than

[2] Giovanni Sartori, "Constitutionalism: A Preliminary Discussion" (1962) 56 *American Political Science Review* 853, 858. Emphasis original.

democratic or liberal mode of constitutionalism is that it relies heavily on a claim to effective government, and only incidentally on other political values. In other words, it represents a distinctive and, in many ways, normatively troubling way to counterbalance the three justificatory logics that sustain modern constitutional authority. In subsequent chapters, I will critically discuss the ways in which key elements of the EU's legal and institutional structure reflect this order of priority.

(I) GROUNDING CONSTITUTIONAL AUTHORITY: A RESTATEMENT

How do constitutions ground their claim to constrain, shape, and regulate the exercise of public power? Thus posed, the question suggests a definitional minimum for what constitutionalism must entail, namely, that all public authority within a political system must conform to a body of stable norms. In Neil MacCormick's words, "[c]onstitutionalism as a *minimal* virtue involves duly respecting the conditional quality of powers conferred ... and involves observing faithfully the (interpreted) conditions of the respective agencies' empowerment."[3] MacCormick's use of the word "minimal" is key: constitutional norms may be infused with a kaleidoscope of political values, including democracy, autonomy, justice, and equality. None of these, however, is unique to constitutionalism; rather, each has a normative content that is analytically distinct from constitutional rule *simpliciter*. MacCormick's point is that constitutionalism, as a vehicle for commissioning political power *and* patrolling its exercise, should not be confused with the various political ideals with which constitutions are inscribed. Holmes and Sunstein identify this nexus of empowerment and limitation as essential to constitutional rule: "the balance of rigidity and flexibility, of permanence and adaptability ... lies at the heart of constitutional government."[4] The defining "virtue" of constitutionalism is that of guiding the exercise of political power in light of principles and norms that are at once stable and mutable.

Starting with this parsimonious conception of constitutionalism allows us to identify a number of competing normative justifications for constitutional authority. In other words, we can imagine constitutional systems that have been shaped in accordance with—and that in turn reinforce—a wide range of principles and ends. While constitutional theorists tend to argue that

[3] Neil MacCormick, *Questioning Sovereignty: Law, State, and Nation in the European Commonwealth* (Oxford University Press 1999) 103. Emphasis original.

[4] Stephen Holmes and Cass R Sunstein, "The Politics of Constitutional Revision in Eastern Europe" in Sanford Levinson (ed), *Responding to Imperfection. The Theory and Practice of Constitutional Amendment* (Princeton University Press 1995) 275.

the proper purpose of constitutionalism is to realize political ideals *x* or *y*, the range of possible justifications as to why political power ought to be subject to a series of stable yet mutable norms is in fact quite broad (though it is not unlimited). In fact, some recent scholarship attends to the ways in which constitutional rule can be used to undermine or hinder the lofty ideals with which it is traditionally associated.[5] To begin, I will briefly outline some of these traditional associations, focusing in particular on the twin ideals of democratic self-rule and individual liberty that guide the modern political discourse of constitutional rule. I will then give an account of the idea of effective government as a normative logic of constitutional authority in its own right, one that has accompanied constitutional practice since some of its earliest instantiations. Finally, I will argue that the EU's constitutional order is premised primarily on this functionalist justification.

Although the term "constitution" did not settle into its contemporary meaning until the eighteenth century,[6] political thinkers of all ages have been preoccupied with accounting for the law's claim to authority, particularly when it comes into conflict with political will. Aristotle famously considered "whether it is more advantageous to be ruled by the best man or by the best laws,"[7] and concluded that good laws require the complement of the expeditious faculty of human judgment.[8] Many medieval and

[5] Alexander Somek, "Authoritarian Constitutionalism: Austrian Constitutional Doctrine 1933 to 1938 and its Legacy" in Christian Joerges and Navraj Singh Ghaleigh (eds), *Darker Legacies of Law in Europe* (Hart 2003); Tom Ginsburg and Alberto Simpser (eds), *Constitutions in Authoritarian Regimes* (Cambridge University Press 2013); Turkuler Isiksel, "Between Text and Context: Turkey's Tradition of Authoritarian Constitutionalism" (2013) 11 *International Journal of Constitutional Law* 702.

[6] For an account tracing the evolution of this term, see Gerald Stourzh, "*Constitution*: Changing Meanings of the Term from the Early Seventeenth to the Late Eighteenth Century" in Terence Ball and JGA Pocock (eds), *Conceptual Change and the Constitution* (University Press of Kansas 1988). In 1733, Bolingbroke wrote: "By constitution we mean, whenever we speak with propriety and exactness, that assemblage of laws, institutions and customs, derived from certain fixed principles of reason, directed to certain fixed objects of public good, that compose the general system, according to which the community hath agreed to be governed ... We call this a good government, when ... the whole administration of public affairs is wisely pursued, and with a strict conformity to the principles and objects of the constitution" (quoted in Stourzh 43). Bolingbroke's is an intermediary position between the Aristotelian idea of the constitution as the frame of government, and the American Revolutionaries' conception of it as the supreme law of the realm. Stourzh pinpoints Emer de Vattel's 1764 writing as the first to "clearly [distinguish] between the constitution and the legislative power, which depended on the former and was inferior to it" 45.

[7] Aristotle, *Politics* (Benjamin Jowett tr and Richard McKeon ed, The Modern Library 2001) 1286a5–10. On this question, also see Plato, *Statesman* (Christopher J Rowe tr, Hackett 1999) 294a–96d.

[8] "The discussion of the first question [what is to be the supreme power in the *polis*] shows nothing so clearly as that laws, when good, should be supreme; and that the magistrate or magistrates should regulate those matters [only] on which the laws are unable to speak with precision owing to the difficulty of any general principle embracing all particulars." Aristotle, *Politics* 1282b1–82b5. I placed the "only" in brackets, because some other translations omit it, changing the meaning of the passage. cf Aristotle, *Politics* (Carnes Lord tr) 103.

early modern thinkers viewed the fundamental laws of the realm, scripture, Roman law, and natural law as binding on the sovereign.[9] Among them, twelfth-century philosopher and theologian John of Salisbury advanced a Christianized version of classical natural law doctrine, rejecting the Roman concept of the prince as *legibus solutus* in favor of the idea that the earthly sovereign "may not lawfully have any will of his own apart from that which the law or equity enjoins, or the calculation of [what] the common interest requires."[10] In a formulation later borrowed by Bracton, Salisbury argued that "the very title *rex* is derived from doing right, that is, acting in accordance with law (*recte*)."[11] The early modern notion of higher law was gradually "sharpened to that of a code distinctively for rulers,"[12] the idea of constitutionalism *en herbe*.

While scripture, natural law, and Roman law provided substantive justifications for the authority of laws binding on the sovereign, other medieval jurists contended that these laws were the logical precondition of sovereignty. Monarchical authority could not be established or recognized as legitimate unless it was conferred by the laws of the realm, making the latter's authority logically anterior to the sovereign's. Using this immanent mode of justification, Bracton emphasized that in order to identify the sovereign as such, it was necessary to make reference to a preexisting law of rule. For this purpose, he singled out the principles and "solemn promises" contained in the coronation oath as constituting the grounds of the king's authority.[13] Unlike the king and his edicts, these laws were immortal, and ensured the continuation of monarchical authority (and thereby of the realm itself) by reinvesting it in his successor. By the same token, the monarch could only violate the fundamental laws of the realm at the cost of contradicting the very basis of his rule. As Bracton put it, "the king … should be subject to [God and] the law, because the law makes the king."[14] Similarly, fifteenth-century French jurist Jean de Terre Rouge submitted that "It is not permissible for the King to change those things which have been ordained *ad statum publicum regni*"; that is, in contradiction of the fundamental laws of the monarchy.[15]

9 JGA Pocock, *The Ancient Constitution and the Feudal Law* (Cambridge University Press 1957).

10 Quoted in Edward S Corwin, "The 'Higher Law' Background of American Constitutional Law" (1928) 42 *Harvard Law Review* 149, 166.

11 ibid 166. 12 ibid 164.

13 Charles Howard McIlwain, *Constitutionalism Ancient and Modern* (Cornell University Press 1940) 74; also see Robert S Hoyt, "The Coronation Oath of 1308" (1956) 71 *The English Historical Review* 353, 356–7.

14 Henry de Bracton, *On the Laws and Customs of England* (Samuel E Thorne tr and ed, Belknap 1968) II, 33. This sentence also appears in Sir William Blackstone, *Commentaries on the Laws of England* (William Carey Jones ed, Bancroft-Whitney Company 1915) §334, 239.

15 Cited in McIlwain, *Constitutionalism Ancient and Modern* 100–1.

As Pocock documents, yet another strategy for justifying the laws' authority over the sovereign came to prominence in early modern England, where jurists invoked the ancient origins of the common law and the timelessness of its prescription to contest the authority of the monarch and defend that of Parliament.[16] Since the common law had been passed down from time immemorial and was "traceable to no original act of foundation,"[17] they argued, it could not be a product of the sovereign's will, and was therefore superordinate to it. English lawyers escaped the potential circularity of using the law to limit sovereign authority by using antiquity as an alternative source of legal authority to sovereign command.[18]

Although early modern constitutionalists traced the authority of the fundamental laws of the realm to a relative abundance of sources, accounts of constitutional rule began to fall into a dichotomous pattern of justification from the eighteenth century onwards. The French Declaration of the Rights of Man and the Citizen enshrined just such a pattern, proclaiming that all power derived from the people, while adding that its chief object was the protection of the natural and imprescriptible rights of man. Constitutional government differed from absolutist rule insofar as it subjected the exercise of public power to the collective and individual autonomy of subjects. However, these twin commitments soon unraveled, yielding a rift between rival models of constitutional rule that respectively emphasized popular sovereignty and the sacrosanct liberties of individual subjects. Benjamin Constant captured this mood when he famously distinguished between the liberty of the ancients, which he associated with collective self-rule and ascribed to Rousseau and leading figures of the French Revolution, and the liberty of the moderns, which he identified with "the enjoyment of security in private pleasures," and "the guarantees accorded by [public] institutions to these pleasures."[19] In truth, both of these conceptions of liberty (if discrete conceptions they indeed were) had been honed as challenges to absolutist monarchy: appealing to the sovereignty of the people and the liberties of individual subjects was a two-pronged attack against the institutions of hereditary privilege. Conceptually, too, the distinction between the collective and individualistic aspects of liberty was overwrought, as Constant himself recognized in his own work.[20] Nonetheless, it captured a very real tension

[16] Pocock, *The Ancient Constitution and the Feudal Law.* [17] ibid 37. [18] ibid 21, 37.

[19] Benjamin Constant, "The Liberty of the Ancients Compared with that of the Moderns" in Biancamaria Fontana (tr and ed), *Political* Writings (Cambridge University Press 1988) 317.

[20] Constant writes that "political liberty" (by which he means the liberty exercised through participation in collective self-rule, as distinct from "individual liberty") not only "enlarges [citizens'] spirit, ennobles their thoughts, and establishes among them a kind of intellectual equality which forms the glory and power of a people," but it is also the "indispensable guarantee" of individual liberty. He writes, "far from renouncing either of the two sorts of freedom ... it is necessary, as I have

between the declared fealty of eighteenth-century constitutional revolutions to popular sovereignty, on the one hand, and limited government, on the other. The appeal to limited government, which had been marshaled to challenge absolutism, could be directed with equal force against the popular sovereign. Rousseau, Constant observed, had simply transferred the "immense power which caused much harm" under monarchical rule to the people, and thereby gave "the most formidable support for all kinds of despotism."[21] Enlisted by Napoleon Bonaparte to draft a constitutional charter, Constant articulated an account of legitimate constitutional authority based on the "right to be subjected only to the laws" and to be immune to "the arbitrary will of one or more individuals."[22]

Although Constant's charter proved short-lived, the accompanying treatise he wrote for the purpose of educating the French public stands as the quintessential manifesto of liberal constitutionalism. According to Constant, "the constitution is the guarantee of the people's liberty" and "anything to do with liberty is constitutional."[23] The task of the constitution is to determine "where independence and individual existence begin," and where "the jurisdiction of sovereignty ends."[24] Under this conception, the most important characteristic of constitutionalism is the *fixity* it introduces into the political system by hoisting individual liberty above the grasping hand of sovereign power. In the words of a contemporary observer who shares Constant's liberal conception, constitutionalism is "a fundamental law, or a fundamental set of principles, and a correlative institutional arrangement" that aims to establish "a system of protected freedom for the individual."[25] According to another, constitutionalism is "the practice of politics according to 'rules of the game,' which insure effective restraints upon governmental and other political action."[26]

At the same time, this emphasis on the fixity of constitutional norms exacerbates the problem of how these "rules of the game" are to be defined, what the nature of the "restraints" should be, and how wide the sphere of "protected freedom" should extend. Without a theory of popular authorization, it is difficult to specify and justify the scope of individual liberty that the constitution must protect against interference. The democratic strand of

shown, to learn to combine the two together." Constant, "The Liberty of the Ancients Compared with that of the Moderns" 327.

[21] Benjamin Constant, "Principles of Politics Applicable to All Representative Governments" [1815] in *Political Writings* 176–7.

[22] Constant, "The Liberty of the Ancients Compared with that of the Moderns" 310.

[23] Constant, "Principles of Politics" 171. [24] ibid 177.

[25] Sartori, "Constitutionalism: A Preliminary Discussion" 854–5. In a similar vein, see Carl J Friedrich, "Constitutions and Constitutionalism" in David L Sills (ed), *International Encyclopedia of the Social Sciences* (Macmillan 1968).

[26] Friedrich, "Constitutions and Constitutionalism".

modern constitutional thought supplies precisely this link by emphasizing the mechanisms of self-revision that subordinate public power to the will of those whom it governs.[27] In contrast to the liberal variant, democratic conceptions of constitutional authority underscore the *reflexivity* of constitutional rule. Immutable laws are potentially heteronomous. As Abbé Sièyes emblematically proclaimed to his fellow revolutionaries, "a nation *should* not subject itself to restrictions of a positive form. To do so would expose it to the irretrievable loss of liberty."[28] However, Sièyes also insisted that "If we lack a constitution, a new constitution must be made, and the Nation alone has a right to do so."[29] As a "sequence of *positive laws*," the constitution was necessary to "regulate the organization and functions of the *legislative* body" and "fix the organization and functions of the various *active* bodies."[30] In other words, despite the risk of heteronomy that attends rules that constrain popular will,[31] collective self-rule relies on fixed procedures, institutions, and norms to identify the popular sovereign and to translate its commands into public power.

Many contemporary constitutional theorists have come to regard the friction between the twin principles of individual and collective autonomy, and the respective emphases of the liberal and democratic conceptions on the fixity and reflexivity of constitutional norms as a creative rather than debilitating tension. In his discourse theoretical account of constitutional democracy, for instance, Jürgen Habermas interprets the constitution's dual role in enabling and constraining popular rule as a reflection of the status of citizens as simultaneously the authors and addressees of the laws.[32] On the one hand, the constitution provides the procedural and substantive framework that

[27] The idea of constitutional rule enjoys an illustrious pedigree in the republican and democratic traditions in political philosophy. Influential contemporary accounts of constitutionalism in a civic republican key include Bruce Ackerman, *We the People. Foundations* (Belknap 1991); Jürgen Habermas, *Between Facts and Norms: Contributions to a Discourse Theory of Law and Democracy* (William Rehg tr, MIT Press 1996); Frank Michelman, "Law's Republic" (1989) 97 *Yale Law Journal* 1493; Richard Bellamy, *Political Constitutionalism: A Republican Defence of the Constitutionality of Democracy* (Cambridge University Press 2007). On the classical republican tradition of constitutionalism, see JGA Pocock, *The Machiavellian Moment. Florentine Political Thought and the Atlantic Republican Tradition* (Princeton University Press 1975); Maurizio Viroli, *Republicanism* (Hill and Wang 2002); Martin van Gelderen and Quentin Skinner (eds), *Republicanism. A Shared European Heritage*, vol I (Cambridge University Press 2002); Philip Pettit, *Republicanism. A Theory of Freedom and Government* (Oxford University Press 1999).

[28] Abbé Sièyes, "What is the Third Estate?" [1789] in Michael Sonenscher (tr), *Political Writings* (Hackett Publishing Co. 2003) 137.

[29] ibid 133. [30] ibid 136.

[31] Alexander Bickel coined the phrase "countermajoritarian difficulty" to question the legitimacy of judicial review, although his expression is often used more broadly to characterize the constraints constitutional norms place on popular will. Alexander Bickel, *The Least Dangerous Branch? The Supreme Court at the Bar of Politics* (Yale University Press 1986).

[32] Habermas, *Between Facts and Norms*; also, Jürgen Habermas, "On the Internal Relation between the Rule of Law and Democracy" (1995) 3 *European Journal of Philosophy* 12, 17; Jürgen Habermas, *The Inclusion of the Other* (Ciaran Cronin and Pablo de Grieff eds, MIT Press 1998) 120.

enables fair and inclusive processes of opinion- and will-formation. On the other hand, this institutionalization of public autonomy relies on a prior recognition of the status of individuals as legal subjects and bearers of inalienable rights. Without basic norms that enshrine the equal moral worth of individuals, it is impossible to put democratic self-legislation into practice or, indeed, to explain why it is a meaningful practice in the first place.[33] In contrast to liberal conceptions that invoke vestiges of natural law to justify the primacy of basic rights, Habermas construes private autonomy as a presupposition and a product of democratic sovereignty. The constitution's task is to translate the irreducible "internal relation" between public and private autonomy into institutional arrangements that enable both.[34]

In similar vein, James Tully construes the promise of constitutionalism as counterpoising two "equiprimordial" or "equally basic" principles, the rule of law and popular sovereignty.[35] In Tully's view, the quest to reconcile the two conceptions of political legitimacy dichotomized by Constant is a red herring: the purpose of the constitution is not to *settle* the bounds of individual and collective autonomy through immutable rules, but to invite citizens to consider and calibrate the principles which form the basis of their civic union. In comparison to Habermas, however, Tully's model of "democratic constitutionalism" places a greater burden of justification on entrenched norms. Constitutionalism, according to Tully, is first and foremost a medium for contestation, dialogue, and democratic *praxis*.[36] No one set of constitutional principles may be fixed for all time; rather, the equiprimordiality of democracy and the rule of law requires that the "procedures," "public reasons," and "practices of governance" which citizens use to deliberate and legislate must remain "open to deliberation and amendment *en passant* (not all at once)."[37] The fixity of constitutional rules is justified only insofar as it is necessary to enable citizens to participate in authoring the laws to which they are subject.[38] As soon as the constitution begins to constrict the range and audibility of arguments that can be raised by citizens, it becomes an "imperial yoke" that hegemonizes rather than liberates.[39]

[33] In his eloquent critique of John Hart Ely's constitutional theory, Tribe argues that without the rich reservoir of substantive values underlying them, constitutional procedures are "radically indeterminate and fundamentally incomplete." See Lawrence H Tribe, "The Puzzling Persistence of Process-Based Constitutional Theories" (1980) 89 *Yale Law Journal* 1063.

[34] Habermas, "On the Internal Relation between the Rule of Law and Democracy."

[35] James Tully, "The Unfreedom of the Moderns in Comparison to their Ideals of Constitutional Democracy" (2002) 65 *MLR* 204, 207.

[36] James Tully, *Strange Multiplicity: Constitutionalism in an Age of Diversity* (Cambridge University Press 1995). Also see Bellamy, *Political Constitutionalism*.

[37] Tully, "The Unfreedom of the Moderns" 217.

[38] Tully, *Strange Multiplicity* 5.

[39] ibid 5.

As both Habermas's and Tully's accounts make clear, the principle of democratic self-rule can be marshaled to justify individual rights and liberties that deserve to be protected against encroachment by the state. Constitutional mechanisms of democratic revision ensure that the substantive norms enshrined in the constitution accord with what a particular society at a particular time considers to be the fundamental and imprescriptible interests of its members, but nevertheless allow those norms to be challenged and modified. Conversely, the fixity of constitutional rules enables the exercise of collective self-rule. It seems neither desirable nor possible to immutably fix the basic normative order of society, or to wholly emancipate the popular sovereign from norms resistant to its will. Rather, constitutionalism's ingenuity rests in its ability to hold the twin commitments to individual and collective autonomy in equilibrium. This is not to say that all constitutions at all times succeed in this task, but that it is their distinctive promise to do so.

(II) CONSTITUTIONAL AUTHORITY AND EFFECTIVE GOVERNMENT

I have so far argued that constitutional authority, which entails a claim to condition and constrain the exercise of public power poses a formidable challenge of legitimation. Since the eighteenth-century constitutional revolutions, that challenge has often been met by appealing to the twin principles of democratic self-rule and individual liberty. The task of reconciling the stylized but nevertheless vexing tension between these principles has absorbed much of the attention of modern constitutional theory. Intellectually fecund as these inquiries are, however, the tension between individual and collective autonomy only captures two sides of what is essentially a tripartite problem of constitutional legitimacy. These twin commitments must be complemented by a third, namely, "the goal of efficient decision-making, unencumbered, if necessary, both by popular participation and by constitutional constraints."[40] Whatever other values a constitutional system might be expected to realize, it must structure the exercise of public power so as to ensure the safety and security of its citizens, resolve conflicts, facilitate material prosperity, collect public revenue, participate in the international system, and fulfill the greater and smaller tasks that define a polity. In short, the constitution's authority at least partially rests on enabling effective government. Although the challenge of constitutional

[40] Jon Elster, "Introduction" in Jon Elster and Rune Slagstad (eds), *Constitutionalism and Democracy* (Cambridge University Press 1988) 1.

rule is often framed as one of calibrating the demands of individual liberty and popular sovereignty, it is more accurate to speak of a three-way balance between the principles of individual and collective autonomy and effective government.

Clearly, this tripartite relationship is not always or necessarily conflictual: for instance, epistemic democrats maintain that democratic procedures offer the most reliable way of reaching decisions conducive to the public welfare;[41] while new institutional economics and constitutional political economy scholars emphasize institutions that safeguard civil liberties, including the rule of law, private property, and the enforcement of contracts as essential for a prosperous and well-functioning polity.[42] Nonetheless, analytically disaggregating these normative logics of constitutional authority helps to observe alternative ways of configuring constitutional mechanisms. It also draws attention to how a constitutional system manages complex trade-offs between protecting individual rights, organizing democratic self-rule, and facilitating effective government. In the rest of this chapter, I will develop an account of this third logic of constitutional authority, and highlight its primacy within the EU's institutional configuration. In the next chapter, I will flesh out the concept of functional constitutionalism to describe this configuration and to distinguish it from conventional liberal and democratic models of constitutional rule.

Although constitutional norms appear to curtail the power of the sovereign, a range of social scientific and legal scholarship emphasizes the ways in which they often work to make public power more effective.[43] As Eskridge and Ferejohn argue, describing constitutions as shielding citizens from government "neglects the reason we have government at all," which is, at a minimum, "to ensure everyone's security, to protect us all against personal harm and collective attack, and to guarantee institutions such as

[41] E.g., Joshua Cohen, "An Epistemic Conception of Democracy" (1986) 97 *Ethics* 26; Josiah Ober, *Democracy and Knowledge: Innovation and Learning in Classical Athens* (Princeton University Press 2008); David Estlund, *Democratic Authority: A Philosophical Framework* (Princeton University Press 2008); Christian List and Robert E Goodin, "Epistemic Democracy: Generalizing the Condorcet Jury Theorem" (2001) 9 *Journal of Political Philosophy* 277; Hélène Landemore, *Democratic Reason: Politics, Collective Intelligence, and the Rule of the Many* (Princeton University Press 2012).

[42] E.g., Douglass C North, "The New Institutional Economics and Third World Development" in John Harriss, Janet Hunter, and Colin M Lewis (eds), *The New Institutional Economics and Third World Development* (Routledge 1997); Daron Acemoglu and James Robinson, *Why Nations Fail: The Origins of Power, Prosperity, and Poverty* (Crown Publishers 2012).

[43] Hilton Root, "Tying the King's Hands" (1989) 1 *Rationality and Society* 240; Douglass C North, "Institutions and Credible Commitment" (1993) 149 *Journal of Institutional and Theoretical Economics* 11; Douglass C North and Barry R Weingast, "Constitutions and Commitment: The Evolution of Institutions Governing Public Choice in Seventeenth-Century England" (1989) 49 *Journal of Economic History* 803; Stephen Holmes, *Passions and Constraint* (University of Chicago Press 1995).

the national market and a stable financial system."[44] Constitutionalism is supposed to enable, not hinder, a living, breathing system of public power, populated by posts, institutions, and rules that deliver the public goods for the sake of which the polity exists. Constitutions allocate power among legislative, executive, and judicial branches of government, distribute competences among local, regional, national, and international institutions, and set out the processes through which offices throughout the land will be filled, laws issued, and disputes resolved.[45]

The idea that the basic "laws of rule" not only constrain the exercise of public power but also help to organize its effective exercise is hardly new. As early as the thirteenth century, Bracton defended his argument that the king must observe the fundamental laws of the realm in the following way:

> [The king] is called *rex* not from reigning but from ruling well ... Let him, therefore, temper his power by law, which is the bridle of power, that he may live according to the laws, for the law of mankind has decreed that his own laws bind the lawgiver ... Nothing is more fitting for a sovereign than to live by the laws, *nor is there any greater sovereignty than to govern according to law*, and he ought properly to yield to the law what the law has bestowed upon him, *for the law makes him king*.[46]

This passage suggests not only that it is desirable for the king to obey the law, but also that obeying the law constitutes and indeed enhances his sovereignty. But how can sovereignty be "greater" when it is exercised in accordance with the law, rather than arbitrarily? In what sense might legal limitation be said to strengthen the sovereign?

In his seminal essays on the enabling role of liberal constitutional constraints, Stephen Holmes elaborates on some of the ways in which constitutional rule does not simply constrain and condition public power but can also render it more effective.[47] Holmes finds in the writings of Jean Bodin, conventionally considered the archetypal theorist of absolutist sovereignty, a proto-constitutional account of laws that are binding on the sovereign but which nevertheless work to augment his power. Among them, for instance, the *leges imperii* command the monarch to respect the right of succession, bar him from appointing a successor, oblige him to safeguard the territorial

[44] William N Eskridge Jr. and John Ferejohn, *A Republic of Statutes. The New American Constitution* (Yale University Press 2010) 1 and 10 respectively. Also see Arthur S Miller, "Toward a Definition of the Constitution" (1982) 8 *University of Dayton Law Review* 633, 646: "the Constitution of 1787 is only ostensibly one of rights and limitations; in fact, it is one of powers and of control."

[45] John Ferejohn and Lawrence Sager, "Commitment and Constitutionalism" (2003) 81 *Texas Law Review* 1929, 1945.

[46] Bracton, *On the Laws and Customs of England*, II, 305–6. Emphasis added.

[47] Holmes, *Passions and Constraint*.

integrity of the realm, and rule out arbitrary transfers of territory.[48] Bodin understood that these laws curtailed the discretion of any one monarch while ensuring the permanence of monarchical power itself; that is to say, they were "authority-reinforcing, will-empowering, and possibility-expanding rules."[49] Along similar lines, Francis Sejersted observes that early modern sovereigns who adhered to legal constraints on the scope of their authority were paradoxically more assured of the durability of their acts than a despot whose power was circumscribed by his own mortality.[50] Legal constraints could enable sovereigns to cash in some of their *de jure* authority for de facto control, that is, the ability to govern effectively.[51]

On these accounts, legal constraints on sovereign discretion help to resolve a key problem known to political scientists as the paradox of commitment, namely the idea that "the ability to commit ... expands one's opportunity set, whereas the capacity to exercise discretion ... reduces it."[52] Thus, in the early modern instance, the absence of limits to the sovereign's authority posed an obstacle to the sovereign's ability to wield its power effectively. Conversely, by curtailing his prerogative in the short term, the monarch could wield greater political power in the longer term. For instance, Hilton Root has argued that the French monarchy in the eighteenth century increased its creditworthiness by repudiating the claim to be above the law, and accepting an obligation to repay its debts.[53] By placing limits on its fiscal discretion, the sovereign reassured lenders that they would not be expropriated, and secured easier access to loans as a result. Property rights proved an excellent way of realizing such self-limitation, and by some accounts, they were expressly "created and maintained by the state to promote the goals of the state."[54]

In their well-known study of the Glorious Revolution of 1688, Douglass North and Barry Weingast advance a similar argument about the enabling effects of constitutional commitment.[55] They argue that the rapacious taxation policies pursued by the English monarchy during the seventeenth century led to constitutional conflict and prompted the introduction of a series of mechanisms for constraining the power of the

48 ibid 106–107. 49 ibid 109–10.

50 Francis Sejersted, "Democracy and the Rule of Law: Some Historical Experiences of Contradictions in the Striving for Good Government" in Elster and Slagstad *Constitutionalism and Democracy*, 144–9.

51 Stephen D Krasner, *Sovereignty. Organized Hypocrisy* (Princeton University Press 1999) 10.

52 Kenneth A Shepsle, "Discretion, Institutions and the Problem of Government Commitment" in Pierre Bourdieu and James Coleman (eds), *Social Theory for a Changing Society* (Russell Sage 1991) 246. Also see Ferejohn and Sager, "Commitment and Constitutionalism."

53 Root, "Tying the King's Hands"; North, "Institutions and Credible Commitment" 14–15.

54 Holmes, *Passions and Constraint* 102.

55 North and Weingast, "Constitutions and Commitment" 803–32.

monarch. These mechanisms included shifting the subject of the sovereign from the king to the king-in-parliament, entrusting fiscal power to a permanent parliament, and reinforcing the independence of the common law courts where claims of expropriation were heard.[56] Although each of these institutions limited the power of the monarch to expropriate his subjects, North and Weingast argue, they increased rather than diminished the solvency of the public purse.

Insofar as these constitutional reforms created pockets of individual liberty, particularly by reinforcing aristocratic property rights, their significance has been described primarily as marking the beginnings of the liberal constitutional tradition. The important point made by Holmes, Root, and North and Weingast is that the constitutional rules in question did not simply *limit* government, they also enlarged and perpetuated its power. Proto-constitutional provisions of a non-fiscal nature had similar effects, expanding the liberties of subjects while simultaneously strengthening the sovereign. For instance, Holmes argues that the French monarchy experimented with policies of religious toleration for essentially pragmatic reasons. Divesting the sovereign from the business of saving souls could help defuse political tensions that threatened domestic peace and monarchical authority.[57] Similarly, devolving more power to local representative assemblies created a safety valve for popular discontent that might otherwise destabilize monarchical authority.[58] Put differently, many proto-constitutional constraints on the absolutist monarch, even when they strengthened the liberties of subjects, ultimately contributed to empowering the sovereign.

North and Weingast's account has been criticized for inferring the motivations behind these constitutional changes from their observed effects.[59] The argument I have made so far does not hinge on the causal accuracy of their account, since I am neither arguing that constitutional constraints such as property rights were instituted with the aim of making government more powerful, nor that constitutional rule is a necessary or sufficient condition of effective government.[60] As Law observes, we can characterize a constitutional mechanism "either on the basis of the goals that it is intended

[56] ibid 816–17. [57] Holmes, *Passions and Constraint* 102, 120–25. [58] ibid 118–20.

[59] Jon Elster, "Don't Burn Your Bridge Before You Come to It: Some Ambiguities and Complexities of Precommitment" (2003) 81 *Texas Law Review* 1751, 1785.

[60] On whether constitutions "matter," see James M Buchanan, "Constitutional Restrictions on the Power of Government" in James M Buchanan (ed), *Choice, Contract, and Constitutions* (Liberty Fund 2001); Torsten Persson and Guido Tabellini, *The Economic Effects of Constitutions* (MIT Press 2003); Donald Lutz, *Principles of Constitutional Design* (Cambridge University Press 2006); Stefan Voigt, "Positive Constitutional Economics: A Survey" (1997) 90 *Public Policy* 205. For an econometric analysis of the effect of constitutional due process provisions on overall human rights observance, see Linda Camp Keith, "Constitutional Provisions for Individual Human Rights (1977–1996): Are they

to serve, or on the basis of the consequences that it actually produces."[61] Accordingly, my claim is of the latter sort: whatever the reasons, intentions, and causes behind these early experiments in constitutional rule, their effect was to "markedly increase [the sovereign's] capacity to govern and to achieve his steady aims."[62] In other words, they suggest that some instances of constitutional commitment reinforce rather than diminish the power of the sovereign.[63] This is what I will call the *functionalist logic of constitutional authority*.

In this context, I use the term *functionalism* to describe a mode of legitimation based on effective rule rather than a mode of causal inference.[64] The functionalist logic of constitutional authority represents a way of justifying political rules and procedures with reference to their role in enabling the effective exercise of public power. As such, it is analytically distinct from the democratic and rights-based accounts of constitutional authority, even though we often invoke all three justifications to defend or contest a given constitutional mechanism: for instance, the separation of powers has been regarded as a security against the arbitrary exercise of power, ensuring that "the same persons, who have the power of making laws" do not "have also in their hands the power to execute them, whereby they may exempt themselves from obedience to the laws they make, and suit the law, both in its making, and execution, to their own private advantage."[65] However, it can also be justified as "a form of the division of labor, permitting—in some cases—a more efficient distribution and organization of governmental functions."[66] Similarly, most well-ordered constitutional systems draw on some combination of all three sources of constitutional legitimacy, democratic, rights-based, and functional. However, the functionalist logic (again, understood as a mode of justification rather than as an explanatory paradigm) is irreducible to either the democratic or rights-based justifications for constitutional rule, just as surely as the latter are analytically distinct from one another.

mere 'Window Dressing'?" (2002) 55 *Political Research Quarterly* 111. On the impact of constitutional provisions on the likelihood of political repression, see Christian A Davenport, "'Constitutional Promises' and Repressive Reality: A Cross-National Time-Series Investigation of why Political and Civil Liberties Are Suppressed" (1996) 58 *Journal of Politics* 627.

[61] David S Law, "The Paradox of Omnipotence: Courts, Constitutions, and Commitments" (2006) 40 *Georgia Law Review* 407, 435.

[62] Holmes, *Passions and Constraint* 111.

[63] Of course, such a calculation could conceivably become a reason for adopting certain constitutional mechanisms, or a normative basis for justifying them.

[64] For a critique, see Jon Elster, *Ulysses Unbound: Studies in Rationality, Precommitment, and Constraints* (Cambridge University Press 2000) 89–90; Elster, "Don't Burn Your Bridge" 1784.

[65] John Locke, *Second Treatise of Government* (CB Macpherson ed, Hackett 1980) ch XII, 76.

[66] Holmes, *Passions and Constraint* 165.

A familiar example can help to sharpen this distinction. Few political debates have showcased the functionalist discourse of justification more prominently than those relating to the framing and adoption of the US Constitution—in fact, functionalist arguments arguably eclipsed appeals to individual rights or popular sovereignty in the same context. As David Hendrickson writes, "the conventional ways of describing the American political inheritance, focusing on its 'liberal' or 'republican' character, need to be supplemented by recognition of a third paradigm of thought ('the unionist paradigm')—one centered on the problem of cooperation among 'the several states in the union of the empire'."[67] Indeed, the imperative of replacing the Articles of Confederation with a new constitutional document was explicitly framed in the latter terms. The 1786 Annapolis Convention to "Remedy Defects of the Federal Government" called on state representatives to "consider how far an uniform system in their commercial intercourse and regulations might be necessary to their common interest and permanent harmony of the several states."[68] The proceedings of the convention appealed not to the necessity of such a system for securing republican freedom or protecting the rights of citizens, but rather to the need to "render the constitution of the Federal Government adequate to the exigencies of the Union."[69]

Many of the arguments summoned by the framers in support of the US Constitution evince a similar concern with commissioning an effective federal government.[70] Prior to the Constitutional Convention, Alexander Hamilton had warned repeatedly of the "feeble and precarious" nature of the union under the Articles of Confederation and had called for a "solid coercive" union to replace it.[71] That concern is also evident in the inaugural essay of the *Federalist Papers*, where Hamilton professes "[a]n enlightened zeal for the *energy* and *efficiency of government*," and vows to show the citizens of New York "[t]he *utility* of the Union to your political prosperity," "the *insufficiency* of the present confederation to preserve that Union,"

[67] David C Hendrickson, *Peace Pact: The Lost World of the American Founding* (University Press of Kansas 2003) xii.

[68] Proceedings of Commissioners to Remedy Defects of the Federal Government, Annapolis, September 11, 1786. Available at http://avalon.law.yale.edu/18th_century/annapoli.asp accessed October 8, 2015.

[69] ibid.

[70] As Skowronek points out, among the framers, Hamilton "pursued a vigorous and wide-ranging program aimed at concentrating power in the national government and centralizing national powers in the executive branch," particularly in areas of "internal taxation, finance, banking, public works, and military organization." Stephen Skowronek, *Building a New American State: The Expansion of National Administrative Capacities 1877–1920* (Cambridge University Press 1982) 22.

[71] Alexander Hamilton, Letter to James Duane dated September 3, 1780. Available at http://press-pubs.uchicago.edu/founders/documents/v1ch5s2.html accessed October 8, 2015.

and "the *necessity* of a government at least equally *energetic* with the one proposed."[72] The term "energetic" crops up frequently in these essays to denote the essential attribute of a government that can govern a large and disparate polity while conforming to the "principles of republican government."[73] Elsewhere, Hamilton argues that founding a "federal government capable of regulating the common concerns and preserving the general tranquility"[74] requires vesting it with "the power of making laws ... attended with a sanction" and not "mere recommendations which the States observe or disregard at their option."[75] The key criterion he proposes for evaluating the proposed constitution is not how avidly it safeguards the liberties of citizens, but whether it secures "the *quantity of power* necessary to the accomplishment of [the *objects to be provided* for by the federal government]."[76]

Perhaps more surprising is the degree to which James Madison joins Hamilton in underscoring the need to remedy the confederation's functional handicaps. On the one hand, Madison stresses that the "general government" is "not to be charged with the whole power of making and administering laws," but limited in "jurisdiction ... to certain enumerated objects, which concern all the members of the republic, but which are not to be attained by the separate provisions of any."[77] However, Madison explains, the framers were called upon to design "a national government, adequate to the exigencies of government, and of the Union."[78] Delegates to the constitutional convention "were deeply and unanimously impressed with the crisis, which had led their country almost with one voice to make so singular and solemn an experiment for correcting the errors of a system by which this crisis had been produced."[79] The crisis at hand was not so much one of defending republican liberty but of establishing a system "of a measure fully commensurate to the national exigencies."[80]

On Hamilton's accounting, these exigencies included securing a lasting internal peace, "the management of foreign affairs, the right of declaring war, of raising armies ... of regulating trade, determining with what countries it shall be carried on, granting indulgencies laying prohibitions on all the articles of export or import ... of coining money, establishing banks ... appropriating funds and doing whatever else relates to the operations of finance, transacting every thing with foreign nations, making alliances offensive and

[72] Alexander Hamilton, "Federalist No. 1" in Alexander Hamilton, James Madison, and John Jay, *The Federalist Papers* (Ian Shapiro ed, Yale University Press 2009) emphasis added.

[73] "Federalist No. 1." [74] "Federalist No. 16." [75] "Federalist No. 15."

[76] "Federalist No. 23." [77] "Federalist No. 14." [78] "Federalist No. 40."

[79] "Federalist No. 40." [80] "Federalist No. 40."

defensive, treaties of commerce &c."[81] As the Constitution's critics were quick to note, the theme of individual liberty is conspicuous in its absence from this list. Protesting the framers' preoccupation with a "strong and energetic" government, Patrick Henry lamented: "When the American spirit was in its youth, the language of America was different; liberty, sir, was then the primary object."[82] "If we admit this consolidated government," he warned at the Virginia ratification convention, "it will be because we like a great, splendid one."[83]

The *Federalist*'s emphasis on energetic (rather than emancipatory) government is partly attributable to the fact that constitutional rule was already associated with the idea of republican liberty in the minds of its intended audience. Having adopted written constitutions, the several states were already converts to the cause of constitutional government. Hamilton went so far as to concede that measures such as a centrally administered army might seem "dangerous to liberty," and yet, he contended, "we run much greater risk of having a weak and disunited federal government, than one which will be able to usurp upon the rights of the people."[84] Arguing against those who attacked the proposed document for entrusting too much power to the federal government, he wrote: "... the absurdity must continually stare us in the face of confiding to a government the direction of the most essential national interests, without daring to trust it to the authorities which are indispensible to their proper and efficient management."[85] Riffing on Alexander Pope, Hamilton declared: "the true test of a good government is its aptitude and tendency to produce a good administration."[86]

In sum, although the US Constitution has variously been cited as an exemplar of liberal, republican, and democratic models of constitutionalism, the *Federalist Papers* suggest that its framers were motivated as much by the imperative of making government *effective* as they were by the principles of popular sovereignty and individual liberty.[87] As Holmes writes, the framers "saw constitutions as instruments of government," and that as such, "their

[81] Letter from Hamilton to Duane.

[82] Patrick Henry, "Shall Liberty or Empire Be Sought?" speech to the Virginia Convention dated June 5, 1788. Available at https://en.wikisource.org/wiki/Henry%27s_speech_in_the_Virginia_Ratifying_Convention accessed October 8, 2015.

[83] ibid. [84] Letter from Hamilton to Duane.

[85] "Federalist No. 23." [86] "Federalist No. 68."

[87] "Perhaps the most important very early effects of the US Constitution were to eliminate military insecurity between the states ("Federalist No. 9") and to increase the scale of the market in which entrepreneurs in the states could trade ("Federalist Nos. 11, 23")." Russell Hardin, "Why a Constitution?" in Bernard Grofman and Donald Wittman (eds), The Federalist Papers *and the New Institutionalism* (Agathon Press 1989) 106.

constitutionalism was basically strategic, ... designed with the hope of enhancing the combined problem-solving capacity of the three branches and two levels of government."[88]

Of course, this does not mean that the framers sought greater federal "problem-solving capacity" for its own sake. Rather, they viewed the imperative of building an effective public authority to replace the deposed old order as a step towards securing the foundations of republican liberty. Unlike their French counterparts, Hannah Arendt has argued, American constitutional revolutionaries did not view public institutions as obstacles to liberty; what they were "afraid of in practice was not power but impotence."[89] According to Arendt, the framers viewed the primary task of constitution-making as "not how to limit power but how to establish it, not how to limit government but how to found a new one."[90] She traces this all-important lesson to Montesquieu, whose system of power arresting power was based on an understanding that "political freedom did not reside in the I-will but in the I-can."[91]

Despite its prominence within the ratification debates, therefore, the rallying cry of the need for an effective federal government was far from being the only guiding commitment of the US Constitution. It was nestled alongside liberal and republican principles, not least the aspiration to "secure the blessings of liberty" (if only for a non-enslaved, white, male, propertied minority) and establish a political community composed of equal citizens (whose scope was, again, severely limited) that would govern itself through "reflection and choice" rather than accident, force, or whim.[92] To say that these principles guided the constitutional framers is not to say that political institutions or officeholders respected them in practice. Rather, these ideals formed the basis for the constitution's claim (and that of the political system established in accordance with it) to the allegiance of those it governed. They were normative aspirations that have gone unfulfilled for much of the republic's citizenry for much of its history. However, their presence has empowered generations of oppressed and marginalized groups to challenge the institutions that flagrantly betrayed them.[93]

*

[88] Stephen Holmes, "To 'Facilitate Future Invasions of the Remainder': Westward Expansion and its Natural Enemies in the *Federalist Papers*" (forthcoming). Draft paper on file with the author.

[89] Hannah Arendt, *On Revolution* (first published 1962, Penguin Books 1977) 153.

[90] ibid 148. [91] ibid 150. [92] "Federalist No. 1."

[93] Famous examples in this vein include Elizabeth Cady Stanton and Lucretia Mott, "The Seneca Falls Declaration of Sentiments" [1848] reproduced in *History of Woman Suffrage* vol I (Fowler & Wells 1881) 70–3; Frederick Douglass, "What to the Slave is the Fourth of July?" [1852] reproduced in David Chesebrough (ed), *Frederick Douglass: Oratory from Slavery* (Greenwood Press 1998).

So far, I have argued that enabling the effective exercise of public power is a central, if often tacit, normative basis for constitutional authority. If true, what does this argument contribute to our understanding of constitutionalism? First, as I hope to have shown, arguments about effective government are a prominent refrain within the modern discourse of constitutional legitimacy. In light of this discussion, what is often framed as the central dilemma of constitutional rule between individual liberty and democratic self-rule must be reconceived as a trilemma: constitutional legitimacy entails striking a delicate balance the imperatives of democratic rule, individual liberty, and effective government. These imperatives do not always pull in the same direction, meaning that they may dispose public institutions towards certain choices rather than others depending on the primacy they are assigned within a particular constitutional order. To take the most familiar example, liberal constitutionalists worry that a singular commitment to the principle of popular sovereignty may endanger the rights of individuals who find themselves outvoted, while democrats point out that constitutional constraints might bar popular challenges to hardened patterns of domination. Equally important, I contend, are potential trade-offs between effective government on the one hand, and democratic self-rule and individual liberty on the other. For instance, critics of democracy since Plato have argued that popular rule can generate irrational, corrupt, or ignorant political decisions, and have sought to circumscribe the arena of participatory politics to ensure constant, effective, and wise leadership.[94] Perhaps more worrisome in the contemporary context are constitutional choices that sacrifice democratic participation or basic individual rights (or both) in the name of effective government, public order, security, or economic stability. At the extreme, such trade-offs might result in a system of authoritarian constitutionalism, which, as I have argued elsewhere, curtails individual and collective autonomy in the name of the unity, stability, and security of the state.[95] At the other extreme, we might imagine a form of anarchical constitutionalism that Hamilton feared the Articles of Confederation had become: a system too hamstrung by a mistrust of centralized power to discharge the basic tasks of statehood.

In their respective ways, the examples of authoritarian and anarchical constitutionalism manifest an extreme miscalibration of competing constitutional commitments. The theory of functional constitutionalism

[94] For a comprehensive critique of aggregative democracy as irrational, unfair, and open to manipulation, see William H Riker, *Liberalism Against Populism: A Confrontation Between the Theory of Democracy and the Theory of Social Choice* (first published 1982, Waveland Press 1988).

[95] Isiksel, "Between Text and Context: Turkey's Tradition of Authoritarian Constitutionalism."

I develop in the rest of the book underscores a less extreme but no less conspicuous miscalibration. In a nutshell, the EU represents an abbreviation and attenuation of democratic control over important political decisions for the sake of more competent policymaking at the supranational level. The concrete objectives pursued through European integration, such as economic productivity, competitive markets, consumer protection, health and safety standards, and sound environmental stewardship, are in and of themselves perfectly defensible, even indispensable. EU member states expect that delegating power from democratically accountable domestic institutions to democratically attenuated supranational institutions will more effectively protect their citizens' interests in each of these arenas. Viewed through this lens, the familiar claim about the EU's "democratic deficit" is in fact a complaint about the EU's failure to strike the right balance between alternate sources of constitutional authority, namely democratic rule on the one hand, and effective government on the other.

From this perspective, the EU throws into high relief the challenge of calibrating competing sources of constitutional authority, and the extent to which these competing sources can be traded off against one another without jeopardizing the overall legitimacy of the system. Furthermore, considering effective government as a source of constitutional authority alongside democracy and individual liberty allows the idea of constitutionalism to "travel" better without forfeiting its connotative precision.[96] Insofar as the EU instantiates neither the democratic nor the liberal models of constitutional rule, it seems to fall outside the constitutional category altogether. However, if the liberal and democratic models of constitutionalism are not the only ones available to us, and if we include within that category regimes that rest primarily on a logic of effective government (as I have argued we must), then we can reclaim constitutionalism as a relevant category of analysis in the context of international institutions that feature recognizable aspects of constitutional rule. The following section offers a sketch of this argument, while the details occupy Chapter 2.

(III) ECONOMIC UNION AND SOVEREIGN COMMITMENT

Although there has always been heated debate over the actors and conditions that explain each twist in the windy path of European integration, competing research programs tend to converge on the observation that integration responds to policy challenges which member states cannot, or can no longer,

[96] Giovanni Sartori, "Concept Misformation in Comparative Politics" (1970) 64 *American Political Science Review* 1033, 1035.

effectively tackle on their own.[97] The empirical literature tends to treat the EU primarily as a way for member states to enhance "legitimacy in functional, political and administrative terms," that is to say, as a power-building exercise that helps to "shore up" the diminishing efficacy of member states "acting in isolation."[98] The list of contemporary problems that "can no longer be solved within the framework of nation-states or by the traditional method of agreements between sovereign states" includes "the globalization of commerce and communication, of economic production and finance, of the spread of technology and weapons, and above all of ecological and military risks."[99]

All of this, however, pertains to the demand side of regional integration. The fact that states would benefit from cooperation or even that they are motivated to cooperate says very little about whether they will be able to do so.[100] Problems of collective action or social cooperation do not automatically

[97] The empirical literature on European integration is conventionally grouped along two major camps, neofunctionalism and intergovernmentalism, with a number of conciliatory approaches in between, most notably, that of multilevel governance. Although the common ground between these approaches can often be quite extensive, the most important point of divergence regards the agents that each theory privileges as the motor of integration. While intergovernmentalists explain the success of integration with reference to the preferences of member states, their relative bargaining power, and their willingness to accept limitations on their sovereignty, neofunctionalist theories tend to highlight the cooperative interaction between sub- and supranational agents and norms, including national courts, litigants, interest groups, and supranational actors such as the Commission, Central Bank, and the Court of Justice in extending the initial concessions made by states in directions neither foreseen nor approved by them. Under both accounts, however, the *capacity to govern* increases as a result of integration: either accruing to the states themselves (under the intergovernmentalist account) or strengthening sub- and supranational authorities at the expense of states (under the neofunctionalist account). The classic texts of intergovernmentalism include Stanley Hoffman, "Obstinate or Obsolete: The Fate of the Nation State and the Case of Western Europe" (1966) 95 *Daedalus* 862; Alan Milward, *European Rescue of the Nation-State* (Routledge 1992); Geoffrey Garrett and Barry R Weingast, *Ideas, Interests and Institutions: Constructing the EC's Internal Market* (University of California Center for German and European Studies 1991); Andrew Moravcsik, "Preferences and Power in the European Community: A Liberal Intergovernmentalist Approach" (1993) 31 *JCMS* 473; Geoffrey Garrett, "The Politics of Legal Integration in the European Union" (1995) 49 *International Organization* 171; Andrew Moravcsik, *The Choice for Europe. Social Purpose and State Power from Messina to Maastricht* (Cornell University Press 1998). Mainstays of the neofunctionalist camp include Ernest B Haas, *The Uniting of Europe* (first published 1968, University of Notre Dame Press 2004); Philippe C Schmitter "Three Neo-Functional Hypotheses about International Integration" (1969) 23 *International Organization* 161; Anne-Marie Burley and Walter Mattli, "Europe Before the Court" (1993) 47 *International Organization* 41; Wayne Sandholtz and Alec Stone Sweet (eds), *European Integration and Supranational Governance* (Oxford University Press 1998); Alec Stone Sweet, Wayne Sandholtz, and Neil Fligstein (eds), *The Institutionalization of Europe* (Oxford University Press 2001); A. Stone Sweet, *The Judicial Construction of Europe* (Oxford University Press 2004). On multilevel governance, see especially: Gary Marks, Liesbet Hooghe, and Kermit Blank, "European Integration from the 1980s: *State-Centric v Multi-level Governance*" (1996) 34 *JCMS* 341; Liesbet Hooghe and Gary Marks, *Multi-level Governance and European Integration* (Rowman & Littlefield 2001).

[98] Anand Menon and Stephen Weatherill, "Transnational Legitimacy in a Globalising World: How the European Union Rescues its States" (2008) 31 *West European Politics* 397, 398.

[99] Jürgen Habermas, *The Inclusion of the Other* (C Cronin and P de Grieff eds, MIT Press 1998) 106.

[100] As Keohane puts it, "It is the combination of the potential *value* of agreements and the *difficulty* of making them that renders international regimes significant. In order to cooperate in world politics on

generate their own solutions. In fact, numerous schemes of international cooperation have failed to get off the ground notwithstanding substantial agreement about the need for joint action between states. As scholars of international relations have long emphasized, interstate cooperation is conditional, among other things, on resolving the problem of credible commitment. In the absence of coercive enforcement, states are motivated to shirk the actions they must take in order to satisfy the terms of international cooperation and reap the reciprocal benefits.[101] The European integration process has required member states to take costly actions such as lifting restrictions to trade, scaling back state subsidies, and dismantling measures that advantage domestic producers or burden commercial mobility. It has been even trickier to promote "positive integration" by formulating harmonized regulatory measures in areas such as competition, agricultural subsidies, state aids, health and safety, environmental, consumer, and labor standards.[102] Moreover, even when states refrain from cheating, informational asymmetries can make it difficult for each state to gauge the extent to which its peers are upholding their end of the deal.[103] For similar reasons, traders and investors may be deterred from engaging in economic activity abroad if they are not confident that the host state will honor its obligations to treat foreigners equitably. Far from attesting to "an absence of conflict," Keohane writes, international cooperation is "highly political" insofar as it requires states to alter their behavior in lasting ways through "negative as well as positive inducements."[104]

In sum, cooperation among states is beset by the "paradox of omnipotence," whereby the lack of constraints on sovereign power (particularly of safeguards against cheating) gets in the way of the sovereign's ability to exercise its power effectively.[105] The EU's supranational governance mechanisms respond to this problem—at least in part—by providing a commitment and monitoring device.[106] The story of Ulysses tying himself to the mast of his ship to avoid future temptation by the sirens, which is

more than a sporadic basis, human beings have to use institutions." Robert O Keohane, "International Institutions: Two Approaches" (1988) 32 *International Studies Quarterly* 379, 386.

[101] Robert Axelrod, *The Evolution of Cooperation* (Basic Books 1984) 11. For a classic account of this problem in the international security context, see Robert Jervis, "Cooperation Under the Security Dilemma" (1978) 30 *World Politics* 167.

[102] Fritz W Scharpf, "Negative and Positive Integration in the Political Economy of European Welfare States" in Gary Marks, Fritz W Scharpf, Philippe C Schmitter, and Wolfgang Streeck (eds), *Governance in the European Union* (Sage 1996).

[103] Robert O Keohane, *After Hegemony. Cooperation and Discord in the World Political Economy* (Princeton University Press 1984) 92–5, 107.

[104] ibid 53. [105] Law, "The Paradox of Omnipotence."

[106] Moravcsik, *The Choice for Europe* 73.

often invoked as an allegory for constitutional constraint, is also apposite in the context of delegating power to supranational institutions.[107] "Governments adopting the rules and principles of international regimes take on future obligations whose costs they cannot accurately calculate," but thereby also "limit their ability to act on the basis of myopic self-interest."[108] Since the collective "self" of a sovereign state is polycephalous and multigenerational, it faces that many more temptations to renege on commitments.[109] Delegating competence over the making, monitoring, and enforcement of policies to an authority beyond member states' immediate control enables states not only to make their commitments credible to one another and to third parties, but also to effectuate those commitments in practice.[110]

Furthermore, the transfer of legislative and judicial authority to the EU is often framed "as a technical necessity: it is a way of binding the hands of national governments in order to insulate policymaking from partisanship and short-term electioneering."[111] Indeed, the European Commission and the Court of Justice invoke this functionalist rationale when their decisions contradict the express preferences of the member states: on this view, the integration project has generated imperatives that must take precedence over state consent if it is to reach its stated goals.[112]

In this respect, supranational governance, like many instances of constitutional constraint, responds to the problem of unlimited power obstructing effective rule. It is supposed to extend the functional capabilities of public institutions by reducing the discretionary scope of sovereign power. Just as the absolutist monarch had short-term incentives to default on his debts, and could only reassure creditors by narrowing his discretion to do so, states can increase the likelihood of following through on their commitments by empowering supranational agents to oversee compliance. These commitments help them to signal their credibility to their peers and to private actors, rendering reciprocal fulfillment of duties

[107] Jon Elster, *Ulysses and the Sirens. Studies in Rationality and Irrationality* (Cambridge University Press 1984). For limitations of the self-binding analogy with respect to constitutional constraints, see Elster, *Ulysses Unbound* 91–5.

[108] Keohane, *After Hegemony* 108.

[109] Jervis, "Cooperation Under the Security Dilemma" 168.

[110] Robert Axelrod and Robert O Keohane, "Achieving Cooperation Under Anarchy: Strategies and Institutions" (1985) 38 *World Politics* 226, 250. The distinction between credible or persuasive and effective commitments draws on Law, "The Paradox of Omnipotence."

[111] Christopher J Bickerton, *European Integration: From Nation-States to Member States* (Oxford University Press 2012) 14.

[112] For an analysis of pragmatic appeals to the effectiveness and uniformity of Community law at the Court of Justice, see Mitchel Lasser, *Judicial Deliberations: A Comparative Analysis of Transparency and Legitimacy* (Oxford University Press 2004) ch 4.

more likely.[113] Substantively, the obligations member states undertake are not static: the EU provides a platform for striking future bargains to address future policy challenges in mutually beneficial ways, and facilitates agreement by linking together a wide spectrum of issues.[114] Last but not least, supranational delegation insulates policymaking from domestic reversal, electoral alternation, and popular mobilization, curtailing democratic autonomy in anticipation of the long-term benefits of interstate cooperation.

What, exactly, are these anticipated benefits? In the following chapters, I will argue that the core commitment that frames the EU's constitutional system is that of establishing an economic union based on "the principle of an open market economy with free competition, favouring an efficient allocation of resources."[115] To realize that broad commitment, the EU has been tasked with, inter alia, "establishing [and] ensuring the functioning of the internal market," understood as "an area without internal frontiers in which the free movement of goods, persons, services and capital is ensured,"[116] coordinating member states' economic policies,[117] and defining and implementing a monetary policy with the cardinal aim of price stability.[118] Although the Treaty on European Union proclaims that the Union is "founded on the values of respect for human dignity, freedom, democracy, equality, the rule of law and respect for human rights, including the rights of persons belonging to minorities [...],"[119] little of the EU's institutional structure pertains directly to realizing these lofty aspirations. Rather, much of that structure has been designed to secure the conditions of material prosperity. Insofar as the EU's competences cluster around the goal of economic union, its constitutional system derives its legitimacy "not from any strong popular backing, but primarily from the economic credibility it claims to generate."[120] This is not to say that the EU does not have or has never enjoyed strong democratic support; it is rather to say that its authority rests firmly on a functionalist footing.

(IV) CONCLUSION

I have argued in this chapter that there are several distinct ways of justifying the authority of constitutional norms. While contemporary constitutional theory tends to emphasize the principles of individual liberty and democratic self-rule, constitutional systems are also expected to facilitate the

[113] Giandomenico Majone, "From the Positive to the Regulatory State: Causes and Consequences of Changes in the Mode of Governance" (1997) 17 *Journal of Public Policy* 139, 153.

[114] Keohane, *After Hegemony* 107. [115] Art 120 TFEU. [116] Art 26(1–2) TFEU.

[117] Art 119(1) TFEU. [118] Art 127(1) TFEU. [119] Art 2 TEU.

[120] Michael A Wilkinson, "The Specter of Authoritarian Liberalism: Reflections on the Constitutional Crisis of the European Union" (2013) 14 *German Law Journal* 527, 548.

effective exercise of political power. In particular, constitutional constraints can help address the paradox of omnipotence, whereby the state's unlimited discretion can hinder the effective exercise of power in matters ranging from securing public credit to engaging in international cooperation.[121] In contrast to a sovereign that disavows all limitations on its power, "a constitutionally-bound government acquires capacity it would not otherwise have by effectively restraining itself."[122] I concluded this discussion by suggesting that the authority of the EU and its legal system derives from precisely such a pragmatic exercise in sovereign commitment.

What I have not yet shown is why this supranational system of sovereign commitment should be considered a constitutional order in its own right. In the next chapter, I will detail the ways in which the EU's institutional and legal structure replicates *and* modifies familiar features of constitutional rule. Just as democratic constitutional systems prioritize norms and procedures that enable popular participation, and liberal constitutional systems protect the individual against arbitrary interference by the state, *functional constitutionalism* privileges effective government over other values and commitments. In the EU's case, the measure of effective government is the establishment of an economic union among member states. The appeal to the demands of economic union is not simply the enduring leitmotif of European integration, but also undergirds the EU's entire legal and institutional configuration and makes it structurally resistant to political contestation and democratic revision.

[121] Law, "The Paradox of Omnipotence."

[122] Ferejohn and Sager, "Commitment and Constitutionalism" 1929.

2

Functional Constitutionalism in the European Union

(I) A NEW LEGAL DISCOURSE FOR A NEW LEGAL ORDER

In some ways, the problem of international cooperation can be analogized to the problem of constitutional rule. Both are instances of sovereign commitment and confront the formidable challenge of getting rulers to observe limits on their power. International agreements, like constitutions, pose "parchment barriers against the encroaching spirit of power,"[1] and stand in need of various mechanisms to elicit the compliance of the sovereign without coercive enforcement.[2] It is obvious, however, that not all international regimes can be described as constitutional systems in their own right. In what sense can the EU be considered a constitutional order? Or does such consideration entail a category mistake?

Although the 1957 Treaty Establishing the European Economic Community (Treaty of Rome) was an agreement among states, over the first few decades of its existence, it evolved into "an integrated legal order that confers rights and obligations on private parties, and one in which the controls on the exercise of public power are similar in nature to those found in nation states."[3] The present-day European Union (EU) replicates many familiar aspects of domestic constitutional rule at the supranational level, including a hierarchically ordered system of legal norms based on the principle of enumerated powers, judicial review, a schedule of directly applicable individual rights, and institutions charged with making policies, implementing them, and monitoring domestic compliance. Accordingly,

[1] James Madison, "Federalist No. 48" in Alexander Hamilton, James Madison, and John Jay, *The Federalist Papers* (Ian Shapiro ed, Yale University Press 2009).

[2] Jeffrey L Dunoff and Joel P Trachtman, "A Functional Approach to International Constitutionalization" in Jeffrey L Dunoff and Joel P Trachtman (eds), *Ruling the World? Constitutionalism, International Law, and Global Governance* (Cambridge University Press 2009) 4, 10.

[3] Paul Craig, "Constitutions, Constitutionalism, and the European Union" (2001) 7 *European Law Journal* 125, 128.

many scholars have argued since the initial decades of integration that the European Community (and its successor, the EU) should be considered in constitutional terms.[4] As early as 1965, Commission President Walter Hallstein submitted that "[i]n [the Treaty of Rome] system we can clearly recognize the features of a federal constitution: a structure that depends on co-operation between the higher entity and constituent States."[5] In Joseph Weiler's classic formulation:

> The constitutional thesis claims that in critical aspects the Community has evolved and behaves as if its founding instrument were not a Treaty governed by international law but, to use the language of the European Court of Justice, a constitutional charter governed by a form of constitutional law.[6]

Most versions of the constitutional thesis cast the Court of Justice of the European Union (CJEU or ECJ) as the leading actor in a decades' long process of evolution. Although it is easy to overstate the influence of the Court in determining the course of European integration,[7] it is important to emphasize its preeminent role in shaping the agreements and compromises struck by the member states into a doctrinally coherent legal structure.[8] This story has been told many times: through its far-reaching interpretation of the relatively sparse provisions of the Treaty of Rome, the Court brought together the distinct legal systems of the member states under a dense canopy of supranational legal norms.[9]

Proponents of the constitutional thesis tend to identify three pillars as holding up this canopy. The first is the doctrine of the supremacy of EU law. In a series of landmark rulings beginning with *Costa v ENEL* in 1964,[10] the Court proclaimed that EC law must take precedence over the laws of member states in the event of a conflict, even when the norm in question

[4] See especially, Hans Peter Ipsen, *Europäisches Gemeinschaftsrecht* (JCB Mohr 1972); Ami Barav, "The Judicial Power of the European Economic Community" (1980) 53 *Southern California Law Review* 461, 466; Eric Stein, "Lawyers, Judges, and the Making of a Transnational Constitution" (1981) 75 *AJIL* 1.

[5] Walter Hallstein, "Some of Our 'Faux Problèmes' in the European Economic Community" (1965) 21 *The World Today* 10, 12.

[6] JHH Weiler, "The Reformation of European Constitutionalism" (1997) 35 *Journal of Common Market Studies* 97.

[7] Andrew Moravcsik, "The European Constitutional Compromise and the Neofunctionalist Legacy" (2005) 12 *Journal of European Public Policy* 349, 363; Peter L Lindseth, *Power and Legitimacy. Reconciling Europe and the Nation-State* (Oxford University Press 2010) 3, 110–11.

[8] Karen Alter, *Establishing the Supremacy of European Law* (Oxford University Press 2001); Alec Stone Sweet, *The Judicial Construction of Europe* (Oxford University Press 2004); Susanne K Schmidt and R Daniel Kelemen, *The Power of the European Court of Justice* (Routledge 2013).

[9] For authoritative accounts of this process, see Joseph Weiler, "The Community System: The Dual Character of Supranationalism" (1981) 1 *Yearbook of European Law* 268; Alter, *Establishing the Supremacy of European Law*; Stone Sweet, *The Judicial Construction of Europe*.

[10] Case 6/64, *Flaminio Costa v ENEL* [1964] ECR 585.

originates in that state's constitution (an assertion that has been and continues to be challenged by national constitutional courts).[11] Within domestic legal systems, the supremacy principle gives EU law entrenched status, a feature that is typically—though not uniformly—associated with constitutional law. No EU norm can be modified unilaterally through any member state's internal legislative or judicial processes. Since most treaty amendments require unanimous approval and ratification by all twenty-eight member states, treaty provisions have a "super-entrenched" status, meaning that they are entrenched at both the national and supranational levels.[12] Even individual opt-outs are a matter to be negotiated and agreed upon by all member states. Although the 2009 Treaty of Lisbon introduced a simplified revision procedure for certain treaty amendments, any amendment proposals must still meet the relatively onerous conditions of a unanimous Council vote and approval by the European Parliament.[13] In fact, one of the key reasons why the CJEU has been able to position itself as an influential institution in the constitutional development of the EU is the difficulty of modifying treaty norms.[14] Even the revision of ordinary EU law is arduous, requiring either a supermajority or unanimity among member states representatives in the Council, along with complex procedures of input by the European Parliament. Taken together, both primary *and* secondary EU law constrains the actions of member state institutions in the manner of entrenched constitutional norms.

Second, the piecemeal and sometimes grudging acceptance of the supremacy doctrine by national courts has resulted in a system of supranational judicial review that integrates EU law into the legal systems of member states as a partially autonomous source of normative authority.[15] Under the preliminary ruling procedure, national courts are empowered

[11] Case 106/77, *Amministrazione delle Finanze dello Stato v Simmenthal SpA* [1978] ECR 629; Case C-213/89, *The Queen v Secretary of State for Transport, ex parte Factortame Ltd and others* [1990] ECR I-2433. More recently, see *R (HS2 Action Alliance Ltd) v Secretary of State for Transport* [2014] UKSC 3, para 207, where the joint concurring opinion by Lord Neuberger and Lord Mance of the UK Supreme Court stated: "The United Kingdom has no written constitution, but we have a number of constitutional instruments. They include Magna Carta, the Petition of Right 1628, the Bill of Rights and (in Scotland) the Claim of Rights Act 1689, the Act of Settlement 1701 and the Act of Union 1707. The European Communities Act 1972, the Human Rights Act 1998 and the Constitutional Reform Act 2005 may now be added to this list ... It is, putting the point at its lowest, certainly arguable (and it is for United Kingdom law and courts to determine) that there may be fundamental principles, whether contained in other constitutional instruments or recognised at common law, of which Parliament when it enacted the European Communities Act 1972 did not either contemplate or authorise the abrogation."

[12] Christine Reh, "The Lisbon Treaty: De-Constitutionalizing the European Union?" (2009) 47 *JCMS* 625, 635.

[13] Art 48(6–7) TEU.

[14] Stone Sweet, *Judicial Construction of Europe* 66.

[15] Alter, *Establishing the Supremacy of European Law*; Water Mattli and Anne-Marie Slaughter, *Constructing the European Community Legal System from the Ground up* (EUI Working Papers 1996).

(and courts of last instance are required) to refer questions about the application of EU law to the Court of Justice.[16] Over time, the CJEU has directed national courts to disregard *any* national legislation that comes into conflict with European law. This mechanism has not only enabled the CJEU to co-opt domestic courts into a European judiciary with a supranational court as its primary guide,[17] but has also given ordinary national courts powers of judicial review normally reserved for constitutional courts, thus revising the domestic constitutional systems of member states in areas falling within the scope of EU law.[18] Moreover, because it is their own judiciaries rather than a distant international court ordering them to comply with EU law, member states have applied the latter more diligently than they otherwise might have.

The third customary pillar of the supranational legal order is the doctrine of direct effect. In 1963, the Court of Justice ruled that certain provisions of the Treaty of Rome gave rise to individual rights that could be relied on by individual litigants before national courts.[19] In the ensuing decades, the Court found more and more supranational norms to be directly

[16] Art 267 TFEU (ex-art 177 TEC).

[17] Stone Sweet, *Judicial Construction of Europe*; Anne-Marie Burley and Walter Mattli, "Europe Before the Court" (1993) 47 *International Organization* 41; Renaud Dehousse, *The European Court of Justice: The Politics of Judicial Integration* (St. Martin's Press 1998).

[18] To highlight some well-known examples: In the *Simmenthal II* case of 1978, the ECJ authorized lower courts to invalidate domestic statute in the event of a conflict with European law, flouting the Italian Constitution's prohibition against judicial review by lower courts. See Case 106/77 *Simmenthal SpA*. In its 1996 *Factortame* judgment, the Court of Justice arguably went further. In Lasser's words, the ECJ held that "the 'full, effective judicial protection' of Community rights justifies overriding the most basic premises of national constitutional law and separation powers doctrine: it requires Member State courts to overturn national legislation that is incompatible with—and therefore represents an 'obstacle' to—Community law, *even in those legal systems that do not grant such powers of review to their judiciaries.*" (Mitchel Lasser, *Judicial Deliberations: A Comparative Analysis of Transparency and Legitimacy* (Oxford University Press 2004) 225; Joined cases C-46/93 and 48/93, *Brasserie du Pêcheur SA v Bundesrepublik Deutschland and The Queen v Secretary of State for Transport* [1996] ECR I-1029, para 33). The British House of Lords, who had sent the original reference to the ECJ, accepted that the UK's EC membership necessitated the recognition of the supremacy of Community law, which in turn required curtailing the implied repeal (*lex posterior*) doctrine which had hitherto been the cornerstone of the British system of parliamentary sovereignty. UK House of Lords, *Factortame Ltd. and others v Secretary of State for Transport* [1991] 1 AC 603. More generally, see Eric Stein, "Lawyers, Judges, and the Making of a Transnational Constitution" (1981) 75 *AJIL* 1, 13; Stone Sweet, *Judicial Construction of Europe* 82–5; Miguel Poiares Maduro, "The Importance of Being Called a Constitution: Constitutional Authority and the Authority of Constitutionalism" (2005) 3 *International Journal of Constitutional Law* 332, 339–40; Miguel Poiares Maduro, "Sovereignty in Europe: The European Court of Justice and the Creation of a European Political Community" in Mary L Volcansek and John F Stack, Jr. (eds), *Courts Crossing Borders: Blurring the Lines of Sovereignty* (Carolina Academic Press 2005).

[19] According to the ECJ, treaty provision must be "clear," "unconditional," must give rise to "a negative obligation" on the part of states, and not be dependent on implementing measures in order to qualify for direct effect. Case 26/62, *Van Gend en Loos v Nederlandse Administratie der Belastingen* [1963] ECR 1. The Court later relaxed these criteria, e.g. Case 43/75 *Defrenne v Sabena* [1976] ECR 455.

effective within national orders. This vested member state nationals with a series of individuated entitlements originating exclusively in supranational law. To the extent that the EU creates rights that citizens can claim before national courts, it is often considered to have "moved ... beyond the traditional separation of international public law and domestic law."[20] This was the ECJ's own famous assessment in the *Van Gend en Loos* decision, where it declared that the European Economic Community "constitutes a new legal order of international law for the benefit of which the states have limited their sovereign rights, albeit within limited fields, and the subjects of which comprise not only member states but also their nationals."[21] The Court did not justify this interpretation of the treaty by invoking any moral duty on the part of the EC to protect individual rights, but did so on the grounds that enabling individuals to invoke certain treaty provisions as rights would help in "ensuring that obligations imposed upon those subject to the Treaty are observed"; bring about the "uniform interpretation of the Treaty by national courts and tribunals"; and enable the "effective supervision" of member state compliance with treaty obligations.[22] In other words, in designating individual citizens as its subjects, the EU legal order treats them as custodians of the obligations member states owe to one another.

In 1986, the ECJ carried the European legal order's three decades of development to its high water mark by calling the Treaty of Rome the "constitutional charter" of the European Community.[23] It declared that "The European Economic Community is a community based on the rule of law, inasmuch as neither its Member States nor its institutions can avoid a review of the question of whether the measures adopted by them are in conformity with the basic constitutional charter, the Treaty."[24] In a formulation it has regularly repeated since, the Court held in its *Les Verts* decision that "the EC Treaty [establishes] *a complete system of legal remedies* and procedures designed to enable the Court of Justice to review the legality of acts of the institutions."[25] Within their functionally delimited sphere of application, the authority of the treaties over the institutions they call into being is seamless and pervasive. In other words, the Court sets out to safeguard what I described in the last chapter, following MacCormick, as

[20] Ernst-Joachim Mestmäcker, "On the Legitimacy of European Law" (1994) 58 *Rabels Zeitschrift für ausländisches und internationals Privatrecht* 615, 622; Pierre Pescatore, "The Doctrine of 'Direct Effect': An Infant Disease of Community Law" (1983) 8 *European Law Review* 155, 158; JHH Weiler, "The Transformation of Europe" (1991) 100 *YLJ* 2403.

[21] Case 26/62, *Van Gend en Loos*. [22] ibid.

[23] Case 294/83 *Partie Ecologiste 'Les Verts' v Parliament* [1986] ECR 1339.

[24] ibid para 23. [25] ibid para 23.

the "minimal virtue" of constitutionalism, demanding that EU institutions "duly [respect] the conditional quality of powers conferred" and "[observe] faithfully the (interpreted) conditions of the respective agencies' empowerment."[26] Every exertion of authority by the EU must filter through the mesh of constitutional validity established by the treaties.

The *Les Verts* decision made constitutional language all but unavoidable in discussions concerning the nature of the supranational polity. In subsequent decisions, the Court has continued to use constitutional terminology, stating that the EU has "its own constitutional framework and founding principles."[27] Furthermore, much of the academic debate over the nature and trajectory of European integration takes place within the discursive parameters of constitutional theory, even when observers *challenge* the idea that the EU is a constitutional regime in its own right. The popularity of this terminology in the scholarship can partly be explained in terms of epistemic empowerment: conceptualizing the EU as a constitutional polity vindicates the relevance of legal and normative inquiry in the realm of international politics, where traditionally only sovereign states and their capacity to exert violence have been held to "matter,"[28] and where the law, either as a factual or normative category, has been regarded as largely epiphenomenal.[29] Nonetheless, this discursive turn did not long remain confined to scholarship. The inauguration of a more ambitious phase of political integration by the 1993 Treaty of Maastricht generated expectations that after many decades spent on the margins of public debate, the EU was finally ready for its own Philadelphian moment, imagined as a democratic act of self-constitution by which the peoples of Europe would re-establish their union on federal terms. Leading the charge, Jürgen Habermas argued that this transformation required—and would in turn be reinforced by—the adoption of a constitutional text that would help democratic politics to finally break the shell of the nation-state.[30] Endorsing Habermas's project in a celebrated 2000 speech, the then German foreign minister Joschka Fischer argued that the time had

[26] Neil MacCormick, *Questioning Sovereignty: Law, State, and Nation in the European Commonwealth* (Oxford University Press 1999) 103.

[27] Opinion 2/13 EU:C:2014:2454 para 158.

[28] As Waltz memorably phrased it: "National politics is the realm of authority, of administration, and of law. International politics is the realm of power, of struggle, and of accommodation." Kenneth Waltz, *Theory of International Politics* (McGraw-Hill 1979) 113.

[29] For an updated articulation of this position, see Jack L Goldsmith and Eric A Posner, *The Limits of International Law* (Oxford University Press 2006).

[30] Jürgen Habermas, *The Inclusion of the Other* (Ciaran Cronin and Pablo de Grieff eds, MIT Press 1998) 161; Jürgen Habermas, "Remarks on Dieter Grimm's 'Does Europe Need a Constitution?'" (1995) 1 *ELJ* 303; Jürgen Habermas, "Why Europe Needs a Constitution" (2001) 11 *New Left Review* 5.

come for Europe to federate.[31] Both of these appeals grounded the need for a "constitution for the EU" on two countervailing considerations: on the one hand, the legitimation problems created by the transfer of power from elected domestic legislatures and democratically accountable executives to supranational institutions attenuated from popular control; and on the other hand, the global forces that necessitated the expansion of supranational decision-making.

The constitutional movement crested with the decision of EU member states at the 2001 European Council meeting in Laeken to explore the possibility of a supranational constitutional document. Although the Council tasked the Convention with finding ways to "increase the democratic legitimacy, transparency [and efficiency] of the *present institutions,*" rather than fundamentally reconfiguring them,[32] the President of the Convention, Valéry Giscard d'Estaing, was quick to redefine its mission in express analogy with the Philadelphia Convention that drafted the US Constitution. The Convention stoked Euro-federalist hopes that the experience of constitution-making would "catalyze" the emergence of a vibrant European *demos* invested in the integration project and eager to make its mark on supranational policy.[33] The concerted effort to abandon the elite-driven, sotto voce manner of European integration in favor of grassroots political participation was evident in the extensive consultations with citizens and civil society groups that accompanied the Convention process.

Alas, the fruit of the Convention's labors, the equivocally entitled "Constitutional Treaty," was summarily rejected by the very *demoi* whose will it was intended to express. Although the French and Dutch referendums that defeated the Constitutional Treaty did not necessarily reflect popular judgment on the merits of the document, they doubtless constituted a kind of popular engagement with the European project. Furthermore, the bombastic billing of the constitution-making enterprise arguably heightened public perceptions of the EU's democratic deficit. Meeting in 2007, the European Council tasked a new intergovernmental conference with salvaging the necessary institutional

[31] Joschka Fischer, "From Confederacy to Federation: Thoughts on the Finality of European Integration," speech delivered at Humboldt University in Berlin, May 12, 2000. Fischer conspicuously borrowed from Habermas in casting the constitution as a solution for Europe's democratic deficit: "These three reforms—the solution of the democracy problem and the need for fundamental reordering of competences both horizontally, i.e., among the European institutions, and vertically, i.e., between Europe, the nation-state and the regions—will only be able to succeed if Europe is established anew with a constitution. In other words, through the realisation of the project of a European constitution centred around basic, human and civil rights, an equal division of powers between the European institutions and a precise delineation between European and nation-state level."

[32] European Council Presidency Conclusions, Laeken December 14–15, 2001 SN 300/1/01 REV 1. Annex I, 22–3, emphasis added.

[33] Habermas, *The Inclusion of the Other* 161.

reforms from the wreckage of the Constitutional Treaty, and unceremoniously consigned the rest to the dustbin of history: "The constitutional concept, which consisted in repealing all existing Treaties and replacing them with a single text called 'Constitution,' is abandoned."[34] These institutional repairs and updates were bundled into the primly intergovernmental Lisbon Treaty, which was adopted and ratified without any of the Philadelphian rhetoric.

To many, the abortive constitutional moment was hardly surprising. According to proponents of the "no-*demos* thesis," the EU lacks the necessary conditions of meaningful democratic engagement and fails to generate the degree of political identification among citizens that a constitutional polity must enjoy.[35] Although supranational institutions constrain states or help to resolve well-defined policy problems, critics have argued, they do not represent "a group of people the vast majority of which feels sufficiently attached to each other to be willing to engage in democratic discourse and binding decision-making."[36] On this view, domestic institutions still hold the key to political legitimacy and command the attention and loyalties of citizens, while "[n]either the Commission, nor the EP, nor the ECJ are understood to embody or express the capacity of a cohesive political community to rule itself through institutions historically constituted for that purpose."[37] The absence of a vibrant public sphere at the supranational level not only precludes the possibility of constitutionalism taking root in the supranational context,[38] but also ensures that attempts to impose a constitutional framework on the EU will result in a Euroskeptic backlash. *Pace* Habermas, adherents of this view insist that the *demos* catalyzes the constitution, not the other way around. As Weiler sums it up, "if there is no *demos*, there can be no democracy."[39] In its absence, the EU's elaborate constitution-like characteristics cannot breathe democratic life into supranational politics.[40]

[34] European Council Presidency Conclusions, Brussels June 21–22, 2007 11177/1/07 REV 1, Annex I, I.1, 15.

[35] Lindseth, *Power and Legitimacy* 10.

[36] Lars-Erik Cederman, "Nationalism and Bounded Integration: What it Would Take to Construct a European Demos" (2001) 7 *European Journal of International Relations* 139, 144.

[37] Lindseth, *Power and Legitimacy* 28.

[38] Dieter Grimm, "Does Europe Need a Constitution?" (1995) 1 *ELJ* 282.

[39] JHH Weiler, *The Constitution of Europe* (Cambridge University Press 1999) 337.

[40] Habermas's idea of the "catalytic constitution" espouses something of the Haasian "spillover" logic: it assumes that the legal procedural model so created will be incrementally filled in by democratic substance. This creates a tension between Habermas's democratic theory and his endorsement of the constitutionalization of the EU. As John McCormick puts it, "Habermas resorts to an unsubstantiated historical narrative and an unreflective ideational construction of the past in comparison with/in contrast to the present so that the present might be grasped more facilely. That Habermas engages in such moves to highlight optimistic rather than Weberianly pessimistic possibilities does not mitigate the undertheorized quality of the moves themselves." John P McCormick, *Weber, Habermas, and Transformations of the European State. Constitutional, Social, and Supranational Democracy* (Cambridge University Press 2007) 180.

Following the failed attempt to reinvent the EU as a supranational democracy, some of the certainty attending the use of constitutional terminology in scholarly debate has ebbed. Leading the charge, Peter Lindseth has argued that it is a category mistake to describe the EU in constitutional terms because:

> [t]he legitimation of supranational regulatory power (its "mandate," so to speak) has never been successfully located supranationally ... Rather, it has been located, however tenuously, in the enabling treaties themselves, akin to enabling legislation on the national level, empowering the supranational exercise of regulatory discretion within the capacious limits defined by those treaties.[41]

In Lindseth's view, constitutional authority has its source in popular will; it is original rather than derivative. By contrast, there is no such *pouvoir constituant* behind the EU's legal order; instead, the EU's legitimacy rests on the ongoing assent and participation of member states while its legal validity derives from special provisions contained in national constitutions. By implication, member states retain the sole true claim to the title "constitutional," while the EU's authority is more accurately understood as an extension of the postwar administrative state that complements, sometimes uneasily, representative democracy at the domestic level.[42]

As Lindseth persuasively argues, supranational governance operates largely in the administrative mode: the EU exercises powers delegated to it by member states; its autonomy extends no further than functionally delimited areas of policy; its decision-making processes privilege technical expertise over partisan bargaining and impartiality over ideology; and it operates at arm's length from majoritarian control. In this respect, Lindseth builds on Giandomenico Majone's long-standing characterization of the EU's supranational elements as continuous with domestic non-majoritarian institutions such as constitutional courts, central banks, and specialized regulatory agencies.[43] Although Lindseth stresses the profoundly contentious nature of the powers delegated to the EU, he maintains that "supranational institutions remain administrative, not constitutional."[44]

However, several important features of the EU's complex institutional landscape complicate the parsimonious binary of administrative and

[41] Lindseth, *Power and Legitimacy* 19. [42] ibid 89.

[43] Giandomenico Majone, "From the Positive to the Regulatory State: Causes and Consequences of Changes in the Mode of Governance" (1997) 17 *Journal of Public Policy* 139, 153; Giandomenico Majone, "The Rise of the Regulatory State in Europe" (1994) 17 *Journal of Public Policy* 77, 84, 92; Giandomenico Majone, *The European Community: An 'Independent Fourth Branch of Government'?* EUI Working Paper SPS No.93/9 (European University Institute 1993).

[44] Lindseth, *Power and Legitimacy* 53.

constitutional modes of authority. Almost since their origins, the power exercised by supranational institutions has outstripped their formal legal mandate, straining the principal–agent relationship implied by the administrative model.[45] The flexibility of the treaties, the CJEU's maximalist interpretations, the expanding scope of supranational competence, the political salience of the EU's powers, and the thorough-going transformation of member states' constitutional systems as a result of the integration process make it increasingly problematic to classify the EU alongside administrative institutions rather than constitutional polities. Most importantly, the EU confounds the analytical distinction between constitutional and administrative paradigms of political authority by fueling the machinery of constitutional rule with an administrative rather than democratic logic of legitimation. Furthermore, this development is not unique to the EU: the essential role that contemporary administrative institutions fulfill within democratic systems often blurs the boundaries between administrative and constitutional rule as mutually exclusive paradigms of political authority. In the US context, Eskridge and Ferejohn have proposed the notion of "administrative constitutionalism" to describe this hybridization, arguing that statutory mechanisms and administrative agencies are indispensable for realizing the abstract commitments enshrined in the US's superannuated, vague, and incomplete "Large 'C' Constitution."[46]

In light of these considerations, the rest of this chapter makes two complementary analytical moves. The first is to highlight the important respects, beyond the formal characteristics outlined above, in which the EU falls within the conventional conceptual parameters of constitutionalism. The second move is to identify the ways in which the EU scrambles these parameters. Taken together, these two analytical moves are intended to show that the EU represents a qualitative variation on the idea of constitutional rule, one that I term *functional constitutionalism*. Functional constitutionalism is not simply an ad hoc interpretive category tailored to the EU; it is a broader attempt to adapt the theoretical premises of constitutionalism to institutions that wield public power beyond the domestic context. The EU's legal system has already effected such an adaptation in practice, but constitutional theory has yet to catch up. A conceptual reckoning is therefore long overdue.

[45] This discussion draws in part on Turkuler Isiksel, "Review of *Power and Legitimacy: Reconciling Europe and the Nation-State*, Peter Lindseth (Oxford University Press, 2010)" (2012) 8 *European Constitutional Law Review* 128. Also see Peter L Lindseth, "Author's Reply: 'Outstripping', or the Question of 'Legitimate for What?' in EU Governance" (2012) 8 *European Constitutional Law Review* 153.

[46] William N Eskridge Jr. and John Ferejohn, *A Republic of Statutes. The New American Constitution* (Yale University Press 2010) 4–5.

(II) FUNCTIONAL CONSTITUTIONALISM, TAKE ONE: WHY CONSTITUTIONAL?

In the last chapter, I argued that unlike natural categories, social science concepts such as constitutionalism, democracy, or citizenship are historically and politically contingent. Attempting to hold their meaning constant in the face of new practices ignores the profound ways in which these concepts are conditioned by the political processes and institutions that instantiate them. This does not mean that ideas like democracy or constitutionalism are infinitely flexible; it is rather to say that applying them in a novel context is not like picking up a yardstick and using it to measure observed phenomena. The no-*demos* thesis exemplifies this fallacy. As a generic claim, it holds that the EU cannot be considered a constitutional system in its own right because constitutional authority properly so-called must be traceable to the will of a self-governing *demos*. As Dieter Grimm puts it, "it is inherent in a constitution in the full sense of the term that it goes back to an act taken by or at least attributed to the people."[47] The EU, by contrast, is not the product of an immediate popular act of self-constitution. Nor has it succeeded in forging a sufficiently proximate correspondence between the people and the supranational institutions that govern their lives. Consequently, it is said to lack several definitional features of constitutional authority, namely that it must be (i) comprehensive, because *all* exercises of political authority within a given body politic must be subject to the sovereign authority of the people as represented by their constitution; (ii) exclusive, because the constitution's authority is not derived from any source other than popular will; and (iii) autonomous, because the will of the people is subject to no other source of authority.

Parsed in this way, the normative lodestar that guides the conception of constitutionalism used by proponents of the no-*demos* thesis is the commitment to popular sovereignty. However, there are several reasons why framing that commitment as the definitive element of constitutionalism is overly restrictive. First, although the ideal of a popular act of self-founding is a fine one, as an empirical matter, it rests on a certain stylized narrative of eighteenth-century constitutional revolutions that few existing constitutional systems would be able to meet. Second, it is not clear that the democratic quality of a constitution hinges on whether it was drafted and ratified through mass participation (whether in the

[47] Dieter Grimm, "Treaty or Constitution? The Legal Basis of the European Union after Maastricht" in Erik Oddvar Eriksen, John Erik Fossum, and Augustin Jose Menendez (eds), *Developing a Constitution for Europe* (Routledge 2004) 75.

form of revolutionary upheavals, constituent assemblies, social mobilization, even referendums).[48] A constitution imposed by a foreign power or a hegemonic elite can evolve into a democratic regime if it institutes effective and inclusive mechanisms of electoral representation, incorporates usable procedures of constitutional amendment, and garners popular engagement and allegiance over time (the German *Grundgesetz* is a good example). Constitutions create *demoi* as much as *demoi* create constitutions, which makes it difficult to rule out the possibility that a supranational legal regime could generate its own bases of democratic legitimacy. For reasons I will explain shortly, the EU's current constitutional configuration makes such jurisgenerativity difficult and unlikely, but that is not a reason to preemptively dismiss the prospects of democratic constitutionalism beyond the state.

Third, and most important, by stipulating popular sovereignty as a necessary condition of constitutional authority, the no-*demos* thesis leaves no clear distinction between sovereign and constitutional authority. Yoking constitutional authority to democratic self-rule *as a definitional matter* leaves the former without distinctive analytical content of its own. Furthermore, this move naturalizes the statist cast within which the constitutional ideal has evolved, without explaining why that association is anything more than a matter of historical contingency. In fact, as intellectual historians have noted, constitutional rule is an idea whose resilience over a remarkably long period is explicable at least partially with reference to the fluidity and adaptability of its meaning.[49] According to Gerald Stourzh, present conceptions of constitutional rule can be traced to at least two distinctive sources, implicating, first, "the application of analogies from nature to politics, or, to be more precise ... the transfer to bodies corporate or political of a term that is usually applied to the physical body"; and second, the Roman and canon law usages of "*constitutio*" in reference to "(fixed) law or regulations."[50] Thus, "in medieval and even early modern English law, the term referred to specific written regulations," distinguishing them from custom or convention.[51] It was around the time of the Glorious Revolution of 1688, Stourzh writes, "that the term 'constitution' was used in a fundamental act

[48] Jeffrey Lenowitz, *Why Ratification? Questioning the Unexamined Constitution-making Procedure* (PhD thesis, Columbia University 2013).

[49] Terence Ball and JGA Pocock (eds), *Conceptual Change and the Constitution* (University Press of Kansas 1988); Charles Howard McIlwain, *Constitutionalism Ancient and Modern* (Cornell University Press 1940); Edward S Corwin, "The 'Higher Law' Background of American Constitutional Law" (1928) 42 *Harvard Law Review* 149.

[50] Gerald Stourzh, "*Constitution*: Changing Meanings of the Term from the Early Seventeenth to the Late Eighteenth Century" in Ball and Pocock, *Conceptual Change and the Constitution*, 43.

[51] ibid 43.

of state … [where] James was charged with having attempted 'to subvert the constitution of the kingdom.'"[52] As late as 1748, however, Montesquieu still used the term *constitution* in a descriptive sense to refer to the frame of government, closely tracking Aristotle's idea of the *politeia*, while reserving the phrase *lois fondamentales* to describe those "fixed and established laws" governing the exercise of public power.[53] According to Stourzh, "The rise of the constitution as the *paramount law*, reigning supreme and therefore invalidating, if procedurally possible, any law of a lower level in the hierarchy of legal norms, including 'ordinary' legislator-made law, is *the* great innovation and achievement of American eighteenth-century constitutionalism."[54] Although this timeline can certainly be contested, Stourzh's conclusion that "it was a long time before the term 'constitution' emerged in documents of a publicly binding character" is surely on point.[55] In view of this complex trajectory, it is problematic to define constitutionalism exclusively in terms of the historically and politically contingent ideal of popular sovereignty as exercised within the territorial state, however appealing that ideal remains in normative terms.

In fact, proponents of the no-*demos* thesis often conflate the conceptual question of the coherence of non-democratic models of constitutional rule with the normative question of their desirability. As I argued in the last chapter, constitutional machinery can be used to advance a wide range of principles and ends, and modern constitutional practice has been shaped by many different justificatory discourses. Natural law, scripture, divine revelation, custom and tradition, national grandeur, and public order are alternative justifications that can yield different (though not necessarily desirable) forms of constitutional rule. In fact, a spate of recent scholarship attends to the ways in which constitutional rule has been used to thwart popular participation, undermine individual rights, and perpetuate illiberal or hegemonic practices.[56] Democracy is not the only basis on which constitutional authority can be built, though we might insist that it is the only *legitimate* basis. Framed in this way, the no-*demos* yields a strong normative argument that the EU's constitutional system is illegitimate to the extent

[52] ibid 42–3.

[53] Charles de Secondat, Baron de Montesquieu, *The Spirit of the Laws* (Anne M Cohler, Basia C Miller, and Harold S Stone trs and eds, Cambridge University Press [1748, 1758] 1989), pt I, bk 2, ch 1, 10; pt I, bk 2, ch 4, 18.

[54] Stourzh, "*Constitution*: Changing Meanings of the Term," 47, emphasis original.

[55] ibid 42.

[56] Alexander Somek, "Authoritarian Constitutionalism: Austrian Constitutional Doctrine 1933 to 1938 and its Legacy" in Christian Joerges and Navraj Singh Ghaleigh (eds), *Darker Legacies of Law in Europe* (Hart 2003); Tom Ginsburg and Alberto Simpser (eds), *Constitutions in Authoritarian Regimes* (Cambridge University Press 2013); Turkuler Isiksel, "Between Text and Context: Turkey's Tradition of Authoritarian Constitutionalism" (2013) 11 *International Journal of Constitutional Law* 702.

that it is insufficiently democratic, but it does not establish that the EU cannot coherently be considered a constitutional system in its own right.

If we persist in treating constitutionalism as an expression of popular sovereignty, with its attendant demands that constitutional authority must be comprehensive, exclusive, and autonomous, many of the EU's member states would arguably also fall short of that conception. The assumption of a world made up of discrete, self-contained, and self-validating constitutional orders is no longer a comprehensive description of empirical reality (if it ever was).[57] It is increasingly difficult to trace the authority exercised by global governance institutions to a single, comprehensive jurisdiction or to any single "metaprinciple of authority."[58] States are subject to *jus cogens* norms; they have become habituated to accommodating competing legal claims raised from within other jurisdictions; they undertake mutual obligations under public international law; they observe the judicial principle of comity, and private and public law obligations towards private actors such as business corporations; and constitutional ideas cross-pollinate among different systems.[59] Even within the domestic context, therefore, the paradigm of comprehensive, exclusive, and fully autonomous constitutional authority is no longer adequate.[60] The qualified nature of sovereignty necessarily constrains the scope of popular sovereignty.[61]

By contrast, extracted from its sovereigntist cast, the constitutional perspective captures a far greater variety of legal form and function. Here, the risk is one of over-inclusion. Gunther Teubner's definition of constitutionalism as the "foundation of an autonomous order and its self-limitation" exemplifies this tendency.[62] Teubner observes that "these two functions of the constitution cannot be limited to politics," and extends the remit of the constitutional idea to spheres of social interaction including the economy, science, religion, or sport.[63] In his view, privileging the political sphere as the proper domain of constitutionalism is not only arbitrary but also reflects

[57] It has been argued that it was not. For a representative sampling of the reasons why, see especially Hent Kalmo and Quentin Skinner (eds), *Sovereignty in Fragments. The Past, Present and Future of a Contested Concept* (Cambridge University Press 2010). Also see Stephen D Krasner, *Sovereignty. Organized Hypocrisy* (Princeton University Press 1999); Lauren Benton, *A Search for Sovereignty: Law and Geography in European Empires, 1400-1900* (Cambridge University Press 2010).

[58] Neil Walker, "Beyond Boundary Disputes and Basic Grids: Mapping the Global Disorder of Normative Orders" (2008) 6 *International Journal of Constitutional Law* 373, 376.

[59] Sujit Choudhry (ed), *The Migration of Constitutional Ideas* (Cambridge University Press 2007).

[60] MacCormick, *Questioning Sovereignty* ch 8.

[61] Anne Peters, "Compensatory Constitutionalism: The Function and Potential of Fundamental International Norms and Structures" (2006) 19 *Leiden Journal of International Law* 579, 592.

[62] Gunther Teubner, *Constitutional Fragments: Societal Constitutionalism and Globalization* (Oxford University Press 2012) 18.

[63] ibid 17.

an impoverished and flawed statist understanding of society. As I argued in the introduction, however, an overly broad conception of constitutionalism fails to take account of "the importance of being called a constitution."[64] In other words, it dulls the critical edge of constitutionalism as a normative ideal and risks reducing it to a sociological marker for the differentiation of social systems.[65]

To avoid the pitfalls of over- and under-inclusiveness, I propose to reserve the terminology of constitutionalism for a system of public institutions whose powers are so extensive as to *constitute* a discrete political community, without, however, stipulating as a definitional matter that any constitutional system properly so-called must be configured in line with strong democratic principles. Eponymously, constitutional systems are constitutive in the sense of laying the foundations of a body politic. Even judged by this criterion, however, the EU at first blush still seems like an addendum to the sovereign states that have brought it into existence, since it rests on a series of revocable agreements between them. At no point in its history has any member state announced any intention to relinquish to the EU its primacy as a political unit and as a source of allegiance for its citizens. Once again, however, we should be wary of presuming an eighteenth-century narrative of constitutive acts that dramatically sweep away the *ancien regime* and replace it with a new order.[66] In practice, radical constitutional shifts often occur at an evolutionary, rather than revolutionary, pace. When, precisely, did the American states cease to be sovereign, or agree to such a cessation? When did Britain become a democracy? When did Russia stop being one? When did France revert from an empire to a nation-state? In each case, it is clear that a constitutive shift has occurred in the nature of political community, but it is artificial, not to say counterfactual, to assign a single revolutionary watershed to each.

By the same token, European integration has surely engendered political transformations that are constitutional in scale, no less so for their incrementalism. As Craig writes, the EU legal order has evolved from "a relationship binding upon the states *qua* states, to an integrated legal order that confers rights and obligations on private parties, and one in which the controls on the exercise of public power are similar in nature to those found in nation states."[67] Although the states that make up the EU have not ceased

[64] Maduro, "The Importance of Being Called a Constitution."

[65] G Sartori, "Concept Misformation in Comparative Politics" (1970) 64 *American Political Science Review* 1033.

[66] Hannah Arendt, *On Revolution* (first published 1962, Penguin Books 1977).

[67] Craig, "Constitutions, Constitutionalism, and the European Union" 128.

to be states, they have become *member* states.[68] A member state, Bickerton argues, is better understood as a "distinctive kind of state where national power is exercised in concert with others" and "whose self-understanding is inseparable from pan-European-level cooperation."[69] Much as marriage or civil partnership transforms two unattached individuals into members of a new social unit, EU membership has redefined constituent polities by occasioning far-reaching institutional, legal, social, political, and cultural transformations. Much of this work has been performed by the EU's legal system, which knits together supranational, national, and subnational norms and applies sophisticated tools to smooth out the snags.[70] The result is a composite polity that is embedded *within* member states as much as it is *above* them. While none of the transformations occasioned by European integration are irreversible, much less inevitable, they are nothing short of constitutive: not because a popular revolution has swept away the *ancien regime* of autarkic nation-states, or because a Promethean assembly of law-givers has solemnly pronounced a new polity into existence, but because integration has gradually established a new configuration of political authority in Europe.

(III) FUNCTIONAL CONSTITUTIONALISM, TAKE TWO: WHY "FUNCTIONAL"?

Functionalism is one of the perennial –isms of social science, and for that reason a challenging term to repurpose. Before I flesh out the distinguishing characteristics of the EU as a system of *functional constitutionalism*, I will delineate my usage of this term from some of its conventional associations.[71] In a nutshell, I use the language of functionalism to convey the

[68] Chris J Bickerton, *European Integration: From Nation-States to Member States* (Oxford University Press 2012).

[69] ibid 4, 49.

[70] Christian Joerges, "Taking the Law Seriously: On Political Science and the Role of Law in the Process of European Integration" (1996) 2 *ELJ* 105.

[71] For a richly detailed intellectual historiography of functionalism as a theory of international law and organizations, see Jan Klabbers, "*EJIL* Foreword: The Transformation of International Organizations Law," (2015) 26 *EJIL* 9. Klabbers characterizes the functionalist paradigm as one that locates a given international organization's legitimacy in the limited grant of authority to it by states for a particular purpose. Put differently, this paradigm premises the legitimacy of an international organization on the consent of the states that have established it, rather than on the values or purposes that it has been established to pursue. By contrast, the functionalist logic I develop here heavily emphasizes the latter. I argue that the EU's claim to authority is not exclusively based on state consent. The EU acts in ways that are sufficiently attenuated from state consent as to require another source of justification, and draws its legitimacy in part from the immanent teleology of the objectives with which it has been charged.

EU's purposive mode of legitimation. This differs from its familiar connotation in the field of comparative constitutionalism, where functionalism is understood as a way of accounting for variation among political institutions with reference to the problems or imperatives of governance to which they respond.[72] In David Kennedy's words, functionalist approaches evaluate and classify "legal cultures according to the different ways they achieve common economic or political functions," and address "social, economic, and political needs and realities."[73] This understanding of functionalism as an epistemic method, as a tool of the knower, contrasts with my use of it as a feature of the thing known. In other words, I use the qualifier "functional" to convey certain distinctive properties of a constitutional system, rather than to denote a particular approach used to understand constitutional systems. Similarly, the phrase *functional constitutionalism* is not intended to suggest that the EU is the functional equivalent of a constitutional system or that it discharges the tasks that constitutional systems might be expected to fulfill. I intend to argue both more and less than this: on the one hand, my claim is that the EU is not merely *analogous to* a constitutional regime; it *is* a particular kind of constitutional regime. On the other hand, I wish to systematically establish the distinctive features of supranational as opposed to domestic constitutionalism, at least as we observe it in the EU.

For their part, social scientists commonly understand functionalism to refer to a disputed manner of causal inference, according to which "specialized structures will evolve to perform new tasks or to fulfill new needs as these arise."[74] Functionalist accounts are typically criticized for deriving causes from observed outcomes, thereby eliding other possible explanatory factors and failing to explain cases in which the same needs have gone unmet. In what follows, I use the terminology of functionalism to denote a species of normative claims rather than causal ones. In other words, the qualifier "functional" describes a normative pattern of justification, not a particular mode of accounting for social change.

By far the most well-established referent of functionalism in the context of EU studies is the still-fecund research program of neofunctionalism. The *locus classicus* of this school is Ernst B Haas's inquiry into the causal

72 Mark Tushnet, "The Possibilities of Comparative Constitutional Law" (1999) 108 *Yale Law Journal*, 1125, 1238. For a critique of the functionalist approach, see Ruti Teitel, "Comparative Constitutional Law in a Global Age" (2004) 117 *Harvard Law Review* 2570 (arguing that a functionalist analysis of constitutionalism is problematic insofar as "a shared understanding of the aims of constitutionalism … has not yet emerged" 2576.).

73 David Kennedy, "New Approaches to Comparative Law: Comparativism and International Governance" (1997) *Utah Law Review* 545, 561, 588 respectively.

74 John Gerard Ruggie, "Collective Goods and Future International Collaboration" (1972) 66 *American Political Science Review* 874, 875.

dynamics of regional integration in Europe, specifically of the European Coal and Steel Community (ECSC) .[75] Although Haas later came to doubt this early account, his work launched a thousand progressions, qualifications, and critiques.[76] In broad outline, neofunctionalist accounts of regional integration tend to stress supra- and subnational dynamics, not least the agency of supranational institutions and the shifting loyalties of domestic groups to explain the gradual erosion of state sovereignty and the sidelining of its classic instruments.[77] Despite the terminological overlap, my argument neither presumes nor questions the validity of the neofunctionalist research program. Here, again, my goal is not to investigate the conditions that explain the EU's institutional trajectory, but to give an interpretive and critical account of the principles underpinning the EU's legal system.

An important point of departure for Haas's neofunctionalist account was a normative paradigm of international politics advanced by David Mitrany in the mid-twentieth century. Mitrany endorsed functionalism as the most promising vehicle towards establishing what he called a "working peace system."[78] He argued that the world had "grown into a yet loose but living social system,"[79] whereby all states shared an interest in social welfare, technological progress, and economic prosperity, and had adopted "similar machinery of administrative practice and controls" to pursue these aims.[80] This "common outlook and purpose," he argued, could be exploited to advance international cooperation and ultimately to institute a system of world government. Over time, "the content and working of sovereignty would be changed effectively by ... inconspicuous and partial transfers of authority to functional organs."[81] Importantly, Mitrany was critical of early attempts at European integration, which he saw as poised to replicate the pathologies

[75] Ernst B Haas, *The Uniting of Europe. Political, Social, and Economic Forces 1950-1957* (first published 1958, University of Notre Dame Press 2004). Also see Leon N Lindberg, *The Political Dynamics of European Economic Integration* (Stanford University Press 1963), which applies and amends Haas's theory in the context of the European Economic Community; Philippe C. Schmitter "Three Neo-Functional Hypotheses about International Integration" (1969) 23 *International Organization* 161.

[76] Ernst B Haas, *The Obsolescence of Regional Integration Theory* (University of California Press 1975). For a sympathetic overview of what is living and what is dead in neofunctionalist integration theory, see Philippe C Schmitter, "Ernst B. Haas and the Legacy of Neofunctionalism" (2005) 12 *Journal of European Public Policy* 255. For a more critical appraisal, see Moravcsik, "The European Constitutional Compromise and the Neofunctionalist Legacy."

[77] Haas, *The Uniting of Europe* ch 1.

[78] See the essays collected in David Mitrany, *The Functional Theory of Politics* (LSE/Martin Robertson 1975).

[79] ibid 109.

[80] David Mitrany, "The Prospect of Integration: Federal or Functional" (1965) 4 *JCMS* 119, 136.

[81] Mitrany, *The Functional Theory of Politics* 121.

of nation-states.[82] Europe, Mitrany maintained, had adopted a federal/constitutional model premised on a fixed political compact among states rather than a dynamic model of functional cooperation based on "working efficiency and flexibility of membership."[83] Since the "cardinal virtue of the functional pattern" was that of "technical self-determination,"[84] Mitrany held, a functional organization had "no obvious need for constitutional division of authority and power"; in fact, "any except the most general formal rules would embarrass the working of the system."[85]

As this passage indicates, Mitrany understood functionalism and constitutionalism as mutually exclusive responses to the problem of international cooperation.[86] Despite the critical reception of Mitrany's empirical assumptions, this dichotomous classification of functionalism and constitutionalism as rival paradigms of political ordering has proved resilient.[87] For instance, according to Murray Forsyth:

> two souls or spirits dwell within the European integration process, as it has developed so far. The most immediately apparent, indeed the dominant one up to now, has been *the technical-functional*, or the programmatic. Alongside this is the *federal-constitutional spirit*, manifesting itself less directly, often masked by the technical-functional language of the official texts, but none the less there, and not a mere fiction or aspiration for the future.[88]

In contrast to Forsyth, who describes these two "spirits" as coexisting uneasily within the EU's institutional structure, the EU is often characterized *either* as a functional *or* as a constitutional polity. Proponents of the constitutional thesis typically maintain that the EU has moved beyond its original, functionalist configuration. By contrast, those who emphasize the functionalist,

[82] Mitrany writes: "if continental unions would tie up certain strands [of a loose but living social system], they would tear up many more, and more promising. The problems which now divide the national states would almost all crop up again in any territorial realignments; their dimensions would be different, but not their evil nature." *The Functional Theory of Politics* 109.

[83] Mitrany, "The Prospect of Integration" 143.

[84] Mitrany, *The Functional Theory of Politics* 118.

[85] ibid 118.

[86] Mitrany, "The Prospect of Integration" 126.

[87] Something of this distinction is also at play in the contrast Hooghe and Marks draw between Type I and Type II governance structures, which they argue embody "alternative responses to fundamental problems of coordination." Type I structures take their cue from federalism, featuring a durable architecture and fixed boundaries, a firm apportionment of jurisdictions, and a mixed bundle of competences; while Type II structures are goal-oriented institutions with task-specific jurisdictions, flexible institutional architecture, and fluid composition. See Liesbet Hooghe and Gary Marks, "Unraveling the Central State, but How? Types of Multi-level Governance" (2003) 97 *American Political Science Review* 233, 234–40.

[88] Murray Forsyth, "The Political Theory of Federalism and the Relevance of Classical Approaches" in Joachim Jens Hesse and Vincent Wright (eds), *Federalizing Europe? The Costs, Benefits, and Preconditions of Federal Political Systems* (Oxford University Press 1996) 40.

regulatory, or administrative nature of the EU's authority tend to question its constitutional credentials. In my view, this dichotomy is easily overdrawn. Instead, I submit that the EU's legal system can and should be understood as both functionalist and constitutional at the same time. An early precursor to this claim is Hans Peter Ipsen's classic account of the Community legal order, set out in his 1972 treatise *Europäisches Gemeinschaftsrecht*.[89] Ipsen was among the first to consider the EC in constitutional terms notwithstanding the functionally delimited nature of its tasks, the gradualism of its development, and the delegated basis of its authority.[90] He carefully distinguished supranational constitutional practice from its domestic variants, pointing to the dynamism of the EC's legal system, which he described as a *Verfassung im Wandel* or as a *Wandelverfassung*. Against European federalists, however, Ipsen contended that the EC was neither designed nor fated to follow a state-building trajectory.[91] Viewing integration as a federal enterprise, he argued, ignores its distinctive character as a purposive association for functional integration (*Zweckverband funktioneller Integration*).[92] This somewhat tautological phrase was meant to foreground a contrast between the limited scope of the EC's powers on the one hand, and the comprehensive authority and ethical totality of the sovereign state on the other.[93] Deepening this contrast, Ipsen described the EC as a utilitarian endeavor rather than an emotive association (*Gefühlsverband*), one that neither required nor generated sentimental attachment on the part of citizens.[94]

Ipsen's key insight was to characterize supranational constitutional authority in purposive or functionalist terms. Although its powers have greatly expanded in the intervening decades, the EU continues to draw its legitimacy from a claim to better govern enumerated domains of policy than member states acting alone.[95] However, Ipsen did not see any fundamental incompatibility between domestic constitutional autonomy and the

[89] Hans Peter Ipsen, *Europäisches Gemeinschaftsrecht* (JCB Mohr 1972). I am grateful to Luise Papcke for her research assistance and many helpful exchanges on Ipsen's work. I am also grateful to Christian Joerges and Michael Stolleis for conversations on Ipsen's biography, and for indulging my questions about how Ipsen's evidently sincere commitment to the Nazi regime might be reconciled with his enthusiastic advocacy of European integration after the war. See especially, Christian Joerges, "Europe a *Großraum*? Shifting Legal Conceptualisations of the Integraiton Project" in Christian Joerges and Navraj Singh Ghaleigh (eds), *Darker Legacies of Law in Europe* (Hart 2003) 182–3 n 92; Michael Stolleis, *A History of Public Law in Germany 1914-1945* (Thomas Dunlap tr, Oxford University Press 2004); Michael Stolleis, *Geschichte des Öffentlichen Rechts in Deutschland 1945-1990* (CH Beck 2012).

[90] Hans Peter Ipsen, *Verfassungsperspektiven der Europäischen Gemeinschaften* (Walter de Gruyter & Co 1970); Hans Peter Ipsen, "Die Verfassungsrolle des Europäischen Gerichtshofs für die Integration" in J Schwarze (ed), *Der Europäische Gerichtshof als Verfassungsgericht und Rechtsschutzinstanz* (Nomos 1983) 32.

[91] ibid 32.

[92] Ipsen, *Europäisches Gemeinschaftsrecht* 196–200.

[93] ibid 197.

[94] ibid 198.

[95] Hans Peter Ipsen, *Europäisches Gemeinschaftsrecht in Einzelstudien* (Nomos 1984) 34.

Zweckverband of the EC, arguing that participation in a functionally delimited legal system left the core of state sovereignty intact.[96] I maintain, by contrast, that Europe's functional constitutionalism has profoundly altered its member states, prompting far-reaching recalibrations of domestic institutions; reshuffling constitutional values; and curtailing member states' ability to pursue a myriad of policy priorities that conflict with their ever-expanding supranational obligations. What is more, these transformative dynamics were immanent in the vague but strikingly ambitious "ever-closer union" pledge enshrined by the Treaty of Rome. While this pledge did not necessarily point towards a federal state, it was from the beginning incompatible with an exclusive model of state sovereignty. In fact, Ipsen's own characterization of the EC as a transformative system militates against any self-contained understanding of a *Zweckverband*.

Most importantly, Ipsen bought into the discourse of supranational institutions as impartial administrators of value-neutral, apolitical, and non-redistributive tasks. However, this technocratic narrative conceals the extent to which supranational governance entails value-laden, contested political choices with deep implications for member states' ability to pursue domestic constitutional values such as social justice and democratic autonomy.[97] Similarly, Ipsen only grudgingly conceded that there may be democratic costs to a *Zweckverband* that cannot be offset by commensurate gains in effective governance. Anticipating other accounts of European integration as a technocratic project, such as the early work of Giandomenico Majone,[98] Ipsen insisted that majoritarian institutions that decide redistributive questions in the domestic context are complemented, not undermined, by supranational institutions whose legitimacy rests on organized knowledge creation (*Wissensbildung*).[99] In the final section of this chapter, and in the chapters that follow it, I will question this happy reconciliation.[100] For now, it is worth noting that as the EC acquired greater power, Ipsen grew more hesitant about the adequacy of the EC's functionalist basis of legitimacy, although he remained unconvinced that the mechanisms of representative democracy were the appropriate remedy in the supranational context.[101] If anything, the intervening decades have magnified these misgivings.

[96] Ipsen, *Verfassungsperspektiven der Europäischen Gemeinschaften* 6.

[97] Lindseth similarly critiques Ipsen for ignoring the deeply political nature of administrative governance. Lindseth, *Power and Legitimacy* 36.

[98] Most notably, Majone, *The European Community: An 'Independent Fourth Branch of Government'?*; Giandomenico Majone, "Europe's 'Democratic Deficit': The Question of Standards" (1998) 4 *ELJ* 5.

[99] Ipsen, *Verfassungsperspektiven der Europäischen Gemeinschaften* 20–21.

[100] On this point, see Christian Joerges, *The Law in the Process of Constitutionalizing Europe* (EUI Working Paper 2002/04) 17.

[101] E.g. Ipsen, *Europäisches Gemeinschaftsrecht in Einzelstudien* 50–1.

With this long train of negations and caveats out of the way, let me state my argument in a nutshell. In this book, the term "functional" conveys three distinctive characteristics of the EU's constitutional system. The first of these is that unlike domestic constitutional systems whose scope extends over the full range of public power within the body politic, the EU's legal system is functionally delimited. Second, this system enshrines the norms necessary to build an economic union between the member states; that is to say, it espouses a specific and detailed teleology compared to conventional constitutional systems, which it elevates above the fray of democratic contestation. Third, its legitimacy depends on the successful realization of these substantive objectives; that is to say, its basis of legitimacy is functionalist rather than democratic or rights-based. In what follows, I will elaborate on each of these characteristics in turn.

Functionally delimited sphere of validity

In the context of the sovereign state, constitutionalism implies "pervasive" authority:[102] exertions of public power are valid only insofar as they fall within the realm of possibility opened up by the constitution. All public power must filter through the mesh of constitutional validity. Put differently, not only is the constitution the highest legal authority, but there must also be "no space for proprietors of public power outside the constitution."[103]

Like a domestic constitutional system, "neither [EU] Member States nor its institutions can avoid review of the conformity of their acts with the basic constitutional charter" consisting of the treaties.[104] However, the EU's constitutional authority is also functionally delimited, meaning that EU law binds member states and their citizens only within the finite domain of policy delineated by the treaties. As Jean Monnet observed in a speech marking the inaugural session of the High Authority of the European Coal and Steel Community, supranational institutions "are sovereign within the limits of their competence—that is to say, [they] are endowed with the right to make decisions and carry them out."[105] If the attribution of sovereignty to

[102] Frank I Michelman, "What do Constitutions Do that Statutes Don't (Legally Speaking)?" in Richard W Bauman and Tzvi Kahana (eds), *The Least Examined Branch: The Role of Legislatures in the Constitutional State* (Cambridge University Press 2006).

[103] Grimm, "Treaty or Constitution?" 72.

[104] Joined Cases C-402/05 P and C-415/05 P *Yassin Abdullah Kadi and Al Barakaat International Foundation v Council of the European Union and Commission of the European Communities* [2008] ECR I-6351, para 281.

[105] Jean Monnet, Speech Inaugurating the High Authority of the European Coal and Steel Community, Luxembourg, August 10, 1952. Available at http://www.cvce.eu/content/publication/1997/10/13/218b0df9-f81d-43d5-aecb-d1c6aecba604/publishable_en.pdf accessed February 17, 2016.

an organization with such a narrow substantive mandate sounds contradictory, it nonetheless captures the tensions endemic to the hybrid legal and institutional structure to which it refers. Although European integration has long since left behind the sectoral approach exemplified by the ECSC, the hybrid configuration of authority identified by Monnet endures. Thus, on the one hand, EU law claims primacy within national legal systems in the way that constitutional norms prevail over statute.[106] On the other hand, this primacy obtains *only* within the sphere of validity delineated by the treaties. Any significant expansion of the EU's authority must be ratified by member states and can (at least in theory) be reduced by them.[107]

The policy goals that simultaneously empower the EU and circumscribe its area of activity radiate outwards from the central project of economic union. Of the senses in which the term *functional constitutionalism* captures the distinctive characteristics of the EU's legal order, then, the first is the functionally delimited rather than comprehensive scope of its authority.[108] Functional delimitation should not be confused with functional *specialization*, since the cardinal objective of economic union is not specialized or self-contained.[109] Quite the contrary, it implicates nearly every area of public policy. As a result, the EU's competences extend over a sprawling constellation of policy domains, prompting regular skirmishes over the scope of supranational authority that are led by the more vigilant national judiciaries, opposition parties, legislatures, administrative bodies, and other domestic political actors.[110] Particularly since EU decisions rely for their implementation on the cooperation of national and subnational authorities, the boundaries of the EU's competence are fuzzy, fluid, and perpetually contested.[111]

[106] "As a consequence of the supremacy of European law, the four economic freedoms, and the injunctions against distortions of competition, have in fact gained constitutional force vis-à-vis member states." Fritz Scharpf, *Governing in Europe: Effective or Democratic?* (Oxford University Press 1999) 58.

[107] Art 48(2) TEU.

[108] Peters, "Compensatory Constitutionalism" 602–3.

[109] In this sense, the EU scrambles the useful typology of units of governance set out by Hooghe and Marks. It is a durable, multilevel community that nevertheless has a task-specific jurisdiction (although one that is unusually broad), flexible design, and fluid boundaries. Hooghe and Marks, "Unraveling the Central State, but How?"

[110] The most recent example of skirmishes over the bounds of the authority granted to EU institutions concerns so-called Outright Monetary Transactions (OMT), which prompted the German Federal Constitutional Court (GFCC) to send its first request for a preliminary ruling to the CJEU. German litigants appealed to the GFCC to challenge the legality of the European Central Bank (ECB)'s program of authorizing the purchase of bonds issued by eurozone states on secondary markets as exceeding the limits of the authority granted to the ECB. In response, the CJEU ruled that no violation of the treaty's prohibition on monetary financing had occurred. Case C-62/14 *Peter Gauweiler and others v Deutscher Bundestag* ECLI:EU:C:2015:400.

[111] Miguel Poiares Maduro, "Europe and the Constitution: What if this Is as Good as it Gets?", in JHH Weiler and Marlene Wind (eds), *European Constitutionalism Beyond the State* (Cambridge University Press 2003) 93.

Although the EU, like typical federal systems, operates on the basis of the principle of enumerated or conferred powers, its constitutional system has a limited scope of authority.[112] By contrast, the authority of federal constitutions tends to be comprehensive in scope. Varying degrees of power and varying rosters of competences are allocated to different levels, but the federal constitution is usually the authoritative basis for this allocation, and the ultimate source of legal validity at all levels. "The constitutional framework of federation," Elazar writes, "provides the frame or bare bones of the structure which is, in turn, fleshed out by formal and informal institutional arrangements often overlapping."[113] Even where the federal government itself is relatively weak vis-à-vis constituent units, the authority of public institutions at all levels typically derives from and is delimited by the federal constitution. By contrast, EU law is situated within a composite constitutional structure that comprises plural, independently valid nodes of authority, and accordingly acknowledges (sometimes grudgingly) the primacy of other legal systems in matters that fall outside of its own scope of authority.

Insofar as it acknowledges its own limited scope but nevertheless operates as a fully fledged constitutional system within that scope, the EU legal order effectively decouples constitutional authority from the attribute of sovereignty. Although it is possible to construe the relationship between the EU's legal order and the constitutional systems of its member states as one of sub- and superordinate, derivative and original authority, doing so flattens the multidimensionality of the EU's legal architecture. As Cohen observes, "[t]he non-derivative character of legal supranationalism is as important to grasp as the non-derivative character of domestic constitutions."[114] This pluralist perspective illuminates shifts in normative authority that rigid conceptions of sovereignty tend to occlude. Rather than trying to shoehorn these complex relationships into stylized dichotomies, it is more useful to trade in the comprehensive conception of constitutional authority in favor of a "pluralist [and dispersed] conception" in which "different persons or bodies [have] the power to decide in different circumstances, without there

[112] I will refrain from foraying into the tangled definitional thicket of federations, confederations, unions of states, and commonwealths. Jean Cohen adroitly unravels this thicket, offering a compelling theory of the EU "as a union of states and peoples" that is not itself a state. See Jean L Cohen, *Globalization and Sovereignty. Rethinking Legality, Legitimacy and Constitutionalism* (Oxford University Press 2012) 85, and ch 2 more broadly.

[113] Daniel J Elazar, "The Role of Federalism in Political Integration" in Daniel J Elazar (ed) *Federalism and Political Integration* (Turtledove Publishing 1979) 16.

[114] Jean L Cohen, "Sovereignty in the Context of Globalization: A Constitutional Pluralist Perspective" in Samantha Besson and John Tasioulas (eds), *The Philosophy of International Law* (Oxford University Press 2010) 273.

necessarily being any single, hierarchical system of decision-making."[115] Constitutional autonomy in Europe's contemporary legal landscape is more helpfully conceived as graduated, intersectional, heterarchical, and pluralistic, rather than exclusive, comprehensive, hierarchical, and monistic.[116]

Clearly, this description reflects neither the domestic constitutional courts' nor the CJEU's respective conceptions of the European legal order and their own position within it. The Court of Justice famously claims exclusive authority to adjudicate the bounds of supranational legal authority, and has long maintained that "national courts have no jurisdiction themselves to declare that measures taken by Community institutions are invalid."[117] Leading the countercharge on the part of national judiciaries, the German Federal Constitutional Court reserves to itself the right to "[examine] whether legal instruments of the European institutions and bodies keep within the boundaries of the sovereign powers accorded to them by way of conferral," that is, to conduct ultra vires review of EU acts where the EU judiciary fails to do so.[118] In a pluralistic constitutional landscape, it is not surprising that questions of autonomy, supremacy, and decisional finality garner competing, even incommensurable answers from the point of view of each legal order. Luckily, the perspective of the observer need not overlap with that of any single participant. Constitutional theory can be multi-perspectival, meaning that it can comprehend the claims raised by each participant on their own terms without assigning to any single one among them the objective primacy that it craves.

Despite their incommensurable perspectives, the Court of Justice and domestic high courts have cultivated a practice of "constitutional toleration" in response to periodic challenges to the autonomy and supremacy of EU

[115] Richard Bellamy and Dario Castiglione, "Building the Union: The Nature of Sovereignty in the Political Architecture of Europe" (1997) 16 *Law & Philosophy* 422.

[116] Key contributions to the debate on constitutional pluralism include MacCormick, *Questioning Sovereignty*; Mattias Kumm, "The Cosmopolitan Turn in Constitutionalism: On the Relationship between Constitutionalism in and beyond the State" in Jeffrey L Dunoff and Joel P Trachtman (eds), *Ruling the World? Constitutionalism, International Law, and Global Governance* (Cambridge University Press 2009); Miguel Maduro, "Contrapunctual Law: Europe's Constitutional Pluralism in Action" in Neil Walker (ed), *Sovereignty in Transition* (Hart 2003); Miguel Maduro, "Courts and Pluralism: Essay on a Theory of Judicial Adjudication in the Context of Legal and Constitutional Pluralism" in Dunoff and Trachtman, *Ruling the World?*; Neil Walker, "The Idea of Constitutional Pluralism" (2002) 65 *MLR* 317; Daniel Halberstam and Eric Stein, "The United Nations, the European Union, and the King of Sweden: Economic Sanctions and Individual Rights in a Plural World Order" (2009) 46 *CMLR* 13; Matej Avbelj and Jan Komárek, "Four Visions of Constitutional Pluralism" (2008) 2 *European Journal of Legal Studies*. Available at http://www.ejls.eu/4/61UK.pdf accessed October 8, 2015.

[117] Case 314/85, *Foto-Frost v Hauptzollamt Lübeck-Ost* [1987] ECR 4199.

[118] German Federal Constitutional Court, Order of 30 June 2009, 2 BvE 2/08 (Lisbon Judgment), para 240. English translation available at http://www.bundesverfassungsgericht.de/SharedDocs/Entscheidungen/EN/2009/06/es20090630_2bve000208en.html accessed October 8, 2015.

law. The guiding maxim of this practice, in Weiler's words, is that "the jurisdictional line (lines) should be a matter of constitutional conversation, not a constitutional *diktat*."[119] As a discursive enterprise, constitutional toleration enables a plurality of relatively autonomous orders to accommodate one another's claims to validity without letting go of their own. It also illustrates the dialectical process by which the EU's legal system has come to be embedded within domestic constitutional orders, while prompting domestic constitutional orders to adjust to their supranational obligations.

Among the EU's most important contributions to constitutional theory is this demonstration of the feasibility (as distinct from the desirability) of constitutional pluralism, a system in which distinct legal systems exercise complementary and occasionally conflictual forms of authority without immediately succumbing to centrifugal dynamics. Just as Diogenes the Cynic is fabled to have refuted Zeno's dichotomy paradox by walking the distance that in theory is impossible to travel, the EU bears out what a sovereigntist conception of constitutionalism dismisses as impossible, namely, a pluralist system of authority in which "[d]istinct systems can co-exist without any one having to deny either the independence or the normative character of another."[120]

Unlike conceptions of constitutionalism that presuppose the attributes of sovereignty, functional constitutionalism allows us to comprehend these dynamics without squeezing them into a hierarchical mold. Under this conception, the EU's legal system is neither an independent supranational tier that floats above constituent political units nor a closely monitored agent of sovereign will. Rather, it is a purposively configured source of public authority that stretches across local, subnational, and national tiers of governance.[121] John McCormick has coined the term "*Sektoralstaat*" to describe this distinctive structure, which simultaneously assembles diverse units of governance around a particular policy issue and disaggregates public power into "functionally limited enumerated powers."[122] For this reason, McCormick argues, "the EU is a qualitatively different and new form of polity" in comparison with the law-governed liberal state (*Rechtsstaat*) of the early twentieth century and the corporatist welfare state (*Sozialstaat*) of the postwar period.[123] Constitutional mechanisms of entrenchment,

[119] JHH Weiler, "European Neo-Constitutionalism: In Search of Foundations for the European Constitutional Order" (1996) 44 *Political Studies* 517, 532.

[120] MacCormick, *Questioning Sovereignty* 75.

[121] In this respect, the idea of functional constitutionalism denotes a model of legal authority engendered by a multilevel governance structure. See especially, Liesbet Hooghe and Gary Marks, *Multi-level Governance and European Integration* (Rowman & Littlefield 2001).

[122] Mestmäcker, "On the Legitimacy of European Law" 633.

[123] McCormick, *Weber, Habermas, and Transformations of the European State* 250.

supremacy, and direct effect help to insulate the enumerated powers of the *Sektoralstaat* against interference by national institutions, including democratic ones. Whereas the *Rechtstaat* was animated by the principle of the rule of law and limited government, and the *Sozialstaat* by the principle of solidarity, the *Sektoralstaat* has its own principles and logics of coordination, most notably expediency, expertise, and power-building. I further discuss these principles in the following sections.

Teleological rigidity

The EU's constitutional evolution has been described as a "continuous, non-teleological process,"[124] one that "accepts contestation and non-fixity as a way of life."[125] This claim is often complemented by an emphasis on the absence of an explicit and intentional, much less agreed-upon, *finalité politique* guiding the integration process. However, mutability does not exclude teleology: teleological processes are defined by movement along a purposive trajectory arching from genesis to culmination, which distinguishes them from directionless motion propelled by happenstance.

Contrary to conventional wisdom, I submit that the EU's constitutional system has a strong teleological orientation, and which further distinguishes it from liberal and democratic models of constitutionalism discussed in the last chapter. The *telos* that guides the EU's legal order is that of economic union, understood in a capacious sense to include market integration, market regulation, and economic and monetary (and perhaps ultimately fiscal) union. As I remarked earlier, economic union is neither a narrow nor self-contained *telos*. The task of governing a multinational, diverse economic space, as the EU sets out to do, implicates a virtually unlimited range of policy questions. However, while most proponents of European integration have regarded economic union as a way station en route to an always-undefined *finalité politique*, this is the EU's central accomplishment to date. Whatever its as-yet unrealized potentialities or prospects, the EU's "really existing" constitutional system coheres around a *finalité economique*.

This purposive orientation marks the second important respect in which the EU's constitutional system differs from conventional models of constitutionalism. Constitutional theorists often distinguish constitutional norms from ordinary legislation or administrative law on the basis of two spectral characteristics: first, constitutional norms are expected to be substantively more open-ended relative to ordinary legislation, and relatively more

[124] Reh, "The Lisbon Treaty: De-Constitutionalizing the European Union?" 627.

[125] Jo Shaw, "Process, Responsibility and Inclusion in EU Constitutionalism" (2003) 9 *European Law Journal* 45, 48. It is important to note that Shaw is speaking here in the normative (and not necessarily descriptive) vein.

difficult to modify. In Holmes and Sunstein's words, "Constitutionalism hinges upon a distinction between the procedures governing ordinary legislation and the more onerous procedural hurdles that must be overcome in order to recast the ground rules of political life."[126] The constitution's role as the normative frame of politics implies that, all things being equal, it should be resistant to abrupt alteration and partisan manipulation for short-term political gain. According to Elster, this "ensures that constitutional change will be slow, compared to the fast lane of ordinary politics."[127] These two characteristics interact: since constitutional norms are resistant to change through the ordinary political process, they must be supple enough to accommodate a range of social, economic, and political priorities, interests, and changing circumstances. For this reason, public choice theorists invoke the metaphor of a sporting competition to analogize constitutional design to "agreements on the rules of a game," and the ordinary policy process to "agreements on the outcomes."[128] "[T]he hallmark of the constitutionalist," according to Buchanan, "is the categorical distinction he makes between outcomes generated within defined rules and the rules themselves."[129]

How to ensure that constitutional norms embody relatively neutral structural choices? Provided that they represent sufficiently diverse interests, Mueller hypothesizes that constitutional framers will choose rules that either reflect shared substantive values or set out procedures that are impartial, since they will not be able to foresee—much less agree on solutions to—policy controversies that might arise in the future.[130] Others cast doubt on Mueller's assumption, pointing out the difficulties of guaranteeing the fairness and impartiality of constitutional choice. For one thing, constitution-makers may be an elite cabal looking to prolong their grip on power at the expense of excluded groups. According to Ran Hirschl, constitutional entrenchment can be a tool for "hegemonic preservation," thwarting the interests of the majority and immunizing elite preferences.[131]

[126] Stephen Holmes and Cass Sunstein, "The Politics of Constitutional Revision in Eastern Europe" in Sanford Levinson (ed), *Responding to Imperfection. The Theory and Practice of Constitutional Amendment* (Princeton University Press 1995) 275.

[127] Jon Elster, *Ulysses Unbound. Studies in Rationality, Precommitment, and Constraints* (Cambridge University Press 2000) 100.

[128] Dennis C Mueller, *Constitutional Democracy* (Oxford University Press 1996) 62.

[129] Geoffrey Brennan and James M Buchanan, *The Reason of Rules. Constitutional Political Economy* (Cambridge University Press 1985) 20.

[130] Mueller, *Constitutional Democracy* 63. Also see James Buchanan and Gordon Tullock, *The Calculus of Consent* (University of Michigan Press 1962).

[131] Ran Hirschl, "The Political Origins of the New Constitutionalism" (2004) 11 *Indiana Journal of Global Legal Studies* 71; Ran Hirschl, *Towards Juristocracy: The Origins and Consequences of the New Constitutionalism* (Harvard University Press 2004).

As a historical matter, Melissa Schwartzberg notes, the strategy of making certain norms immutable has "a rich legacy of protecting narrow, instrumental decrees, such as treaties, and unjust laws against religious toleration and, most notoriously, slavery."[132] Furthermore, constitutions are invariably shaped by contingent bargains, power imbalances, and past injustices.[133] A constitutional norm, just like any other legal norm, can be unjust, oppressive, or illiberal; but it is often that much more difficult to change.[134]

Although this line of critique casts doubt on the likelihood that constitutional choice will be more impartial and accommodating toward different interests than the ordinary policy process, it paradoxically speaks in favor of reinforcing that distinction in practice. Assuming that the framers of a constitutional document are likely to prefer constitutional rules favorable to their own interests, as Charles Beard contended with regard to the US Constitution,[135] then constitutional norms should either be sufficiently mutable to allow marginalized individuals and groups to seek redress, substantively open-ended in order to allow such contestation to take place at the level of the ordinary political process, or both. To be sure, no constitutional regime is indifferent with regard to outcomes, and the purest proceduralism is not free of substantive presuppositions.[136] However, the compatibility of constitutionalism with individual and collective autonomy presumes the possibility of an analytical distinction between the rules and outcomes of the political process, and partly depends on the constitution's ability to maintain that distinction in practice.

The EU's system of functional constitutionalism is substantively elaborate in the way of ordinary legislation, but entrenched in the manner of constitutional law. On the one hand, as I argued in the last chapter, supranational law exists to hold states to their long-term policy commitments. For this reason, treaty provisions have super-entrenched status, and secondary EU law has entrenched status vis-à-vis domestic legal norms. Whereas constitutional entrenchment is reconciled with democratic autonomy with reference to its role in *enabling* collective self-rule, however, the EU's legal system has been configured to *constrain* the ability of member

[132] Melissa Schwartzberg, *Democracy and Legal Change* (Cambridge University Press 2007) 25.

[133] Courtney Jung, Ellen Lust-Okar, and Ian Shapiro, "Problems and Prospects for Democratic Settlements: South Africa as a Model for the Middle East and Northern Ireland?" (2005) 33 *Politics & Society* 277.

[134] Richard Bellamy, *Political Constitutionalism: A Republican Defence of the Constitutionality of Democracy* (Cambridge University Press 2007) 4.

[135] Charles A Beard, *An Economic Interpretation of the Constitution of the United States* (first published 1913, Macmillan Company 1921).

[136] Lawrence H Tribe, "The Puzzling Persistence of Process-Based Constitutional Theories" (1980) 89 *Yale Law Journal* 1063.

states to revise their commitments. Thus, "the constitutionalization of the treaties has 'frozen' certain specific goals by shielding them from political redefinition."[137] On the other hand, EU law is far more demanding in terms of detailed outcomes and obligations relative to the standard to which democratic theorists hold constitutional norms. As Forsyth writes, the EU differs from most federal constitutional systems in part because "the treaty base of the whole technical edifice expands into an immense tract ... that mixes the fundamental with the secondary, the general with the highly specific."[138] Procedurally, EU law is deeply entrenched, while substantively, it is overloaded with the kind of detailed prescription that would typically be left to ordinary legislative or even administrative processes.[139] In other words, the EU's system of functional constitutionalism collapses the distinction between defining the rules of the policy process and stipulating its outcomes.

Furthermore, supranational institutions such as the Commission, the Court, and even the European Parliament reflect this purposive configuration: they can push the integration project forward, but not backward; they can expand it, but do little to constrain it. As creatures of the treaties, these institutions lack the authority to revise, question, or curtail the objectives enshrined in them, however intense democratically expressed popular preferences may be in favor of doing just that. The combination of procedural and substantive fixity creates a powerful ratchet effect.[140] To paraphrase Robert Lecourt, former president of the ECJ, supranational law lacks a reverse gear because the treaties chart a one-way path towards integration.[141] In sum, EU law instantiates a system of functional constitutionalism not only on account of its functionally delimited scope, but also because it has a more pronounced teleological orientation relative to conventional constitutional systems.

Functionalist basis of legitimation

As I showed in the previous chapter, higher order norms that constrain, shape, and regulate the exercise of political power appeal to a variety of sources for their authority. Although the principles of democratic

[137] Stefano Bartolini, *Restructuring Europe. Center Formation, System Building, and Political Structuring between the Nation-State and the European Union* (Oxford University Press, 2005) 165.

[138] Forsyth, "The Political Theory of Federalism and the Relevance of Classical Approaches" 42.

[139] Dieter Grimm, "The Democratic Costs of Constitutionalisation: The European Case" (2015) 21 *ELJ* 460, 464.

[140] The ratchet metaphor is borrowed from Burley and Mattli, "Europe before the Court" 60.

[141] "Les traités ne prévoient aucun mécanisme d'aller et retour... On a parfois parlé d'Europe à deux vitesses, mais jamais d'un droit communautarie à marche arrière." Robert Lecourt, *L'Europe des Juges* (Bruylant 1976) 303–304.

self-rule and individual liberty have served as the lodestars of modern, secular systems of constitutional rule, they are not equally central to the EU's constitutional system. Rather, the EU's authority rests primarily on a functionalist pattern of justification. Far from being unique to the EU, this pattern is at work whenever institutions are valued primarily with reference to their conduciveness to expeditious decision-making, competent administration, the efficient provision of public goods, or superior epistemic quality. In the previous chapter, I discussed a long list of constitutional mechanisms that have been explained and/or defended in terms of enabling public institutions to effectively fulfill tasks that might otherwise elude them, such as ensuring political stability, securing cheap credit, encouraging private industry, or pacifying sectarian struggle.[142] As Alfred Stepan points out, power building is a particularly prominent rationale for the establishment of "coming-together federations" in which "previously sovereign polities agree to give up part of their sovereignty in order to pool their resources to increase their collective security and to achieve other goals, including economic ones."[143] As I argued in the last chapter, Alexander Hamilton's defense of the proposed US Constitution is emblematic of this line of argument. Hamilton stresses "[t]he utility of the Union to your political prosperity," "the insufficiency of the present confederation to preserve that Union," and "the necessity of a government at least equally energetic with the one proposed."[144] This parallel was also explicitly drawn by Altiero Spinelli, one of the key early leaders of the European integration process: "when it comes to the supranational unification of certain aspects of political life," Spinelli observed in 1957, "one cannot fail to take into account the American model, because the logic of the American system is the very logic of political power building."[145]

[142] This argument is developed in Chapter 1, section (ii), drawing on Hilton Root, Root, "Tying the King's Hands" (1989) 1 *Rationality and Society* 240; Douglass C North, "Institutions and Credible Commitment" (1993) 149 *Journal of Institutional and Theoretical Economics* 11; Douglass C North and Barry R Weingast, "Constitutions and Commitment: The Evolution of Institutions Governing Public Choice in Seventeenth-century England" (1989) 49 *Journal of Economic History* 803; Stephen Holmes, *Passions and Constraint* (University of Chicago Press 1995).

[143] Alfred Stepan, "Federalism and Democracy: Beyond the US Model" (1999) 10 *Journal of Democracy* 19, 21.

[144] Alexander Hamilton, "Federalist No. 1" in Alexander Hamilton, James Madison, and John Jay, *The Federalist Papers* (Ian Shapiro ed, Yale University Press 2009) emphasis added. On this rationale, see David C. Hendrickson, *Peace Pact: The Lost World of the American Founding* (University of Kansas Press 2003).

[145] Altiero Spinelli, "The American Constitutional Model and Attempts at European Unification" (first published 1957) (2005) 47 *The Federalist* 115. Available at http://www.thefederalist.eu/site/files/PDF/EN/2000/2005-2-EN.pdf accessed October 8, 2015.

As these examples suggest, functionalist justifications often make reference to specific *teloi* to be achieved, such as internal and external security, public order, wealth maximization, territorial expansion, or efficient use of scarce resources. The 1957 Treaty of Rome aimed to create a shared economic space capable of generating prosperity and, ultimately, a peaceful political order among European nation-states.[146] Although the EU has amassed a formidable portfolio of policy competences over time, "[t]he enhanced effectiveness generated by the supranational regulation of transnational economic exchange," not to mention the benefits of a competitive, integrated, and expanding market in goods, services, and capital, "represents an important legitimizing function of supranationalism."[147] Member states have delegated extensive powers to the EU in order to reap the efficiency gains of an integrated and competitive market, respond to the pressures of global economic interdependence, project their collective influence abroad, coordinate labor and other regulatory standards, and address shared challenges such as environmental stewardship. The promise of sustainable economic growth, and of a variety of public goods associated with an integrated marketplace, remains the primary justification for the EU's claim to bind member states and their citizens.[148] Above all, the term *functional constitutionalism* captures the EU's character as a political and constitutional system that is justified primarily with reference to producing public goods that states acting alone cannot guarantee.

In the parlance of EU scholars, the EU's technocratic pattern of legitimacy is known, following Fritz Scharpf's coinage, as "output legitimacy," according to which "political choices are legitimate if and because they effectively promote the common welfare of the constituency in question."[149] By contrast, Scharpf argues, an input-oriented conception of legitimacy considers political choices to be legitimate "if and because they reflect the 'will of the people'—that is, if they can be derived from the authentic preferences of the members of a community."[150] In constitutional democracies, what transforms the brute power of the state into normatively validated acts of public authority are the guarantees of individual and collective autonomy,

[146] On the economic focus of EU law, see, among others, Miguel Poiares Maduro, *We the Court: The European Court of Justice and the European Economic Constitution* (Hart Publishing, 1998); Christian Joerges and Michelle Everson, "Law, Economics and Politics in the Constitutionalization of Europe" in Erik Oddvar Eriksen, John Erik Fossum, and Augustin Jose Menendez (eds), *Developing a Constitution for Europe* (Routledge 2004).

[147] Anand Menon and Stephen Weatherill, "Transnational Legitimacy in a Globalising World: How the European Union Rescues Its States" (2008) 31 *West European Politics* 397, 402.

[148] Renaud Dehousse, *Rediscovering Functionalism* (Harvard Jean Monnet Working Paper No.7/00 2000) 8.

[149] Scharpf, *Governing in Europe: Effective or Democratic?* 6.

[150] ibid 6.

equal participation, and due consideration built into constitutional democratic procedures.[151]

According to Scharpf, input- and output-oriented modes of legitimation constitute "two dimensions of democratic self-determination."[152] Scharpf invokes Lincoln's famous characterization of democracy in the Gettysburg address as a system of "government of the people, by the people, for the people": governing "*for* the people" denotes output legitimacy, while government "of and by the people" stands in for the input dimension.[153] He writes that "plausible legitimacy arguments cannot be based on purely input-oriented (or 'populist'—Riker 1982) notions of democracy," but must include considerations of how well state institutions serve the public interest.[154] On this account, non-majoritarian institutions such as judicial review, independent central banks, and expert administrative agencies should be considered no less democratic than elected legislatures.[155]

There are several grave problems with assimilating the functionalist justification of constitutional legitimacy into the democratic paradigm, however. As I argued in the previous chapter, not all forms of political legitimacy are democratic: public institutions appeal to sources as diverse as divine right, antiquity, custom, morality, and class interests to justify their power over those whom they govern. A regime can fulfill its purposes without being democratic in any recognizable sense. In fact, the empowerment of institutions designed to ensure effective government often comes at the expense of participatory decision-making and electoral oversight. Conversely, democratic institutions do not necessarily make the best policy choices among those available. Even if democracy offers the best procedural device for generating good policy outcomes as epistemic democrats have claimed,[156] these two expectations should be held analytically distinct.

[151] Jürgen Habermas, *Between Facts and Norms: Contributions to a Discourse Theory of Law and Democracy* (William Rehg tr, MIT Press 1996).

[152] Scharpf, *Governing in Europe: Effective or Democratic?* 2.

[153] Fritz W Scharpf, "Democratic Legitimacy under Conditions of Regulatory Competition: Why Europe Differs from the United States" in Kalypso Nicolaïdis and Robert Howse (eds), *The Federal Vision* (Oxford University Press 2001) 358; McCormick, *Weber, Habermas, and Transformations of the European State* 270.

[154] Scharpf, *Governing in Europe: Effective or Democratic?* 7.

[155] This is the conclusion drawn by Giandomenico Majone, who opposes "populist" or "majoritarian" understandings of democracy to a "Madisonian" conception that aims to "share, disperse, delegate and limit power" in order to protect the public interest from majoritarian excess. Majone, "From the Positive to the Regulatory State" 159–60.

[156] Joshua Cohen, "An Epistemic Conception of Democracy" (1986) 97 *Ethics* 26; Josiah Ober, *Democracy and Knowledge: Innovation and Learning in Classical Athens* (Princeton University Press 2008); David Estlund, *Democratic Authority: A Philosophical Framework* (Princeton University Press 2008); Christian List and Robert E Goodin, "Epistemic Democracy: Generalizing the Condorcet Jury Theorem" (2001) 9 *Journal of Political Philosophy* 277; Hélène Landemore, *Democratic Reason: Politics, Collective Intelligence, and the Rule of the Many* (Princeton University Press 2012).

While it is attractive to think of effective government as a dimension of democratic rule rather than as a criterion external to it, doing so can have the effect of defining democracy in a way that is actively hostile to the idea of participatory rule. After all, few would recognize the image of democracy in being ruled by an omnicompetent, benevolent autocrat. Democracy is a contested and supple concept to be sure,[157] but institutions whose *raison d'être* is to limit the influence of citizens on policymaking are better understood as complements to democratic rule or as vehicles for realizing other important values and principles.[158] As Gutmann notes, the "democratic ideal, no matter how inclusive, cannot credibly lay claim to maximizing all the human goods at issue in ... political choices."[159] Furthermore, associating democracy with muscular epistocratic or technocratic criteria has what Nadia Urbinati calls a "disfiguring" effect on the concept.[160] The question of "whether the people should be permitted to rule on complicated matters even when they lack the knowledge of experts" is a serious and enduring theoretical problem within democratic theory, not one that can be "presumed away" by stretching the concept.[161] Rather than cramming effective government into a bloated conception of democracy, therefore, I characterize it as the central criterion of a distinct, *functionalist*, standard of legitimation. This is not to say that considerations of competence and epistemic quality are irrelevant for democratic institutions, much less that non-majoritarian bodies are incompatible with democracy; it is rather to observe that quality of "output" is not a democratic criterion per se.

Furthermore, while Scharpf maintains that the input- and output-oriented dimensions of legitimacy are "generally complementary," the EU is riven by a deep tension between democratic and functionalist modes of legitimation. Present since the origins of the European integration process, this tension has only grown as the EU's competences have expanded. Despite their deep commitment to democratic rule, member states themselves acknowledge that transferring power from domestic representative institutions to supranational institutions entails a trade-off when they appeal to the latter's greater problem-solving capacity.

Acknowledging the distinction between democratic and functionalist bases of legitimacy is essential for grasping why the EU represents a distinct mode of political ordering. In the previous chapter, I argued that modern

[157] WB Gallie, "Essentially Contested Concepts" (1956) 56 *Proceedings of the Aristotelian Society* 167.

[158] G Sartori, "Constitutionalism: A Preliminary Discussion" (1962) 56 *American Political Science Review* 853.

[159] Amy Gutmann, "Democracy" in Robert E Goodin and Philip Pettit (eds), *A Companion to Contemporary Political Philosophy* (Blackwell Reference Online 1995).

[160] Nadia Urbinati, *Democracy Disfigured* (Harvard University Press 2014).

[161] Gutmann, "Democracy" 521.

constitutional systems are expected to strike a three-way balance between commitments to democratic self-rule, individual liberty, and effective government. Each constitutional system weights these commitments differently. In contrast to democratic and rights-based models, the EU's constitutional system relies disproportionately on a commitment to effective government. Put another way, it posits economic objectives such as productivity, competitiveness, and higher standards of living as superordinate goods whose pursuit takes precedence over democratic self-rule by citizens, which is enshrined in the EU's institutional architecture only to the extent that it will minimally hinder the provision of these superordinate goods.[162]

The following chapters substantiate this claim in greater detail. Here, I will illustrate it with reference to a key treaty provision that broadly defines the EU's scope of competence, namely the principle of subsidiarity. Although the EU's competences are limited to those explicitly delegated to it by the member states, this principle, together with that of proportionality, helps to locate their outer bounds. According to the subsidiarity principle:

> in areas which do not fall within its exclusive competence, the Union shall act only if and in so far as the objectives of the proposed action *cannot be sufficiently achieved* by the Member States, either at central level or at regional and local level, but can rather, by reason of the *scale* or *effects* of the proposed action, *be better achieved* at Union level.[163]

More simply put, if EU action in an area not explicitly assigned to it by the treaties is unlikely to be more effective in attaining a given object than member states acting singly, then the EU has no valid reason to act. By contrast, if the EU's authority were premised on democratic principles, its mandate would be delineated on the basis of whether its actions would be likely to enjoy greater democratic legitimacy by comparison to member states acting alone. In fact, according to many observers, supranational institutions can claim just such a justification insofar as they oblige states to take into account the effects their decisions have on non-citizens.[164] Clearly, however, the subsidiarity principle represents a conflicting presumption that decisions taken at the national or subnational levels are more democratic than those made at the supranational level, but that considerations of effective policymaking may outweigh that presumption. In other words, far from awarding competences to the EU based on the democratic

[162] The distinction between subordinate and superordinate goods draws on Ian Shapiro, *Democratic Justice* (Yale University Press 1999) 23.

[163] Art 5(3) TEU, emphasis added.

[164] For instance, Maduro argues that European integration helps to "[correct] the constitutional limits of national political communities." Maduro, "Sovereignty in Europe" 57.

value-added of supranational decision-making, the treaties themselves acknowledge a trade-off between legitimation based on effective government versus that based on democratic self-rule.

(IV) THE VULNERABILITIES OF FUNCTIONAL LEGITIMACY

To argue as I have done here that the EU's constitutional authority is premised principally on a claim to functional effectiveness is not to say that supranational institutions are, as an empirical matter, more effective policymakers than member states. Absolutist monarchies have successfully appealed to divine sanction without any actual instances of celestial annunciation. The EU's legal order instantiates a system of functional constitutionalism because functional effectiveness, rather than democracy or individual liberty, predominantly frames its appeal to the allegiance of member states and citizens, whether or not that claim is borne out in practice. The commitment to effective government should accordingly be understood as an "aspiration and not fact."[165]

Nonetheless, the functionalist claim to legitimacy comes with a number of distinctive vulnerabilities. Any regime that consistently fails to fulfill the basic tasks assigned to it is liable sooner or later to lose the allegiance of those it governs. However, political systems whose legitimacy rests on democratic principles might be able to survive such crises if their members persist in their commitment to live together as a self-governing community of equals. By contrast, if the EU consistently fails to deliver the public goods expected of it, it stands to forfeit its very claim to exist. As Majone observes, "The legitimacy of non-majoritarian institutions depends ... on their capacity to engender and maintain the belief that they are the most appropriate ones for the functions entrusted to them."[166] To take a current example, discussed in greater detail in the conclusion, the EU's inability to swiftly resolve the economic and financial crisis that has roiled its member states since 2010 has not only jeopardized its monetary union, but has also dealt a severe blow to the promise of economic prosperity on which its legitimacy largely rests.[167]

Functional effectiveness is often a perfectly adequate basis on which to premise the authority of more narrowly tailored institutions. The same cannot be said of an entity whose powers are as significant and wide-ranging as the EU's. Although its decisions are massively consequential, the EU still

[165] Hendrickson, *Peace Pact* 21.

[166] Giandomenico Majone, "Europe's 'Democratic Deficit'" 22.

[167] See especially, Joerges, *The Law in the Process of Constitutionalizing Europe*.

casts controversial policy questions as problems to be solved rather than compromises to be struck between competing and sometimes incommensurable interests.[168] Its central justificatory standard remains one of Pareto-efficiency, whereby policies are claimed to be legitimate not because they express the will of the people or their representatives, but because they are supposed to make everyone better off.[169] This line of argument short-circuits pleas for greater democratic control over EU decision-making. Since no rational person could possibly object to being made "better off," it is by implication superfluous to consult citizens.[170] The very terminology of regulation, harmonization, and convergence used by EU institutions conveys the fiction that each policy question admits of one correct answer, and that the EU is capable of finding it. The prevalence of the term "governance" over "government" conceals the contested, redistributive, and mandatory nature of the EU's decisions.

The idea that any public institution is capable of ruling in a way that always leaves everyone better off is utopian, and very likely at odds with the very nature of politics. The exercise of power necessarily benefits some at the expense of others, or at least creates asymmetric gains. Supranational institutions are no exception. In domains as varied as competition policy, structural funding, agricultural subsidies, counterterrorism sanctions, and enlargement, not to mention the administration of the internal market and monetary policy, the EU makes decisions that rival any nation-state in their stakes, scope, and degree of obligation.[171] As Moravcsik and Sangiovanni contend, input legitimacy is inseparable from output legitimacy in the sense that it is impossible to assess whether policies are really in the public interest in the absence of robust democratic mechanisms for determining what is in the public interest.[172] This does not mean that no analytical distinction exists between functional and democratic legitimacy (a distinction, we might note, that is as old as Plato's *Republic,* and nowhere as sharply drawn). Rather, it means that the claim to effective rule is increasingly inadequate as a freestanding basis of legitimation for the EU.[173] The extent and significance of the EU's

[168] Scharpf, *Governing in Europe: Effective or Democratic?* 10–13.

[169] Simon Hix, *What's Wrong with the European Union and How to Fix it* (Polity Press 2008) 90–1.

[170] Jürgen Habermas, *Europe. The Faltering Project* (Ciaran Cronin tr, Polity 2009) 82–3.

[171] Hix, *What's Wrong with the European Union and How to Fix it* 94–6.

[172] Andrew Moravcsik and Andrea Sangiovanni, "On Democracy and 'Public Interest' in the European Union" in Wolfgang Streeck and Renate Mayntz (eds), *Die Reformierbarkeit der Demokratie. Innovationen und Blockaden* (Campus 2002).

[173] Richard Bellamy, "Democracy Without Democracy: Can the EU's Democratic 'Outputs' be Separated from the Democratic 'Inputs' Provided by Competitive Parties and Majority Rule?" (2010) 17 *Journal of European Public Policy* 2.

powers undermine its ability to make decisions that "avoid or at least minimize conflict,"[174] while its claim to make everyone better off rings hollow in the face of stiffening popular opposition to further integration. However desirable its objectives may be in the abstract, their attenuation from the processes of democratic authorization that give them meaning undermines the EU's claim to political obligation on the part of citizens.

(V) CONCLUSION

In this chapter, I outlined what I term the EU's system of *functional constitutionalism*. I argued that it has three distinguishing features, namely, the functionally delimited scope of its authority, its teleological fixity, and its functionalist pattern of legitimation. While the EU constrains sovereign power in the manner of a constitutional regime, and employs many conventional constitutional mechanisms in doing so, its legitimacy is premised primarily on a claim to make government more effective. This marks it out from constitutional systems whose legitimacy is rooted in their claim to facilitate democratic self-rule, protect individual liberty, or to achieve some other end altogether.

In the following chapters, I will delve into substantive areas of EU law to deepen the contrast between functional constitutionalism and other models of constitutional rule. Although the EU has been associated with far more noble ideals than the vulgar one of economic union, not least those enshrined in article 2 of the Treaty on European Union, these are at best indirectly pursued by its legal and institutional structure. Aspirational conceptions of supranational authority underestimate the extent to which the teleology of economic union constrains the EU's constitutional horizons and thwarts attempts at broadening them.

174 Scharpf, *Governing in Europe: Effective or Democratic?* 25.

3

Disentangling Fundamental Rights and Market Freedoms

Safeguarding basic individual rights is one of the defining tasks of modern constitutional rule. In the postwar period, however, many international organizations have also claimed this function.[1] This overlap does not necessarily imply redundancy: constitutional and international systems of rights protection can be complementary. While domestic constitutional systems build rights safeguards into the system of public power they call into being, international human rights regimes typically provide external oversight over domestic institutions.[2] (Of course, the success of neither type of oversight is assured!) The European Union (EU) appropriates elements of both models: on the one hand, like a constitutional state, it establishes a new system of public power on the basis of a schedule of individual freedoms, while on the other, it is an international (or supranational) body that patrols member state compliance with individual rights norms.

This sketch is accurate enough, but it elides a series of distinctions that are crucial for understanding how individual rights figure within the EU's constitutional system and, in turn, the characteristics of the system itself. The protection of certain individual rights is indeed foundational to the supranational constitutional system, meaning that certain rights norms condition and guide the exercise of power by the EU and its member states. Second, the EU does indeed

[1] For an early account and impassioned defense of this process, see Hersch Lauterpacht, *International Law and Human Rights* (first published 1950, Archon Books 1968).

[2] It is important not to overstate the dichotomy between external versus internal constraints. Extensive social science research suggests that the effectiveness of external mechanisms of human rights protection depends critically on their synergies with domestic mechanisms. See especially, Mark Goodale and Sally Engle Merry (eds), *The Practice of Human Rights: Tracking Law between the Global and the Local* (Cambridge University Press 2007); Ryan Goodman and Thomas Pegram (eds), *Human Rights, State Compliance, and Social Change: Assessing National Human Rights Institutions* (Cambridge University Press 2011); Beth A. Simmons, *Mobilizing for Human Rights: International Law and Domestic Politics* (Cambridge University Press 2009), 125–47; Margaret E Keck and Kathryn Sikkink, *Activists Beyond Borders* (Cornell University Press 1998); Seyla Benhabib, *Another Cosmopolitanism. The Berkeley Tanner Lectures* (Oxford University Press 2006).

constitute an autonomous source of individual rights guarantees for its citizens; that is to say, it creates novel entitlements that do not fully overlap with the guarantees found in domestic legal systems. However, the rights that have an exclusively supranational source are *not* those conventionally understood as human rights; rather, they are rights to engage in cross-border economic activity, and are derived from treaty provisions on the freedom of movement of goods, services, capital, and persons. In the discursive universe of EU law, these *fundamental freedoms* (*libertés fondamentales*) are quite clearly distinguished from *fundamental rights* (*droits fondamentaux*), which refer to the conventional set of basic human interests enshrined in most domestic constitutions, the European Convention on Human Rights, and the EU Charter of Fundamental Rights. The Court of Justice of the EU (CJEU)'s jurisprudence of market freedoms predates its appropriation of a supranational mandate to protect conventional basic rights, and has been far more demanding and exhaustive in comparison to the latter.

This distinction clearly poses the perennial question of what should and should not be categorized as human rights proper, which I will address in due course.[3] Most observers will agree, however, that not all individual rights claims rise to the level of *human* rights. It is too easy and sometimes quite convenient to elide this point, particularly if one is eager to celebrate the EU's pioneering success as an effective supranational regime of individual rights. Having chosen the loaded terminology of fundamental freedoms to describe the treaty provisions enabling commercial mobility, the Court of Justice bears some responsibility for this confusion. However, the Court's own jurisprudence clearly bifurcates the EU's rights regime into two relatively independent strands that have developed along separate paths and embody different rationales. This chapter contends that rights of commercial mobility still form the nucleus of the EU's constitutional system, occupying the place in the supranational normative hierarchy that a conventional constitutional system would reserve for rights such as the right to life and bodily integrity, the freedom of speech and conscience, or the right to vote and stand for election. However, commercial mobility rights are treated as fundamental not on account of their moral urgency, but because they are indispensable to forging an economic union among member states. In other words, they not only reflect the EU's purposive configuration, they are also the centerpiece of the EU's system of functional constitutionalism.[4]

[3] Philip Alston, "Conjuring up New Human Rights: A proposal for Quality Control" (1984) 78 *AJIL* 607; Maurice Cranston, "Human Rights, Real and Supposed" in Patrick Hayden (ed), *The Philosophy of Human Rights* (Paragon House 2001); Henry Shue, *Basic Rights. Subsistence, Affluence, and US Foreign Policy* (2nd edn, Princeton University Press 1996).

[4] According to the Court of Justice, "the objectives of the treaty" include, "in the first place, the establishment of a common market," which is defined as "the elimination of all obstacles to intra-Community trade in order to merge the national markets into a single market bringing about

To be sure, the incorporation of the Charter of Fundamental Rights into the EU's primary law in 2009 has given the protection of traditional fundamental rights an explicit and permanent basis within the supranational constitutional system. The potential effects of this incorporation on the EU's spectrum of competences have been carefully circumscribed, however. For instance, the EU lacks the authority to exercise human rights oversight over its member states except when their actions come within the material scope of the treaties, which is still largely conditioned by the teleological aim of economic union. Unless a human rights violation by a member state occurs within a policy domain that implicates the EU's competences, it will likely fall through the cracks of supranational protection. Notwithstanding its rhetorical power, therefore, the Charter of Fundamental Rights does not make the EU into a human rights organization, since its legal effect is conditioned by the EU's functionalist priorities.[5]

This is not to say that human rights are ornamental within the EU's legal system. It is, however, to caution that the presence or absence of a documentary commitment to human rights says little about the relative priority of human rights protection among the ends pursued by an organization, much less does such presence predict or ensure that organization's success in protecting and upholding human rights.[6] We must be careful not to mistake the constitutional text for the institutional matrices of power it calls into being. In the extreme instance, we can think of many political systems in which the principles ceremoniously enshrined in the constitution are manifestly violated in practice.[7] Although the EU is not such a system, it does evince a form of constitutional dysfunction whereby its documentary foundations pledge far more than what its current institutions are empowered

conditions as close as possible to those of a genuine internal market." Case 15/81 *Gaston Schul Douane Expediteur BV v Inspecteur der Invoerrechten en Accijnzen, Roosendaal* [1982] ECR 01409, para 33.

[5] The debate over whether the EU should be considered a human rights organization is a longstanding one. The question was posed and answered in the negative in an influential article by Armin von Bogdandy, "The European Union as a Human Rights Organisation? Human Rights and the Core of the European Union" (2000) 37 *CMLR* 1307. Bogdandy has since shifted his position and maintains that "Fundamental rights protection, once a sideshow, has become of central importance for the EU." Armin von Bogdandy, Matthias Kottmann, Carlino Antpöhler, Johanna Dickschen, Simon Hentrei, and Maja Smrkolj, "Reverse Solange—Protecting the Essence of Fundamental Rights against EU Member States" [2012] 49 *CMLR* 489. See also Philip Alston (ed), *The EU and Human Rights* (Oxford University Press 1999); Samantha Besson, "The European Union and Human Rights: Towards a Post-National Human Rights Institution?" (2006) 6 *Human Rights Law Review* 323.

[6] Linda Camp Keith, "Constitutional Provisions for Individual Human Rights (1977-96): Are They Mere 'Window Dressing'?" (2002) 55 *Political Research Quarterly* 111. On the impact of constitutional provisions on the likelihood of political repression, see Christian A Davenport, "'Constitutional Promises' and Repressive Reality: A Cross-National Time-Series Investigation of why Political and Civil liberties Are Suppressed" (1996) 58 *Journal of Politics* 627.

[7] David S Law and Mila Versteeg, "Sham Constitutions" (2013) 101 *California Law Review* 863.

to deliver. By itself, the statement that the EU is "founded on the values of respect for human dignity, freedom, democracy, equality, the rule of law and respect for human rights" does not endow the EU with the institutional or political capacity to make good on those principles.[8] Similarly, although the Charter of Fundamental Rights tasks the EU with guaranteeing a generous range of human rights, the functional delimitation of the EU's powers allows it to guarantee the enjoyment of a far narrower set of individual rights. These rights relate primarily to commercial mobility.

When it comes to protecting human rights proper, the role of supranational institutions is mostly intramural. The supranational judiciary, the Charter of Fundamental Rights, and the Fundamental Rights Agency are well-suited to monitoring the EU's own human rights compliance. Even so, however, the EU is relatively deficient when it comes to other constitutional devices that can ensure the observance of basic individual rights. As the EU's powers expand into ever more consequential domains of policy, its capacity to ensure a high level of rights protection will need to be expanded not only through documentary and doctrinal means, but through more robust mechanisms of checks and balances, the separation of powers, and democratic representation. The chapter develops each of these arguments in turn.

(I) FUNDAMENTAL RIGHTS OR MARKET FUNDAMENTALISM?

As drafted in 1957, the Treaty Establishing the European Economic Community (Treaty of Rome or EC Treaty)[9] contained no bill of rights. Although it guaranteed workers' rights to accept employment[10] and pursue self-employed activities in another member state,[11] these rights were designed as policy objectives that member states hoped to achieve rather than immediate, subjective entitlements. The treaty provided for procedures for fleshing out, adapting, and expanding these objectives and

[8] Art 2 TEU.

[9] The original EC Treaty has been amended many times, and has been officially renamed the "Treaty on the Functioning of the European Union" (TFEU) in 2009. For reasons of historical accuracy, I mostly refer to the EC Treaty or Treaty of Rome in this chapter, and provide updated references in the footnotes.

[10] Art 45 TFEU (ex-art 48 TEC) establishes the right of workers "to accept offers of employment actually made; (b) to move freely within the territory of Member States for this purpose; (c) to stay in a Member State for the purpose of employment in accordance with the provisions governing the employment of nationals of that State laid down by law, regulation or administrative action; (d) to remain in the territory of a Member State after having been employed in that State [...]"

[11] Art 49 TFEU (ex-art 52 TEC) provides that "Freedom of establishment shall include the right to take up and pursue activities as self-employed persons and to set up and manage undertakings, in particular companies or firms [...]"

supervising their implementation. The European Economic Community was not designed to function as a regime of individual rights, much less as a comprehensive human rights regime.[12]

In the seminal *Van Gend en Loos* decision of 1963, the European Court of Justice (ECJ) famously qualified the EC Treaty's interstate paradigm. It ruled that individuals could rely on certain treaty provisions before national courts to challenge member state acts they believed to be contrary to those provisions.[13] This establishment of the doctrine of direct effect is a classic declarative speech act, and a revolutionary one at that. The Court not only converted reciprocal obligations between states into standards of treatment owed to their (and one another's) citizens, but also recast the system established by the founding treaties as a "new legal order under international law."[14] In the decades following *Van Gend en Loos*, the Court of Justice ruled that some provisions of regulations,[15] directives,[16] the Treaty of Rome,[17] and certain other treaties,[18] have direct effect under the right conditions,[19] establishing a de facto supranational regime of rights.[20]

[12] There are two rival explanations as to why the Treaties of Paris and Rome lacked basic rights provisions. According to the orthodox account, rights protection was understood to fall within the domain of member state competence and to be guaranteed under other international rights documents, including the ECHR. On Gráinne de Búrca's revisionist account, by contrast, the omission was a temporary strategic move in line with the gradualist method of integration favored by Monnet and Spaak as distinct from more ambitious designs espoused by Spinelli and the framers of the failed European Political Community. De Búrca argues that the Communities were meant to acquire a human rights function all along, though this was expected to occur as a result of the expanding process of integration. Gráinne de Búrca, "The Road Not Taken: The European Union as a Global Human Rights Actor" (2011) 105 *AJIL* 649.

[13] Case 26/62 *Van Gend en Loos v Nederlandse Administratie der Belastingen* [1963] ECR 1.

[14] John R Searle, *Speech Acts: An Essay in the Philosophy of Language* (Cambridge University Press 1969).

[15] The EC Treaty provided that regulations would be "directly applicable," meaning that they would be binding on member states and valid in domestic legal systems without having to be transposed into statute. Although the immediate enforceability of regulations in domestic systems made them capable, in theory, of being invoked as individual rights before domestic courts, it remained unclear how direct applicability would play out in practice, particularly given that each member state had its own rules for the reception of international law. Ex-art 189 TEC (art 288 TFEU).

[16] Case 41/74 *Yvonne Van Duyn v Home Office* [1974] ECR 1337.

[17] *Van Gend en Loos.*

[18] Case 12/86 *Meryem Demirel v Stadt Schwäbisch Gmünd* [1987] ECR 3719.

[19] According to the ECJ, treaty provision must be "clear," "unconditional," must give rise to "a negative obligation" on the part of states, and not be dependent on implementing measures in order to qualify for direct effect. *Van Gend en Loos*. The Court later relaxed these criteria, choosing to give direct effect to the "principle" of equal pay for equal work contained in art 119 TEC (now art 157 TFEU), which obligation was rather general, imprecise, and not necessarily "negative." See Case 43/75 *Defrenne v SABENA* [1976] ECR 00455.

[20] The process by which the EC Treaty came to be interpreted as containing a schedule of individual rights has been told many times. For authoritative accounts, see especially Pierre Pescatore, "The Doctrine of 'Direct Effect': An Infant Disease of Community Law" (1983) 8 *European Law Review* 155, 158; Joseph HH Weiler, "Eurocracy and Distrust: Some Questions Concerning the Role of the European Court of Justice in the Protection of Fundamental Human Rights within the Legal Order of the

Shortly after its inception, therefore, the EC legal order staked a claim to be an external source of rights for member state citizens. More importantly, by positioning itself as the warden of supranational rights, the Court of Justice instituted a "decentralized enforcement mechanism" that relied on domestic courts and individuals with interests at stake to identify and challenge member state measures inconsistent with EC law.[21] Together with the Court's equally important doctrine of supremacy, according to which supranational law was to be accorded primacy over domestic law (including constitutional norms),[22] the doctrine of direct effect initiated a process that left EC law looking and behaving more and more like a constitutional system, particularly insofar as it constrained the prerogatives of member state institutions in their treatment of individuals.[23]

What this well-rehearsed account neglects to mention is that substantively, the rights norms that originate exclusively in the supranational legal order protect a narrower constellation of values and interests compared to conventional constitutional and international human rights documents. The Court of Justice reserves the term "fundamental rights" for the freedoms of movement of persons, goods, services, and capital and the freedom of establishment in another member state.[24] These rights translate the treaty's central objective of market integration into individuated entitlements.

What, if anything, distinguishes the commercial mobility rights that the ECJ found in the Treaty of Rome from rights enshrined in conventional

European Communities" (1986) 61 *Wash L Rev* 1103, 1111–119; Joseph HH Weiler, "The Transformation of Europe" (1991) 100 *YLJ* 2403; Federico Mancini and David T Keeling, "Democracy and the European Court of Justice" (1994) 57 *MLR* 175; Karen Alter, *Establishing the Supremacy of European Law. The Making of an International Rule of Law in Europe* (Oxford University Press 2001) 88–96; R Daniel Kelemen, "The EU Rights Revolution: Adversarial Legalism and European Integration" in Tanja Börzel and Rachel A Cichowski (eds), *The State of the European Union, vol.6: Law, Politics, and Society* (Oxford University Press 2003); Alec Stone Sweet, *The Judicial Construction of Europe* (Oxford University Press 2004).

21 Stone Sweet, *Judicial Construction of Europe* 69. Also see Kelemen, "The EU Rights Revolution"; Alter, *Establishing the Supremacy of European Law*; Anne-Marie Burley and Walter Mattli, "Europe Before the Court" (1993) 47 *International Organization* 41.

22 Case 6/64 *Flaminio Costa v ENEL* [1964] ECR 585; Case 106/77 *Amministrazione delle Finanze dello Stato v Simmenthal SpA* [1978] ECR 629; Case C-213/89 *The Queen v Secretary of State for Transport, ex parte: Factortame Ltd and others* [1990] ECR I-02433.

23 JHH Weiler, *The Constitution of Europe* (Cambridge University Press 1999) 221.

24 For the right of establishment as a "fundamental right conferred by the Treaty on Community subjects," see Case 340/89 *Vlassopoulou v Ministerium für Justiz, Bundes und Europaangelegenheiten Baden-Württemberg* [1991] ECR 2357, para 22. For "the fundamental right of free access to employment which the Treaty confers individually on each worker in the Community," see Case C-415/93 *Union Royal Belge de Société de Football Association v Bosman* [1995] ECR I-4921, para 129. For the freedom of movement of capital as a "fundamental freedom," see Case 203/80 *Casati* [1981] ECR 2595, para 8. For the free movement of goods as a fundamental freedom, see Case C-112/00 *Schmidberger v Austria* [2003] ECR I-05659, para 23(2).

constitutional and/or human rights documents? So posed, the question opens several teeming cans of worms. Specifying the precise conceptual, legal, and historical relationship between *constitutional* rights and *human* rights raises complex normative and institutional questions that extend beyond the scope of this chapter.[25] Similarly, adjudicating what is and is not properly speaking a human right is a philosophical quagmire from which there is no graceful exit.[26] However, there is a more pragmatic alternative to reflecting a priori about whether market freedoms belong in the domain of human rights proper, which is to assess whether any of the existing arguments to that effect are persuasive. According to Sir David Edward, a former judge of the ECJ:

> the freedoms guaranteed by the Treaties are *not* just secondary "economic" rights to be relegated to an annexe ... They are rights that are in every sense as fundamental and important for the average citizen as those enshrined in the European Convention on Human Rights.[27]

For Edward, what makes the commercial mobility rights protected by EU law "in every sense as fundamental and important" as human rights is that they entail "legally enforceable guarantees that [member state citizens] will be treated equally and without discrimination, and that they will not be subjected to arbitrary decisions."[28] In other words, like human rights, these

[25] According to Moyn's historical reconstruction, eighteenth-century constitutional revolutionaries appealed to rights that would be "achieved through the construction of spaces of citizenship," whereas "the central event in human rights history is the recasting of rights as entitlements that might contradict the sovereign nation-state from above and outside rather than serve as its foundation." Samuel Moyn, *The Last Utopia: Human Rights in History* (Belknap 2012) 13. Cf Benhabib, who argues that universal human rights norms do not emanate from an exclusive supranational *nomos*, but should rather be understood as anchored in domestic processes of democratic contestation. On this view, international human rights and domestic constitutional rights exist in a complementary and mutually constitutive relationship. Benhabib, *Another Cosmopolitanism*.

[26] Theories of human rights that are derived from hypotheses concerning the essential features of humanity or of human flourishing include James Griffin, *On Human Rights* (Oxford University Press 2008); Alan Gewirth, *Human Rights. Essays on Justification and Applications* (University of Chicago Press 1982); John Finnis, *Natural Law and Natural Rights* (Oxford University Press 1980); Jack Donnelly, *The Concept of Human Rights* (Oxford University Press 1985). By contrast, political or non-foundationalist conceptions of human rights understand human rights not as entitlements derived from any inherent features of humanity but as standards of treatment codified by international law that condition state sovereignty and make violations a matter for international concern. See especially, Michael Ignatieff, *Human Rights as Politics and Idolatry* (Princeton University Press 2001); Joseph Raz, "Human Rights without Foundations" in Samantha Besson and John Tasioulas (eds), *The Philosophy of International Law* (Oxford University Press 2010); Charles R Beitz, *The Idea of Human Rights* (Oxford University Press 2009); Joshua Cohen, "Minimalism about Human Rights: The Most We Can Hope for?" (2004) 12 *J Pol Phil* 190.

[27] Sir David Edward, Acceptance Speech for the UACES Award for Lifetime Achievement by a Practitioner delivered at the University Association for Contemporary European Studies Annual Conference, Edinburgh, UK, September 2, 2008. On file with the author.

[28] ibid.

norms protect individuals against sovereign caprice, and expand the nation-state's scope of concern to encompass the interests of foreigners. As Edward rightly observes, this is a remarkable achievement given the bloody history of European nation-states. The fact that the substantive scope of these rights is limited to market activity (or that it hardly overlaps traditional human rights documents) is, in Edward's account, largely incidental to these more weighty considerations.

Ernst-Ulrich Petersmann takes this claim further by highlighting what he argues are substantive overlaps between the rights of commercial mobility protected by the EU, on the one hand, and basic rights norms protected by constitutional and international human rights documents, on the other.[29] According to Petersmann, "transnational 'market freedoms' for movements of goods, services, persons, capital, and related payments" constitute part of a "transnational 'cosmopolitan law'" that "corresponds to the Kantian insight that market freedoms are indispensable complementary conditions of individual autonomy, self-determination, and peaceful cooperation across frontiers."[30] "Most policy objectives of specialized agencies (such as monetary stability, trade liberalization and health protection)," Petersmann argues, "can be understood as protecting liberty, property, non-discrimination and other human rights values across frontiers."[31] Although Petersmann proposes a philosophical justification for considering commercial mobility rights as human rights, the weight of his argument rests partly on the causal claim that "market integration law can promote human rights."[32] On his account, free trade is not only abstractly derived from Kant's

[29] Petersmann's argument on this score falls within the tradition of German "Ordnungspolitik" or ordoliberalism (see especially, Ernst-Ulrich Petersmann, *Constitutional Functions and Constitutional Problems of International Economic Law* (University Press Fribourg, Switzerland 1991) 63–6. With deep roots in the modern natural law tradition, ordoliberalism views economic activity as a privileged expression of individual autonomy that justifies insulating the conditions of free market competition from the vicissitudes of politics by means of constitutional entrenchment and other extra-majoritarian mechanisms. As David Gerber writes, "[t]he market economy could work properly only if the laws related to it were applied within a constitutional framework, and this framework would then assure that government could not interfere with the operations of the economy." David J Gerber, "Constitutionalizing the Economy: German Neo-Liberalism, Competition Law, and the 'New Europe'" (1994) 42 *American Journal of Comparative Law* 25, 56. See also Christian Joerges, *The Law in the Process of Constitutionalizing Europe* (EUI Working Paper 2002/04) 11; Christian Joerges and Michelle Everson, "Law, Economics and Politics in the Constitutionalization of Europe" in Erik Oddvar Eriksen, John Erik Fossum, and Augustin Jose Menendez (eds), *Developing a Constitution for Europe* (Routledge 2004) 166, 172.

[30] Ernst-Ulrich Petersmann, "How to Constitutionalize International Law and Foreign Policy for the Benefit of Civil Society?" (1999) 20 *Michigan J of International Law* 1, 17.

[31] Petersmann, "Time for a United Nations 'Global Compact'" 634.

[32] ibid 629.

categorical imperative but also advances human development and well-being as an empirical matter.

Even assuming that this deeply contested empirical proposition is broadly accurate, however, the welfare-enhancing effects of markets can be harnessed without framing market freedoms as human rights. In view of the intense controversies and conflicts of interest that swirl around trade liberalization, it seems wiser to entrust the accommodation of these interests to democratic processes than settle them through a priori exercises of the categorical imperative. By comparison to the dry dock of philosophical contemplation, the political arena has the virtue of having inclusive procedures for hearing and deciding between competing values, interests, and public goods. Using the democratic process to determine the proper scope of market freedoms wherever possible is both normatively more appealing and more prudent than locking them away in the forbidding crypt of constitutional entrenchment.

It is important to note that the observance of extensive commercial mobility rights such as those protected by the EU are neither legally mandated nor logically entailed by existing international human rights documents. Thus, constitutional states that do not recognize an individual right to buy and sell goods and services across borders without the encumbrance of quotas, tariffs, and border controls are not normally considered violators of human rights for that reason. And if they ought to be, then the EU is equally guilty on this score insofar as it restricts or regulates commercial border across *its* external borders. Similarly, if the right to labor mobility guaranteed by article 45 TFEU were to be considered a human right as much as a market freedom, it would surely be a violation to restrict its enjoyment to citizens of member states rather than granting them to all workers regardless of nationality. In general, however, EU commercial mobility rights are reserved for member state citizens unless explicitly extended to third country nationals.[33]

The foregoing point indicates an important structural difference between the two categories of rights: supranational rights of commercial mobility originate in member states' reciprocal commitments to grant one another's citizens unhindered market access, whereas human rights guarantees tend to have the character of universal obligations on the part of states towards human beings irrespective of their nationality. As the European

[33] For instance, art 15 (2) of the Charter of Fundamental Rights provides that "Every citizen of the Union has the freedom to seek employment, to work, to exercise the right of establishment and to provide services in any Member State," while art 15(3) adds that "Nationals of third countries who are authorised to work in the territories of the Member States are entitled to working conditions equivalent to those of citizens of the Union." I will further discuss the status of third country nationals with respect to the EU's guarantees of mobility in Chapter 5.

Commission of Human Rights has held, each signatory to the European Convention on Human Rights (ECHR):

> undertakes, vis-à-vis the other High Contracting Parties, to secure the rights and freedoms defined in [the Convention] to every person within its jurisdiction, regardless of his or her nationality or status ... in short, it undertakes to secure these rights and freedoms not only to its own nationals and those of other High Contracting Parties but also to nationals of States not parties to the Convention and to stateless persons.[34]

By contrast, the freedoms of movement guaranteed under EU law have the character of "club goods," duties towards fellow member states and their citizens that rest on reciprocity, and that are consequently not owed to outsiders unless special provision has been made to extend them.

For our purposes, the most obvious reason for resisting the attempt to shoehorn commercial mobility rights into the rubric of human rights is that the EU's own judiciary meticulously upholds the distinction between the two categories of rights. As previously noted, the CJEU pointedly reserves the term *fundamental rights* to refer to conventional civil, political, and social rights, including the freedom of expression and association, the right to a fair hearing, and the right to peaceful enjoyment of property, demarcating them from what it terms *fundamental freedoms* of movement. This discursive bifurcation is clearly in evidence in the *Schmidberger*[35] and *Omega*[36] disputes, which brought the two sets of rights into conflict and forced the Court to articulate the relationship between them. In the *Schmidberger* case, a trucking company sued Austria for obstructing the freedom of movement of goods by temporarily shutting down an important transport route between Italy and Germany in order to enable a popular protest against the environmental effects of road transport. In its judgment, the ECJ held that the temporary restriction of the freedom of movement of goods (a fundamental freedom) was justified by the public interest in protecting the freedoms of expression and assembly (a fundamental right). In *Omega*, a German gaming arcade contested the Bonn police authority's prohibition against gaming equipment that allowed users to simulate homicide using fake submachine guns. The German Federal Administrative Court upheld the prohibition on

[34] *Austria v Italy App no 788/60* (1961) CD 18–19. Similarly, the International Law Commission's Articles on State Responsibility characterize human rights norms as obligations of "a nonreciprocal character and are not only due to other States but to the individuals themselves." Draft Articles on Responsibility of States for Internationally Wrongful Acts, with Commentaries, Chapter II, Commentary to "Countermeasures," 129, para 5, in Report of the International Law Commission on the Work of its Fifty-Third Session, UN GAOR 56th Sess., Supp No 10, UN Doc A/56/10 (2001).

[35] Case C-112/00 *Schmidberger v Austria*, para 77.

[36] Case C-36/02 *Omega Spielhallen- und Automatenaufstellungs-GmbH v Oberbürgermeisterin der Bundesstadt Bonn* [2004] ECR I-9609.

the basis that the game violated the principle of human dignity protected by the German Basic Law. Because the equipment had been supplied by a UK-based manufacturer, the company that owned the arcade contended that the prohibition amounted to a restriction of the freedom of movement of goods and the freedom to provide services in another member state. In response, the ECJ held that the German authorities had in fact curtailed these fundamental freedoms of movement, but were justified in doing so by the overriding interest in protecting the fundamental value of human dignity.[37]

Cases such as *Omega* and *Schmidberger* clearly show that regardless of philosophical squabbles over whether market freedoms belong in the category of human rights proper, the two constitute separate categories of rights as a matter of EU law. At the same time, the Court of Justice has itself encouraged confusion by appropriating the qualifier "fundamental" to describe market freedoms. This choice of terminology has fueled a long-standing, vociferous debate among scholars concerning the hierarchy of values in the EU's constitutional order. Critics charge that the Court treats "the principles of free movement of goods and freedom of competition" as "norms of equal qualitative significance" to those enshrined in human rights instruments such as the ECHR.[38] According to an influential essay by Jason Coppel and Aidan O'Neill, describing market freedoms as "fundamental" represents an ideological maneuver designed to reshape European society in the image of the market, wrest greater authority for EU law, and broaden the Court's own interpretive turf. These authors charge that the Court has failed to "take rights seriously,"[39] and has gravely compromised its credibility as an institution tasked with ensuring the conformity of EU law with basic rights.[40] Similarly, Martti Koskenniemi has argued that the Court fastidiously protects economic rights such as "entitlement to property and land as well as the confidentiality of business information," and does so at the expense of other rights including those relating to asylum, racial discrimination, and environmental protection.[41] In his view, the description of market freedoms as "fundamental" is emblematic of the way EU law

[37] According to the Court, "the protection of [fundamental] rights is a legitimate interest which, in principle, justifies a restriction of the obligations imposed by Community law, even under a fundamental freedom guaranteed by the Treaty such as the freedom to provide services." *Omega* para 35, emphasis added.

[38] Jason Coppel and Aidan O'Neill, "The European Court of Justice: Taking Rights Seriously?" (1992) 12 *Legal Studies* 227, 243.

[39] ibid. [40] ibid 243.

[41] Martti Koskenniemi, "The Effect of Rights on Political Culture" in Philip Alston, Mara Bustelo, and James Heenan (eds), *The EU and Human Rights* (Oxford University Press 1999) 107.

elevates economic freedom to the level of a human right and thereby destabilizes the societal values enshrined in member state constitutions.

Others have defended the Court of Justice by pointing out that its case law does not, in fact, establish "normative equivalence" between commercial mobility rights and human rights.[42] In a 1995 essay, Weiler and Lockhart maintain that the ECJ is well aware of the relative moral weight of human rights and market freedoms, and has been willing to strike a judicious balance between the two sets of norms, restricting market freedoms in the light of overriding normative considerations where necessary.[43] The *Omega* and *Schmidberger* decisions in which the Court curtailed market freedoms to ensure the exercise of conventional civil and political rights support this claim.

Unlike either set of observers, I contend that the Court's discursive choice of describing market freedoms as fundamental while doctrinally separating them from conventional human rights norms is neither a disingenuous maneuver nor an innocuous sleight of hand. Rather, the consecration of commercial mobility rights as *fundamental* freedoms is indicative of the deeply teleological orientation of the EU's legal system. As Advocate General Trstenjak puts it, "the Court understands the fundamental freedoms primarily as instruments for opening up markets" rather than morally weighty principles in their own right.[44] Emblematically, when the ECJ announced the direct effect doctrine in the famous *Van Gend en Loos* decision, it did not premise its decision on any moral duty on the part of the EC to protect individual rights; rather, it cited the need to ensure the effectiveness of the treaties by enlisting "the vigilance of individuals concerned to protect their rights."[45] Giving direct effect to treaty provisions within national legal systems, the ECJ reasoned, would help in "ensuring that obligations imposed upon those subject to the Treaty are observed"; encourage the "uniform interpretation of the Treaty by national courts and tribunals"; and enable the "effective supervision" of member state compliance with treaty obligations.[46] In other words, individuals were called upon to stand guard over the European legal order, not vice versa. In line with this basic framework, market freedoms have come to enjoy the status of fundamental norms not because they instantiate some universal human interest, but because they are instrumental for

[42] JHH Weiler and Nicolas JS Lockhart, "'Taking Rights Seriously' Seriously: The European Court and its Fundamental Rights Jurisprudence," Parts I & 2 (1995) 32 *CMLR* 61 and 579, 594.

[43] ibid 595–6.

[44] Opinion of AG Trstenjak in Case C-81/09 *Idrima Typou AE v Ipourgos Typou kai Meson Mazikis Enimerosis* [2010] ECR I-10161, para 75.

[45] Case 26/62 *Van Gend en Loos* 13.

[46] ibid.

achieving the "fundamental objectives"[47] that frame the EU's legal system, not least that of economic union.

That said, the discursive move of describing the commercial mobility provisions of the Treaty of Rome as fundamental freedoms has several implications. In the first place, the language of fundamental freedoms raises the threshold of justification for domestic measures that member states may have adopted in the public interest (such as a ban on video games simulating murder) but which impinge on transnational commercial mobility rights (such as the right of a manufacturer to sell such games and the right of an arcade to buy them). Although the Court of Justice has been careful to decide conflicts between market freedoms and measures taken in the public interest on the relative merits, borrowing the interpretive framework of proportionality analysis from the context of domestic human rights jurisprudence for the purpose, it has construed permissible restrictions on market freedoms narrowly.[48] Nonetheless, the qualifier "fundamental" unmistakably positions commercial mobility at the center of the universe of value established by the treaties. What informs the consideration of commercial mobility rights as *fundamental* freedoms in the EU's legal order is not any intrinsic human interest, Kantian morality, divine sanction, or democratic will; it is rather the *telos* of economic union that frames this normative system.

(II) THE EU'S HUMAN RIGHTS COMPETENCE: AN AFTERTHOUGHT

Like market freedoms, basic rights initially entered into the supranational legal order through the case law of the Court of Justice.[49] While the Treaty of Rome exhaustively enumerated the obligations of member states with respect to market integration, it scarcely included any conventional fundamental rights norms.[50] For its part, the Court of Justice framed market

[47] For instance, in its *Heylens* decision, the ECJ ruled that the right to free access to employment in another member state constitutes a "fundamental right" under art 48 of the Treaty of Rome because of its importance in fulfilling the "fundamental objectives" of the Treaty, in this case, the free movement of workers across borders. Case 222/86 *UNECTEF v Heylens* [1987] ECR 4097, para 12.

[48] Alec Stone Sweet, *Governing with Judges: Constitutional Politics in Europe* (Oxford University Press 2000) 165–70.

[49] The ECJ first alluded to a responsibility to protect fundamental rights in 1969. See Case 29/69 *Stauder v City of Ulm* [1969] ECR 419. Later decisions where the Court more firmly committed itself to vetting the human rights compatibility of measures (and omissions) falling under Community law include, among others, Case 11/70 *Internationale Handelsgesellschaft* [1970] ECR 1125; Case 4/73 *Nold v Commission* [1974] ECR 491; Case C-260/89 *Elliniki Radiophonia Tiléorassi AE v Dimotiki Etairia Pliroforissis and Sotirios Kouvelas* [1991], ECR I-02925.

[50] A possible exception was the ex-art 119 requirement that member states apply "the principle that men and women should receive equal pay for equal work." Although it was not phrased as an

freedoms as an essential and non-negotiable requirement of supranational law from its earliest days, but its foray into the domain of human rights came largely as a strategic and defensive move. Asked as early as 1959 to adjudicate an alleged conflict between a decision by the High Authority of the European Coal and Steel Community (ECSC) and the basic constitutional rights of a German plaintiff,[51] the ECJ held that it was "not competent to apply the national law of the Member States," in this case, the German Basic Law's guarantees of human dignity and the free choice of profession.[52] In other words, during the founding period, the Court of Justice did not consider itself the guarantor of fundamental rights, particularly since these were absent from the legal instruments it was asked to interpret. Although the EU legal order has accumulated an extensive corpus of human rights norms in the ensuing decades, the ad hoc foundations of its human rights mandate are reflected in the limited role its institutions have in protecting and promoting basic individual rights, particularly when considered against their extensive powers in the domain of economic union.

The story of the ECJ's spontaneous "arrogation"[53] of a human rights mandate is familiar. When the ECJ proclaimed that supranational law must prevail over member state laws in the event of conflicts,[54] national constitutional courts expressed concern over the lack of basic rights safeguards in EC law. In its 1973 *Frontini* ruling, the Italian Constitutional Court interpreted article 11 of the Italian Constitution, which sets out the conditions under which Italy may relinquish partial sovereignty to international bodies, as requiring that Community competences must not infringe on fundamental rights.[55] More famously still, in its 1974 *Solange I* decision, the German Federal Constitutional Court (GFCC) reserved the right to review the conformity of EC acts with the Basic Law "as long as the integration process has not progressed so far that Community law also receives a catalogue of fundamental rights decided on by a parliament and of settled validity, which is adequate in comparison with the catalogue of fundamental rights contained in the [German] Constitution."[56]

Concerned that national courts might begin unilaterally derogating from supranational law on human rights grounds, the ECJ began expanding the nascent jurisprudence of basic rights it had debuted a few years

individual right, the Court interpreted this provision as having direct effect. For references and a further discussion, see Chapter 6.

[51] Case 1/58 *Friedrich Stork and Cie v High Authority of the ECSC* [1959] ECR 17.
[52] ibid para 4(a).

[53] Weiler, 'The Transformation of Europe' 2417.
[54] *Costa v ENEL*.

[55] *Frontini v. Ministero delle Finanze* (Case No 183/73) [1974] 2 CMLR 372; Francesco P Ruggieri Laderchi, "Report on Italy" in Anne-Marie Slaughter, Alec Stone Sweet, and Joseph Weiler (eds), *The European Courts and National Courts* (Hart Publishing 1998).

[56] Case 2 BVL 52/71 *Internationale Handelsgesellschaft mbH v Einfuhr- und Vorratstelle für Getreide und Füttermittel* (Decision of May 29 1974) 37 BVerfGE 271, [1974] CMLR 540.

earlier. In its *Internationale Handelsgesellschaft* (*IHg*) ruling, it appointed itself the guardian of a patrimony of individual rights rooted in the "constitutional traditions of Member States" and which, it argued, had always been an "integral part" of Community law as "general principles of law," even if they were absent from the treaties.[57] The Court held that "the protection of such rights, whilst inspired by the constitutional traditions common to the Member States, must be ensured within the framework of the structure and objectives of the Community."[58] In other words, the Court pulled the rug from under domestic courts by claiming that basic rights norms in question had their source of validity within the supranational legal order, and monopolized the power to strike down "measures which are incompatible with fundamental rights."[59] In subsequent decades, it affirmed that rights ranging from the right to human dignity and integrity[60] to the freedom of expression[61] and the rights of defense[62] were among the general principles of supranational law.

In sum, human rights norms were introduced into the market-oriented legal system of the EC as a judicially affixed band-aid, intended to preserve its unity and autonomy against the threat of defection by national courts. In the words of one observer, "Human rights were gradually introduced as limits to the discretion of the supranational institutions. They did not, however, alter the aims, focus, or activity of the Union's legal order and institutions."[63] Up until the Treaty on European Union (TEU) gave legal recognition to the ECJ's de facto incorporation of basic rights into supranational law, basic rights guarantees had only an ad hoc place within the EU's constitutional system.[64] Moreover, even when the TEU established an obligation to respect the basic rights set out in the ECHR and member state constitutions, the EU continued to lack a formal bill of rights until 2009. For these reasons, the declaration in article 2 TEU that the EU is "founded on … respect for human rights" rings false as a historical claim, and must instead be regarded as a future-oriented aspiration. The EU is founded on respect for *market-related* rights, and its constitutional system remains anchored there today. In what follows, I will argue that the role

[57] *Internationale Handelsgesellschaft.* [58] ibid para 4. [59] *Nold* para 13.

[60] For instance, Case C-377/98 *Kingdom of the Netherlands v European Parliament and Council of the European Union* [2001] ECR I-07079, para 6.

[61] The emblematic case is *ERT*, which also expanded the scope of the Court's review of member state acts falling within the scope of Community law. *ERT*, paras 6, 44, 45.

[62] For instance, see Case C-270/99 *Z v European Parliament* [2001] ECR I-09197, para 44. For a detailed taxonomy and consideration of these rights, see Gráinne de Búrca, "The Language of Rights and European Integration" in Jo Shaw and Gillian More (eds), *New Legal Dynamics of European Union* (Clarendon Press 1995) 31–4.

[63] von Bogdandy, "The European Union as a Human Rights Organisation?" 1308.

[64] Ex-art F TEU, now art 6 TEU.

of human rights in the EU's institutional structure remains mostly intramural, that is to say, limited to patrolling the EU's own exercise of power.

(III) THE INTRAMURAL ROLE OF SUPRANATIONAL HUMAN RIGHTS NORMS

The Charter of Fundamental Rights gives the EU what it lacked at its founding, namely an extensive schedule of rights guarantees modeled on the ECHR and national constitutions, supplemented and updated with provisions such as those relating to the protection of personal data, the right to conscientious objection, and prohibitions on human cloning and eugenics. According to the member states, the Charter responds to "a need, at the present stage of the Union's development ... to make [the] overriding importance and relevance [of fundamental rights] more visible to the Union's citizens."[65] Despite this mission, however, the Charter has been designed to preclude any new human rights competence on the part of the EU. In giving legal effect to the Charter, article 6(1) of the TEU emphasizes that its provisions "shall not extend in any way the competences of the Union as defined in the Treaties." Article 51(1) of the Charter provides that "The provisions of this Charter are addressed to the institutions and bodies of the Union with due regard for the principle of subsidiarity and to the Member States *only when* they are implementing Union law."[66] Clearly, then, the Charter's primary purpose is to patrol the acts of EU institutions, and its scope is not intended to cover only those actions that member states have taken in pursuit of EU obligations.[67] Unlike the ECHR, therefore, neither the Charter nor the EU judiciary can be relied on by member state citizens (or other aggrieved parties) to challenge domestic abuses of basic rights so long as the offending measures do not fall within the material scope of EU law.

[65] Conclusions of the Cologne European Council Presidency, June 3–4, 1999, Annex IV.

[66] Emphasis added. Charter of Fundamental Rights of the European Union (2007/C 303/01) Title VII, art 51 reads in full:

1. The provisions of this Charter are addressed to the institutions and bodies of the Union with due regard for the principle of subsidiarity and to the Member States only when they are implementing Union law. They shall therefore respect the rights, observe the principles and promote the application thereof in accordance with their respective powers.
2. This Charter does not establish any new power or task for the Community or the Union, or modify powers and tasks defined by the Treaties.

For good measure, Declaration 1 annexed to the Treaty of Lisbon declares that "The Charter does not extend the field of application of Union law beyond the powers of the Union or establish any new power or task for the Union, or modify powers and tasks as defined by the Treaties."

[67] Precisely what counts as "implementation of Union law" is intensely contested, of course. For an early but comprehensive assessment, see Piet Eeckhout, "The EU Charter of Fundamental Rights and the Federal Question" 39 *CMLR* [2002] 945.

If past experience is any guide, however, the Court of Justice can be counted on to exploit ambiguities in the framing of the EU's human rights mandate in order to erode the limitations on the Charter's application and expand its authority into matters only tenuously related to the EU's area of competence. If the Charter were to be transformed into "the nucleus of a federal-type constitution"[68] applicable to *all* member state actions, this would decisively expand the functionally delimited horizons of the EU's constitutional system. Following US constitutional law, this is sometimes referred to as the question of incorporation[69] or "the federal question."[70] This question catches the EU in a bind: on the one hand, a systematic move towards incorporation would dramatically alter the demarcation of competences between the EU and its member states; while on the other hand, the limitations of the Charter's scope of application ensure that member states can stay within the letter of EU law as long as their domestic human rights violations do not pose a systemic threat to constitutional democracy or hinder any of the substantive policy objectives enumerated in the treaties.[71]

The question of extending the EU's role of human rights supervision beyond the substantive scope of the treaties came into play in the *Centro Europa 7* case that implicated, inter alia, the guarantee of pluralism in the broadcasting sector.[72] Although the ECJ did not decide this case on fundamental

[68] Eeckhout, "The EU Charter of Fundamental Rights and the Federal Question" 991.

[69] Weiler, "Eurocracy and Distrust" 1136–7; Miguel Poiares Maduro, "The Double Constitutional Life of the Charter of Fundamental Rights of the European Union" in Tamara K Hervey and Jeff Kenner (eds), *Economic and Social Rights under the EU Charter of Fundamental Rights—A Legal Perspective* (Hart Publishing 2003) 290.

[70] Eeckhout, "The EU Charter of Fundamental Rights and the Federal Question."

[71] Currently, art 7 TEU allows for a sanctioning mechanism for systematic human rights violations by which the Council can suspend the voting rights and other treaty-based rights of a member state in the event of a "serious and persistent breach" of the principles enumerated in art 2, including democracy, respect for human rights, and the rule of law. In recent years, other proposals have been advanced for circumventing the Charter's limited scope of application without activating the art 7 procedure, adding new institutional competences, or amending the treaties. See especially, von Bogdandy and others, "Reverse Solange—Protecting the Essence of Fundamental Rights against EU Member States" 505 (arguing that art 2 TEU and the status of EU citizenship can be interpreted as substantive safeguards of core human rights that empower the EU "to protect its citizens against excesses even of their member states of origin which would deprive that status of practical meaning"); Kim Lane Scheppele, "Enforcing the Basic Principles of EU Law through Systemic Infringement Procedures" in Dimitry Kochenov and Carlos Closa (eds), *Reinforcing the Rule of Law Oversight in the European Union* (Cambridge University Press 2016) (arguing that the art 258 procedure, which allows the European Commission to bring infringement actions against member states, could be used to establish a supranational judicial oversight mechanism whereby the Commission would "bundle" a number of complaints against a member state that commits serious and persistent breaches of democratic, human rights, and rule of law standards).

[72] Case C-380/05 *Centro Europa 7 Srl v Ministero delle Comunicazioni e Autorita per le Garanzie nelle Comunicazioni* [2008] ECR I-00349. The principle of media pluralism is enshrined in art 11(2) of the Charter, though the case was brought and decided before the Charter's formal incorporation into primary law.

rights grounds, its Advocate General proposed an interesting reconstruction of the relationship between fundamental rights and the objectives of the EU. In his opinion, AG Maduro rejected the claim that human rights protection falls outside "the Core of the European Union."[73] Instead, he submitted that "[p]rotection of the 'common code' of fundamental rights" constitutes "an *existential requirement* for the EU legal order."[74] "[T]he very existence of the European Union," Maduro contended, "is predicated on respect for fundamental rights."[75] Notwithstanding his rights-based interpretation of the EU's legal system, however, the Advocate General urged the Court to "remain faithful to its conventional approach," which is to review member state compliance with human rights norms *only when* these measures fall within the EU's substantive scope of competence.[76] To maneuver around this restriction, Maduro argued that the Court should consider violations of fundamental rights a matter for EU law when they become so pervasive as to deter the citizens of member states from exercising their mobility rights. While resourceful, however, this logic appears to contradict Maduro's own claim that fundamental rights guarantees are an "existential requirement for the EU legal order," since it persists in treating a human rights violation as noteworthy only insofar as it affects the freedom of movement. Even on this more aggressive construction, then, the EU's protection of fundamental rights would be premised on the effects of their violation on other, more "existential" rights, namely those associated with commercial mobility.[77]

As long as the EU's human rights mandate remains restricted to the general domain of economic union, the EU is still best understood as a system of functional constitutionalism. While this may disappoint advocates of a wider EU competence to ensure human rights compliance by member states, however, it is far from clear that the benefits of extending the Charter's scope of application would outweigh its tectonic effects on the allocation of constitutional authority between the EU and its member states. Ever since *Van Gend en Loos*, the supranational judiciary has leveraged the discourse of individual rights to propel integration forward, while the concerns of the individuals concerned have often been secondary to questions of supremacy and competence allocation.[78] In the long run, therefore, the Charter's primary political significance may be as an opportunity for the expansion of the CJEU's interpretive authority at the

[73] Opinion of Advocate General Poiares Maduro, *Centro Europa 7*, delivered on 12.09.2007, paras 18–21. Maduro tacitly responds to von Bogdandy, "The EU as a Human Rights Organisation?"

[74] Maduro, *Centro Europa*, para 19, emphasis added. [75] ibid para 19. [76] ibid paras 21–2.

[77] The Court did not adopt the Advocate General's construal of the role of human rights within the EU's legal system in *Centro Europa 7*.

[78] Coppel and O'Neill, "The European Court of Justice: Taking Rights Seriously?"

expense of member state autonomy. The 2013 *Fransson* decision illustrates this point.[79] The Court of Justice was asked to consider a complaint by a Swedish citizen concerning tax avoidance penalties levied against him under Swedish law, which the claimant complained violated the principle of double jeopardy (*ne bis in idem*) enshrined in the Charter. The Court used the occasion of Fransson's complaint to expand its conception of what counts as a national measure "implementing Union law" under article 51(1) of the Charter. Alarmed by this interpretation of a provision that was clearly meant to limit the CJEU's forays into domestic law, the GFCC swiftly responded to *Fransson* in an otherwise unrelated judgment of its own, warning against treating "any connection of a provision's subject-matter to the merely abstract scope of Union law, or merely incidental effects on Union law, [as] sufficient for binding the Member States by the Union's fundamental rights set forth in the EUCFR."[80]

In fact, expanding the EU's human rights role might even *depress* the overall standard of human rights protection that member states afford their citizens.[81] In *Melloni*, the Court of Justice ruled that member states can opt for higher standards of domestic human rights protection than those required by the EU Charter of Fundamental Rights *only* if they can do so in a way that does not hinder their compliance with EU obligations or undermine the effectiveness of EU law.[82] In the case at hand, the European Arrest Warrant legislation instructed Spanish authorities to extradite Mr. Melloni to Italy where he had been tried *in absentia* and convicted. However, Spanish constitutional law forbade extraditing individuals if they had been convicted *in absentia* with no possibility of appeal. The Court of Justice held that domestic standards of human rights protection could not be so high as to compromise "the primacy, unity and effectiveness of EU law."[83] In other words, rather than providing a floor below which human rights standards must not fall, EU law may end up as a ceiling that constrains domestic human rights standards, at least in policy matters that fall within the scope of the EU's competence.[84]

The most serious institutional mechanism available to the EU for addressing grave and systematic infringements of human rights by its member states has lain dormant since its adoption. Introduced by the Treaty of

[79] Case C-617/10 *Åklagaren v Hans Åkerberg Fransson* ECLI:EU:C:2013:105.

[80] Bundesverfassungsgericht Case No.1 BvR 1215/07, April 24, 2013, Section IV C.

[81] Eeckhout, "The EU Charter of Fundamental Rights and the Federal Question" 993.

[82] Case C-399/11 *Stefano Melloni v Ministerio Fiscal* ECLI:EU:C:2013:107. [83] ibid para 60.

[84] An eloquent account of this problem and possible solutions is given by Leonard Besselink, "Entrapped by the Maximum Standard: On Fundamental Rights, Pluralism, and Subsidiarity in the European Union" (1998) 35 *CMLR* 629.

Amsterdam, article 7 TEU allows the Council acting unanimously (excluding the state concerned) to suspend the voting rights of a member state in the event of a "serious and persistent breach" of the standards enumerated in article 2 TEU, which include "respect for human dignity, freedom, democracy, equality, the rule of law and respect for human rights, including the rights of persons belonging to minorities." Not only has the article 7 procedure never been used, it is often described as unusable.[85] In fact, even a modified "pre-article 7" procedure requiring a four-fifths majority in the Council to declare a "clear risk" of a serious breach of article 2 standards on the part of a member state has never been invoked, and certainly not for lack of such risks.[86] If used, the so-called nuclear option of article 7 is likely to create deep, acrimonious political rifts between member states of the kind that the European integration process was intended to heal. As a de facto and *de jure* mechanism of ostracism, it requires member state governments to sit in judgment of one another's domestic political affairs. In sum, the article 7 mechanism is not so much the nuclear option as the boomerang option: member state governments have reason to fear that once activated, it may in the future be invoked against them, or, more likely, disrupt their future prospects of using a legislative forum that depends so much on consensus and comity.

In sum, although human rights norms have gradually risen within the EU's hierarchy of values, they constrain, but do not define, the EU's constitutional ethos. While *all* member state infringements of market freedoms are a matter for EU law, and are subject to stringent standards of compliance and enforcement, member state violations of human rights do not constitute infringements under EU law *unless* they also implicate a member state's substantive obligations under the treaties. For these reasons, it is more accurate to characterize the EU as a system of functional constitutionalism, the basis of whose authority is defined in terms of economic union, rather than as the supranational approximation of a liberal or rights-based model of constitutionalism.

(IV) GUARDING THE GUARDIAN: HUMAN RIGHTS COMPLIANCE BY THE EU

Given their limitations vis-à-vis monitoring the actions of member states, how effective are the EU's human rights instruments in preventing infringements by the EU's own institutions? Such oversight is particularly necessary

[85] Ulrich Sedelmeier, "Anchoring Democracy from Above? The European Union and Democratic Backsliding in Hungary and Romania after Accession" (2014) 52 *JCMS* 105, 108.

[86] ibid 108.

given the EU's growing competences alongside member states in areas that call for human rights scrutiny, including immigration, asylum and border control, law-enforcement and criminal matters, multilateral intelligence and data-sharing, and the prevention of terrorist financing, to name a few. The *Kadi* saga that preoccupied the EU's judiciary for the better part of a decade perfectly illustrates both the need for, and the limitations of, human rights protection at the EU level.[87] This line of cases concerned (among other plaintiffs) Yassin Abdullah Kadi, a Saudi investor stripped of access to his financial assets by several UN Security Council (UNSC) resolutions that named him among individuals and institutions suspected of providing financial support to a terrorist organization.[88] During the initial stages of the sanctions regime, the UNSC did not make available remedies for blacklisted individuals and entities wishing to challenge the measures taken against them. Although the resolutions were addressed to signatories of the UN Charter (which excludes the EU), EU member states chose to implement the asset freezing measures required by the resolutions by cooperating under the EU's Common Foreign and Security Policy umbrella.[89]

In 2001, Mr. Kadi challenged these regulations before the EU's Court of First Instance (CFI) with a request for their annulment, on the grounds that they violated his right to property and his rights of defense, including the right to be heard and the right to effective judicial review.[90] However, the

[87] Court of First Instance of the European Communities Case T-315/01 *Kadi v Council and Commission* [2005] ECR II-3649; Case T-306/01 *Yusuf and Al Barakaat International Foundation v Council and Commission* [2005] ECR II-3533; European Court of Justice, Joined Cases C-402/05 P and C-415/05 P *Yassin Abdullah Kadi and Al Barakaat International Foundation v Council of the European Union and Commission of the European Communities* [2008] ECR I-6351; Case T-85/09 *Kadi v Commission* [2010] ECR II-5177.

This case (and the scholarly debate it sparked) is discussed at greater length in Turkuler Isiksel, "Fundamental Rights in the EU after *Kadi and Al Barakaat*" (2010) 15 *ELJ* 551. Notable interventions directly concerning the ECJ's *Kadi* ruling include Gráinne de Búrca, "The European Court of Justice and the International Legal Order after *Kadi*" (2010) 51 *Harvard International Law Journal* 1; WT Eijsbouts and Leonard Besselink, "'The Law of Laws'—Overcoming Pluralism" (2008) 4 *European Constitutional Law Review* 395; Stefan Griller, "International Law, Human Rights and the European Community's Autonomous Legal Order: Notes on the European Court of Justice Decision in *Kadi*" (2008) 4 *European Constitutional Law Review* 528; Daniel Halberstam and Eric Stein, "The United Nations, the European Union, and the King of Sweden: Economic Sanctions and Individual Rights in a Plural World Order" (2009) 46 *CMLR* 13; Bjørn Kunoy and Anthony Dawes, "Plate Tectonics in Luxembourg: The *Ménage à Trois* between EC Law, International Law and the European Convention on Human Rights following the UN Sanctions Cases" (2009) 46 *CMLR* 73.

[88] The most important of these are UN Security Council Resolutions 1267 (1999), 1333 (2000), 1390 (2002), 1452 (2002).

[89] Specifically, Council Regulation (EC) No 881/2002 of 27 May 2002 imposing certain specific restrictive measures directed against certain persons and entities associated with Usama bin Laden, the Al-Qaida network and the Taliban OJ L139/9. Joined Cases C-402/05 P and C-415/05 P *Kadi and Al Barakaat*, paras 67–8.

[90] Case T-315/01 *Kadi v Council and Commission*; Case T-306/01 *Yusuf and Al Barakaat International Foundation v Council and Commission*.

CFI rejected his application, finding that it had no ability to review UNSC resolutions except where these breached *jus cogens* norms.[91] In this case, the CFI held that no such violation had taken place.[92] On appeal, the ECJ overruled the CFI's decision and set forth a quite different line of reasoning: it held that the EU's actions had indeed violated the appellant's rights, because neither the EU legislation in question nor the UNSC resolutions gave him adequate opportunity to challenge the measures that adversely affected him. Invoking its long-standing doctrine that "the EC Treaty [establishes] *a complete system of legal remedies* and procedures designed to enable the Court of Justice to review the legality of acts of the institutions," the Court of Justice held that "neither its Member States nor its institutions can avoid review of the conformity of their acts with the basic constitutional charter, the EC Treaty."[93] Respect for the rule of law and the primacy of fundamental rights within the EU's normative structure required voiding the EU measures in question as they applied to Mr. Kadi, even if this would make it more difficult for member states to fulfill their obligations under other international organizations.

In many respects, the *Kadi* saga is symptomatic of the challenges of constitutionalism beyond the state, not least of a worrying implication of the post-World War II rights revolution. While cosmopolitans have broadly welcomed the growing recognition of individuals as subjects of international law in their own right,[94] the UNSC resolutions singled out specific individuals in order to deprive them of the safeguards provided by domestic legal systems. As the ECJ noted in its *Kadi* decision, the UNSC measures in question were " 'smart' sanctions of a new kind, a feature of which is that there is nothing at all to link the sanctions to the territory or the governing regime of a third country."[95] Denying the appellants adequate opportunities to challenge the sanctions brought against them,[96] the ECJ held, contradicted the constitutional principle against the arbitrary use of public power. By insisting that the EU's actions, even if taken in furtherance

[91] CFI, *Yusuf* para 277; *Kadi* para 226. It is nevertheless remarkable that the CFI found *any* competence at all to review UN Security Council Resolutions.

[92] On the CFI's rulings, see Jessica Almqvist, "A Human Rights Critique of European Judicial Review. Counter-Terrorism Sanctions" (2008) 57 *International and Comparative Law Quarterly* 303; Mielle Bulterman, "Fundamental Rights and the United Nations Financial Sanction Regime: The *Kadi* and *Yusuf* Judgments of the Court of First Instance of the European Communities" (2006) 19 *Leiden Journal of International Law* 753; Christina Eckes, "Judicial Review of European Anti-Terrorism Measures—The *Yusuf* and *Kadi* Judgments of the Court of First Instance" (2008) 14 *ELJ* 74; Piet Eeckhout, "Community Terrorism Listing, Fundamental Rights, and UN Security Council Resolution. In Search of the Right Fit" (2007) 3 *European Constitutional Law Review* 183; Julia Hoffman, "Terrorism Blacklisting: Putting European Human Rights Guarantees to the Test" (2008) 15 *Constellations* 543.

[93] *Kadi and Al Barakaat* para 281, emphasis added.

[94] E.g. Lauterpacht, *International Law and Human Rights*.

[95] *Kadi and Al Barakaat* para 60.

[96] ibid para 334.

of member states' obligations under international law, must be subject to judicial review, the Court signaled that the delegation of governance functions to international organizations must be accompanied by constitutional guarantees.[97]

The *Kadi* saga therefore illustrates the need to incorporate constitutional mechanisms into the structure of international institutions in order to make up for the slackening of domestic constitutional supervision.[98] The eager adoption of UN-mandated national security laws in the aftermath of 9/11 exemplifies a willingness on the part of sovereign states to use international institutions to evade domestic checks and consolidate political control at home.[99] Although the EU and the UNSC are not part of the same legal system, the ECJ assumed an impromptu judicial review function against the unchecked exercise of executive power by the latter body, however indirectly. Clearly, the EU's judiciary cannot and should not be expected to function as an appellate court for the UN, but its refusal to allow the EU to carry out the smart sanctions did prompt the UNSC to adopt some remedies, however superficial, for blacklisted individuals and entities.

Although *Kadi* represents an encouraging instance of supranational human rights protection at work, the systematic impact of the Charter of Fundamental Rights on the EU's overall human rights standards is harder to gauge. For one thing, the Court of Justice only rarely holds EU institutions responsible for failing to comply with basic rights norms.[100] Its first-ever judgment invalidating an EU act on the explicit basis of human rights guarantees was not until 1998.[101] A notable addition to its thin record in this area is the decision invalidating the Data Protection Directive for disproportionate interference with the rights to privacy and data protection enshrined in the Charter.[102] However, the tokenism of decisions scrutinizing

[97] Anne Peters, "Compensatory Constitutionalism: The Function and Potential of Fundamental International Norms and Structures" (2006) 19 *Leiden Journal of International Law* 579.

[98] Peters, "Compensatory Constitutionalism."

[99] Kim Lane Scheppele, "The International Standardization of National Security Law" (2010) 4 *Journal of National Security Law and Policy* 437.

[100] Recent cases in which the Court of Justice has found EU acts to be incompatible with basic rights norms include Case C-236/09 *Test-Achats* [2011] ECR I-773, which invalidated the part of Directive 2004/113/EC on the principle of equal treatment between the sexes (art 5(2)) that allowed for gender-based discrimination in the pricing of insurance policies; and Case C-92 and 93/09 *Volker und Markus Schecke and Hartmut Eifert* [2010] ECR I-11063, in which the Court declared art 44a of Regulations 1290/2005 and 259/2008 requiring the publication of the names of recipients of agricultural aid as incompatible with the right to private life and data protection guarantees of the Charter on Fundamental Rights.

[101] Case C-185/95 *Baustahlgewebe v Commission* [1998] ECR I-8417.

[102] Joined Cases C-293 and 594/12 *Digital Rights Ireland Ltd and Seitlinger and others* 8 April 2014. For an excellent commentary, see Orla Lynskey, "The Data Retention Directive is Incompatible with the Rights to Privacy and Data Protection and Is Invalid in its Entirety: *Digital Rights Ireland*" (2014) 51 *CMLR* 1789.

the EU's own actions in light of Charter standards stands in contrast with the Court's aggressive and expansive championship of market freedoms against member states. Furthermore, the restrictive standing rules of EU law mean that individuals cannot directly take their fundamental rights complaints to the supranational judiciary except in a narrowly defined set of instances.[103] This further limits the ability of the Court of Justice to assume the role of a human rights court and, by implication, any claim that the EU instantiates a supranational constitutional system founded on the protection of basic rights.

The limitations of the EU's human rights mandate have amplified calls for a more encompassing supranational human rights policy.[104] The establishment in 2007 of an Agency for Fundamental Rights (FRA) is a notable outcome of this effort. The FRA is charged with providing EU institutions and member states "with information, assistance and expertise on fundamental rights in order to support them when they take measures or formulate courses of action within their respective spheres of competence to fully respect fundamental rights."[105] Despite its ambitious title, however, the FRA is empowered only to "act only within the scope of application of Community law," meaning that it may not monitor the acts of member states in areas falling outside of supranational competence.[106] Like the Charter, its primary purpose is to ensure an internal monitoring function over the EU, not to scrutinize the actions of member states in the domain of their reserved competences.

Perhaps the most visible item on the EU's human rights policy agenda is its relations with non-member countries or countries seeking membership.[107] Respect for fundamental rights is a central element of the Copenhagen political criteria that candidate countries must meet in order to accede to the

[103] The Treaty of Lisbon has somewhat liberalized the restrictive standing rules for bringing a direct action before the EU judiciary, most notably by removing the requirement that applicants must demonstrate that a supranational regulatory act poses "individual concern" to them (ex-art 230 TEC and Case 25/62 *Plaumann and Co. v Commission of the European Economic Community* [1962] ECR 126). Art 263 TFEU requires that an applicant be "directly concerned" and that the regulatory act in question require no implementing measures. See Treaty of Lisbon amending the Treaty on European Union and the Treaty Establishing the European Community, OJ C306/42 of 17.12.2007, art 2, para 214. On whether this shift in standing rules is likely to allow a greater range of fundamental rights complaints, see Paul Craig, "EU Accession to the ECHR Competence, Procedure, and Substance" (2013) 36 *Fordham International Law Journal* 1114, 1130.

[104] Philip Alston and JHH Weiler, "An 'Ever Closer Union' in Need of a Human Rights Policy: The European Union and Human Rights" in Philip Alston (ed), *The EU and Human Rights* (Oxford University Press 1999).

[105] See Council Regulation (EC) No 168/2007 of 15 February 2007 establishing a European Union Agency for Fundamental Rights OJ L53/1 of 22.02.2007.

[106] ibid.

[107] de Búrca, "The Road Not Taken: The European Union as a Global Human Rights Actor" 673.

EU. Through its yearly reports, the European Commission closely monitors the human rights performance of candidate countries, and further progress on accession negotiations is closely tied to improvements in the candidate country's human rights record. These reports lend visibility to shortcomings of liberal democratic standards in candidate countries and can empower domestic agents in their pursuit of greater political liberalization. More generally, the EU's external action, including development cooperation, humanitarian aid, cooperation in economic, financial, and technical areas, and common commercial policy must be conditioned by a common core of "principles and objectives" that include respect for fundamental rights.[108]

It is telling that the most robust role that EU institutions have in ensuring domestic human rights compliance involves non-EU countries rather than member states. While the EU can and should use its influence to champion human rights standards abroad, this external leadership role is seriously undermined by the constitutional fetters that prevent the application of the same standards to member states. Contrasted with lax domestic enforcement, the EU's eagerness to trumpet human rights in other, often poorer states and erstwhile colonial dominions can smack of a form of imperial hypocrisy that the latter recognize all too well.

The final major piece of the EU's human rights regime is its mandate to accede to the ECHR.[109] Like the EU's own Charter, ECHR accession primarily has what I have referred to as an intramural role, intended to ensure the compliance of EU institutions with human rights norms. While it would not add to the EU's human rights functions, however, accession to the ECHR would give the EU's judiciary an incentive to be more diligent in its application of the relevant human rights law. At present, the Court of Justice has a sparse jurisprudence of fundamental rights relative to domestic courts of last instance. This is certainly not for lack of violations: in areas such as asylum law and extradition, it is far from obvious that the standards prevailing in the EU are up to ECHR standards.[110] Furthermore, the CJEU's

[108] TFEU art 205.

[109] Art 6(2) of TEU proclaims that "the Union shall accede to the European Convention for the Protection of Human Rights and Fundamental Freedoms."

[110] On the discrepancies between the ECHR's standards of refugee reception conditions and those enumerated by the CJEU, see Paul Gragl, "The Shortcomings of Dublin II: Strasbourg's *MSS* Judgment and its Implications for the European Legal Order" (2012) *European Yearbook on Human Rights* 123; Minos Mouzourakis, "'We Need to Talk About Dublin': Responsibility under the Dublin System as a Blockage to Asylum Burden-Sharing in the European Union" (Oxford Refugee Studies Centre Working Paper Series No. 105, 2014); Joanna Lenart, "'Fortress Europe': Compliance of the Dublin II Regulation with the European Convention for the Protection of Human Rights and Fundamental Freedoms" 28 (2012) *Merkourios: Utrecht Journal of International and European Law* 4. On the alleged complicity of some EU member states in practices of "extraordinary rendition" by

reasoning in decisions touching on fundamental human rights issues has been curt, stipulative, and tacit. While some of this can be attributed to the parsimonious rhetorical style of the civil law tradition that has inspired the design of the supranational judiciary, the expansion of the EU's powers creates the need for more extensively reasoned judicial engagement with fundamental rights concerns.[111] By formalizing a substantive judicial dialogue on the rich normative issues raised by rights-based review, Convention membership is likely to draw the CJEU out of its reticence on these issues and foster the development of a more deliberate and deliberative fundamental rights jurisprudence in EU law.

Since the ECHR was drafted by and for state parties, the EU's accession agreement has had to be tailored in light of "the specific characteristics of the Union and Union law," and the limited nature of the Union's competences.[112] Alas, the CJEU declared the agreement drafted through a lengthy inter-institutional process to be incompatible with "the specific characteristics of EU law and its autonomy."[113] While the constitutional issues at stake in the accession agreement controversy are complex, the Court's objections suggest that it views the EU's internal framework for enforcing human rights norms to be sufficient. Furthermore, as de Búrca has shown, the Court of Justice has made "very occasional and increasingly selective use of the case law of the European Court of Human Rights"[114] since the entry into force of the EU Charter, which suggests a deliberate move on the part of the Luxembourg court to develop an autonomous jurisprudence in this arena. Ironically, the CJEU's reluctance to submit to human rights supervision by Strasbourg suggests that just like the sovereign states it has been set up to constrain, the EU itself needs an external source of human rights supervision.

In fact, the role of peer judiciaries, including national courts and the European Court of Human Rights (ECtHR) in ensuring the EU's compliance with human rights norms bears emphasis. To accord with Europe's

the US, see the European Parliament Report on the alleged use of European countries by the CIA for the transportation and illegal detention of prisoners A6-0020/2007 (2006/2200(INI)); available at http://www.europarl.europa.eu/sides/getDoc.do?type=REPORT&reference=A6-2007-0020&language=EN accessed February 19, 2016.

[111] Vlad Perju, "Reason and Authority in the European Court of Justice" (2009) 49 *Virginia Journal of International Law* 308; Gráinne de Búrca, "After the EU Charter of Fundamental Rights: The Court of Justice as a Human Rights Adjudicator?" (2013) 20 *Maastricht Journal of European and Comparative Law* 168, 176–7.

[112] Protocol No. 8 TEU.

[113] Opinion 2/13, EU:C:2014:2454, 18 December 2014, para 200.

[114] de Búrca, "After the EU Charter of Fundamental Rights" 173–4. de Búrca reports that between 2009 and the end of 2012, "out of 122 cases involving the Charter, the CJEU referred to the ECHR in just 18, with only 10 of these involving some mention or discussion of ECtHR case law, the other 8 making mention only of the Convention provision." 175.

pluralist constitutional architecture, any external human rights review over the EU's actions must be configured in a non-hierarchical fashion.[115] For instance, although the CJEU contests the proposition that member state high courts are empowered to exercise external oversight over EU law (for conformity with human rights or any other principle), in practice, it has for decades been engaged in collective constitutional *bricolage* with domestic courts.[116] After all, what prompted the ECJ to take up the cause of human rights in the first place was pressure from national constitutional courts. This experience suggests that competition and overlap among judiciaries, each of which is anxious to prove its own commitment to human rights, might generate a higher standard of human rights protection overall.[117] EU accession to the ECHR would not only give the EU's judiciary a strong incentive to be more diligent in its application of the relevant human rights norms, but would also encourage the Luxembourg court to be more judicious in assigning relative weight to the market objectives of the EU vis-à-vis other important ends, values, rights, and freedoms.[118]

(V) CONCLUSION

Basic rights norms were appended to the EU's constitutional system as a strategic buttress and, while they uphold the integrity of the structure, they remain largely auxiliary to the market norms that constitute its foundations. Compared to the extensive legal and institutional edifice that guarantees the freedoms of movement of goods, services, capital, and persons,

[115] "[T]he constitutional discourse in Europe must be conceived of as a conversation of many actors in a constitutional interpretive community rather than a hierarchical structure with the ECJ at the top … A feature of neo-constitutionalism in this case would be that the jurisdictional line (or lines) should be a matter of constitutional conversation, not a constitutional *diktat*." JHH Weiler, "European Neo-Constitutionalism: In Search of Foundations for the European Constitutional Order" (1996) 44 *Political Studies* 517, 532.

[116] JHH Weiler, "In Defence of the Status Quo: Europe's Constitutional *Sonderweg*" in JHH Weiler and Marlene Wind (eds), *European Constitutionalism beyond the State* (Cambridge University Press 2003).

[117] For a sanguine analysis of the potential benefits of a well-managed system of constitutional pluralism, see especially Nico Krisch, "The Open Architecture of European Human Rights Law" (2008) 71 *MLR* 183.

[118] In a series of recent decisions including *Laval* (Case C-314/05 *Laval un Partneri Ltd v Svenska Byggnadsarbetareförbundet* [2007] ECR I-11767) and *Viking* (Case C-438/05 *International Transport Workers' Federation and Finnish Seamen's Union v Viking Line ABP and OÜ Viking Line Eesti* [2007] ECR I-10779), the CJEU has drawn considerable criticism for privileging the EU's constitutional values of commercial mobility and undermining long-standing forms of corporatist social consensus venerated in member states such as Sweden, Germany, and Finland. See Alicia Hinarejos, "*Laval* and *Viking*: The Right to Collective Action versus EU Fundamental Freedoms" (2008) 8 *Human Rights Law Review* 714; Christian Joerges and Florian Rödl, "Informal Politics and Formalised Law: Reflections after the Judgments of the ECJ in *Viking* and *Laval*" (2009) 15 *ELJ* 1; Koskenniemi, "The Effect of Rights on Political Culture."

the EU's mandate for ensuring human rights compliance looks thin. The bifurcation of the EU's individual rights regime into two unequal strands, comprising constitutionally foundational guarantees of commercial mobility rights on the one hand, and auxiliary guarantees of basic rights on the other, is a clear indication of the enduring economic teleology guiding its overall constitutional system.

Once we abstract away from its largely economic content, however, EU law represents a web of commitments designed to constrain sovereign prerogative. From this perspective, the EU is not a *sui generis* regime; to the contrary, it exemplifies a prominent postwar strategy of bolstering the structure of domestic constitutional democracy by surrounding it with a robust exoskeleton of legal and political safeguards at the international level.[119] Nonetheless, it would be naïve to assume that principles such as democracy, human rights, and the rule of law are immanent to inter-national organizations. Constructed by states to serve their ends, international institutions can reflect and reinforce some of the most troubling aspects of sovereign prerogative. They can enable governments to shrug off domestic constitutional constraints while throwing a veneer of legitimacy over arbitrary uses of power.[120] In such cases, international cooperation is likely to erode rather than enhance the liberal democratic credentials of participating states. Much depends, therefore, on their design and the tasks with which they are charged.

From this perspective, where the EU's human rights mandate can make the most difference is in patrolling uses and misuses of supranational authority. Thanks to its mechanisms of individual rights protection and judicial review, the EU can ensure a higher standard of human rights in its own operations relative to an international organization that lacks these constitutional features. In the *Kadi* dispute, these constitutional mechanisms blocked the attempt by member state executives to mobilize EU institutions to implement the UN's unaccountable sanctions regime.[121]

Despite that token victory, however, the EU has in many ways come to reinforce the walls of the sovereign fortress. Member states increasingly rely on EU institutions to pursue their restrictive policy preferences regarding terrorism, immigration and asylum, organized crime, extradition, border control, and intelligence and data gathering. The EU is torn between helping to create a meticulously policed, disciplined, and regulated political

[119] Jan-Werner Müller, *Contesting Democracy: Political Ideas in Twentieth-Century Europe* (Yale University Press 2011) 148–9; Andrew Moravcsik, "The Origins of Human Rights Regimes: Democratic Delegation in Postwar Europe" (2000) 54 *International Organization* 217.

[120] Scheppele, "The International Standardization of National Security Law."

[121] *Kadi and Al Barakaat*.

space at the supranational level and the open, inclusive, and pluralistic one that its founding treaties demand. For these reasons, the EU itself needs the kinds of internal and external constitutional safeguards that it was designed to provide vis-à-vis its member states. Just as European nation-states have proven themselves prone to forms of ethnic exclusion and nationalist aggression, the EU has its own endemic biases that stand in need of correction, not least its single-minded adherence to the market-building project at the expense of other equally important goals and values. With its universe of values still firmly anchored in the project of economic union, the EU's constitutional system has struggled to give due recognition to competing principles. The relative weakness of its legal and institutional mandate in the domain of fundamental rights protection illustrates this enduring imbalance.

4

Law, Democracy, and Citizenship in the European Union

Although the control that citizens of modern constitutional democracies wield over the institutions that govern them is modest, it is nevertheless meaningful: public authority ultimately derives from the collective will of citizens. From the late eighteenth century onwards, the nation-state has played host to attempts to recover and update the ancient ideal of democratic self-rule, most importantly (but not exclusively) by means of electoral representation.[1] Representative institutions help to transform the brute coercive power of the state into legitimate authority, and enable citizens to regard the laws as being authorized by them and deserving of their allegiance.[2]

The delegation of public power to international institutions disrupts this neat circuit. Although international institutions are increasingly autonomous and possess authority over deeply significant policy matters, they typically widen the distance between decision-makers and citizens, anonymizing, obscuring, and complicating the exercise of power. The diffusion and fragmentation of norm-making authority at the transnational level not only strains conventional models of democratic representation and accountability, but also makes it difficult to identify who should be held to account for a given outcome. The omnipresence of the term *governance* in contemporary public and academic discourse is indicative of this shift, as it allows the speaker to conveniently elide the question of *who* or *what* is doing the governing. Given unavoidable problems of attenuation, diversity, and coordination at the international level, democratic legitimation may well be the

[1] Nadia Urbinati, *Representative Democracy. Principles and Genealogy* (University of Chicago Press 2006).

[2] Habermas expresses this duality as a tension between the facticity and normativity of the law: on the one hand, law is the contingent and coercively enforced command of the lawgiver, while on the other, it makes a moral claim to our obedience. The discourse theory of constitutional democracy is an attempt to reconcile this tension in a way that preserves the autonomy of the individual. See Jürgen Habermas, *Between Facts and Norms: Contributions to a Discourse Theory of Law and Democracy* (William Rehg tr, MIT Press 1996) 447.

most pressing and least tractable of the challenges posed by transferring power to institutions beyond the state.[3]

The knee-jerk response to this challenge is to attempt to scale up domestic mechanisms of democratic control to the level of international institutions. This is easier said than done, however: existing standards of democratic legitimacy and the institutions designed to realize them have largely taken shape within the nation-state context. Once again, European Union (EU) scholarship has been a dynamic tributary to the vigorous debate over the democratic "standards" that are relevant for evaluating, designing, and reforming institutions beyond the state.[4] Most observers acknowledge a need to modify the traditional framework of parliamentary democracy in view of the particular characteristics of international institutions.[5] Alongside proposals for adapting traditional mechanisms of electoral contestation to the EU's hybrid institutional structure[6] stand normative accounts that emphasize alternative criteria of democratic legitimacy, including the deliberative-epistemic quality of decision-making,[7] processes of reason-giving and justification,[8] avenues of participation for those with interests at stake,[9] procedural guarantees and opportunities to contest decisions,[10] and mechanisms of transparency and accountability.[11] Many of these proposals are inspired by the legitimation mechanisms built into administrative institutions.[12] The challenge, these scholars argue, is to devise procedural hacks to hold policymakers to account in ways that do not presuppose elections and other traditional forms of democratic opinion- and will-formation on which democratic states rely.

[3] Robert A Dahl, "Can International Organizations Be Democratic? A Skeptic's View" in Ian Shapiro and Casiano Hacker-Cordón (eds) *Democracy's Edges* (Cambridge University Press 1999).

[4] Giandomenico Majone, "Europe's 'Democratic Deficit': The Question of Standards" (1998) 4 *ELJ* 5.

[5] Ruth W Grant and Robert O Keohane, "Accountability and Abuses of Power in World Politics" (2005) 99 *APSR* 29; Joshua Cohen and Charles Sabel, "Directly-Deliberative Polyarchy" (1997) 3 *ELJ* 313.

[6] Simon Hix, *What's Wrong with the European Union and How to Fix it* (Polity 2008).

[7] Christian Joerges and Jurgen Neyer, "From Intergovernmental Bargaining to Deliberative Political Processes: The Constitutionalisation of Comitology" (1997) 3 *ELJ* 273.

[8] Jürgen Neyer, *The Justification of Europe: A Political Theory of Supranational Integration* (Oxford University Press 2012).

[9] Cohen and Sabel, "Directly-Deliberative Polyarchy".

[10] Renaud Dehousse, "Towards a Regulation of Transnational Governance? Citizen's Rights and the Reform of Comitology Procedures" in Christian Joerges and Ellen Vos (eds), *EU Committees: Social Regulation, Law and Politics* (Hart Publishing 1999).

[11] Grant and Keohane, "Accountability and Abuses of Power in World Politics"; Joshua Cohen and Charles F Sabel, "Global Democracy?" (2005) 37 *International Law and Politics* 763.

[12] Martin Shapiro, "The Giving Reasons Requirement" (1992) *University of Chicago Legal Forum* 179; Dehousse, "Towards a Regulation of Transnational Governance? Citizen's Rights and the Reform of Comitology Procedures."

In contrast to those who see the empowerment of institutions beyond the state as heralding the attenuation or transformation of democratic standards, many cosmopolitan scholars view these institutions as creating opportunities for "deepening and widening democracy both within and across state boundaries, as well as insinuating democratic practices into all levels of political activity."[13] Jürgen Habermas has embraced what he regards as an opportunity to craft "a democratic politics beyond the nation-state" that can liberate the ideal of collective autonomy from its reliance on prepolitical, exclusive forms of political allegiance.[14] Habermas contends that "democratically structured opinion- and will-formation make possible rational agreement even between strangers"[15] and that the link between "*demos*" and "nation" is one of historical contingency rather than empirical necessity.[16] In his view, mobilizing the framework of constitutional democracy to "catalyze" postnational forms of political community would be a way to overcome the ethical particularism of the nation-state, which has at best been an awkward vehicle for realizing the principles of constitutional democracy.[17] As culturally and ethnically delimited communities, nation-states make political agency contingent on the privileged status of membership. By contrast, the normative claim to be included in democratic processes of opinion- and will-formation derives from the autonomy of the individual who is subject to the authority of public institutions, rather than on contingent aspects of her identity such as nationality.[18] Similarly, while most modern constitutions espouse a seemingly universal commitment to basic individual rights, the nation-state's scope of moral concern and legal protection is limited, for the most part, to its own citizens.[19] In short, the inclusive impulses of constitutional democracy come into tension with the exclusivity of the nation-state as a political unit.

[13] Richard A Falk, Robert C Johansen, Samuel S Kim, "Global Constitutionalism and World Order" in Richard A Falk, Robert C Johansen, Samuel S Kim (eds), *The Constitutional Foundations of World Peace* (SUNY Press 1993) 9.

[14] Jürgen Habermas, *The Postnational Constellation: Political Essays* (Max Pensky tr and ed, MIT Press 1998) 88.

[15] Jürgen Habermas, *The Inclusion of the Other* (Ciaran Cronin and Pablo de Grieff eds, MIT Press 1998) 137–8.

[16] ibid.

[17] ibid 161. Also see Daniele Archibugi and David Held (eds), *Cosmopolitan Democracy: An Agenda for a New World Order* (Polity Press 1995).

[18] Liberal nationalists and some civic republicans contest the proposition that having interests at stake constitutes a sufficient basis for claiming inclusion in the decision-making processes of a political community. They argue that certain aspects of an individual's identity (most notably, her political membership) are a morally relevant basis for claims of inclusion and exclusion. See especially, David Miller, *Citizenship and National Identity* (Polity Press 2000); Yael Tamir, *Liberal Nationalism* (Princeton University Press 1995).

[19] Hannah Arendt, *The Origins of Totalitarianism* (Harcourt Inc. 1967). For an unpacking of this dilemma, see Seyla Benhabib, *The Rights of Others. Aliens, Citizens, and Residents* (Cambridge University Press 2004); Seyla Benhabib, *Another Cosmopolitanism. The Berkeley Tanner Lectures* (Oxford University Press, 2006).

As global interdependence in the economic, political, social, and cultural domains intensifies, the lack of fit between the fixed scope of national membership and the contingent circle of stakeholders in any political decision becomes particularly troubling. Domestic policy has what Somek calls "transnational effects":[20] as citizens, we are affected by the decisions of institutions from which we are formally excluded, while the decisions of the institutions that represent us have far-reaching consequences for those to whom they are not accountable. Institutions beyond the state hold out the possibility of drawing the circle of moral inclusion more widely and more flexibly than the typical nation-state, alleviating marginalization, and reorienting domestic legal systems in a more cosmopolitan direction.

Finally, proponents of postnational democracy highlight the important challenges that global interdependence poses to the efficacy of the state as a reason for investigating alternative forms of political community.[21] Although the world is carved up into nominally sovereign territorial units, contemporary political, social, and economic forces often elude the control of any one state.[22] To be sure, cross-border problems such as global economic shocks, transnational criminal networks, environmental degradation, and climate change do not come with obvious supranational solutions, but they do undermine the once-useful fiction of the state's plenipotence within its territory. Furthermore, as Anne Peters writes, "this general loss of effectiveness reduces in turn the effectiveness of self-determination, or democratic output."[23] In the postnational context, constitutional mechanisms could facilitate cooperation among interdependent political communities, allocate the benefits and burdens of their interdependence more equitably, and establish a more robust correspondence between public institutions and those whom they govern.[24] Layered across supra- and subnational levels, democratic decision-making institutions would be able to extend and contract the

[20] Alexander Somek, "The Argument from Transnational Effects I: Representing Outsiders through Freedom of Movement" (2010) 16 *ELJ* 315; "The Argument from Transnational Effects II: Establishing Transnational Democracy" (2010) 16 *ELJ* 375. Somek is critical of this argument as an adequate justification for the far-reaching normative force of the EU's free movement provisions within domestic systems.

[21] Jürgen Habermas, *The Divided West* (tr Ciaran Cronin, Polity 2008) 176; David Held, *Political Theory and the Modern State. Essays on State, Power, and Democracy* (Polity Press 1989); David Held, *Democracy and the Global Order: From the Modern State to Cosmopolitan Governance* (Stanford University Press 1995); Daniele Archibugi, David Held, and Martin Köhler (eds), *Reimagining Political Community: Studies in Cosmopolitan Democracy* (Stanford University Press 1998).

[22] David Held, Anthony McGrew, David Goldblatt, and Jonathan Perraton, *Global Transformations. Politics, Economics, and Culture* (Polity Press 1999).

[23] Anne Peters, "Compensatory Constitutionalism: The Function and Potential of Fundamental International Norms and Structures" (2006) 19 *Leiden Journal of International Law* 579, 592.

[24] David Held, "Democracy and the International Order" in Daniele Archibugi and David Held (eds), *Cosmopolitan Democracy. An Agenda for a New World Order* (Polity Press 1995).

scope of decision-making to fit the affected constituency instead of confining democratic participation to the rigid and, on this view, increasingly arbitrary boundaries of states.[25]

Although we may debate whether the EU can be treated as anything other than idiosyncratic,[26] it has nevertheless been regarded as a pilot project in postnational constitutional democracy and an occasion to assess whether it can realize these hopes. To many, European integration represents an attempt to remedy the moral arbitrariness and decreasing efficacy of national boundaries. Its institutions are expected not only to restore democratic self-rule by patching up the "leaky vessel" of national democracy,[27] but also to stabilize democracies by ensconcing them within a firm external framework of norms.[28] According to David Edward, "a major preoccupation of the politicians of Western Europe after the Second World War was the search for mechanisms to compensate for the shortcomings of democracy in the nation-state."[29] Compared to nation-states, it is argued, supranational institutions hold out the possibility of framing political community in more inclusive ways. Postwar advocates of European integration believed that "[t]he taming of the nation-state through democratic constitutions has its limits," especially when it comes to "[ensuring] that 'foreign' identities and their interests are taken into account within their decision-making processes."[30] Supranational decision-making processes afford "a new form of voice to national disempowered groups and often [reintroduce] true deliberation in areas of the national political process that have become prisoner of a certain composition of interests or of certain unchallengeable definitions of the public good."[31] In each of these respects, European integration is viewed not only as an extension of domestic constitutional democracy, but also its *conditio sine qua non*.

[25] David Held, "Principles of Cosmopolitan Order" in Gillian Brock and Harry Brighouse (eds), *The Political Philosophy of Cosmopolitanism* (Cambridge University Press 2005) 26–7.

[26] James Caporaso, Gary Marks, Andrew Moravcsik, and Mark Pollack, "Does the European Union Represent an *n* of 1?" (1997) X *ECSA Review* 1.

[27] Charles Bright and Michael Geyer, cited in Peter Lindseth, "Author's Reply: 'Outstripping', or the Question of 'Legitimate for What?' in EU Governance" (2012) 8 *European Constitutional Law Review* 153, 163.

[28] Jan-Werner Müller, *Contesting Democracy: Political Ideas in Twentieth-Century Europe* (Yale University Press 2011); Robert O Keohane, Stephen Macedo, and Andrew Moravcsik "Democracy-Enhancing Multilateralism" (2009) 63 *International Organization* 1.

[29] David Edward, "Nations, States, People and Commerce" in Geraldine Prince (ed), *A Window on Europe* (Canongate 1993) 53.

[30] Joerges and Neyer, "From Intergovernmental Bargaining to Deliberative Political Processes" 293. Also see Anand Menon and Stephen Weatherill, "Transnational Legitimacy in a Globalising World: How the European Union Rescues its States" (2008) 31 *West European Politics* 397, 404.

[31] Miguel Poiares Maduro, "Contrapunctual Law: Europe's Constitutional Pluralism in Action" in Neil Walker (ed), *Sovereignty in Transition* (Hart 2003) 523.

Against the background of several decades of agonizing about the EU's so-called democratic deficit, the proposition that the EU could improve on national democracy may seem downright odd. Spurred into action by concerns over the democratic legitimacy of supranational governance, EU member states have spent the past few decades devising new mechanisms for citizen participation in EU decision-making and expanding existing ones. The result is a complex, composite, often fiendishly complicated system that comprises numerous avenues of popular participation, public accountability, and oversight. How do existing EU institutions stack up against the democratic hopes fastened to the European integration project in particular and postnational constitutional democracy in general? To what extent does the EU rely on democratic self-rule as its legitimating principle? Are its democratic mechanisms commensurate with its vast scope of authority?

These questions have motivated voluminous commentary, and the grounds of the democratic deficit debate are too well trodden to warrant yet another comprehensive mapping.[32] In this chapter, I will argue, against conventional wisdom, that the dearth of citizen participation is not the EU's primary democratic problem. More troubling, I contend, is the fact that the EU's most effective avenues of citizen participation exemplify and reinforce its system of functional constitutionalism, and undermine the principle of equal political inclusion as a result. While the EU gives citizens important means for exercising agency in its decision-making processes, the most effective of these means are configured to advance the substantive commitment to market integration, leaving little room for the pursuit of competing aims and shutting out of the political arena those who do not share this commitment. The most significant participatory mechanisms that enable private parties to register their interests at the supranational level are neither inclusive nor necessarily democracy-enhancing. To the contrary, they leave large constituencies of citizens with few effective channels through which to contest the economic policy decisions that affect them. Political agency in the EU is increasingly asymmetric and functionally fragmented,

[32] Few other EU-related themes have received more attention in the past two decades than the EU's so-called "democracy deficit." Seminal interventions include David Beetham and Christopher Lord, *Legitimacy and the European Union* (Longman 1998); Phillippe Schmitter, *How to Democratize the EU—and Why Bother?* (Rowman and Littlefield 2000); Larry Siedentop, *Democracy in Europe* (Columbia University Press 2001); Richard Bellamy and Alex Warleigh (eds), *Citizenship and Governance in the European Union* (Continuum 2001); Erik Oddvar Eriksen and John Erik Fossum (eds), *Democracy in the European Union: Democracy Through Deliberation?* (Routledge 2000); Habermas, *The Inclusion of the Other*; Hix, *What's Wrong with the European Union and How to Fix It*; Beate Kohler-Koch and Berthold Rittberger (eds), *Debating the Democratic Legitimacy of the European Union* (Rowman & Littlefield 2007). Skeptical perspectives include Andrew Moravcsik, "In Defence of the 'Democratic Deficit': Reassessing Legitimacy in the European Union" (2002) 40 *JCMS* 603; Majone, "Europe's 'Democratic Deficit.'"

and these changes come at the expense of domestic democratic institutions that ensure equal participation.

(I) SCALING UP DEMOCRACY OR SCALING DOWN EXPECTATIONS?

In 2009, the Lisbon Treaty mooted the elaborate scholarly debate about which standards of democracy are best suited to supranational institutions by enshrining a capacious set of democratic principles as the EU's founding commitments. The new treaty provisions affirm "the right [of every citizen] to participate in the democratic life of the Union," and emphasize that "citizens are directly represented at Union level in the European Parliament." They underline the role of political parties as "expressing the will of citizens of the Union."[33] Title II of the Treaty on the Functioning of the European Union (TFEU) confers duties on Union institutions to "give citizens and representative associations the opportunity to make known and publicly exchange their views in all areas of Union action" and to maintain "dialogue with representative associations and civil society."[34] Like many aspirational constitutional documents, however, Title II is vague with regard to the institutions needed to instantiate these ideals. In fact, as I will argue in this chapter, the EU's decision-making mechanisms in their current form can only partially realize the ambitious democratic commitments enshrined in the treaties. For now, let us note the multiplicity of competing conceptions of democratic government packed into these provisions, which emphasize representation, popular will, civic dialogue, deliberation, partisanship, and civil society without dwelling on their compatibility. Like the relevant academic scholarship, the treaties evince a lack of consensus about the defining characteristics of democracy as a political principle and a regime type.[35]

To clear up some of the analytical confusion, I will analyze the EU's assorted mechanisms of democratic legitimation in light of three major conceptions of democratic rule, which I define broadly enough to capture new institutional variations. First, *representative* democratic institutions enable the selection of political office-holders through free and fair elections that feature partisan competition and in which each citizen gets an equal vote. I refer to *participatory* democracy to denote procedures that enable citizens to directly voice their opinions and preferences in formalized policymaking processes. Third, *deliberative* democratic institutions enable

[33] Arts 10–11 TEU. [34] ibid.

[35] WB Gallie famously considers democracy as a prime examplar of "essentially contested concepts." WB Gallie, "Essentially Contested Concepts" (1956) 56 *Proceedings of the Aristotelian Society* 167.

decision-making through reasoned reflection, exchange of ideas, and persuasion rather than manipulation, hegemony, and bargaining. Although these working definitions lack the degree of precision that they have acquired in the prodigious democratic theory literature, they differentiate between the various respects in which we can and cannot consider the EU's institutions as democratic. Furthermore, although they can be distinguished from one another analytically, these conceptions are by no means mutually exclusive in theory or practice. Any given democratic institution is likely to instantiate several of them at once. Parliamentary democracy is meant to combine all three. Elections embody both representative and participatory dimensions of democratic rule, but have been criticized for being hostile to deliberation.[36] The US Administrative Procedure Act requires administrative bodies to be both participatory *and* deliberative by setting out procedures of public consultation and reason-giving.[37] However, a deliberative body can also thwart participation if it is elite-driven and secretive.

In what follows, I will critically evaluate the extent to which EU decision-making instantiates these three dimensions of democratic self-rule. Instead of comprehensively reviewing the EU's many and varied democratic mechanisms, however, I will attend to those that reflect and respond to the distinctive circumstances of supranational governance. Discussions of the EU's democratic credentials often focus on the adequacy of the means of electoral control in general, and the promises and limitations of the European Parliament (EP) in particular. By contrast, I maintain that the EU's system of democratic legitimation is far more complex than what this discussion reflects, and it is has some remarkably creative features. Despite its institutional attempts to approximate the representative, participatory, and deliberative ideals, however, I will argue that the EU's composite system of democratic legitimation is ultimately insufficient to realize the ambitious democratic commitments enshrined in the Treaty on European Union (TEU). This is not to rehash the platitude that the EU fails to meet normatively demanding standards of democratic rule. As I observed earlier, such a conclusion is not only unsurprising but also unfair, since these standards have mostly been tailored to nation-states, if not the ethically coherent *polies* of the ancient world. My point is rather that the EU's democratic mechanisms illuminate the distinctive configuration of its system of functional constitutionalism, whose normative claim to authority is founded primarily on the promise of effective government rather than on the principle of collective autonomy in any of its guises.

[36] Philip Pettit, "Depoliticizing Democracy" 2004 17 *Ratio Juris* 52.

[37] Shapiro, "The Giving Reasons Requirement."

The limits of supranational representative democracy

Attempts to adapt standard institutions of democratic legitimation to the supranational context have had mixed results. The configuration of the EU's legislative and executive powers has little in common with a conventional democratic system, whether presidential or parliamentary, and it is unlikely to evolve in that direction any time soon.[38] Its primary legislative organ, the Council, comprises cabinet-level representatives of member state governments; in other words, it assigns legislative functions to office-holders from the executive branch. While the Council increasingly shares legislative authority with the EP, and while its members answer to their respective national parliaments, as an institution, it lacks supranational parliamentary or electoral accountability in the manner of a cabinet. Nonetheless, the Council fulfills a representative democratic function. Major pieces of EU legislation are not decreed by faceless bureaucrats in Brussels, but are in fact negotiated and approved by the duly elected or democratically accountable representatives of national *demoi*.[39] However, unlike parliamentary assemblies, which can represent a wide spectrum of political viewpoints, the effect of ministerial representation on the Council is to filter out domestic pluralism concerning EU matters, since each Council member represents her government's stance as *the* national view. Furthermore, since governments are typically elected on domestic policy platforms, votes cast in national election campaigns hardly add up to a meaningful exercise of *supra*national democratic agency. Finally, entrusting supranational legislative functions to members of the domestic executive branch weights the composite system of European governance in favor of the executive.[40]

While the Council provides an attenuated form of democratic representation, the involvement of national parliaments in EU decision-making brings a more traditional element of representative democracy to the EU's composite system. Compared to EU institutions, national and subnational legislative assemblies have deeper "legitimacy resources":[41] citizens tend to view them

[38] For a bold proposal for further parliamentarizing the EU by combining the representative power of domestic assemblies and the EP, see Andrew Duff, "Building a Parliamentary Europe" (1994) 29 *Government and Opposition* 147, 161–4.

[39] Andrew Moravcsik, "In Defence of the 'Democratic Deficit'"; Armin von Bogdandy, "A Disputed Idea Becomes Law: Remarks on European Democracy as a Legal Principle" in Kohler-Koch and Rittberger, *Debating the Democratic Legitimacy of the European Union*. Bogdandy describes the sharing of legislative power between the indirectly elected Council and the directly elected Parliament as "a principle of dual legitimacy" 36–7.

[40] Deirdre Curtin, *Executive Power of the European Union. Law, Practices, and the Living Constitution* (Oxford University Press 2009).

[41] Fritz Scharpf, *Governing in Europe: Effective or Democratic?* (Oxford University Press 1999) 23; Peter L Lindseth, *Power and Legitimacy. Reconciling Europe and the Nation-State* (Oxford University Press 2010) 11.

as the primary locus of democratic self-rule, and they in turn represent relatively cohesive and well-institutionalized democratic publics of the kind notably absent at the supranational level. Although member states have varying procedures for soliciting their input into the EU's legislative process, the treaties call for national parliaments to remain apprised of (and sometimes to review) draft legislative acts, discuss proposals for treaty revision, and establish inter-parliamentary dialogue with other member states and the EP.[42] In addition, national parliaments are expected to monitor the limits of the EU's competences and ensure the application of the principle of subsidiarity.[43] Although national parliaments' involvement in the EU policy process has increased, such engagement shows variation across member states.[44] Most national parliaments have not made extensive use of existing channels of engagement with the EU.[45] Importantly, the scrutiny exercised by national parliaments preserves the EU's state-centric model of democratic accountability, ensuring that supranational issues are refracted through domestic publics.[46]

Directly elected by member state citizens since 1979, the EP is the main institutional vehicle of representative democracy at the supranational level. Originally designed as a consultative assembly, it now shares the Council's legislative prerogatives in a range of policy areas. Moreover, following the 2014 elections, the EP assumed the important role of selecting the President of the Commission by majority vote, against opposition by some member states.[47] Nonetheless, the EP lacks legislative authority or powers of oversight comparable to a domestic legislative assembly. While it can sack the Commission for misconduct, it cannot hold the Council accountable. Consequently, elections to the EP do not have the power to sway the Union's political agenda to the same extent as a parliamentary system, but they can affect the overall direction of policy.[48]

[42] TEU art 12(a), (d), and (f) respectively.

[43] TEU art 12(b).

[44] For a selected cross-country comparison and analysis, see Katrin Auel and Tapio Raunio, "Debating the State of the Union? Comparing Parliamentary Debates on EU Issues in Finland, France, Germany, and the UK" (2014) 20 *The Journal of Legislative Studies* 13. For a more general comparison, see Thomas Winzen, "National Parliamentary Control of EU Affairs: A Cross-country and Longitudinal Comparison" (2012) 35 *West European Politics* 657.

[45] A range of reasons, including information problems, the fragmented nature of supranational decision-making, and domestic partisan dynamics, have been proposed in explanation. For a brief comparison across fifteen member states, see Torbjörn Bergman, Wolfgang C Müller, Kaare Strøm, and Magnus Blomgren, "Democratic Delegation and Accountability" in Kaare Strøm, Wolfgang C Müller, and Torbjörn Bergman (eds), *Delegation and Accountability in Parliamentary Democracies* (Oxford University Press 2003).

[46] Lindseth, *Power and Legitimacy* 226.

[47] Art 17(7) TEU provides that the President of the Commission "shall be elected by the European Parliament by a majority of its component members."

[48] Karlheinz Reif and Hermann Schmitt, "Nine Second-Order Elections. A Conceptual Framework for the Analysis of European Election Results" (1980) 8 *European Journal of Political Research* 3; Hermann Schmitt, "The European Parliament Elections of June 2004: Still Second-Order?" (2005) 28 *West European Politics* 650.

As a whole, then, the EU's composite institutional structure complements intergovernmental decision-making mechanisms with majoritarian ones, establishing an incomplete system of democratic representation in which elections cannot produce or dismiss governments, but can nevertheless affect the composition of one or more institutions.[49] For instance, when elections in a member state result in the alternation of power, only a single seat on the twenty-eight-strong Council changes hands. Similarly, although European elections can change the party bloc that holds the majority in the EP, "there is no real sense in which the European political process allows the electorate 'to throw the scoundrels out'."[50] This is not to say that transforming the EU into a parliamentary system would improve the democratic legitimacy of its political system. On the contrary, the primary attachment of European *demoi* to their domestic political institutions, the desire on the part of member states to preserve the EU's intergovernmental features, and the relative weakness of the European public sphere speak against further parliamentarizing EU decision-making.[51] Even the former Secretary-General of the EP, Hans Nord, argued in 1965 that:

> attempts should not be made to solve the problem of European parliamentary control merely by trying to make the European Parliament look more like a national one. We are faced with a new and original phenomenon and the future role of the Parliament should be assessed in the light of the distribution of power within the Community.[52]

Though written a half-century ago, Nord's observation pinpoints the contemporary impasse of representative democracy at the supranational level: institutional reforms that would increase electoral control over EU policymaking would contradict the essential intergovernmental and technocratic elements of its constitutional structure. As I argued in the first chapter, the EU has been designed to isolate certain areas of policy from majoritarian influence in the name of ensuring more effective decision-making in those domains. The attenuation of supranational governance from electoral control is a feature, not a bug. However, to say that the EU's

[49] Numerous democratic theorists privilege the electoral alternation of power, rather than the expression of some transcendent idea of the general will, as democracy's defining feature and its advantage over other methods of appointing political leaders. See especially, Joseph Schumpeter, *Capitalism, Socialism, and Democracy* (George Allen & Unwin Ltd 1942) ch XXII; Adam Przeworski, "Minimalist Conception of Democracy: A Defense" in Ian Shapiro and Casiano Hacker-Cordon (eds), *Democracy's Value* (Cambridge University Press 1999).

[50] JHH Weiler, Ulrich R Haltern, and Franz C Mayer, "European Democracy and its Critique" (1995) 18 *West European Politics* 4, 8.

[51] Lindseth, *Power and Legitimacy* 53.

[52] HR Nord, "The Role of the Parliament of the European Communities" *Internationale Spectator* (The Hague, April 8, 1965) 685, 689.

decision-making mechanisms fall short of conventional democratic criteria is not to say that they are illegitimate per se. Rather, the intergovernmental and technocratic elements hardwired into the EU underline the difficulty of reimagining what democratic rule might mean outside the nation-state. Several features of the EU's institutional framework respond to this challenge in creative ways. The remainder of the chapter attends to these, and assesses their democratic value-added.

Participatory democracy through market citizenship?

Formally instituted in 1993, EU citizenship is the supranational adaptation of a conventional mechanism of democratic participation. Among other things, it gives member state nationals the right to vote and run for office in European and local elections even if they lack the citizenship of the member state in which they reside.[53] Unlike guest worker programs that treat migrant laborers simply as factors of production, Union citizenship lends recognition to Europeans who live in member states other than their own as political agents, and attempts to remedy the disenfranchisement that attends the exercise of mobility rights.[54] Furthermore, by requiring member states to extend certain domestic rights of political participation to one another's citizens, it mitigates the exclusion built into national communities of membership. For these reasons, EU citizenship has been welcomed as partially decoupling political rights from nationality, and creating a supranational basis for democratic *praxis*.[55]

At present, however, the political significance of Union citizenship lags far behind its symbolic import. At the very least, democracy demands that citizens be able to understand themselves as having collectively authorized the laws by which they are bound.[56] Union citizenship instantiates a far more modest form of public autonomy at the supranational level, since the collective will of citizens as expressed through their elected representatives is tempered by a number of other political forces and institutional actors in the EU's legislative process. Similarly, Union citizenship cannot conjure the strong public sphere

[53] For a comprehensive analysis of the rights and entitlements created by EU citizenship, see Dimitry Kochenov, "*Ius Tractum* of Many Faces: European Citizenship and the Difficult Relationship Between Status and Rights" 2008–9 15 *Columbia Journal of European Law* 169.

[54] Jo Shaw, *The Transformation of Citizenship in the European Union. Electoral Rights and the Restructuring of Political Space* (Cambridge University Press 2007) 95.

[55] Antje Wiener, *"European" Citizenship Practice: Building Institutions of a Non-State* (Westview Press 1999); Shaw, *The Transformation of Citizenship in the European Union*; Benhabib, *The Rights of Others* ch 4; Willem Maas, *Creating European Citizens* (Rowman & Littlefield Publishers 2007).

[56] Jürgen Habermas, "On the Internal Relation between the Rule of Law and Democracy" (1995) 3 *European Journal of Philosophy* 12, 15; Habermas, *Between Facts and Norms* 122–3, 408–25.

that sustains democratic institutions and gives elections their meaning in the domestic context.[57] In the wake of the abortive attempt to stage its own "constitutional moment,"[58] the EU's prospects of rallying greater civic momentum behind supranational policymaking look dim. Even the indefatigable Jürgen Habermas has expressed his pessimism about the democratizing potential of European elections by describing EU citizenship as an "empty shell."[59]

I will defer a more detailed discussion of EU citizenship until the next chapter. Here, I would like to focus on a juridical relationship between the EU and member state citizens that was forged on the basis of market freedoms. This relationship far predates the introduction of a formal citizenship status. As I discussed in Chapter 2, the ECJ's decision to allow member state citizens to invoke EC law before national courts enabled the development of a new, supranational tier of individual rights, most of which related to commercial mobility.[60] Although EU citizenship formally ensconced this relationship within a civic canopy and expanded its scope, it did not significantly add to its substantive content. In fact, the attention paid to the symbolism of EU citizenship has obscured the deep political significance of the EU's extensive regime of commercial mobility rights. The freedoms of movement of goods, services, and capital are often left out of analyses of supranational democracy because they appear to belong in the economic rather than the political sphere. In practice, however, these rights have enabled private actors to exercise a consequential form of political agency in the development of the supranational legal system. Some observers have described this process as nothing short of a democratic transformation for the EC. As David Keeling and Federico Mancini, a former judge of the ECJ, contend:

> [T]he Court recognized in *Van Gend en Loos* that the two aspects of democratic legitimacy—namely, the right of the people to participate in the law-making function through representative bodies and the ability of individuals to vindicate their rights in judicial proceedings—are intimately linked: one of the reasons given for upholding direct effect was that "the nationals of the States brought together in the Community are called upon to cooperate in the functioning of this Community through the intermediary of the European Parliament and the Economic and Social Committee."[61]

[57] On the role of the public sphere in sustaining electoral democracy, see Habermas, *Between Facts and Norms* ch 8. For a critical application of that theory to the EU, see Dieter Grimm "Does Europe Need a Constitution?" (1995) 1 *ELJ* 282.

[58] Bruce Ackerman, *We the People. Foundations* (Belknap 1991).

[59] Jürgen Habermas, *Europe. The Faltering Project* (Ciaran Cronin tr, Polity 2009) 81, 87.

[60] Case 26/62 *Van Gend en Loos v Nederlandse Administratie der Belastingen* [1963] ECR 1. Michelle Everson, "The Legacy of the Market Citizen" in Jo Shaw and Gillian More (eds), *New Legal Dynamics of European Union* (Clarendon Press 1995) 79.

[61] Federico Mancini and David T Keeling, "Democracy and the European Court of Justice" (1994) 57 *MLR* 175, 183–4.

On this view, the ECJ's shrewd move to grant member state nationals the status of rights-bearers under supranational law was a major democratizing innovation. "[T]he effect of *Van Gend en Loos*," the authors write, "was to take Community law out of the hands of politicians and bureaucrats and to give it to the people. Of all the Court's democratising achievements none can rank so highly in practical terms."[62] At first glance, this seems an overstatement. After all, the legal norms that the ECJ allowed individuals to claim against member states pertained to cross-border economic activity; they did not establish any of the political rights characteristic of democratic citizenship. As McCormick points out, democratic citizenship, whether within or beyond the state, is "characterized by the substantive social, public, and political *exercise* of formal rights rather than the mere *enumeration* or even *observance* of them."[63] Weiler's quip that "[l]ong before women and Jews were made citizens they enjoyed direct effect"[64] gets at the same idea: a citizen, unlike a subject, is more than the passive recipient of a bundle of rights. She is also a political agent who has meaningful opportunities to exercise her public autonomy by participating in the political process.

Although the commercial mobility rights protected by EC law did not initially have such explicit civic content, the doctrine of direct effect clearly enabled member state citizens to exercise a form of supranational political agency. Above all, it allowed them to participate in the integration process by pushing for the faithful application of EC law by member states. Translated into rights owed by member states to individuals, supranational norms empowered member state citizens to challenge quotas, tariffs, regulatory burdens, and myriad other domestic restrictions that interfered with cross-border economic activity. In what is a well-known story, the ECJ enlisted the "vigilance of individuals concerned to protect their [Community] rights,"[65] aided by the cooperation of national courts (especially lower-ranking ones), to establish a "decentralized enforcement mechanism for EC law" that has proved strikingly coherent and effective.[66] Once this process was set in motion, the ECJ found more and

[62] ibid 183.

[63] John P McCormick, *Weber, Habermas, and Transformations of the European State* (Cambridge University Press 2007) 197, emphasis original.

[64] JHH Weiler, *The Constitution of Europe* (Cambridge University Press 1999) 337.

[65] Case 26/62 *Van Gend en Loos*.

[66] Alec Stone Sweet, *The Judicial Construction of Europe* (Oxford University Press 2004) 69; Anne-Marie Burley and Walter Mattli, "Europe Before the Court" (1993) 47 *International Organization* 41; Walter Mattli and Anne-Marie Slaughter, *Constructing the European Community Legal System from the Ground up* (EUI Working Papers 1996); Karen Alter, *Establishing the Supremacy of European Law* (Oxford University Press 2001); R Daniel Kelemen, *Eurolegalism: The Transformation of Law and Regulation in the European Union* (Harvard University Press 2011) ch 3.

more provisions of the treaties and directives as directly effective within national legal orders. Domestic courts were asked to invalidate national laws that interfered with those requirements, and occasionally even to ignore domestic constitutional restrictions against judicial review.[67] National courts, in turn, took up this invitation with unanticipated zeal as more and more workers, traders, investors, and service providers resorted to litigation to eliminate domestic measures inhospitable to commercial mobility. "The more the legal system actually remove[d] barriers to markets, the more subsequent litigation [was] stimulated," since "traders and producers had both the incentive and the resources" to challenge national measures which adversely affected their commercial activity.[68] In Alter's words, "the European legal system has become part of the policymaking process appealed to by those actors who lose during political negotiations over policy."[69] Litigation fostered massive mobilization of interest groups in favor of market integration both at the level of member states and EU institutions.[70] As the judicial process broke down barriers to trade across member states, market actors in greater numbers demanded measures furthering economic integration, and used all available channels, including litigation and aggressive pro-integration lobbying, to do so.[71] The ECJ gave further encouragement to litigation by establishing a principle of state liability under EC law, which obliged member states to compensate individuals or firms that suffer commercial losses as a result of a member state's non-compliance with supranational rules.[72] The cluster of judicial doctrines that have come to be viewed as defining the EU legal order, including vertical and horizontal direct effect, indirect effect, supremacy, mutual recognition, preemption, state liability, and fundamental rights were all developed in response to litigation by member state nationals with

[67] Case 107/77 *Simmenthal II* (1978) ECR 629. Stone Sweet, *The Judicial Construction of Europe* 84–5.

[68] Stone Sweet, *The Judicial Construction of Europe* 129, 109.

[69] Alter, *Establishing the Supremacy of European Law* 28.

[70] Neil Fligstein, *Euroclash: The EU, European Identity, and the Future of Europe* (Oxford University Press 2008) ch 2.

[71] Neil Fligstein and Alec Stone Sweet, "Constructing Polities and Markets: An Institutionalist Account of European Integration" (2002) 107 *American Journal of Sociology* 1206; Sonia Mazey and Jeremy Richardson, "The Logic of Organization: Interest Groups" in Jeremy Richardson (ed), *European Union: Power and Policy-Making* (Routledge 1996).

[72] R Daniel Kelemen, "The EU Rights Revolution: Adversarial Legalism and European Integration" in Tanja Börzel and Rachel A Cichowski (eds), *The State of the European Union, vol 6: Law, Politics, and Society* (Oxford University Press 2003) 228. Landmark decisions in this arena include Joined cases C-6/90 and C-9/90 *Francovich and others v Italy* [1991] ECR 5357; Joined cases C-46/93 and C-48/93 *Brasserie du Pêcheur SA v Bundesrepublik Deutschland and The Queen v Secretary of State for Transport, ex parte: Factortame Ltd and Others* [1996] ECR 1029; Case C-224/01 *Köbler v Austria* [2003] ECR I-10239.

interests at stake.[73] In sum, "trade litigation quickly generated much of the context for legal integration."[74]

Given the momentous political consequences of litigation, it is beyond doubt that commercial mobility rights were not simply passive entitlements but provided a legal framework for political participation. If citizenship entails exercising authorship of the laws by which one is governed, then this is precisely what producers, traders, service-providers, and investors did by invoking their supranational rights in court. Michelle Everson has used the phrase "market citizenship," coined by German jurist Hans Peter Ipsen, to capture the role that private economic actors have played in catalyzing the process of legal and market integration.[75] As Ipsen observed, the individual political status established by direct effect doctrine was confined to the functionally delineated sphere of EC law.[76] Member state nationals became market citizens by transacting in the economic domain established by the treaty.[77] While the concept itself hearkens back to "older notions of the burgher, bourgeois, or economic citizen,"[78] therefore, it differs from member state citizenship due to its functionally circumscribed nature. Market citizenship is a teleological form of political agency; it furthers the goal of economic union.[79]

Although it enables the participation of private actors in the integration process, therefore, the democratic value added of market citizenship open to question. Nonetheless, many scholars have advanced a *faute*

[73] Maduro writes: "Litigation was the fuel of the process of constitutionalization but, at the same time, molded the European Constitution arising from that process. Many of the important developments in the European Economic Constitution and Art 30 have been triggered by individuals and national courts." Miguel Poiares Maduro, *We the Court: The European Court of Justice and the European Economic Constitution* (Hart Publishing 1998) 28.

[74] Stone Sweet, *Judicial Construction of Europe* 109.

[75] Hans Peter Ipsen, *Europäisches Gemeinschaftsrecht* (JCB Mohr 1972) 715–70, 767–70.

[76] Hans Peter Ipsen, "Die Bundesrepublik Deutschland in den Europäischen Gemeinschaften" in Josef Isensee and Paul Kirchhof (eds), *Handbuch des Staatsrechts der Bundesrepublik Deutschland*, vol VII (Müller 1992) 802–3.

[77] Hans Peter Ipsen, "Die Verfassungsrolle des Europäischen Gerichtshofs für die Integration" in J Schwarze (ed), *Der Europäische Gerichtshof als Verfassungsgericht und Rechtsschutzinstanz* (Nomos 1983) 35, 56.

[78] Everson, "The Legacy of the Market Citizen" 84. Also see Shaw, *The Transformation of Citizenship* 45; Tony Downes, "Market Citizenship: Functionalism and Fig-leaves" in Bellamy and Warleigh, *Citizenship and Governance in the European Union*. Saskia Sassen uses the term "economic citizenship" to denote the rights and entitlements that multinational corporations draw from global economic institutions. Saskia Sassen, *Losing Control? Sovereignty in an Age of Globalization* (Columbia University Press 1996) ch 2; Saskia Sassen, *Territory, Authority, and Rights. From Medieval to Global Assemblages* (Princeton University Press 2006) ch 6.

[79] Ipsen, "Die Bundesrepublik Deutschland in den Europäischen Gemeinschaften" 802.

de mieux defense of participation through litigation. In this vein, Martin Shapiro argues:

> Procedural law and judicial review under such law are more or less natural vehicles for the attainment of greater transparency and participation and also a halfway house between the famous democratic deficit and a democratized legislative process. If statute-making cannot be fully democratic, at least the tertiary law-making and implementation of the various lesser organs of Union governance can be pursued through more transparent and participatory procedures.[80]

Insofar as member state citizens used the judicial route to make their mark on the integration process, litigation has been viewed as a qualified substitute for democratic participation, particularly given the dearth of traditional representative institutions at the supranational level. As Gráinne de Búrca writes:

> the European Community's political system remains elitist, largely undemocratic, and beyond the influence of large sections of the population which comprises it. In this context, rather than undermining the democratic process, it is possible that the language of rights gives voice to interests which are largely excluded from the political processes and which might not otherwise be heard.[81]

Although de Búrca is careful to speak broadly of rights rather than market freedoms, she regards rights-based judicial review as an effective way for citizens to challenge decision-makers, and one that helps open the policy process to citizen participation.

This democratic account of rights litigation has special relevance in federal settings. In systems that bring together several semiautonomous jurisdictions, courts are said to protect the interests of those who transact in a jurisdiction other than their own. As John Hart Ely has argued in the American context, judicial review provides "virtual representation" for those who are disadvantaged by the decisions of the host state in which they reside or do business.[82] On this view, federal courts are the sole channel through which "out-of-staters" can raise and enforce claims against discriminatory

[80] Martin Shapiro, "The European Court of Justice" in Paul Craig and Gráinne de Búrca (eds), *The Evolution of EU Law* (Oxford University Press 1999) 343.

[81] Gráinne de Búrca, "The Language of Rights and European Integration" in Shaw and More, *New Legal Dynamics* 53.

[82] John Hart Ely, *Democracy and Distrust. A Theory of Judicial Review* (Harvard University Press 1980) 83. Alexander Somek has also drawn a parallel between Ely's constitutional theory and what he calls "the argument from transnational effects." According to Somek, this encompasses political claims that foreigners make on other states on the basis of affected interests. Somek contests the use of this line of argument in favor of supranational democracy and at the expense of nation-states. See Somek, "The Argument from Transnational Effects."

or unfavorable treatment. A significant portion of the core jurisprudence of the EU's judiciary parallels the logic Ely reads into the Privileges and Immunities Clause of Article IV of the US Constitution, namely, "state legislatures cannot by their various regulations treat out-of-staters less favorably than they treat locals."[83] According to Ely, this rule reflects the framers' recognition that "nonresidents are a paradigmatically powerless class politically."[84] On this interpretation, the Court of Justice of the European Union (CJEU) protects the interests of mobile EU citizens against discrimination or abuse that might result from their political disenfranchisement in the member state in which they do business. Echoing this virtual representation argument, Majone argues that "one of the unanticipated consequences of economic integration has been the growth of an impressive body of rules and decisions protecting diffuse interests that often lacked effective representation or protection at national level," most notably "the economic and social rights … created by the Treaties."[85] Similarly, Miguel Maduro construes free movement rights as "political" rather than economic rights that "[enhance] the representation of the interests of nationals of other Member States within national political processes."[86] By subjecting member states to a system of supranational constitutional scrutiny, EU law rectifies the discriminatory effects of bounded political communities.

In order to evaluate these claims, let us return to Ely's argument that in constitutional democracies in general, and in federal systems in particular, judicial review enables the disenfranchised to redeem procedural and participatory safeguards. Do rights of commercial mobility in the EU "[give] voice to interests which are largely excluded … and which might not otherwise be heard"?[87] This question reveals the democratic problems raised by the exercise of market freedoms as a form of political agency (rather than solely as a basis for economic activity): while these rights allow individuals to voice their interests through litigation, they only enable the expression of pro-integration preferences. As Burley and Mattli point out, in defending the rights of market actors, the CJEU has been "careful to create a one-way ratchet by permitting individual participation in the system only in a way that would advance Community goals."[88] Litigation "reflect[s] the interest of parties who have a major economic or personal stake in increased factor or personal mobility as well as the financial and organizational resources

[83] Ely, *Democracy and Distrust* 83. [84] ibid 83.

[85] Majone, "Europe's 'Democratic Deficit'" 12. Also see Menon and Weatherill, "Transnational Legitimacy in a Globalising World" 407.

[86] Maduro, *We the Court* 167.

[87] de Búrca, "The Language of Rights and European Integration" 53.

[88] Burley and Mattli, "Europe before the Court" 60.

to pursue this interest by seeking judicial redress against national laws and regulations."[89] As Lisa Conant has documented, "the EU legal system is most often effectively engaged by economic enterprises and, through national courts, by societal groups that are well organized domestically or supported by government-sponsored organizations."[90] By contrast, "the less mobile majority of European individuals and firms and, even more significantly, cases representing the interests that benefit from existing national laws and regulation" have little access to the privileged portal of political contestation opened up by market freedoms.[91] In sum, market citizenship has created new outsiders in those who draw limited benefits from the new, supranational legal order. This is not to impugn the project of market integration per se, but to note that a functionally specialized regime of political participation is deeply at odds with the promise of political equality and inclusion associated with democratic citizenship.[92]

The controversial *Laval*[93] and *Viking*[94] decisions of the Court of Justice illustrate these qualms. Both cases pitted supranational commercial mobility rights against domestic collective bargaining arrangements, as well as the freedom of association and right to collective action of workers. In *Laval*, a Latvian firm claimed that the Swedish Workers' Union's decision to strike against insufficient pay was preventing it from carrying out a government contract in Sweden, and therefore violated its right to offer services in another member state, guaranteed by article 49 of the EC Treaty (now art 56 TFEU). In *Viking*, a Finnish shipping company providing ferry services between Finland and Estonia sued the International Transport Workers' Federation for preventing it from re-registering its craft in Estonia, where it would be subject to lower wage requirements, and argued that the Federation's boycott infringed on its freedom of establishment under article 43 of the EC Treaty (now art 49 TFEU). In both of these cases, the Court held that trade unions must refrain as far as possible from interfering with the enjoyment of the "fundamental freedoms" of commercial mobility guaranteed to firms under EU law.[95] Although it paid lip service to the importance of rights of association and collective action, the Court argued that the

[89] Fritz W Scharpf, "The Asymmetry of European Integration, or, Why the EU Cannot Be a Social Market Economy" (2010) 8 *Socio-Economic Review* 211, 221, internal reference omitted.

[90] Lisa Conant, "Europe's No Fly Zone? Rights, Obligations, and Liberalization in Practice" in Börzel and Cichowski, *The State of the European Union* 249–50.

[91] Scharpf, "The Asymmetry of European Integration" 221, internal reference omitted.

[92] TH Marshall and Tom Bottomore, *Citizenship and Social Class* (first published 1950, Pluto Press 1992).

[93] Case C-438/05 *International Transport Workers' Federation and Finnish Seamen's Union v Viking Line ABP and OÜ Viking Line Eesti* [2007] ECR I-10779.

[94] C-314/05 *Laval un Partneri Ltd v Svenska Byggnadsarbetareförbundet* [2007] ECR I-11767.

[95] *Viking* paras 58–61, *Laval* paras 90–108.

exercise of these rights must not unduly restrict the freedom of establishment and the freedom to provide services in another member state.

Decisions like *Laval* and *Viking* enable employers to leverage EU law to circumvent or undermine "crucial features of national labor law, industrial relations law and wage setting practices"[96] that are among the essential features of European social welfare states.[97] More broadly, they illustrate the ways in which commercial mobility rights allow firms incorporated in other member states "to evade national rules of corporate governance,"[98] giving them not only an additional bargaining chip against labor unions, but also an advantage over domestic employers. They also open the door for similarly placed firms to claim damages from trade unions for losses suffered as a result of legally sanctioned industrial action.[99] As the ILO Committee of Experts noted with "serious concern," the *Laval* and *Viking* decisions impose "practical limitations on the effective exercise of the right to strike," particularly since "the omnipresent threat of an action for damages" by employers against trade unions in the light of these decisions "creates a situation where the rights under the Convention [Concerning Freedom of Association and Protection of the Right to Organise] cannot be exercised."[100] In each of these respects, the ECJ's *Laval* and *Viking* decisions illustrate how the rights of market citizens under EU law weaken the domestic socioeconomic safeguards on which old-fashioned citizens rely. In other words, they illustrate how the EU's system of functional constitutionalism empowers some constituencies at the expense of others. Market freedoms protect mobile economic actors against protectionism, but in doing so, they demote a wide range of interests that hamper the teleology of economic union. They also constrain the extent to which democratic publics can manage the social consequences (burdens as well as benefits) of the single market. Rather than buttressing member states' institutional capacity to manage transnational economic forces, the EU's functional constitutionalism

[96] Scharpf, "The Asymmetry of European Integration" 236.

[97] Christian Joerges and Florian Rödl, "Informal Politics and Formalised Law: Reflections after the Judgments of the ECJ in *Viking* and *Laval*" (2009) 15 *ELJ* 1, 17–18.

[98] Scharpf, "The Asymmetry of European Integration" 236.

[99] Alicia Hinarejos, "*Laval* and *Viking*: The Right to Collective Action versus EU Fundamental Freedoms" (2008) 8 *Human Rights Law Review* 714, 729. In fact, following the ECJ's judgment, the Swedish labor court ordered the trade unions concerned to pay approximately €50,000 in punitive damages to Laval. See Directorate General for Internal Policies, "The Impact of the ECJ Judgments on *Viking, Laval, Rüffert*, and *Luxembourg* on the Practice of Collective Bargaining and the Effectiveness of Social Action" IP/A/EMPL/ST/2009-11 (European Commission, May 2010) 9.

[100] Committee of Experts on the Application of ILO Conventions and Recommendations, Report of the Committee of Experts (International Labour Office 2010) 209. Available at <http://www.ilo.org/wcmsp5/groups/public/@ed_norm/@relconf/documents/meetingdocument/wcms_123424.pdf> accessed November 28, 2015.

frequently aligns with those forces, further straining beleaguered welfare states and domestic democratic institutions.[101]

*

As a bundle of rights and participatory practices, market citizenship is an intrinsically fraught concept: whereas modern democratic citizenship, among other things, is a recognition of civic equality and a license to register one's views in the political process, and only minimally prejudices the content of the views its holder is allowed to express, *market* citizenship instantiates a purposive form of political agency. It gives cross-border market actors a privileged platform from which to influence policymaking and implementation. The EU's rights regime offers far fewer resources for countervailing constituencies, such as trade unions, domestic social welfare recipients, or environmental activists, who must rely for the most part on the vulnerable shield of member state laws to protect their interests in the supranational legal process. In this respect, market citizenship contrasts with the expansive and egalitarian dynamic of citizenship rights stressed by TH Marshall.[102] The irony of market citizenship in the EU is that while it establishes a genuinely effective mode of individual participation in supranational governance, it disproportionately favors the functionally circumscribed constituency of cross-border economic actors.

To be sure, market citizenship is now one dimension of what has become a more complex relationship between the EU and its citizens.[103] Nonetheless, it deserves attention as the form of political agency that is indigenous to the EU's system of functional constitutionalism and a symptom of its deep democratic ambivalence. On the one hand, the EU's regime of commercial mobility rights has prompted member states to widen their scope of moral concern and legal protection to one another's citizens and firms. Nic Shuibhne warns against an artificial tendency "to constrain the capacity of the market and to overlook the normative as well as economic capacity of a constitutional market" and the citizenship practices it engenders.[104] On the other hand, however, the EU's system of functional constitutionalism redraws the boundaries of political inclusion by confining opportunities for effective political participation to well-resourced actors with an interest in market

[101] Wolfgang Streeck, *Buying Time. The Delayed Crisis of Democratic Capitalism Union* (Patrick Camiller tr, Verso 2014) 102.

[102] Marshall and Bottomore, *Citizenship and Social Class* 18; Benhabib, *The Rights of Others* 172–4; Andrew Linklater, "Citizenship and Sovereignty in the Post-Westphalian European State" in Archibugi, Held, and Köhler, *Re-imagining Political Community* 124.

[103] For a maximalist interpretation of the civic promise of EU citizenship, which contrasts with the market-centered perspective presented here, see Dora Kostakopoulou, "Ideas, Norms, and European Citizenship: Explaining Institutional Change" (2005) 68 *MLR* 233.

[104] Shuibhne, "The Resilience of EU Market Citizenship" 1609.

integration.[105] Supranational political agency is fractured not along national lines but along functional ones. In other words, the kind of political agency fostered by functional constitutionalism is a closed circuit: it reinforces the project of economic union, but remains inert or, worse, counterproductive, for those whose interests run contrary to that objective. The EU's persistent teleological configuration disappoints hopes for a more capacious postnational democracy. Even in the absence of more effective democratic institutions at the supranational level, market citizenship is no substitute for inclusive and equitable forms of political participation.

Deliberative technocracy: Democracy without the demos?

In addition to problems of size, diversity, and enduring civic allegiance to national political institutions, the task of adapting traditional models of democratic representation and participation to the EU is hampered by the inscrutably technical nature of many of its tasks. Not only are institutions such as the European Commission and the European Central Bank designed to work at arm's length from majoritarian influence,[106] but the subject matter of supranational decision-making is also often forbiddingly complex. In response, many observers turn to proceduralist, pluralist, or associative conceptions of legitimacy tailored to administrative institutions, which often address policy questions requiring specialized expertise. Under a proceduralist conception of legitimation, Dehousse argues, "administrative bodies must consider the interests affected by individual decisions" and must guarantee "transparency and participation or consultation rights" for those with interests at stake.[107] In a similar manner, the EU can promote "an extensive dialogue with the various segments of civil society," which "would obviate some of the shortcomings of representative democracy at the European level."[108] In short, if EU decision-making cannot be fully participatory or representative, then it can at least be *deliberative*; that is to say, committed to hearing all sides, impartially considering interests, risks, and evidence, engaging in justification and reason-giving, and fostering non-coercive agreement among participants.

One pillar of the EU's complex decision-making structure has been singled out as exemplifying this alternative, proceduralist mode of legitimacy,

[105] Lisa Conant, "Europe's No Fly Zone?"; Lisa Conant, *Justice Contained. Law and Politics in the European Union* (Cornell University Press 2002).

[106] Giandomenico Majone, "The Rise of the Regulatory State in Europe" (1994) 17 *Journal of Public Policy* 77; Majone, "Europe's 'Democratic Deficit.'"

[107] Dehousse, "Towards a Regulation of Transnational Governance?" 115. Dehousse is reserved about the democratizing potential of the procedural model, and argues that it should be backed up by parliamentary control mechanisms wherever possible. 122–3.

[108] Renaud Dehousse, "Comitology: Who Watches the Watchmen?" (2003) 10 *Journal of European Public Policy* 798, 807.

namely its extensive archipelago of committees. From inception to implementation, EU legislation goes through a bewildering array of committees, many of which have ad hoc functions, mandates, compositions, and accountability structures. In the absence of a comprehensive supranational bureaucracy to flesh out and implement EU decisions, these committees serve as important sites of norm-production and elaboration.[109] They are also expected to keep EU rules in line with member state preferences,[110] and to enable member state citizens, civil society groups, businesses, and relevant experts to register their views.

The most influential branch of the committee system is the Committee of Permanent Representatives, or COREPER, which consists of ambassadors of member states and assists the Council in drafting legislation. The permanent representatives are in turn assisted by a host of working groups comprising "low-ranking national administrators," who undertake "the hard work of examining, discussing, and negotiating consensus on specific Commission proposals."[111] By one estimate, these working groups (sub-sub delegates of member state ministers represented on the Council) decide 90 per cent of Council legislation.[112]

Each branch of the EU's dense system of committees claims to instantiate a different mode of deliberative decision-making. Expert groups set up by the Commission provide assistance and non-binding advice during the initiative and implementing stages of legislation and in the preparation of delegated acts.[113] Alongside member state appointees, their participants can include representatives of firms, industry groups, trade unions, international organizations or third parties, and individual experts, academics, or practitioners.[114] Their role is to serve as "a forum for discussions, providing high-level input

[109] For this reason, committees have been described as "a form of action through which the [EU] executes long-term policy goals." Christian Joerges, "Bureaucratic Nightmare, Technocratic Regime and the Dream of Good Transnational Governance" in Joerges and Vos, *EU Committees* 9.

[110] Mark A Pollack, "Deliberative Democracy? Two Images of Comitology" (2003) 36 *Comparative Political Studies* 125; Gijs Jan Brandsma and Jens Blom-Hansen, "Negotiating the Post-Lisbon Comitology System: Institutional Battles over Delegated Decision-making" (2012) 50 *JCMS* 939.

[111] Mark Rhinard, "The Democratic Legitimacy of the European Union Committee System" (2002) 15 *Governance* 185, 195.

[112] Rometsch and Wessels (1994) cited in Rhinard, "The Democratic Legitimacy of the European Union Committee System" 195.

[113] Introduced by the Treaty of Lisbon, "delegated acts" enable the Council to delegate the fleshing out of technical details and other specific aspects of EU legislation to the Commission by specifying the goals, content, scope, and duration of the delegated decision-making competence. See art 290 TFEU.

[114] The Commission sets out a template for a decision to set up an expert group, a standard call for applications to participate, and standard rules of procedure for the operation of the committee in European Commission Staff Working Document on the *Framework for Commission Expert Groups*, SEC(2010) 1360 Final, Brussels 10.11.2010. Available at ec.europa.eu/transparency/regexpert/PDF/SEC_2010_EN.pdf accessed February 20, 2016.

from a wide range of sources and stakeholders in the form of opinions, recommendations and reports."[115] Ultimately, however, the Commission decides whether to initiate legislation based on a committee proposal.

A third and final type of committee, namely those constituted under the so-called "comitology" procedures, assists and monitors the Commission in fleshing out Council decisions. Comitology was improvised in the 1960s to administer the European Community's politically sensitive Common Agricultural Policy and formalized by the Single European Act of 1986. After a long struggle, it was opened up to scrutiny and legislative input from the EP. Typically composed of civil servants appointed by member state governments,[116] these committees assist and monitor the Commission's efforts to implement and "fill in the details of the legislation enacted by the Council."[117] Although it lacks a direct legislative mandate, the comitology system has broad public policy implications for all member states: it is estimated that "two-thirds of all directives, regulations and decisions in force today have been made by the Commission in comitology, while about one-third only has been made by the Council and the European Parliament."[118]

Despite its bureaucratic nature, the EU's committee system has attracted scholarly attention as an experiment in epistemic and deliberative democracy. Joerges and Neyer view EU committees as collegial forums in which member state representatives, assisted by technical experts and civil society groups, engage in "mutual reflection about preferences, and social integration by means of discourse."[119] Unlike standard forums of negotiation and bargaining among states, whose outcomes often reflect disparities of power, committee governance is characterized by "rationality," impartiality, and an "ability to consider (and often accommodate) minority interests."[120]

[115] European Commission, "Expert Groups Explained." Available at ec.europa.eu/transparency/regexpert/index.cfm?do=faq.faq&aide=2 accessed February 20, 2016.

[116] Although formal committee membership under comitology is limited to member state representatives, Rhinard points out that smaller member states appoint experts from domestic industries or interest groups to represent them on specialized matters. He also observes significant overlap between the members of Commission expert groups (which advise the Commission at the initiative stage) and comitology groups (who collaborate with the Commission on the implementation of the legislation). Rhinard, "The Democratic Legitimacy of the European Union Committee System."

[117] Martin Shapiro, "The Institutionalization of European Administrative Space" in Alec Stone Sweet, Wayne Sandholtz, and Neil Fligstein, *The Institutionalization of Europe* (Oxford University Press 2001) 111.

[118] Catherine Moury and Adrienne Héritier, "Shifting Competences and Changing Preferences: The Case of Delegation to Comitology" (2012) 19 *Journal of European Public Policy* 1316, 1316–17.

[119] Christian Joerges and Jurgen Neyer, "Transforming Strategic Interaction into Deliberative Problem-solving: European Comitology in the Foodstuffs Sector" (1997) 4 *Journal of European Public Policy* 609, 621.

[120] JHH Weiler, "Epilogue: 'Comitology' as Revolution—Infranationalism, Constitutionalism, and Democracy" in Joerges and Vos, *EU Committees* 347.

Committees socialize member state representatives to "recognize one another as moral agents entitled to be treated as equals," and foster a deliberative context in which "actors' preferences and identities change in the course of their joint reasoning."[121] Furthermore, whereas the national positions represented at formal venues such as the Council are "frequently captured by powerful sectarian domestic interests masquerading as national," committee processes are said to be "most effective in exposing and stripping" these vested interests.[122] Last but not least, the receptiveness of some committees to input from stakeholders in civil society is viewed as opening up EU decision-making to a diverse array of preferences and demands from organized citizen groups. As Joseph Weiler playfully observes:

> Lurking in the background in this unlikeliest of places—comitology ... is St. Jürgen's noble vision of a deliberative and communicative process through which, and only through which, true democratic discourse can take place. In comitology, Joerges and Neyer find the Habermassian promised land.[123]

Do the committees that generate much of the EU's executive and legislative activity *democratize* supranational decision-making? If they do not give a wide range of interested parties opportunities for participation, do EU committees nevertheless afford "virtual representation" to the full spectrum of stakeholders?[124] Do they enable well-reasoned, fair, and impartial policy decisions that might elide majoritarian assemblies? How significant is the deliberative value which the committee system brings to EU decision-making?

All modern bureaucracies, domestic as well as postnational, face the challenge of reconciling the demands of technocratic competence with the ideal of democratic self-rule.[125] The technical complexity of many contemporary policy questions—not least in the economic sphere—makes them unwieldy subjects of democratic debate. This generic problem is compounded in the international and supranational context by persistent diversity between societies, interests, and institutions, and the elongation of the chain of custody linking decision-makers to citizens.[126] In a series of essays that draws inspiration from the EU's system of governance, Joshua Cohen and Charles

[121] Joshua Cohen and Charles F Sabel, "Sovereignty and Solidarity: EU and US" in Jonathan Zeitlin and David M Trubek, *Governing Work and Welfare in a New Economy* (Oxford University Press 2003) 363.

[122] Weiler, "Epilogue: 'Comitology' as Revolution" 347.

[123] ibid 347.

[124] Ely, *Democracy and Distrust* 85.

[125] For a valiant attempt by a leading contemporary democratic theorist to resolve this dilemma, see Pierre Rosanvallon, *Democratic Legitimacy: Impartiality, Reflexivity, Proximity* (Princeton University Press 2011).

[126] Dahl, "Can International Organizations Be Democratic?"

Sabel have argued that the most promising way to democratize postnational governance is "not by creating institutions of electoral accountability for a global government, but, in the first instance, by forming the people and public sphere that lie at the heart of democracy."[127] They contend that eighteenth-century notions of democracy that presuppose a unified popular sovereign are inapplicable in the context of international institutions. Instead, they ask us to:

> Consider ... a world in which sovereignty—legitimate political authorship—is neither unitary nor personified, and politics is about addressing practical problems and not simply about principles, much less performance or identity. In this world, a public is simply an open group of actors, nominally private or public, which constitutes itself as such in coming to address a common problem, and reconstitutes itself as efforts at problem solving redefine the task at hand. The polity is the public formed of these publics: this encompassing public is not limited to a list of functional tasks (police powers) enumerated in advance, but understands its role as empowering members to address such issues as need their combined attention.[128]

The authors describe this as a model of "deliberative polyarchy," and argue that it is a more appropriate model for the EU than parliamentary democracy. While most commentators have argued that the EU's problem of democratic legitimacy necessitates strengthening or scaling up the *demos* (whether by fostering a postnational politics of constitutional patriotism,[129] greater partisan mobilization,[130] or reinvigorating national *demoi* for supranational "demoicracy"),[131] the deliberative polyarchy model moves away this traditional emphasis on the *demos*. Under deliberative polyarchy, each political decision would have its own relevant public, and parties with an important stake in any proposed measure would be called upon to contribute

[127] Cohen and Sabel, "Global Democracy?" 766.

[128] Cohen and Sabel, "Sovereignty and Solidarity" 362.

[129] Habermas, *Inclusion of the Other* ch 4.

[130] Andreas Føllesdal and Simon Hix, "Why there Is a Democratic Deficit in the EU: A Response to Majone and Moravcsik" (2006) 44 *JCMS* 533; Hix, *What's Wrong with the European Union*; Jonathan White, "Europe and the Common" (2010) 58 *Political Studies* 104; Myrto Tsakatika, "Governance vs Politics: The European Union's Constitutive 'Democratic Deficit'" (2007) 14 *Journal of European Public Policy* 867.

[131] Lindseth, *Power and Legitimacy* ch 5; Kalypso Nicolaïdis, "European Demoïcracy and its Crisis" (2012) 51 *JCMS* 351; Francis Cheneval and Frank Schimmelfennig, "The Case for Demoicracy in the European Union" (2012) 51 *JCMS* 334. Having formerly advocated supranational democratic politics, even Habermas himself seems to have shifted in favor of a demoicratic view, advancing a conception of "originally shared popular sovereignty," which "precludes the possibility of ... a supreme constitutional authority ... at the European level." Instead, he argues that "through their participation in the founding process, the European peoples ensure that their respective states survive within the federal polity *in their freedom-guaranteeing function* of constitutional states." Jürgen Habermas, *The Crisis of the European Union: A Response* (Ciaran Cronin tr, Polity 2012) 39, emphasis original.

to its drafting.[132] In contrast to clunky parliamentary systems that grant each citizen one vote to elect an all-purpose legislative assembly, policymaking would be tailored to the relevant constituency as far as possible.

Deliberative polyarchy represents an unusually compelling attempt to reimagine what democratic legitimacy might mean in the context of powerful administrative and regulatory institutions operating across multiple levels of governance. Rather than resigning themselves to administrative empowerment and the triumph of technocracy over collective self-rule, its authors seek to reshape these institutions in the light of democratic principles, including the participation of affected interests and a commitment to dialogue and reason-giving. At the same time, deliberative polyarchy seems to be at odds with a basic presupposition of democratic rule, namely that of a self-legislating *demos*. The exercise of collective self-rule both presupposes and reproduces a stable political community, preferably one that recognizes the political equality of its members. In order to view decisions arrived at through the political process as legitimate, a diverse body of citizens must be able to imagine the community of their peers and count on one another's willingness to participate in a scheme of long-term social cooperation and to observe the terms of their union.[133] If the duration, membership composition, procedures, and substantive mandate of decision-making institutions are ad hoc, it is difficulty to see what remains of political community. In turn, weakening the regulative idea of the *demos* extinguishes the promise of civic solidarity, which is essential for the stability of political institutions and provides the moral basis of political obligation.

Finally, deliberative polyarchy's overreliance on the principle of affected interests contradicts the principle of equal participation or *isonomia* on which traditional ideas of democratic legitimacy rest.[134] When it is conceived of as a freestanding criterion for political participation (rather than one that complements equal membership in a stable political community), the principle of affected interests licenses unequal and asymmetric forms of power. While

[132] For applications of the principle of affected interests as a criterion of political participation in different governance contexts, see Cohen and Sabel, "Directly-Deliberative Polyarchy"; Cohen and Sabel, "Sovereignty and Solidarity"; Cohen and Sabel, "Global Democracy?" For critiques of the affected interest principle as a justification for greater supranational decision-making, see McCormick, *Weber, Habermas, and Transformations of the European State*; Somek, "The Argument from Transnational Effects," parts I and II.

[133] The notion of an "imagined" group of peers invokes Benedict Anderson, *Imagined Communities: Reflections on the Origin and Spread of Nationalism* (Verso 1983). The idea of a scheme of long-term social cooperation loosely alludes to John Rawls's idea of society as a stable and fair "scheme of social cooperation" or a "cooperative venture for mutual advantage." John Rawls, *A Theory of Justice* (Harvard/Belknap 1999) 3–6.

[134] Nadia Urbinati, "Competing for Liberty: The Republican Critique of Democracy" (2012) 106 *American Political Science Review* 607, 609.

the EU's system of committees is hardly a perfect instantiation of deliberative polyarchy, it illustrates this problem. Although the Commission asks expert groups to "consult as many stakeholders as possible," it still gets to choose which interests "matter" in a given policy decision, and is likely to exercise that choice in favor of already influential actors.[135] For instance, while firms operating in a polluting industry can show a concentrated interest in the regulation of that industry, the diffuse and long-term interests of citizens might not command equal weight on the affected interest metric. Since committees are not answerable to a parliamentary assembly that represents a wider spectrum of views among the body politic, they can be "a mere blank check for more powerful pluralist groupings to pursue their particularist aims."[136] Furthermore, the voluntarism inherent in this system pegs the outcome of the deliberative process on the organizational resources of stakeholders, potentially excluding those who are not sufficiently mobilized or resourced.[137] Empirical surveys have shown "structural imbalances" in terms of access to EU decision-making that favor businesses or groups that possess "technical expertise" and "economic clout."[138] Just as openness does not guarantee equal participation, it cannot safeguard against institutional bias in the distribution of benefits and burdens.[139] In sum, a participatory system based on affected interests poses with renewed urgency the perennial question of *who* determines the relevant circle of interests and *who* gauges the intensity of the interests at stake.[140] The absence of a supranational political community against the background of which the various stakeholders' claims may be judged makes the question of the latter's compatibility with the public interest difficult to adjudicate.[141]

[135] Sonia Mazey and Jeremy Richardson, "Institutionalizing Promiscuity: Commission-Interest Group Relations in the European Union" in Stone Sweet, Sandholtz, and Fligstein, *The Institutionalization of Europe* 86, 89.

[136] Michelle Everson, "The Constitutionalization of European Administrative Law: Legal Oversight of a Stateless Internal Market" in Joerges and Vos, *EU Committees* 297.

[137] Sabine Sarugger, "Interest Groups and Democracy in the European Union" (2008) 31 *West European Politics* 1274.

[138] Rainer Eising, "The Access of Business Interests to EU Institutions: Towards Elite Pluralism?" (2007) 14 *Journal of European Public Policy* 384, 399.

[139] Mazey and Richardson, "Institutionalizing Promiscuity" 93.

[140] Frederick G Whelan, "Democratic Theory and the Boundary Problem" in J Roland Pennock and John W Chapman, *Nomos XXV: Liberal Democracy* (New York University Press 1983).

[141] Everson, "The Constitutionalization of European Administrative Law." Everson argues that "though divorced from the traditional state and its unitary political will," "the novel internal market polity need nevertheless be directed to some form of acceptable and accepted public interest," which may be guaranteed by "European law" 294-95. I am not equally sanguine that European law could, like Baron von Munchhausen pulling himself out of a swamp by his own ponytail, temper its own market teleology by espousing a broader conception of European public interest. For one thing, it is doubtful that the public interest could be considered genuinely public if it is decided solipsistically by the privileged interpreters and interlocutors of the legal system.

(II) CONCLUSION: CAN A PURPOSIVE UNION BE DEMOCRATIC?

Without a doubt, the most important contribution of European integration to democracy is its role in pacifying the relations among nation-states jostling for primacy on a congested continent. European integration must have more than a walk-on part in any account of the peace, prosperity, and stability that Western European societies have enjoyed in the postwar period and in which many East Central European societies have come to partake since the fall of Communist regimes. There is also little doubt that the mundane, even pedantic discipline of supranational decision-making has accustomed member states to acting in concert and resolving disputes through dialogue, bargaining, and consensus. To the extent that the EU discourages states from unilaterally deciding matters that concern their neighbors, it has replaced the solipsism of national frames of reference with a more inclusive perspective that Tocqueville called "self-interest well understood."[142]

As I argued in the introduction, however, there is a serious disjunction between the political aims of integration and the economic mechanisms mobilized to realize them. Although European integration is an ambitious experiment to substitute the anarchic system of nation-states with a more enlightened form of political ordering, its legal and institutional framework has taken shape in response to a narrower problem: that of forging a single market (and, later, monetary union) between its member states. The EU's most sophisticated rules and procedures have these objectives in view, and it remains most powerful in the economic domain. Despite the democratic aspirations fastened to it, therefore, the EU's supranational legal order—unlike many modern constitutional systems—does not take democratic self-rule as its cardinal objective. Not only do attempts to adapt the institutional framework of modern representative democracy to the EU founder on issues of size, diversity, and the absence of a shared public sphere.[143] More importantly, democratic attenuation is a systemic feature of supranational governance, which curtails electoral control over policy-making in order to enable member states to credibly commit to long-term policy decisions. As I have sought to show in this chapter, although the EU affords various innovative channels for citizen participation in decision-making, these still reflect and reinforce the cardinal objective of forging a

[142] Alexis de Tocqueville, *Democracy in America*, (HC Mansfield and D Winthrop tr and ed, University of Chicago Press 2000) vol II, part II, chs 4, 8.

[143] Dahl, "Can International Organizations Be Democratic?"; Grimm, "Does Europe Need a Constitution?"

common economic space. The functionalist framing of these participatory mechanisms means that they cannot be mobilized by citizens to challenge and revise the constitutional tenets of economic union. It is this foreclosing of the domain of democratic contestation, rather than any failure to replicate the traditional institutions of representative democracy, that is the EU's essential democratic flaw.

5

A Citizenship of Aliens: Markets, Mobility, Solidarity

(I) PEOPLE VERSUS COMMODITIES: DISTINGUISHING THE OBJECTS OF MOBILITY

Commercial mobility rights have played a key role in transforming the 1957 Treaty of Rome Establishing the European Community from an interstate agreement into a supranational constitutional system.[1] The European Court of Justice (ECJ) set this process into motion by designating individuals as immediate subjects of supranational law and by translating the treaty provisions on commercial mobility into a de facto supranational bill of rights.[2] In the legal terminology of the European Union (EU), these rights are referred to as "fundamental freedoms," not primarily on account of their moral urgency, but because they are essential to the market teleology of the EU's legal system. In other words, they are justified with reference to the functional imperative of creating and maintaining an economic union. In this respect, they exemplify the EU's system of functional constitutionalism, whose normative claim to authority is premised primarily on the effective administration of the economic tasks delegated to it.

In my analysis so far of this constitutional system, I have considered commercial mobility rights as a coherent bundle, without distinguishing between the various objects of mobility, namely goods, services, capital, and persons. By contrast, many political theorists tend to single out the legal framework of *personal* mobility as the kernel of a postnational political community in the making. What reasons are there to distinguish between the freedom of movement of persons across state borders and mobility rights that pertain to inanimate factors of production (goods, services, and capital)? Nineteenth-century

[1] Alec Stone Sweet, The Judicial Construction of Europe (Oxford University Press 2004); C Barnard, *The Substantive Law of the EU. The Four Freedoms* (3rd edn, Oxford University Press 2010); R Daniel Kelemen, *Eurolegalism: The Transformation of Law and Regulation in the European Union* (Harvard University Press 2011).

[2] For a more detailed discussion of this process, see Chapter 3.

laissez-faire liberalism made no such distinction, advocating the cross-border mobility of persons alongside commodities.[3] The 1889 International Emigration Conference affirmed "the right of the individual to come and go and dispose of his person and his destinies as he pleases."[4] Today, however, the global movement towards economic liberalization aims for the unhindered movement of money, goods, and services, but steadfastly excludes the free movement of *people*. There are countless ways of differentiating and de-differentiating between mobility rights: some have argued that if we liberalize the circulation of factors of production, we ought to liberalize migration, while others maintain that collapsing the two categories commodifies people and obscures the humanitarian and democratic dimensions of personal mobility.

This apparent need to adjust our prescriptions about mobility in terms of *what* exactly is moving through borders (from people to animals, germs, goods, money, and ideas) requires some analytical explication. After all, commercial mobility rights, like those of personal mobility, are *individual* rights: even though they have inanimate factors of production as their object, the holders of the rights in question are still persons (with the important caveat that they are often legal persons such as corporations). For instance, Title II of the Treaty on the Functioning of the EU (TFEU) gives producers and merchants the right to market their goods in another member state without discrimination or hindrance. Similarly, treaty provisions concerning the free movement of services create subjective rights on the part of providers and recipients of services (who may be natural or legal persons).[5] In fact, as I argued in the previous chapter, the phrase "market citizen" is not a flat-out contradiction in terms precisely because commercial mobility rights have allowed traders, service providers, industry groups, and other commercial actors to exercise political agency in the supranational arena by contesting hindrances to cross-border economic activity. If all rights of commercial mobility have the character of individual rights, and all of them carry political as well as economic significance, on what grounds can we distinguish the constitutional significance of personal mobility from other free movement rights?

The original text of the Treaty of Rome affords some clues. Although this document focused on market integration, article 3 listed among its aims "the abolition, as between Member States, of obstacles to the free movement of … *persons*,"[6] rather than merely of *workers* or *labor*.[7] This intimates a

[3] Robert E Goodin, "If people were money …" in Brian Barry and Robert E Goodin (eds), *Free Movement. Ethical Issues in the Transnational Migration of People and of Money* (The Pennsylvania State University Press 1992).

[4] ibid 13. [5] Title IV, ch 3 TFEU. [6] Ex-art 3 (1)(c) TEC, emphasis added.

[7] Catherine Barnard, *The Substantive Law of the EU. The Four Freedoms* (2nd edn, Oxford University Press 2007) 249.

regard for individuals not merely as factors of production but also as potential co-constituents of a shared political and juridical space. In fact, as Willem Maas shows, framers of the European integration project imagined personal mobility as a strategy for integration.[8] Whereas international agreements rarely require states to open their borders to one another's citizens (except with respect to specific classes of people such as diplomats, business administrators, refugees, or stateless persons), constitutional unions typically allow for personal mobility as a juridical bond between constituent units of a composite body politic. For these reasons, personal mobility bolsters an interpretation of the EU as a political community in the making rather than a loose alliance of states.

For their part, political theorists have found much to praise in the EU's personal mobility regime. On alternate accounts, the free movement of persons germinates a postnational civic identity, portends the decline of the European nation-state, and/or heralds the advent of cosmopolitan right. One thing is certain: the supranational regime of personal mobility represents a startling departure for modern European politics. First, insofar as borders have been constitutive sites of sovereign authority, rights to free movement represent a significant abridgement of sovereign power.[9] As Menéndez observes, "[i]n the first half of the twentieth century, European nation-states had perfected the institutional and normative instruments with which they controlled the flows of people in and out of their borders."[10] This effort to homogenize the national group and secure its fabled homeland resulted in the deep scars that the European project was meant to heal. Against that background, supranational mobility rights represent a remarkable step towards reconfiguring the European political space.

Second, when human beings can move with ease from one country to another, they act as agents of political, cultural, and social cross-pollination, challenging rigid notions of bounded communities. Personal mobility can be expected to amplify the integrative effects of commercial exchange, since people, unlike commodities, are capable of forging transnational forms of political consciousness and solidarity. Although EU personal mobility rights clearly have a market rationale, therefore, their significance goes beyond their role in promoting economic union.

[8] Willem Maas, *Creating European Citizens* (Rowman & Littlefield 2007) 21.

[9] Wendy Brown, *Walled States, Waning Sovereignty* (MIT Press 2010).

[10] Augustín José Menéndez, "European Citizenship after *Martínez Sala* and *Baumbast*: Has European Law Become More Human but Less Social?" ARENA Online Working Paper No. 11 (ARENA 2009) 3. Available at http://www.sv.uio.no/arena/english/research/publications/arena-publications/workingpapers/working-papers2009/WP11_09_Online.pdf

Since political communities are made up of people and not commodities, people crossing borders generate dynamics that the mobility of factors of production cannot. However, it is another thing to ask whether personal mobility, as a bundle of legal entitlements and socioeconomic activities, provides a sufficient basis for postnational citizenship. This, in effect, is what the EU has set out to do. As a historical and legal matter, personal mobility is the nucleus of EU citizenship.[11] The main task of this chapter is to evaluate the civic potential of a citizenship regime based on mobility, most importantly, to assess the extent to which personal mobility can move the EU beyond its configuration as a system of functional constitutionalism. I will warn against overstating this transformative potential, whether in terms of democratizing the EU or for forging a postnational political community. Despite the ECJ's expansive interpretation of the relevant treaty provisions over the past two decades, EU citizenship is still anchored in personal mobility rights, which is in turn anchored in the project of economic union. Accordingly, the developmental path by which personal mobility rights have expanded into a formal status of EU citizenship has yielded a model of political agency modeled on market participation.[12] The resulting institutional relationship between the EU and its citizens falls short on all-important dimensions of political obligation, solidarity, and civic trust. Furthermore, insofar as it is premised on transnational mobility, EU citizenship instantiates a distinctive civic status I propose to call (adopting Linda Bosniak's phrase) a *citizenship of aliens*.[13] As long as its benefits remain tied to mobility, EU citizenship will remain a citizenship of aliens, one that protects and empowers those who move, but remains mostly inert for those who stay.

The chapter will begin by sketching the expansion of personal mobility rights from a qualified freedom of movement for coal and steel workers to a general right of Union citizenship. I will then illustrate the resilient market logic of EU citizenship by examining the implications of personal mobility rights for national schemes of social solidarity. As a historical matter, the free movement of workers was included in the scope of the treaty partly in order to alleviate the burden of mass employment in

[11] Jo Shaw, *The Transformation of Citizenship in the European Union. Electoral Rights and the Restructuring of Political Space* (Cambridge University Press 2007); Niamh Nic Shuibhne, "The Resilience of EU Market Citizenship" (2010) 47 *CMLR* 1597, 1611.

[12] Michelle Everson, "The Legacy of the Market Citizen" in Jo Shaw and Gillian More (eds), *New Legal Dynamics of European Union* (Clarendon Press 1995).

[13] Bosniak describes alien citizenship as entailing "a demand for [the] fair treatment and social empowerment" of noncitizens, particularly those who reside within a political community without enjoying full recognition under its laws. Linda Bosniak, "The Citizenship of Aliens" (1998) 56 *Social Text* 29, 33.

some regions and to relieve labor market shortages in others. Today, the EU still treats personal mobility as a substitute for more capacious social policy by encouraging people to move where the jobs are and entitling them to benefits there, rather than stimulating job-creation in recession-prone economies or providing social assistance to the unemployed. This substitution is also evident in the insistence of the Court of Justice that member states must extend social benefits to mobile Europeans regardless of whether they have contributed to the funding of those schemes. Intended as the germ of transnational civic solidarity, personal mobility risks jeopardizing domestic social assistance schemes that depend on long-term reciprocity between contributors and recipients and, perversely, erodes support for the integration project amongst non-mobile EU citizens.

In the final section, I will show that the EU's system of personal mobility rights is equally deficient from a cosmopolitan perspective. While supranational free movement law mitigates the exclusionary framing of national political communities, it has helped to fashion a new, equally bounded legal space by excluding third country nationals from its scope. As a result, the mobility rights associated with EU citizenship promote "the transformation of external relations between a number of states into an internal market,"[14] creating "a corporate entity with a distinct boundary vis-à-vis the outside world."[15] It is not coincidental that extensive personal mobility rights for EU citizens have been accompanied in recent years by restrictive measures against refugees and migrants from third countries.

(II) FREE MOVEMENT IN MOTION: THE MOBILITY RIGHTS OF PERSONS FROM ROME TO MAASTRICHT

At the inception of the European integration project, any special importance that the free movement of persons may have had was expertly hidden. The 1952 Treaty of Paris founding the European Coal and Steel Community (ECSC) pledged free movement for workers in relevant sectors,[16] but left the realization of this modest commitment to further action by member states. Indeed, its implementation proved difficult to negotiate, and before the ECSC could make good on the treaty's personal mobility provisions,

[14] Murray Forsyth, *Unions of States. The Theory and Practice of Confederation* (Holmes & Meier Publishers 1981) 183.

[15] Murray Forsyth, "The Political Theory of Federalism and the Relevance of Classical Approaches" in Joachim Jens Hesse and Vincent Wright (eds), *Federalizing Europe? The Costs, Benefits, and Preconditions of Federal Political Systems* (Oxford University Press 1996) 40.

[16] Art 69 of the ECSC Treaty committed member states to lifting restrictions on the mobility of qualified workers in the coal and steel industries.

the same group of member states signed the Treaty of Rome Establishing the European Economic Community (EEC).[17] Abandoning the sectoral approach of the ECSC, the EEC set out to extend the scope of free movement to all workers with the exception of civil servants.[18]

Worker mobility was only one objective within a general framework of market integration set out by the Treaty of Rome, which aimed for the free circulation of goods,[19] services,[20] and capital.[21] The rationale for including labor within the scope of the treaty was political as well as economic. Facing a chronic labor surplus, Italy insisted that economically productive citizens be allowed to "move freely from regions where jobs were hard to find to those areas needing extra workers."[22] Furthermore, workforce mobility would address labor market disparities among member states and regions. In this respect, labor mobility was treated just like other factors of production, that is, in terms of its conduciveness to market efficiency. Notwithstanding this emphasis on economic reasons, however, the treaty took a broader view of worker mobility, promising rights of residence to workers even after the end of their period of active employment.[23]

After the treaty's entry came into force in 1958, member states had a transitional period of ten years to remove restrictions on the movement of workers and to adopt the necessary implementing legislation. At the expiry of this period, however, all restrictions on the movement of workers among member states were to be lifted. Directive 68/360, adopted in October 1968, required member states to "abolish restrictions on the movement and residence of nationals and of members of their families."[24] Regulation 1612/68 complemented it by requiring host states to treat workers from other member states no less favorably than their own citizens "in respect of any conditions of employment and work," including conditions of remuneration and dismissal, tax advantages, vocational training, housing, and trade union membership.[25] It also granted family reunification

[17] Maas, *Creating European Citizens* 16.

[18] Ex-art 39 TEC, art 45 TFEU.

[19] Ex-art 28 TEC, art 34 TFEU.

[20] Ex-art 49 TEC, art 56 TFEU.

[21] Ex-art 56 TEC, art 63 TFEU.

[22] Barnard, *The Substantive Law of the EU* 250. Willem Maas, "The Genesis of European Rights" (2005) 43 *JCMS* 1009.

[23] Art 48(3)(d) TEC. The continued right of residence did, however, have some market justifications; for instance, encouraging workers to retire in the same country as their economic activity would make pensions and other social benefits easier to administer.

[24] Council Directive 68/360/EEC of October 15, 1968 on the abolition of restrictions on movement and residence within the Community for workers of member states and their families [1968] OJ L257/13, art 1.

[25] Council Regulation (EEC) 1612/68 on freedom of movement for workers within the Community [1968] OJ L257/2 (since replaced by Regulation (EU) 492/2011 of the European Parliament and of the Council on freedom of movement for workers within the European Union [2011] OJ L141/1).

rights to migrant workers.[26] Most notably, the regulation framed the freedom of movement in the constitutional language of a "fundamental right of workers and their families."[27] Lastly, Commission Regulation 1251/70 gave workers and their families the right to remain in the host state after the end of the worker's period of economic activity, further expanding the scope of mobility beyond active labor market participation.[28]

The transformation of personal mobility from a policy objective into a subjective right received its greatest boost from the jurisprudence of the European Court of Justice. As discussed in previous chapters, the ECJ used its interpretive authority to transform the interstate commitments codified in the treaties into rights that individual citizens could invoke in national courts, often in the absence of implementing legislation. Of the original freedoms of movement codified by the treaty, the Court interpreted provisions relating to the free movement of workers,[29] services,[30] and the freedom of establishment for self-employed persons[31] as creating personal mobility rights.[32] To be sure, these judgments did not add up to the overnight abolition of all restrictions on the mobility of Community nationals, but they empowered litigants to challenge obstacles to mobility before domestic courts by interpreting the relevant treaty provisions as directly effective within domestic legal systems.[33] In other words, the Court extended the "decentralized enforcement mechanism" of individual litigation to the area of personal mobility.[34]

Since its origins, personal mobility rights have expanded along two equally important axes, namely with respect to the scope of persons entitled to them, and the entitlements that attend personal mobility. Faced with

[26] Regulation 1612/68, arts 10–12.

[27] For instance, the operative part of Regulation 1612/68 began with: "Any national of a Member State, shall, irrespective of his place of residence, have the right to take up an activity as an employed person ..." ibid art 1.

[28] Commission Regulation (EEC) 1251/70 on the right of workers to remain in the territory of a Member State after having been employed in that State [1970] OJ L142/24.

[29] Case 41/74 *Yvonne Van Duyn v Home Office* [1974] ECR 1337.

[30] Joined Cases 110 and 11/78 *Ministère Public and Chambre Syndicale des Agents Artistiques et Impresarii de Belgique ASBL v Willy van Wesemael and others* [1979] ECR 35; Case 279/80 *Webb* [1981] ECR 3305.

[31] Case 2/74 *Jean Reyners v Belgian State* [1974] ECR 631.

[32] Barnard, *Substantive Law of the EU* 249.

[33] Stone Sweet, *The Judicial Construction of Europe*; R Daniel Kelemen, "The EU Rights Revolution: Adversarial Legalism and European Integration" in Tanja Börzel and Rachel A Cichowski (eds), *The State of the European Union, vol.6: Law, Politics, and Society* (Oxford University Press 2003); Karen Alter, *Establishing the Supremacy of European Law. The Making of an International Rule of Law in Europe* (Oxford University Press 2001); Anne-Marie Burley and Walter Mattli, "Europe Before the Court" (1993) 47 *International Organization* 41.

[34] Stone Sweet, *Judicial Construction of Europe* 69.

successive cases concerning *who* qualifies as a "worker" within the meaning of the treaty, the ECJ adopted successively broader definitions of the term, while litigants seeking the benefits of mobility brought cases testing its new limits.[35] Over time, the Court interpreted the category of workers so expansively as to cover, inter alia, part-time workers earning less than the minimum wage,[36] job seekers,[37] and even a member of a religious community receiving only room and board in exchange for his services.[38] Over time, the prerequisite of engaging in gainful economic activity has been all but abandoned, vesting everyone from self-employed persons to, retirees, persons of independent means, students, and tourists with the right to circulate among member states. The right of personal mobility is subject only to minimal constraints of public policy, public security, and public health,[39] which are in turn narrowly interpreted by the Court of Justice.[40]

The second axis along which personal mobility rights have expanded concerns the ever-expanding entitlements of mobile Europeans with respect to host states and their countries of origin.[41] As the ECJ has stressed in its rulings, Europeans would be unlikely to exercise their rights of free movement if doing so put them at a significant disadvantage in terms of their quality of life.[42] If intra-EU workers are denied access to social benefits in the host

[35] Barnard, *Substantive Law of the EU* 87–9. This dynamic has been described by Stone Sweet in other areas of EU law as a feedback effect. Stone Sweet, *Judicial Construction of Europe* 164–5; Alec Stone Sweet, *Governing with Judges: Constitutional Politics in Europe* (Oxford University Press 2000) 19. Also see Rachel A Cichowski, *The European Court and Civil Society: Litigation, Mobilization, and Governance* (Cambridge University Press 2007); Neil Fligstein, *Euroclash: The EU, European Identity, and the Future of Europe* (Oxford University Press 2008).

[36] Case 53/81 *DM Levin v* Staatssecretaris van Justitie [1982] ECR 1035.

[37] Case C-138/02 *Collins v Secretary of State for Work and Pensions* [2003] ECR I-2703.

[38] Case 196/87 *Steymann v Staatssecretaris van Justitie* [1988] ECR 6159.

[39] Art 45(3) TFEU (ex-art 39 TEC). In addition, art 45(4) enables member states to limit access to employment in the public service.

[40] For instance, the Court has held that a criminal conviction is not in and of itself sufficient to deport a Union citizen. See Case 67/74 *Bonsignore v Oberstadtdirektor of the City of Cologne* [1975] ECR 297. It also requires that the member state's response (e.g. deportation, refusal of admission) must be proportionate to the public policy end being pursued, and that it respect the fundamental rights of the person in question.

[41] Adrian Favell argues that the term "mobility" rather than "immigration" is more appropriate for capturing the distinctiveness of the EU experience. Unlike traditional patterns of migration, which, according to Favell, are usually understood as a permanent act of relocation and assimilation, mobility better describes the ease of temporary relocations enabled by EU law, whether for study, work, or retirement. Adrian Favell, *Eurostars and Eurocities. Free Movement and Mobility in an Integrating Europe* (Blackwell 2008).

[42] In *Even*, the Court argued that the question of whether or not to extend certain national advantages to migrant workers had to be construed, among other factors, in the light of the potential of those advantages to "facilitate ... mobility within the Community." In this case, however, the Court ultimately approved the limitation of certain national benefits to citizens. The benefit in question was an early retirement pension adjustment that Belgium granted to Belgians who had rendered military service in World War II, and the Court reasoned that it was not discriminatory to deny it to migrant

state, their families are unable to join them, or their children are barred from educational opportunities afforded to nationals, they will be less likely to exercise their treaty rights. In legislation adopted over several decades, the EC/EU has sought to make personal mobility attractive and convenient. To this effect, the Council adopted several pieces of legislation in the 1970s to eliminate major discrepancies between member state laws that made free movement disadvantageous to would-be migrant workers.[43] Member states agreed to grant equal treatment to workers from other member states with regard to a comprehensive range of work-related benefits, including but not limited to retirement, illness, disability, and maternity benefits.[44] They ensured that workers would retain those benefits when they took employment abroad or returned to their host state after a period of work.[45] Other legislation secured the rights of residence of self-employed persons in their host state and enabled their families to join them.[46] Each of these measures protects member state citizens against a plethora of disadvantages that they may experience as a consequence of their mobility, whether in the host state or in their member state of origin.

For its part, the Court of Justice elaborated on the public benefits to which migrant member state nationals are entitled, from the right of dependent relatives of migrant workers to pensions and welfare subsidies[47] to the

workers who did not have a record of wartime service to Belgium, in this case, to Mr. Even who had served in the war as a French national. Case 207/78 *Ministère Public contre Gilbert Even et Office National des Pensions pour Travailleurs Salariés* [1979] ECR 2019.

[43] Marlene Wind, "Post-National Citizenship in Europe: The EU as a 'Welfare Rights Generator'?" (2009) 15 *Columbia Journal of European Law* 239, 248–50.

[44] Council Regulation 1408/71 on the application of social security schemes to employed persons, to self-employed persons and to members of their families moving within the Community [1971] OJ L149/2.

[45] ibid.

[46] Council Directive 75/34/EEC of 17 December 1974 concerning the right of nationals of a Member State to remain in the territory of another Member State after having pursued therein an activity in a self-employed capacity [1975] OJ L14.

[47] In *Cristini*, the Court ruled that the family of a deceased Italian national who had worked in France was entitled to a transport subsidy granted by the French railways. In *Castelli*, it found that the principle of equal treatment for migrant workers requires member states to grant pension benefits to the relatives of workers. In *Collins*, the Court found that member states could not exclude Union citizens from an allowance granted to job seekers on the basis of nationality. Finally, in *Grzelczyk*, the Court found that the Belgian state discriminated against Union citizens because it granted the minimum subsistence allowance to all Belgian *nationals* (not workers) whereas it only granted it to member state nationals who were *workers*. Thus, Union nationals had to jump the extra hurdle of being economically active, which Belgian nationals did not. Respectively: Case 32/75 *Anita Cristini v Société Nationale des Chemins de Fer Français* [1975] ECR 1085; Case 261/83 *Carmela Castelli v Office National des Pensions pour Travailleurs Salariés (ONPTS)* [1984] ECR 3199; Case C-138/02 *Collins v Secretary of State for Work and Pensions* [2003] ECR I-2703; Case C-184/99 *Rudy Grzelczyk v Centre Public d'Aide Sociale d'Ottignies-Louvain-la-Neuve* [2001] ECR I-6193.

right of students to training programs and financial support in their host state.[48] Through a stringent application of the constitutional principle of non-discrimination on the basis of nationality, which will be the topic of the next chapter, the Court's jurisprudence progressively curtailed the ability of member states to deny social advantages to noncitizens who exercise their supranational mobility rights.[49]

In the early 1990s, however, this inflationary trend in personal mobility rights came up against the functional bounds of the Treaty of Rome. In the *Konstantinidis* case, the ECJ was asked to interpret the freedom of movement not simply as a market freedom, but as a civil status held by member state nationals regardless of gainful economic activity. In response, the Court stopped discernibly short of severing the nexus between economic activity and personal mobility.[50] The case concerned a Greek citizen resident in Germany who complained that the German authorities had made an error in transliterating his name. The Court was faced, inter alia, with the question of whether the transliteration merely hindered Mr. Konstantinidis from practicing his trade, or whether it amounted to a more serious infringement of his fundamental rights. In its submission to the court, the Commission took a market-based view, arguing that the clerical mistake was likely to confuse the plaintiff's clients and create administrative burdens, thereby interfering with his supranational rights as a cross-border economic actor. By contrast, in his non-binding opinion to the ECJ, Advocate General Jacobs submitted that Germany's treatment of Mr. Konstantinidis was a violation of EC law not primarily because it caused him economic disadvantage but because it violated his basic rights, including respect for his dignity and individuality. "[A] Community national who goes to another member-State as a worker or self-employed person ... is entitled not just to pursue his trade or profession and to enjoy the same living and working

[48] In *Gravier*, the Court held that member states could not discriminate against the nationals of other member states vis-à-vis access to vocational training and invalidated an enrollment fee Belgium charged foreign students. In *Matteucci*, the Court extended to an Italian national a scholarship that Germany, through a bilateral agreement, had reserved for Belgian and German nationals. In *Lair*, the Court held that individuals who had previously exercised their free movement rights as workers in a member state were entitled to maintenance grants to pursue studies in that member state. Finally, in *Bidar*, it required the UK to extend maintenance grants and student loans to a French student, privileging the student's status as a Union citizen over and above his rather more limited rights as a student. See, respectively, Case 293/83 *Françoise Gravier v City of Liège* [1985] ECR 593; Case 235/87 *Annunziata Matteucci v Communauté Française of Belgium* [1988] ECR 5589; Case 39/86 *Sylvie Lair v Universität Hannover* [1998] ECR 3161; Case C-209/03 *The Queen, on the application of Dany Bidar v London Borough of Ealing and Secretary of State for Education and Skills* [2005] ECR I-2119.

[49] Michael Blauberger and Susanne K Schmidt, "Welfare Migration? Free Movement of EU Citizens and Access to Social Benefits" (2014) *Research and Politics* 1.

[50] Case C-168/91 *Christos Konstantinidis v Altensteig-Standesamt* [1993] ECR I-1191.

conditions as nationals of the host State," he argued, but also "to say *'civis europeus sum'* and to invoke that status in order to oppose any violation of his fundamental rights."[51] In other words, Jacobs urged the Court to interpret free movement as something broader and more fundamental than a contingent benefit of market participation.

Despite its expansive jurisprudence of personal mobility rights, the Court of Justice pointedly refused to follow AG Jacobs's recommendation, and decided the case on the basis of economic disadvantages resulting from faulty orthography.[52] This choice is important, because it illustrates the intrinsic limits of market rights and, by implication, the system of functional constitutionalism that provides their normative context. As long as personal mobility rights were rooted in the project of economic union, the decisive consideration was the protection of the person's status as an economic actor, rather than his dignity or individuality as the member of a supranational political community. In other words, the *Konstantinidis* decision suggested that expanding a market right into a supranational civic status would require a constitutional transformation.

(III) MOBILITY AND EU CITIZENSHIP: FROM MARKET FREEDOM TO POLITICAL RIGHT

To be sure, the symbolic, sociological, and political significance of personal mobility goes far beyond expanded opportunities for market participation. Even when immigrants lack political rights, they are agents in the public sphere and contribute to their respective social milieu by engaging in the workforce, joining associations, raising children, and participating in civic life. Although free movement rights gave individuals legal claims to presence and protection in other member states, however, they neither established political equality for mobile Europeans in their host state nor gave them a supranational civic status. Although the economic preconditions for exercising freedoms of movement were gradually loosened, the civic potential of human mobility was kept in check by the narrow teleology of market integration.

The formal introduction of EU citizenship should be understood primarily as an attempt to transcend those limits and to imbue the supranational enterprise with democratic content.[53] The 1993 Treaty of Maastricht crossed the threshold that the ECJ had avoided in *Konstantinidis* by recognizing

[51] Case C-168/91 *Konstantinidis*, Opinion of AG Jacobs, para 46.

[52] Case C-168/91 *Konstantinidis*, para 16.

[53] Shaw, *The Transformation of Citizenship in the European Union* 45–7.

member state nationals as citizens of a supranational political community rather than mere beneficiaries of an economic union between states. Furthermore, it rearticulated personal mobility as a citizenship right rather than a market freedom, giving all member state nationals the right to take up residence or employment in another member state, be joined by their families, and access education, health, social insurance, and pension schemes on a par with citizens of the host member state.[54]

This shift prompted legislative activity geared towards updating legislation adopted under the market integration paradigm of personal mobility in the 1960s and 1970s.[55] Most notably, the 2004 Citizens' Rights Directive consolidated four decades of prior legislation, subsuming the free movement rights of workers, self-employed persons, students, and others under the blanket status of Union citizenship and codifying the ECJ's jurisprudence in this area.[56]

Has EU citizenship fully assimilated the economic content of mobility rights into a civic paradigm of supranational membership, or did it simply give a fancier title to the market freedoms that member state nationals already enjoyed? Which is the dog, and which the tail? To fully assess the significance of the transition from labor mobility to supranational political status, it is helpful to distinguish between the *civil* and *civic* dimensions of citizenship.[57] The civil dimension of modern citizenship denotes rights and

[54] Art 21 TFEU (ex-art 18 TEC) provides: "Every citizen of the Union shall have the right to move and reside freely within the territory of the Member States."

[55] Inter alia, see Directive 2014/67/EU of the European Parliament and of the Council on the enforcement of Directive 96/71/EC concerning the posting of workers in the framework of the provision of services [2014] OJ L159/11; Directive 2014/54/EU of the European Parliament and of the Council of 16 April 2014 on measures facilitating the exercise of rights conferred on workers in the context of freedom of movement for workers [2014] OJ L128/8; Directive 2014/50/EU of the European Parliament and of the Council of 16 April 2014 on minimum requirements for enhancing worker mobility between Member States by improving the acquisition and preservation of supplementary pension rights OJ L128/1; Regulation (EU) 492/2011 of the European Parliament and of the Council of 5 April 2011 on freedom of movement for workers within the European Union [2011] OJ L141/1; Directive 2005/36/EC of the European Parliament and of the Council on the recognition of professional qualifications [2005] OJ L255/22; Directive 96/71/EC of the European Parliament and of the Council of 16 December 1996 concerning the posting of workers in the framework of the provision of services [1997] OJ L018.

[56] Directive 2004/38/EC of the European Parliament and of the Council of 29 April 2004 on the right of citizens of the Union and their family members to move and reside freely within the territory of the Member States amending Regulation (EEC) 1612/68 and repealing Directives 64/221/EEC, 68/360/EEC, 72/194/EEC, 73/148/EEC, 75/34/EEC, 75/35/EEC, 90/364/EEC, 90/365/EEC, and 93/96/EEC [2004] OJ L158/77.

[57] I intentionally refer to the civil versus civic dichotomy as *dimensions* of citizenship rather than separate bundles of rights as per TH Marshall's influential distinction between civil and political rights. The same right often has a civil *and* a political dimension: religious liberty is the quintessential civil right, but also forms the basis of very effective forms of political agency, particularly when wielded as a basis for constitutional review of statute, not just in the US, but in virtually any constitutional

liberties that draw the outer bounds of an individual's "private autonomy" as a subject of the laws, though not necessarily as an author of them. By contrast, the civic dimension of citizenship establishes the conditions of "public autonomy," by which citizens can "understand themselves, in the exercise of their civic rights, as authors of just those rights which they are supposed to obey as addressees."[58] According to Jürgen Habermas, private and public autonomy should be construed as mutually presupposing in theory and reciprocally reinforcing in practice.[59] The distinguishing promise of constitutional democracy, Habermas argues, is to institutionalize that reciprocal relationship.

Prior to the introduction of EU citizenship, the relationship between the EU and member state citizens was restricted to the civil dimension. As supranational subjects, individuals enjoyed rights but could not "understand themselves … as authors of just those rights,"[60] and therefore lacked political agency commensurate with their market freedoms. Of course, as I argued in the previous chapter, these freedoms enabled a form of political agency by which "market citizens" could participate in domestic and supranational policy processes.[61] Even so, however, the EU's individual rights regime had no explicit civic content. By contrast, EU citizenship attempted to ensconce the predominantly civil rights member state nationals held under supranational law within a civic canopy.

Unfortunately, this civic canopy is flimsier than many celebratory analyses of EU citizenship acknowledge. Its central pillar is article 20(2)(b) TFEU, which provides that EU citizens shall have "the right to vote and to stand as candidates in elections to the European Parliament and in municipal elections in their Member State of residence, under the same conditions as nationals of that State." This, however, does not establish a freestanding right to vote as an entailment of EU citizenship. Whatever right EU citizens can claim to participate in the political process originates primarily in each member state's respective constitutional system. As the ECJ held in *Eman*

democracy where the public status of religion is contested. TH Marshall and Tom Bottomore, *Citizenship and Social Class* (first published 1950, Pluto Press 1992).

[58] Jürgen Habermas, *The Inclusion of the Other* (Ciaran Cronin and Pablo de Grieff ed, MIT Press 1998) 258.

[59] cf James Tully, *On Global Citizenship: James Tully in Dialogue* (Bloomsbury 2014). Tully posits a far more demanding ideal of civic citizenship than the one I set out here. He defines civil citizenship as "a status defined by rights and guaranteed by the institutions of the constitutional rule of law" (including rights of democratic participation and representative institutions), while he associates the former with "actual participation in civic activities" (37); the former as defined by institutions and law, and the latter by activities and relationships (38–41). By Tully's definition, civic citizenship is almost wholly at odds with the political model of supranationalism, which is defined by democratic attenuation, technocratic complexity, and failure to inspire grassroots activism.

[60] Habermas, *The Inclusion of the Other* 258.

[61] Everson, "The Legacy of the Market Citizen."

and Sevinger, "in the current state of Community law, the definition of the persons entitled to vote and to stand for election falls within the competence of each Member State in compliance with Community law."[62] Provided that they apply *the same criteria* to citizens of other member states who are resident in their territory, member states get to determine *who* is eligible to vote and how.[63] A hypothetical *denial* by a member state of a right to vote would only be a violation of EU citizenship rights if it were applied in a discriminatory manner to citizens of other member states.

Since EU citizenship does not create so much as a right to vote, its most important civic function is to compensate mobile Europeans for the disenfranchisement that would otherwise result from taking up residence in another state. As the 1993 Directive on electoral rights associated with EU citizenship put it: "the right to vote and to stand as a candidate in elections to the European Parliament in the Member State of residence ... is an instance of the application of the principle of non-discrimination between nationals and non-nationals and a corollary of the right to move and reside freely."[64] In other words, rather than creating a freestanding form of political agency, the driving rationale of EU citizenship and associated rights is still that of accommodating mobility, which is in turn motivated, more often than not, by economic reasons.

Despite its billing as a supranational civic status, the real value added of EU citizenship was to expand the *civil* dimension of the relationship between the EU and its citizens. Based on article 20(2) TFEU, which provides that "citizens of the Union shall enjoy the rights and be subject to the duties provided for in the Treaties," Kochenov observes, "any right to be found in the EC Treaty is potentially a citizenship right."[65] Most notably, EU citizenship established the right of *all* member state nationals (rather than simply cross-border market participants) to move to and reside in another member state, expanding the scope of their private autonomy without significantly upgrading their capacity to exercise democratic control over the institutions that govern them. As Nic Shuibhne contends, "EU citizenship has been principally substantiated, so far, by consolidating and building upon

[62] Case C-300/04 *M.G. Eman and OB Sevinger v College van Burgemeester en Wethouders van Den Haag* [2006] ECR I-8060, para 45.

[63] For this reason, litigants in cases such as *Eman and Sevinger* have relied on art 3 of Protocol 1 of the European Convention on Human Rights on the right to free elections in order to establish their freestanding right to vote. Case C-300/04 *Eman and Sevinger*.

[64] Council Directive 93/109/EC laying down detailed arrangements for the exercise of the right to vote and stand as a candidate in elections to the European Parliament for citizens of the Union residing in a Member State of which they are not nationals [1993] OJ L329.

[65] Dimitry Kochenov, "*Ius Tractum* of Many Faces: European Citizenship and the Difficult Relationship Between Status and Rights" 2008–9 15 *Columbia Journal of European Law* 169, 193.

legal rights that relate almost exclusively to transnational movement."[66] In similar vein, Advocate General Maduro has observed that "the freedoms of movement must be understood to be one of the essential elements of the 'fundamental status of nationals of the Member States'" and "represent the cross-border dimension of the economic and social status conferred on European citizens."[67]

Nonetheless, once mobility rights were rearticulated as EU citizenship entitlements, the Court of Justice began progressively to weaken the economic nexus previously required to claim benefits in a host state. In a seminal case, a Spanish national resident in Germany successfully relied on EU citizenship to claim social benefits even though she was not economically active in Germany at the time.[68] Prior to the introduction of EU citizenship, she would most likely have been denied the protections of Community law.[69] In a subsequent decision, the Court affirmed that "the Treaty on European Union does not require that citizens of the Union pursue a professional or trade activity, whether as an employed or self-employed person, in order to enjoy the rights provided in Part Two of the EC Treaty, on citizenship of the Union."[70] In other words, member state nationals could rely on their supranational membership status to take advantage of EU law, without having to meet a threshold of productive economic activity.[71] Although "admittedly" member states could require Union citizens exercising their right to free movement have adequate sickness insurance, the Court emphasized that their discretion was subject to narrow limits.[72]

Although the market participation requirement for enjoying rights associated with EU citizenship has mostly fallen away, the mobility nexus has

[66] Nic Shuibhne, "The Resilience of EU Market Citizenship" 1609.

[67] Joined Cases 158/04 and 159/04 *Alfa Vita Vassilopoulos AE and Carrefour Marinopoulos AE v Elliniko Dimosio and Nomarchiaki Aftodioikisi Ioanninon* [2006] I-8137, Opinion of AG Maduro, para 40.

[68] Case C-85/96 *Martinez Sala v Freistaat Bayern* [1998] ECR I-2691, para 61. However, the Court declined to address the question of whether ex-art 8 on Union citizenship gave rise to "a new right to *reside* in the territory of the Member State concerned" (para 60, emphasis added). In Ms. Martinez Sala's case, the legality of her residence in Germany was not in question.

[69] Menendez, "European Citizenship after *Martinez-Sala* and *Baumbast*" 12.

[70] Case C-413/99 *Baumbast v Secretary of State for the Home Department* [2002] ECR I-7091, para 83.

[71] Several other decisions reinforced this conclusion. In *Zhu and Chen*, Ms. Chen, who was a Chinese citizen, claimed the right to reside in the UK by virtue of the Irish citizenship of her infant daughter. The ECJ ruled against the UK's decision to deny Ms. Chen leave to remain, holding that the baby's Union citizenship gave her an entitlement to move freely within the Union under art 21 TFEU (ex-art 18(1)). However, the Court made it clear that this right was "subject to limitations and conditions laid down by the Person of Independent Means Directive 90/364." Thus, although ex-art 18(1) enabled the baby *and* her non-EU citizen mother to reside in the UK, they were still subject to the condition of having adequate sickness insurance and financial resources. Case C-200/02 *Zhu and Chen v Secretary of State for the Home Department* [2004] ECR I-9925.

[72] *Zhu and Chen*, paras 91 and 86, respectively.

been more resilient.[73] Most notably, the benefits associated with EU citizenship remain largely inert for non-mobile citizens. In its *Ruiz Zambrano* decision, the ECJ took a big step towards severing the connection between the enjoyment of EU citizenship rights and mobility.[74] The case concerned a Colombian couple whose claims for asylum in Belgium were denied despite the Belgian citizenship of their two young children. After the parents lost their right to reside in Belgium, they invoked the rights of their young children as EU citizens to claim a derivative right of residence and employment in that country. Several member states submitted briefs to the Court insisting that EU citizenship had been intended to protect the rights of member state nationals who moved from one member state to another, which the Ruiz Zambrano children had not done. The Court reasoned that denying the right to residence to their parents would "have the effect of depriving citizens of the Union," in this case, the minor children, "of the genuine enjoyment of the substance of the rights conferred by virtue of their status as citizens of the Union."[75] If Belgian law failed to honor the rights of the Ruiz Zambrano children to remain in Belgium (which they could not do unless their parents were granted the permission to stay and take up gainful employment), then EU law would step up to the plate to ensure that they could remain in the EU as they had a right to do. However, in subsequent decisions, the Court shied away from the broader implications of this expansionary move.[76]

In accordance with the EU's long-standing pattern of constitutional development, the CJEU is likely to be called upon to further disentangle

[73] Prior to *Ruiz Zambrano* (see below), the decision in which the Court accepted arguably the most tenuous commercial mobility link to date in allowing for a right of residency is *Carpenter* (Case C-60/00 *Mary Carpenter v Secretary of State for the Home Department* [2002] ECR I-6279). In that decision, the Court held that a British deportation order for the Philippine wife of Mr. Carpenter breached the latter's rights to family reunification, given that Mr. Carpenter traveled to other member states from time to time for business. The Court found that "the separation of Mr. and Mrs. Carpenter would be detrimental to their family life and, therefore, to the conditions under which Mr. Carpenter exercises a fundamental freedom" (para 39). Although this case was *not* decided under the treaty's Union citizenship provisions, it nevertheless shows the Court relaxing the criteria of economic activity to ensure the widest possible reach for free movement provisions.

[74] Case C-34/09 *Ruiz Zambrano v Office National de l'Emploi* [2011] ECR I-01177.

[75] *Ruiz Zambrano*, para 42, citing art 20 TFEU.

[76] In *McCarthy*, the Court argued that the UK government's decision to refuse a residence permit to the Jamaican husband of a UK citizen did not have "the effect of depriving her of the genuine enjoyment of the substance of the rights associated with her status as a Union citizen." Case C-434/09 *Shirley McCarthy v Secretary of State for the Home Department* [2011] ECR I-03375, para 49. In *Dereci*, the Court carefully circumscribed the criterion set out in *Ruiz Zambrano*, arguing that the "denial of the genuine enjoyment of the substance of the rights conferred by virtue of European Union citizen status refers to situations in which the Union citizen has, in fact, to leave not only the territory of the Member State of which he is a national but also the territory of the Union as a whole." Case C-256/11 *Murat Dereci and others v Bundesministerium für Inneres* [2011] ECR I-11315, para 66.

the latent paradoxes of a civic status that is still essentially a citizenship of aliens.[77] However, it is still the case that the exercise of mobility rights activates the protections of Union citizenship, rather than the other way around. Furthermore, since EU citizenship has been built around a pre-existing regime of rights designed to encourage transnational market participation, economic activity remains a relevant determinant of the strength of a Union citizen's claims against a host state. As Barnard observes, "A non-economically active migrant continues to be in the most precarious position,"[78] not least because their continued right to residence in the event of financial hardship is contingent on the host state's generosity. EU law still lays out the brightest welcome mat for member state nationals who are either active market participants or possess ample personal resources, disappointing the expectation of civic equality associated with citizenship status.[79] In short, the adoption of EU citizenship has neither sublimated the commercial origins of personal mobility rights nor superseded the essentially economic nature of the relationship between the EU and its citizens.[80]

(IV) MOBILITY VERSUS SOLIDARITY: ALTERNATIVE APPROACHES TO SOCIAL POLICY

The freedom of movement must be seen not only as a personal right created by the European integration process, but also as part of the elusive commitment to building a "Social Europe." That commitment has been present since the very beginnings of European integration, when France's socialist prime minister Guy Mollet sought to include the harmonization of social policy and welfare spending among the original aims of the Treaty of Rome.[81] Mollet did not get his wish, however. Although the Preamble of

[77] Predictions are also mixed. Shaw argues that the share of market logic in constituting Union citizenship rights is likely to diminish further: "In the future, the Court could intervene to uphold the EU law rights of EU citizens in more situations which are not directly or even indirectly linked to the inter-state and market dimensions of the EU," as it did in the *Ruiz Zambrano* and *Eman and Sevinger* decisions (Shaw, *The Transformation of Citizenship in the European Union* 234). By contrast, Tryfonidou interprets the Court's post-*Zambrano* jurisprudence as evincing a "backward-moving trend" towards *limiting* the scope of Union citizenship entitlements (Alina Tryfonidou, "Case Note: (Further) Signs of a Turn of the Tide in the CJEU's Citizenship Jurisprudence" (2013) 14 *Maastricht Journal* 302, 320). Kochenov has criticized this line of decisions for leaving the scope and substance of the rights of EU citizenship in a muddle, having apparently "moved beyond the market-driven rationale of the past" without, however, further specifying its essence. Dimitry Kochenov, "The Right to Have *What* Rights? EU Citizenship in Need of Clarification" (2013) 19 *ELJ* 502, 515.

[78] Barnard, *Substantive Law of the EU*, 445.

[79] Kochenov, "*Ius Tractum* of Many Faces" 195.

[80] Nic Shuibhne, "The Resilience of EU Market Citizenship."

[81] Fritz Scharpf, "The European Social Model: Coping with the Challenges of Diversity" (2002) 40 *JCMS* 645, 646.

the EEC Treaty dutifully expressed the desire of signatory states to promote the "improvement of the living and working conditions of their peoples" and "ensure [the] harmonious development [of their economies] by reducing the differences existing between the various regions and the backwardness of the less favored regions," it did not create the institutional structure required to further these commitments.[82] In the ensuing decades, integration in the social domain has been clipped by member states' insistence on preserving their prerogatives over national welfare provision.[83] With limited power to issue binding rules, and lacking any significant redistributive capacity, the EU's role in this area has been limited to benchmarking objectives, articulating best practices, and comparatively assessing outcomes. As a consequence, "the course of European integration from the 1950s onward has created a fundamental asymmetry between policies promoting market efficiencies and those promoting social protection and equality."[84] Since the 1990s, a growing chorus of scholars has expressed concern that the singular emphasis on market integration and competitiveness is eroding the domestic social protections and delicate corporatist bargains that define the European social model.[85] Although the EU has shored up protections in areas such as labor law and consumer protection, a detailed compliance study finds that "liberalizing measures of the single market program certainly had a much larger effect on the member states," concluding that "EU social policy still is on an unequal footing with European integration."[86] Unquestionably, Social Europe has made far less headway than Market Europe.

The EU's existing competences in the area of social policy have been described as a "composite patchwork of constitutive elements, anchored to different levels of government of a compound and internally diverse

[82] This passage rephrases the ECSC Treaty's preambular pledge to "raise the standard of living" by expanding productivity. See also, Maas, "The Genesis of European Rights" 1018.

[83] Stephan Leibfried, "Social Policy: Left to the Judges and the Markets?" in Helen Wallace, Mark A Pollack, and Alasdair R Young (eds), *Policy-Making in the European Union* (7th edn, Oxford University Press 2015).

[84] Scharpf, "The European Social Model" 665.

[85] Especially, Fritz Scharpf, "Economic Integration, Democracy, and the Welfare State" (1997) 4 *Journal of European Public Policy* 18; Claus Offe, *The Democratic Welfare State. A European Regime Under the Strain of European Integration* IHS Political Science Series no 68 (Institute for Advanced Studies 2000); Claus Offe, *Europe Entrapped* (Polity 2015); Wolfgang Streeck, "Competitive Solidarity: Rethinking the 'European Social Model'" in Karl Hinrichs, Herbert Kitschelt, and Helmut Wiesenthal (eds), *Kontingenz und Krise: Institutionenpolitik in Kapitalistischen und Postsozialistischen Gesellschaften. Claus Offe zu seinem 60. Geburstag* (Campus 2000); Alexander Somek, *Individualism. An Essay on the Authority of the European Union* (Oxford University Press 2008); Menéndez, "European Citizenship after *Martínez Sala* and *Baumbast*."

[86] Gerda Falkner, Oliver Treib, Miriam Hartlapp, and Simone Leiber, *Complying with Europe: EU Harmonisation and Soft Law in the Member States* (Cambridge University Press 2005) 346–7.

polity."[87] According to Maurizio Ferrara, this patchwork has four main elements: first, the individual social protection systems of member states; second, the "social citizenship space" constituted by free movement and equal treatment rights; third, the "ensemble of sub-national [or regional] social schemes"; and fourth, the bundle of "supranational policies that have an explicit social purpose," whether regulatory or redistributive.[88] These components, Ferrara points out, do not add up to a coherent social policy and are often in tension with one another.

In this section, I would like to take Ferrara's claim one step further by showing that the "social citizenship space" established by personal mobility rights (the second component) is in fact intended to *substitute for* a redistributive social policy at the EU level (the fourth component) due to the political unfeasibility of the latter. As Maas has shown, the inclusion of labor among the mobility provisions of the Paris and Rome Treaties was chiefly a concession to Italy to "permit export of its surplus labor."[89] As Giubboni argues, the apparent "flimsiness of the social provisions of the Treaty of Rome" is symptomatic of the postwar "compromise of embedded liberalism,"[90] whereby multilateral institutions of economic liberalization would be counterbalanced by strong domestic institutions guaranteeing social cohesion.[91] In the classic formula coined by Robert Gilpin, embedded liberalism meant "Smith abroad" and "Keynes at home."[92] In the European Community, member states were in charge of providing the social protections necessary to cushion the impact of greater market competition. The Community, in turn, would support their efforts by enabling citizens to seek employment in other member states if their industries succumbed to the rigors of market competition. In other words, labor mobility was auxiliary to domestic social welfare protections, but it was an essential instrument in the supranational social justice toolkit from the beginning. This reliance on labor mobility as a strategy for relieving mass unemployment illustrates the way in which the EU entrusts the objective of social justice to the efficient operation of the market.

The adequacy of labor mobility as a social policy instrument has been called into question by the simultaneous weakening of the European social model and the imperviousness of global capital flows to regulation over the

[87] Maurizio Ferrara, "Social Europe and its Components in the Midst of the Crisis: A Conclusion" (2014) 37 *West European Politics* 825, 839.

[88] ibid 828. [89] Mason, quoted in Maas, "The Genesis of European Rights" 1012.

[90] Stefano Giubboni, *Social Rights and Market Freedom in the European Constitution: A Labour Law Perspective* (Rita Inston tr, Cambridge University Press 2006) 16.

[91] John Gerard Ruggie, "International Regimes, Transactions, and Change: Embedded Liberalism in the Postwar Economic Order" (1982) 36 *International Organization* 379.

[92] Robert Gilpin, *The Political Economy of International Relations* (Princeton University Press 1987) 355.

past few decades.[93] The balance of embedded liberalism has been thrown off kilter by the erosion of domestic welfare provision, while the EU continues to lack the social policy mandate and fiscal capacity that would complement the strict regime of budgetary discipline member states must follow. Although the 2009 Treaty of Lisbon enumerated the building of a "competitive *social* market economy"[94] among the EU's aims, and listed justice and solidarity among its founding values,[95] it nevertheless preserved the domestic basis of welfare provision, thereby creating a "disjunction ... between lofty Treaty proclamation[s] and lack of law-making instruments."[96] Similarly, while it introduced means for the EU to "encourage cooperation" among member states on social policy, it left it up to member states to design, implement, and fund it.[97] Similarly, a new general obligation that the EU "take into account requirements linked to the promotion of a high level of employment, the guarantee of adequate social protection, the fight against social exclusion" is not accompanied by any new supranational competences.[98] Instead, it merely enjoins the EU from stepping on member states' toes as they walk a tightrope between the socioeconomic needs of their citizens, on the one hand, and the imperatives of market liberalization, on the other.

The choice of commercial mobility over social solidarity is starkly at play in the Court of Justice's case law on personal mobility. Since the late 1980s, the Court has interpreted free movement provisions as obligating member states to extend social and welfare coverage to citizens of other member states who were legally present in their territory, touching off a debate about the impact of mobility on domestic welfare entitlements. In its seminal *Cowan* decision, the ECJ ruled that a British tourist in France was entitled to the same crime compensation scheme as the host state's own citizens.[99] The repackaging of personal mobility as an EU citizenship right has led the Court to further relax the requirements of gainful economic activity and financial self-sufficiency built into the pre-Maastricht rules. For instance, in the *Martinez Sala* decision discussed earlier, the Court ruled that an EU citizen who became unemployed while exercising her right to free movement in another member state was entitled to childcare benefits on the same basis

[93] Maurizio Ferrara, "Modest Beginnings, Timid Progresses: What's Next for Social Europe?" in Bea Cantillon, Herwig Verschueren, and Paula Ploscar (eds), *Social Inclusion and Social Protection in the EU: Interactions Between Law and Policy* (Intersentia 2012).

[94] Art 3(3) TEU. Emphasis added.

[95] Art 2 TEU.

[96] Mark Dawson and Bruno de Witte, "The EU Legal Framework of Social Inclusion and Social Protection: Between the Lisbon Strategy and the Lisbon Treaty" in Cantillon, Verschueren, and Ploscar *Social Inclusion and Social Protection in the EU*, 54.

[97] Art 153(1) and (2).

[98] Art 9 TFEU.

[99] Case 186/87 *Cowan v Le Trésor Public* [1989] ECR 195.

as nationals of the host state.[100] In its *Grzelczyk* decision, the Court obliged Belgium to extend the minimum living allowance to a French exchange student, and deflected anticipated objections against expanding the pool of recipients without expanding that of contributors.[101] According to the Court, an EU citizen is entitled to social assistance schemes in her country of residence even if she is unable to contribute to their maintenance (for instance, because she has never been engaged in gainful employment). It reasoned that a sufficient "degree of financial solidarity" exists among member states to justify the extension of certain types of social assistance to all EU citizens legally resident in the member state.[102]

While this jurisprudence has made life easier for mobile EU citizens, the Court's generosity leaves national and municipal authorities to shoulder the burden of intra-EU mobility.[103] "What the Court cannot do," Scharpf underlines, "is to establish a common European regime that would respond to some of the values and policy purposes, which as a consequence of its decisions, can no longer be realized at the national level."[104] Many observers have rightly questioned whether such an approach is sustainable or, indeed, fair. Given the asymmetry between contributors and recipients, the more Union citizens exercise their right to free movement, the less member states may be able to afford generous welfare provisions.[105] Streeck argues that the "imbalance between a potentially rising number of beneficiaries and potentially shrinking number of payers ... is bound to exert pressure on national systems to cut back or, at the very least, not to expand their provisions of social citizenship."[106] This is not a nativist objection to mobility, but a warning that certain rights, especially those whose enjoyment depends on finite social and economic resources, are only feasible if they entail corresponding duties.

In this respect, the EU's internal mobility regime brings two key commitments espoused by progressive scholars into tension. While personal mobility law mitigates the nation-state's exclusive scope of moral concern and raises hopes of postnational democratic politics, it also increases the pressure

[100] Case C-85/96 *Martinez Sala*. [101] Case C-184/99 *Rudy Grzelczyk*, para 44.

[102] ibid para 44. Barnard, *The Substantive Law of the EU* 438–9.

[103] Martin Höpner and Armin Schäfer, "Embeddedness and Regional Integration: Waiting for Polanyi in a Hayekian Setting" (2012) 66 *International Organization* 429, 431.

[104] Fritz W Scharpf, "The Asymmetry of European Integration, or Why the EU cannot be a 'Social Market Economy'" (2010) 8 *Socio-Economic Review* 211, 223.

[105] Menéndez, "European Citizenship after *Martínez Sala* and *Baumbast*" 27, 31.

[106] Wolfgang Streeck, "Citizenship under Regime Competition" in Klaus Eder and Bernhard Giesen (eds), *European Citizenship between National Legacies and Postnational Projects* (Oxford University Press 2001) 128.

on the European social model by disrupting "the reciprocity of social rights and obligations."[107] Nonetheless, it is easy to exaggerate the magnitude of the challenge posed by intra-EU mobility to welfare states. First, the total volume of intra-EU migration remains relatively small: according to 2011 Eurostat data, only 2.5 per cent of the combined population of twenty-seven member states were intra-EU migrants, which amounted to only a third of the total immigrant population.[108] More importantly, the labor market participation rate for intra-EU migrants in 2012 was 80.7 per cent, nearly 4 percentage points higher than the native population average.[109] Another report estimated that economically non-active EU migrants made up less than 1 per cent of the total EU population, and the expenses associated with their healthcare were estimated at a median of 0.2 per cent of total health spending in the host state.[110] In sum, an overwhelming number of intra-EU migrants contribute to public revenues, and are less likely than a state's own citizens to claim unemployment and disability benefits.[111]

The upshot of this critique is therefore not so much the material strain that intra-EU migration places on domestic employment opportunities and welfare resources as the dubious wisdom of placing the burden of social justice on the operations of the market. Expecting people to move where the jobs and social benefits are is a woefully inadequate way to compensate for the constraints the EU imposes on member states in terms of social spending. This is particularly true in view of the tight fiscal discipline required by Europe's monetary union. The EU's social policy programs are "utterly unequipped to face the challenges of strengthened Stability and Growth rules and of the asymmetric social shocks that the crisis has inflicted on the various member states."[112] While member states are expected to bring

[107] Höpner and Schäfer, "Embeddedness and Regional Integration" 450.

[108] Katya Vasileva, "Nearly Two-thirds of the Foreigners Living in EU Member States Are Citizens of Countries outside the EU-27" (Eurostat Statistics in Focus No 31/2012) 2. Available at http://ec.europa.eu/eurostat/documents/3433488/5584984/KS-SF-12-031-EN.PDF/be48f08f-41c1-4748-a8a5-5d92ebe848f2 accessed October 3, 2015.

[109] Eurostat, "Migrant Integration Statistics—Employment" (April 2015). Available at: http://ec.europa.eu/eurostat/statistics-explained/index.php/Migrant_integration_statistics_-_employment#Unemployment accessed September 1, 2015.

[110] ICF GHK in association with Milieu Ltd., "A fact finding analysis on the impact on the Member States' social security systems of the entitlements of non-active intra-EU migrants to special non-contributory cash benefits and healthcare granted on the basis of residence," Report submitted to the European Commission Directorate-General for Employment, Social Affairs, and Inclusion, 14 October 2013, at 13, 92 respectively. Available at http://bookshop.europa.eu/en/a-fact-finding-analysis-on-the-impact-on-the-member-states-social-security-systems-of-the-entitlements-of-non-active-intra-eu-migrants-to-special-non-contributory-cash-benefits-and-healthcare-granted-on-the-basis-of-residence-pbKE0413060/ accessed September 1, 2015.

[111] ibid 61, 202.

[112] Ferrara, "Social Europe and its Components in the Midst of the Crisis" 834.

their fiscal and budgetary policies into conformity with strict EU rules, they retain sole responsibility for funding social welfare schemes and absorbing the costs of mobility.

The financial and sovereign debt crisis of the past decade has increased the lopsidedness of intra-EU migration. The Eurogroup's insistence on tackling the recession by means of endless fiscal belt-tightening has left the social safety nets of debtor states threadbare and hampered their ability to use public expenditure for job creation.[113] As a result, job seekers in greater numbers have left recession-plagued economies to seek opportunities in more prosperous member states.[114] Meanwhile, attractive destinations for intra-EU migrants such as the UK, Germany, the Netherlands, Belgium, and Austria have witnessed ever-louder domestic calls to end "benefits tourism,"[115] contributing to negative public sentiment towards the core EU objective of free movement.[116] Hostile political responses to crisis-driven mobility and the added strain (real or perceived) on local, regional, and national resources are a reminder that relying on labor market mobility to solve structural economic problems "risks the financial viability of national welfare systems and the legitimacy of the EU enterprise at the same time."[117] Even the Commission concedes that "intra-EU mobility can relieve only a minor part of the labour market pressure" that is the legacy of the crisis and of the austerity policies pursued in response to it.[118] This substitution of labor market mobility for greater fiscal solidarity between member states illustrates

[113] The OECD estimates that social spending-to-GDP ratios have declined by 1.5 to 3.5 percentage points in Germany, Hungary, Ireland, the United Kingdom, Estonia, and Greece since their peak in 2009, and plateaued for the EU overall. OECD Directorate for Employment, Labour, and Social Affairs, "Social Expenditure Update" (November 2014) 2. Available at <http://www.oecd.org/els/soc/OECD2014-Social-Expenditure-Update-Nov2014-8pages.pdf> accessed December 5, 2015. A collaborative 2012 study argues that "the obsession with cutting public expenditure is undermining or even blocking the road to recovery and the revitalisation of socio-economic models" in many of the countries studied, including Ireland, Italy, Hungary, Spain, and Greece. Steffen Lehndorff (ed), *A Triumph of Failed Ideas. European Models of Capitalism in the Crisis* (European Trade Union Institute 2012).

[114] In 2012, the Commission reported that "Due to the high unemployment rate in Southern European countries, mobility intentions are high (especially among young people) and labour mobility from those countries has increased, in particular to Germany." European Commission, "EU Employment and Social Situation: Quarterly Review" (June 2012) 6, 33. Available at http://ec.europa.eu/social/BlobServlet?docId=7830&langId=en accessed October 3, 2015.

Also see Meghan Benton and Milica Petrovic, *How Free is Free Movement? Dynamics and Drivers of Mobility within the European Union* (Migration Policy Institute Europe 2013) 10.

[115] James Fontanella-Khan, Gerrit Wiesmann, and Helen Warrell, "UK Seeks EU Support over 'Benefits Tourism'" *Financial Times* (London, March 7, 2013); Andrew Byrne, "Free Flow of Labour Stemmed as Belgium Cracks Down on Migrants" *Financial Times* (London, March 16, 2014).

[116] Dorte Sindbjerg Martinsen and Hans Vollaard, "Implementing Social Europe in Times of Crises: Re-established Boundaries of Welfare?" (2014) 37 *West European Politics* 677.

[117] Blauberger and Schmidt, "Welfare Migration?" 6.

[118] European Commission, "EU Employment and Social Situation: Quarterly Review" (June 2012) 6.

Streeck's provocative contention that the EU has worked to "enshrine the institutional hegemony of market justice over social justice."[119]

Finally, the same substitution also exacerbates the asymmetry between the legal entitlements of mobile and non-mobile Europeans. Since intra-EU migration is not buttressed by a supranational benefits scheme, non-mobile Europeans must effectively underwrite Europe's mobility regime. Lisa Conant finds that some member states have responded to the CJEU's extension of domestic social benefits to intra-EU migrants by paring down generous social assistance arrangements in favor of US-style "workfare" schemes that require labor-market participation.[120] In other words, others' mobility may cause non-mobile Europeans to lose some of the benefits they enjoy. This not only casts doubt on the fairness of a market-based model of social solidarity, but also illustrates the unequal distribution of the benefits of EU citizenship. According to Scharpf, the personal mobility regime "violates the norms of reciprocity" among member states by creating "special burdens for national welfare states with high levels of collectively financed services and transfers."[121] Others have gone further, contending that "the main effect of European integration remains the freeing of individuals from collectively imposed obligations."[122]

Although its political viability remains virtually nil for the foreseeable future, it is difficult to see what, aside from a well-resourced supranational social policy, could redress these imbalances. A consideration of alternative designs for a more robust Social Europe[123] and the various compelling reasons why member states are unlikely to commit to it[124] is beyond the scope of this chapter. Without it, however, beleaguered national welfare states will be left to address the social externalities of market integration, and may

[119] Wolfgang Streeck, *Buying Time. The Delayed Crisis of Democratic Capitalism* (Patrick Camiller tr, Verso 2014) 103.

[120] Lisa Conant, "Rights and the Limits of Transnational Solidarity in Europe" in Donald W Jackson, Michael C Tolley, and Mary L Volcansek (eds), *Globalizing Justice: Critical Perspectives on Transnational Law and the Cross-border Migration of Legal Norms* (SUNY Press 2010) 142.

[121] Scharpf, "The Asymmetry of European Integration" 238.

[122] Höpner and Schäfer, "Embeddedness and Regional Integration" 432. Also see Somek, *Individualism*; Menéndez, "European Citizenship after *Martínez Sala* and *Baumbast*."

[123] For a list of different options, ranging from a European "baby bond" to a social insurance scheme for mobile Europeans, see Ferrara, "Modest Beginnings, Timid Progresses: What's Next for Social Europe?" 36.

[124] Member states' reluctance to transfer social policy competences to the EU stem from many reasons, including ideological differences between member state governments, entrenched historic differences between national welfare state models, concerns over further attenuating democratic control over policy, fears of a bloated and inefficient supranational bureaucracy, popular attachment to existing welfare institutions, and desire for sovereign control of national resources. For an overview, see Philippe C Schmitter and Michael W Bauer, "A (Modest) Proposal for Expanding Social Citizenship in the European Union" (2001) 11 *Journal of European Social Policy* 55, 55.

struggle to sustain the level of assistance to which their citizens are accustomed. The extensive economic interdependence between EU member states and the harsh fiscal discipline imposed by their monetary union strengthen the imperative for a cushioning supranational social solidarity scheme. Such a scheme would also deepen the social content of EU citizenship, particularly if it created an individual entitlement to social assistance that needy EU citizens could access regardless of mobility.[125] However unlikely for political and institutional reasons, entrusting the EU with a social mandate equal in scope and prominence to that of market liberalization would go beyond a simple recalibration of values: it would fundamentally alter the functionalist nature of the EU's constitutional system.

(V) THE LIMITS OF FREE MOVEMENT: INTEGRATION WITHIN, DIFFERENTIATION WITHOUT

Modern borders are expressions of sovereign authority. European states have sought to render the political and national units congruent in part by tightly controlling flows of people, commodities, and currency across their respective territories.[126] Insofar as it gives the bearer "the right to move and reside freely within the territory of the Member States," and requires host states to treat one another's citizens no less favorably than their own, the EU's personal mobility regime is also significant from a cosmopolitan perspective. Some scholars have gone so far as to argue that this regime embodies Immanuel Kant's idea of cosmopolitan right (*ius cosmopoliticum*) as a universal right to seek contact with foreigners.[127] Like the discoverers and merchants whose globetrotting bravado inspired Kant, the EU encourages the cultivation of transnational solidarities by enabling member state nationals to "move and reside freely" in states other than their own.[128] In fact, by establishing an entitlement not only to visit but also to settle in another state, access social benefits, and participate in elections, EU citizenship goes far beyond the limited claim to hospitality allowed under Kant's scheme of cosmopolitan right.[129]

[125] E.g. the "Euro-stipendium" proposed by Schmitter and Bauer aims to eliminate extreme poverty by providing a supranational social assistance scheme to member state nationals and permanent residents. ibid, 56.

[126] "Nationalism is primarily a political principle, which holds that the political and the national unit should be congruent." Ernest Gellner, *Nations and Nationalism* (Cornell University Press 1983) 1.

[127] Alexander Hoogenboom, "In Search of a Rationale for the EU Citizenship Jurisprudence" (2015) 35 *Oxford Journal of Legal Studies* 301.

[128] Immanuel Kant, "Perpetual Peace. A Philosophical Sketch" in Hans Reiss (ed), *Political Writings* (HB Nisbet tr, 2nd edn, Cambridge University Press 1997).

[129] ibid 105–6.

Without question, the EU's internal mobility regime eases the legal, moral, and political salience of borders between member states. Considering the Continent's history, that achievement is as heartening as it is improbable. That it heralds the arrival of a cosmopolitan legal order, however, is doubtful. Most notably, if the principle guiding the EU's free movement norms were one of cosmopolitan regard, we would expect these norms to apply equally to all individuals within the EU's jurisdiction. However, mobility rights are not universal entitlements of this sort. They belong to EU citizens as nationals of member states rather than as *polites* of the *cosmos*. In other words, free movement rights amount to a new, exclusive membership status.

Although the EU's free movement regime by no means heralds a cosmopolitan legal order, its supranational organs have often voiced a relatively more inclusive stance towards external migration relative to most member states, and have occasionally succeeded in tempering the latter's exclusionary reflexes.[130] In particular, the European Commission mediates between member state preferences in favor of stricter controls over the admission and residency of third-country nationals, and the EU's established norms of liberal internal mobility. The Commission has long sought to shift the focus towards the human rights and social inclusion issues raised by external immigration,[131] reminding member states that "most of the rights enumerated in the Charter [of Fundamental Rights] are conferred on all persons regardless of their nationality or place of residence."[132] Furthermore, the Commission pushed unsuccessfully for

[130] Up until recently, the European Parliament had displayed a relatively inclusive attitude towards third-country nationals. See, for instance, European Parliament, *Resolution on the Communication from the Commission on Immigration, Integration and Employment* [2004] OJ C92, 390–9; European Parliament, *Resolution on the Free Movement of Persons* A3 0199/91, June 1991; European Parliament, *Report on Immigration Policy* A3-0280/92, November 1992, 5, 10. See also, Kostakopoulou, "Invisible Citizens?" 186; Mario Martiniello, "Citizenship of the European Union: A Critical View" in Rainer Bauböck (ed), *From Aliens to Citizens* (Avebury 1994). As Mouzourakis observes, however, the recent expansion of the co-decision mechanism and "increasing legislative authority has rendered the European Parliament more convergent with the Council and less liberal with regard to immigration and asylum policies." Minos Mouzourakis, "'We Need to Talk About Dublin': Responsibility under the Dublin System as a Blockage to Asylum Burden-Sharing in the European Union" (University of Oxford Refugee Studies Centre Working Paper Series No 105, 2014) 15–16.

[131] For a detailed account of immigration-related bargaining between the Council and the Commission, see J Niessen, *Five Years of EU Migration and Asylum Policymaking under the Amsterdam and Tampere Mandates* (Migration Policy Group 2004) 44.

[132] In addition, the Commission argued that the Charter "reflects the European Union's traditions and positive attitude to equal treatment of citizens of the Union and third country nationals." European Commission, *Proposal for a Council Directive Concerning the Status of Third Country Nationals who are Long-Term Residents* COM (2001) 127, [2001] OJ C240 E/79. This proposal formed the basis of Council Directive 2003/109/EC on the status of third-country nationals who are long-term residents.

a "civic citizenship"[133] status for long-term resident third-country nationals that would guarantee them some form of political participation at the local level[134] as well as providing "certain core rights and obligations to immigrants which they would acquire gradually over a period of years, so that they are treated in the same way as nationals of their host state, even if they are not naturalised."[135] Although the civic citizenship proposal foundered on member state opposition,[136] Directive 109, adopted in 2003,[137] created a harmonized status for third-country nationals who are long-term residents. Accordingly, after five years' uninterrupted residence, member states are obliged to grant long-term resident status to third-country nationals and treat them on a par with their own citizens as regards access to employment and working conditions, education and vocational training and assistance, access to social security, social assistance, housing, freedom of association, and free movement within the member state.[138] Still, the grant of long-term resident status is conditional on the applicant's ability to show proof of "stable resources" and sickness insurance, and member states retain the discretion to impose additional requirements, such as language proficiency.

In addition, while member states retain the prerogative to determine the number of immigrants they are willing to admit, the European Commission has urged member states to adopt more permissive policies on this front.[139] Tellingly, however, the Commission frames the case for a more liberal admissions policy as a matter of "growing market needs"[140] such as combatting economic stagnation and labor market shortages, promoting growth,[141]

[133] The European Commission, *Communication on a Community Immigration Policy* COM (2000) 757, 19, 22.

[134] The European Commission, *Communication on Immigration, Integration and Employment*, s 4.3.

[135] The European Commission, *Communication on Immigration, Integration and Employment* COM/2003/0336 final, s 3.3.6.

[136] It is worth noting that member states as well as municipal administrations regularly take the initiative on civic citizenship, efforts which are approvingly documented by the Commission in its annual reports on migration and immigration.

[137] Council Directive 2003/109/EC of 25 November 2003 concerning the status of third-country nationals who are long-term residents [2003] OJ L16/44.

[138] Directive 109, art 11.

[139] Communication from the Commission to the European Parliament, the Council, the European Economic and Social Committee and the Committee of the Regions, *Towards a Common Immigration Policy* COM (2007) 780 final; Communication from the Commission to the European Parliament and the Council, *4th Annual Report on Immigration and Asylum (2012)* COM (2013) 422 final, 4–7.

[140] European Commission, *Towards a Common Immigration Policy.*

[141] The European Commission, *Communication on Immigration, Integration and Employment* 112.

and sustaining expansive national welfare provisions in the face of an aging workforce.[142] Third-country nationals, to a greater extent than EU citizens, are valued primarily as factors of production. Similarly, discrepancies between member states' immigration regimes disrupt the smooth functioning of the internal market and complicate the Commission's governance tasks. These are among the reasons why the Commission has pushed for harmonized criteria and procedures for admission for economic migrants.[143] The liberal treatment of third-country nationals under EU law is therefore creditable to the imperatives of economic union. In other words, rather than instantiating a principled commitment to cosmopolitan ideals, it reflects the EU's system of functional constitutionalism. The case of third-country nationals is perhaps the clearest instance in which the market paradigm has helped to advance legal guarantees favorable to individual freedom and equality before the law.[144]

The development of separate regimes of mobility pertaining to member state nationals and third-country citizens was neither a necessary nor a foreordained consequence of liberalizing internal mobility. The original Treaty of Rome did not explicitly exclude third-country nationals from the scope of its free movement provisions, which could have been interpreted as applying to all legal residents or workers.[145] Moreover, as the Commission has repeatedly pointed out, "an internal market without frontiers in which the free movement of persons is ensured logically implies the free movement of all legally resident third-country nationals for the purpose of engaging in economic activities."[146] Although legislation in recent years shows a trend towards aligning the rights and entitlements of legally resident third-country nationals with those of EU citizens, however, the Council

[142] E.g. European Commission, *Communication on a Community Immigration Policy* COM (2000) 757; European Commission, *Communication on an Open Method of Coordination for the Community Immigration Policy* COM (2001) 387.

[143] European Commission, *Green Paper on an EU Approach to Managing Economic Migration* COM (2004) 0811 final.

[144] Nic Shuibhne argues that the market framework is a normatively more capacious one for advancing EU citizenship claims than it is usually given credit for, and contains untapped potentialities. This conclusion seems more warranted in the case of third-country nationals, who arguably enjoy a wider range of rights within their member states thanks to the EU's market rationale. Nic Shuibhne, "The Resilience of EU Market Citizenship" 1609, 1619.

[145] The Treaty of Rome provided that "Freedom of movement for workers shall be secured within the Community" (ex-art 48(1) TEC). It did, however, specify that "discrimination based on nationality" would be abolished "between workers of the Member States" (ex-art 48(2) TEC). Theodora Kostakopoulou, "Invisible Citizens? Long-term Resident Third-country Nationals in the EU and their Struggle for Recognition" in Richard Bellamy and Alex Warleigh (eds), *Citizenship and Governance in the European Union* (Continuum 2001) 183; Also, Tamara K Hervey, "Migrant Workers and their Families in the European Union: The Pervasive Market Ideology of Community Law" in Jo Shaw and Gillian More (eds), *New Legal Dynamics of European Union* (Clarendon Press 1995) 97–9.

[146] European Commission, "European Social Policy—A Way forward for the Union: A White Paper" COM (94) 333, 29–30.

has insisted on distinguishing and spelling out the rights and obligations of third-country nationals separately from those of EU citizens.[147]

Perhaps more importantly, the liberalization of movement within the Union has prompted further securitization of Europe's external borders. Article 3 of the Treaty on European Union captures the dramatic contrast between internal freedom of movement and external border security, declaring in the same breath that "the Union shall offer its citizens an area of freedom, security and justice without internal frontiers, in which the free movement of persons is ensured in conjunction with appropriate measures with respect to external border controls, asylum, immigration and the prevention and combating of crime."[148] Particularly during the post-9/11 period, member states have chosen to emphasize the security risks associated with immigration, and have mobilized the EU's euphemistically named "Area of Freedom, Security, and Justice" to minimize these perceived risks.[149] EU-level coordination on immigration and asylum policy represents an instrument for setting and enforcing common limits on external border policy, however open a particular member state's own policy with regard to migrants and refugees may be.

Most importantly, many of the EU's policies in this area reflect a law-enforcement approach that contrasts dramatically with the extensive protections the EU affords to mobile member state citizens.[150] There is a deep

[147] In a 2005 Communication, the Commission stated its intent to "progressively present a set of legislative proposals concerning the conditions of entry and residence for third-country nationals in employment." (Commission of the European Communities, *Communication from the Commission—Policy Plan on Legal Migration* SEC (2005) 1680, COM (2005) 0669 final). The legislative proposals that have been adopted in light of that goal include the so-called Blue Card Directive on the entry of high-skilled workers (Council Directive 2009/50/EC of 25 May 2009 on the conditions of entry and residence of third-country nationals for the purposes of highly qualified employment [2009] OJ L155/17); the Single Permit Directive enabling a single application procedure for residence and employment (Directive 2011/98/EU of the European Parliament and of the Council of 13 December 2011 on a single application procedure for a single permit for third-country nationals to reside and work in the territory of a Member State and on a common set of rights for third-country workers legally residing in a Member State [2011] OJ L343/1); Directive 2014/36/EU of the European Parliament and of the Council of 26 February 2014 on the conditions of entry and stay of third-country nationals for the purpose of employment as seasonal workers [2014] OJ L94/375; Directive 2014/66/EU of the European Parliament and of the Council of 15 May 2014 on the conditions of entry and residence of third-country nationals in the framework of an intra-corporate transfer [2014] OJ L157/1.

[148] Art 3(2) TEU.

[149] The high water mark of a relatively liberal Council approach to immigration was the Tampere European Council summit in 1999, where member states stressed the need for "fair treatment of third country nationals," and stated the desire to approximate their legal status with those enjoyed by member state nationals. Tampere European Council, *Presidency Conclusions*, 15–16 October 1999, Section A.III, paras 18 and 21 respectively. Available at <http://www.consilium.europa.eu/uedocs/cms_data/docs/pressdata/en/ec/00200-r1.en9.htm>.

[150] See especially, Directive 2009/52/EC of the European Parliament and of the Council of 18 June 2009 providing for minimum standards on sanctions and measures against employers of illegally

duplicity at work in the denigration of "economic migrants" in a continent so deeply committed to the ideal of unhindered commercial mobility. The right to seek a better livelihood abroad is considered a "fundamental freedom" under EU law, but only if the claimant in question is an EU citizen to begin with.[151] As part of the resolute march towards economic union, EU institutions have encouraged member state citizens to seek employment abroad by removing obstacles to mobility between member states and compensating for its disadvantages. Plucky Europeans who cross borders to snag a labor contract are hailed as the standard-bearers of a new, cosmopolitan work ethic, and if they falter, EU law ensures that the host state's welfare system will be there to catch them. However, when it comes to the thousands of civilians drowning in the Mediterranean, suffocating in trucks, and being trafficked by criminals to escape civil conflagrations on Europe's peripheries, the EU takes a preventive approach geared towards minimizing unauthorized entry.[152] This dual migration regime, which assigns privileges to some and consigns others to precarity, disappoints the inclusive potential of the European integration project. In view of the EU's success in relaxing the iron grip that European nation-states have exerted on their territory and populations, it is particularly dispiriting that the EU's coordination mechanisms are marshaled to enforce the exclusionary reflexes of its member states. Liberalized mobility within the EU has been a vehicle towards the "permanent linking together of states to form a corporate entity with a distinct boundary vis-à-vis the outside world."[153] Far from heralding a cosmopolitan regime of free movement, therefore, the EU often replicates policies of exclusion familiar from the nation-state context.

staying third-country nationals [2009] OJ L168/24; Directive 2008/15/ EC of the European Parliament and of the Council of 16 December 2008 on common standards and procedures in Member States for returning illegally staying third-country nationals [2008] OJ L348/98; Kostakopoulou, "Invisible Citizens?" 188.

[151] Case C-340/89 *Vlassopoulou v Ministerium für Justiz, Bundes- und Europaangelegenheiten Baden-Württemberg* [1991] ECR-I 2357, para 22; Case C-60/00 *Mary Carpenter* para 38.

[152] For instance, the Dublin procedures for allocating responsibility for processing asylum claims in the EU have been criticized for evincing a paradigm of *assigning blame* over a member state's failure to secure its borders against unauthorized entry, and as a "burden and a punishment for the Member State which permitted the individual to arrive in the Union." See, respectively, Mouzourakis, ' "We Need to Talk About Dublin' " 11 and Elspeth Guild, "The Europeanisation of Europe's Asylum Policy" (2006) 18 *International Journal of Refugee Law* 630, 637.

[153] Forsyth, "The Political Theory of Federalism" 40.

6

The Non-discrimination Principle: Unbounding the State?

Although the 1957 Treaty of Rome enumerated the steps necessary for the establishment of a common market amongst the six member states of the European Economic Community, the European integration project has always been associated with a more capacious normative vision. However, precisely what that vision entails is fiercely contested. According to a cosmopolitan interpretation, the ethos guiding European integration is "the inclusion of the other,"[1] that is to say, the expansion of the nation-state's scope of moral concern to embrace those who are not its citizens. The legal framework of market integration, which constrains the ability of member states to privilege their own producers, firms, service providers, and workers at the expense of foreigners, is often regarded as a step towards the unbounding of political community. On this view, the immanent cosmopolitan potential of commerce is encapsulated by article 7 of the original Treaty of Rome, which provided categorically that "Within the scope of application of this Treaty … any discrimination on grounds of nationality shall be prohibited."[2]

Without question, the principle of non-discrimination on the basis of nationality enjoys a dual justification. The first is rooted in the objective of market integration. The logic of uniting member states into a shared space of economic activity militates against measures that favor domestic market participants. In addition to this functionalist justification, however, "in so far as [fundamental freedoms of movement] lay down prohibitions on discrimination … they are to be considered a specific means of expression of the general principle of equality before the law."[3] Even more

[1] Jürgen Habermas, "On the Internal Relation between the Rule of Law and Democracy" in *The Inclusion of the Other* (Ciaran Cronin and Pablo de Grieff eds, MIT Press 1998).

[2] Minimally revised, the relevant part of art 18 TFEU now reads: "Within the scope of application of the Treaties … any discrimination on grounds of nationality shall be prohibited."

[3] Case C-36/02 *Omega Spielhallen- und Automatenaufstellungs-GmbH v Oberbürgermeisterin der Bundesstadt Bonn* [2004] ECR I-9609, Opinion of AG Stix-Hackl, para 50.

importantly, the EU's non-discrimination rules apply to a set of relationships where the principle of equal protection is often deemed inapplicable or weakly applicable, namely the treatment owed by a state to foreigners. For one thing, the system of sovereign states legitimizes discriminatory treatment: members of a polity usually have claims on one another that non-members do not. Many liberal political philosophers who espouse a strong commitment to the equal moral worth of individuals have argued that it is morally permissible for bounded communities to reserve certain privileges for their citizens, and have described the duties we owe to humanity in general as less demanding than those we owe to compatriots.[4] For many, liberal universalism is fully compatible with differentiated treatment between members and non-members of the political community. This underlines the radicalism of the EU's commitment to extending domestic entitlements ranging from social security to consular protection and voting rights to citizens of other member states.[5]

The prohibitions against nationality-based discrimination enshrined in EU law have also been described as extending the emancipatory project of constitutionalism, at least insofar as constitutional rule requires curbing the arbitrary exercise of public power. On this view, the constitutional ideal can only be partially realized at the national level, which leaves the exercise of sovereign power over noncitizens unfettered. As Joerges and Neyer write, "the legitimacy of governance within constitutional states is flawed in so far as it remains inevitably one-sided and parochial or selfish."[6] Insofar as it requires member states to treat noncitizens no less favorably than citizens and prohibits the discretionary use of power over the former, EU law dovetails with the cosmopolitan aspiration to "[correct] the constitutional limits of national political communities,"[7] and makes good on the universalistic promise of constitutional rights.

[4] Most notably, John Rawls, *The Law of Peoples* (Harvard University Press 1999); David Miller, *National Responsibility and Global Justice* (Oxford University Press 2007); David Miller, *Citizenship and National Identity* (Polity Press 2000); Thomas Nagel, "The Problem of Global Justice" (2005) 33 *Philosophy & Public Affairs* 113; Andrea Sangiovanni, "Global Justice, Reciprocity, and the State" (2007) 35 *Philosophy & Public Affairs* 3. For cosmopolitan arguments that cast nationality as an impermissible basis for moral differentiation, see Charles Beitz, *Political Theory and International Relations* (Princeton University Press 1979); Joseph Carens, "Aliens and Citizens: The Case for Open Borders" (1987) 49 *Review of Politics* 251; Thomas Pogge, "An Egalitarian Law of Peoples" (1994) 23 *Philosophy and Public Affairs* 195; Andrew Kuper, "Rawlsian Global Justice: Beyond the Law of Peoples to a Cosmopolitan Law of Persons" (2000) 28 *Political Theory* 640.

[5] Seyla Benhabib, *The Rights of Others: Aliens, Residents, and Citizens* (Cambridge University Press 2004).

[6] Christian Joerges and Jurgen Neyer, "From Intergovernmental Bargaining to Deliberative Political Processes: The Constitutionalisation of Comitology" (1997) 3 *ELJ* 273, 294.

[7] Miguel Poiares Maduro, "Sovereignty in Europe: The European Court of Justice and the Creation of a European Political Community" in Mary L Volcansek and John F Stack Jr. (eds), *Courts Crossing Borders: Blurring the Lines of Sovereignty* (Carolina Academic Press 2005) 57.

Furthermore, having initially been designed to "[ensure] that competition in the common market is not distorted"[8] by protectionist measures, the EU's non-discrimination norms have been extended deep into the domain of social policy. Most notably, the original prohibition against wage discrimination on the basis of sex, articulated in article 119 of the Treaty of Rome, catalyzed a pioneering supranational mandate to combat sex discrimination, which far outpaced most domestic labor laws during the 1970s and 1980s in terms of its progressive quality. On the heels of this early success, the non-discrimination principle has guided extensive supranational legislation adopted to combat disadvantages arising from personal attributes other than nationality and sex, including racial or ethnic origin, religion and belief, disability, age, and sexual orientation. Although the EU generally lacks the power to review member state acts for conformity with human rights norms in purely domestic matters, it nevertheless has the power to "take appropriate action" to combat discriminatory treatment, particularly when such treatment occurs in market-relevant domains of member state policy including employment, education, and social protection.[9] Since the Treaty of Amsterdam, new treaty provisions and attendant legislation have brought a wider constituency of member state citizens under the protection of EU law, making it relevant even to those who have not exercised mobility rights.[10] To use a distinction developed in the last chapter, these provisions pad the civil, if not the civic, content of EU citizenship. As a result, the principle of equal treatment is applicable in nearly every substantive area of EU action, "whether it be taxation, maternity rights, or production quotas for ferrous scrap."[11] The evolution of the non-discrimination principle into a constitutional mandate for equal protection strengthens the EU's claim to reproduce conventional constitutional protections in a postnational context, and expands its teleological scope beyond economic union.

This chapter assesses the evolution of the market-based non-discrimination principle into a constitutional framework for equal treatment that cuts across much of EU and member state law. My aim is not to give a comprehensive account of the complex developments in EU anti-discrimination law, but to use it as a lens through which to observe and evaluate the transformation

[8] Art 3(g) EC. As amended by the Lisbon Treaty, the relevant passage in art 3(b) TFEU reads: "the establishing of the competition rules necessary for the functioning of the internal market" art 3(b) TFEU.

[9] Ex-art 13 TEC, art 19 TFEU.

[10] Mark Bell, *Anti-Discrimination Law and the European Union* (Oxford University Press 2002) 13.

[11] Gillian More, "The Principle of Equal Treatment: From Market Unifier to Fundamental Right?" in Paul Craig and Gráinne de Búrca (eds), *The Evolution of EU Law* (Oxford University Press 1999) 517.

of the EU's system of functional constitutionalism. I will argue that although the EU's non-discrimination regime represents an ambitious attempt to re-establish core constitutional protections in a postnational setting, prohibiting discrimination does not necessarily engender universal inclusion or equal treatment. Nor does it make for a particularly assertive or comprehensive framework of social policy. First, the non-discrimination principle does not amount to a universalistic framework of equality before the law, since third country nationals (TCNs) are excluded from its scope in many respects. A cosmopolitan interpretation of it is therefore misplaced. More interestingly still, protecting mobile EU citizens from discrimination has occasioned *internal* lines of exclusion by allowing member states to treat their own citizens less favorably than the citizens of other member states. Finally, equality and inclusion often demand more than the mere cessation of discrimination, not least the elimination of structural disadvantages, the affirmation of difference, and the elevation of the baseline for social protection and civic engagement. By extrapolating market-based rules against discriminatory treatment to govern other, more complex human relations, the EU has opted for a weak, voluntarist, and negative norm of equality over richer conceptions of social inclusion that might include reciprocity, stronger social assistance, and fair equality of opportunity.

(I) COMMERCIAL MOBILITY: EQUAL TREATMENT OR MARKET ACCESS?

In Chapter 3, I argued that "fundamental freedoms" of commercial mobility, rather than fundamental rights in the conventional sense, occupy the EU's constitutional core. In theory as well as in practice, however, an integrated market requires mobility rights to be complemented by a commitment on the part of member states to extend domestic standards of treatment to one another's workers, producers, investors, and service providers. In view of its guiding aim of eliminating protectionism, "the entire EC Treaty" can be read as "simply the principle of equal treatment for nationals 'writ large'."[12] This is borne out by the belt-and-suspenders approach espoused by the Treaty on the Functioning of the European Union (TFEU), which not only couples each free movement provision with a national treatment requirement, but also articulates a general prohibition on nationality-based discrimination.[13] The comprehensive reach of the non-discrimination principle and its strict application by the Court of Justice of the European Union (CJEU) have played a

[12] Advocate General Francis Jacobs relates this statement (whose source is not indicated) but suggests it is exaggerated. See FG Jacobs, "Introduction" in Elspeth Guild (ed.), *The Legal Framework and Social Consequences of Free Movement of Persons in the European Union* (Kluwer Law International 1998) 3.

[13] Art 18 TFEU (ex-art 12 TEC) (ex-art 7 of the Treaty of Rome).

stabilizing role particularly in view of the EU's spasmodic constitutional development.[14] Former Advocate General Francis Jacobs has argued that even though article 18 TFEU prohibits discrimination on the basis of nationality only within the scope of application of the treaty:

> a case could be made for saying that virtually all activities of the State are subject to the prohibition of discrimination; in other words, that different treatment of the State's nationals and of nationals of other Member States is *always* unlawful unless it can be objectively justified.[15]

In short, the principle of non-discrimination on the basis of nationality is the golden rule of European integration.

Like the golden rule, however, it leaves considerable room for interpretation. The CJEU has treated non-discrimination as "one of the fundamental legal provisions of the Community," and has cited its importance for the uniformity and effectiveness of EU law in narrowly tailoring permissible exceptions to it.[16] In addition to disallowing directly discriminatory national measures, the Court has targeted indirect discrimination generated by domestic measures that are applicable regardless of nationality, but have the effect of disadvantaging goods, services, or workers from other member states.

Although the non-discrimination principle is essential to market integration, it is to some degree also compatible with the social embedding of the market. In other words, while it advances market *integration*, it does not necessarily imply *deregulation*. To appreciate this point, compare the principle of non-discrimination with an alternative interpretation of the treaty's commitment to commercial mobility as requiring unhindered market access.[17] According to the Court's famous *Dassonville* decision, "All trading rules enacted by member states, which are capable of hindering, directly or indirectly, actually or potentially, intra-Community trade are to be considered as measures having an effect equivalent to quantitative restrictions,"[18] which are illegal under the treaty. The so-called "*Dassonville* formula" is remarkably broad in

[14] More, "The Principle of Equal Treatment" 522.

[15] Jacobs, "Introduction" 4, emphasis original.

[16] In *Even*, the Court held that it was not discriminatory for Belgium to deny an early retirement pension adjustment to Belgians who had rendered military service in World War II to migrant workers who did not have a record of wartime service to Belgium. The plaintiff in this case, Mr. Even, had served in the war as a French national. Case 207/78 *Ministère Public contre Gilbert Even et Office National des Pensions pour Travailleurs Salariés* [1979] ECR 2019.

[17] Niamh Nic Shuibhne, *The Coherence of EU Free Movement Law: Constitutional Responsibility and the Court of Justice* (Oxford University Press 2013) 235; Catherine Barnard, *The Substantive Law of the EU. The Four Freedoms* (3rd edn, Oxford University Press 2010) 259–61.

[18] Case 8/74 *Procureur du Roi v Benoît and Gustave Dassonville* [1974] ECR 837. For more recent reaffirmations of this doctrine, see Case C-405/98 *Konsumentombudsmannen v Gourmet International Products AB (GIP)* [2001] I-01795, para 38; Case C-110/05 *Commission v Italy* [2009] I-00519, para 37.

many respects; in particular, it implies that a national measure does not have to be shown to hinder intra-EU mobility to be considered incompatible with EU law—the mere *risk* of hindrance is enough. It has been enormously consequential in targeting and eliminating member state measures that could be shown, however tenuously, to chill cross-border economic activity, and has been extended to other mobility provisions including those relating to persons, services, establishment, and capital.[19]

As Catherine Barnard and Niamh Nic Shuibhne have respectively shown, EU law oscillates between these two alternative conceptions of what market integration requires.[20] On the first, non-discrimination-based approach, economic union entails extending domestic standards of treatment to cross-border commercial actors in order to establish a market "without internal frontiers in which the free movement of goods, persons, services and capital is ensured."[21] The domestic measures in question may be demanding in terms of standards so long as those demands do not disproportionately burden market actors from other member states. By itself, therefore, this approach is less invasive towards market-correcting measures employed by member states. On the second interpretation, by contrast, the relevant consideration for determining the compatibility of a member state measure with the EU's commercial mobility provisions is whether it is likely to hinder market activity full stop. This way of understanding the aims of economic union, implicit in the *Dassonville* formula, casts a far broader net that can "effectively snare *any* national rule as a possible restriction of free movement rights."[22] Even measures that are indistinctly applicable to domestic and foreign actors are suspect "if they affect access to the market of the State, also expressed as hindering or impeding or being liable to prohibit or otherwise inhibit freedom of movement."[23] This leaves member states having to "account under EU law for more national regulatory choices than they might have anticipated."[24] Under the market access approach, the EU aims not simply at market *integration* but also market *liberalization*: the commercial mobility regime is a battering ram with which to demolish state

[19] For a list of examples in each area of mobility, see Nic Shuibhne, *The Coherence of EU Free Movement Law* 210–11.

[20] ibid ch 7; Catherine Barnard, *The Substantive Law of the EU. The Four Freedoms* (2nd edn, Oxford University Press 2007) 250; Eleanor Spaventa, "From *Gebhard* to *Carpenter*. Towards a (Non-) Economic European Constitution" (2004) 41 *CMLR* 743, 745–47; Eleanor Spaventa, "Leaving *Keck* Behind? The Free Movement of Goods after the Rulings in *Commission v Italy* and *Mickelsson and Roos*" (2009) 34 *European Law Review* 914.

[21] Art 26 (2) TFEU.

[22] Nic Shuibhne, *The Coherence of EU Free Movement Law* 212. Emphasis original.

[23] ibid 235.

[24] ibid 230.

interference with economic activity, whether or not the measures in question are protectionist in intent or effect.

The choice between these alternatives has generated a heated debate among scholars and institutional actors.[25] In a widely cited 1993 opinion to the European Court of Justice (ECJ), Advocate General Tesauro warned against the market access approach, arguing that the EC Treaty aimed "to ensure the free movement of goods in order to establish a single integrated market, eliminating therefore those national measures which in any way create an obstacle to or even mere difficulties for the movement of goods."[26] Its purpose was not, he maintained, "to strike down the most widely differing measures in order, essentially, to ensure the greatest possible expansion of trade."[27] To interpret it otherwise would be tantamount to "invoking nothing more or less than the *right to the unhindered pursuit of ... commercial activity*,"[28] which would be an ideological use of the treaty provisions on commercial mobility. By contrast, Advocate General Jacobs has interpreted commercial mobility as requiring that "all undertakings should have unfettered access to the whole of the Community market."[29] National rules that inhibit the volume of trade are prima facie suspect, he maintained, even if they do not disproportionately burden imported products relative to domestic equivalents.[30] According to Jacobs, "from the point of view of the Treaty's concern to establish a single market, discrimination is not a helpful criterion ... the fact that a Member State imposes similar restrictions on the marketing of domestic goods is simply irrelevant."[31] Instead, what counts is whether there is a "substantial restriction" on "unfettered access to the whole of the Community market."[32] Clearly, the interpretation proposed by Jacobs has far greater deregulatory implications than the principle of non-discrimination enshrined in the treaties, which allows member states to regulate the market as long as foreign and domestic producers are similarly affected. In a pointed opinion, AG Tizzano rejected the market access approach for "bending the Treaty to a purpose for which it was not intended: that is to say, not in order to create an internal market in which conditions are similar to those of a single market and where operators can move freely, but in order to establish a market without rules."[33] Finally, AG Maduro contended in a later case

[25] Spaventa, "Leaving *Keck* Behind?"

[26] Case C-292/92 *Hünermund v Landesapothekerkammer Baden Württemberg* [1993] ECR I-6802, Opinion of AG Tesauro, para 28.

[27] ibid, para 28. [28] ibid, para 27, emphasis original.

[29] Case C-412-93 *Leclerc-Siplec v TF1 Publicité and M6 Publicité* [1997] ECR I-182, Opinion of AG Jacobs, para 42.

[30] ibid paras 39–40. [31] ibid para 40. [32] ibid para 42.

[33] Case C-442/02 *Caixa Bank France v Ministère de l'Economie, del Finances et de l'Industrie* [2004] ECR I-8963, Opinion of AG Tizzano, paras 58 and 63, respectively.

that while commercial mobility provisions "aim to guarantee the opening-up of national markets, offering producers and consumers the possibility of fully enjoying the benefits of a Community internal market," they are not intended "to encourage a general deregulation of national economies" or to create "an absolute right to economic or commercial freedom."[34]

This long-standing controversy evinces the sharp contrast between the underlying principles that guide each interpretation. Although their original rationale has to do with market integration, non-discrimination rules concretize a general commitment to equal treatment by the law. By contrast, the market access approach seeks to carve out special consideration and protection for market actors and helps them escape regulation. These competing interpretations reveal an unexpected tension between non-discrimination and commercial mobility, two bedrock principles of market integration that are often thought to be consonant: if commercial mobility is interpreted as requiring unhindered market access, it discriminates in favor of market actors and against other public interests and erodes rules that cushion the externalities of the market. By contrast, the non-discrimination approach is compatible with a wider range of public policy objectives since it impugns only those rules that disproportionately disadvantage cross-border commerce. This broad normative scope is evidenced by the fact that EU non-discrimination rules have not only been used to dismantle disadvantage resulting from national origin, but have also been extended to counter disadvantage resulting from sex, sexual orientation, race, ethnic or religious identity, age, and disability. Although this model of social inclusion leaves much to be desired, as I will argue in the last section, the non-discrimination principle is compatible with, and goes some way towards, the social embedding of the market.[35]

(II) PERSONAL MOBILITY: NON-DISCRIMINATION AS A CITIZENSHIP RIGHT

The social dimension of the non-discrimination principle is clearly in evidence in the area of personal mobility.[36] Freedom from discrimination on grounds of nationality has been described as "the most fundamental

[34] Joined Cases 158/04 and 159/04 *Alfa Vita Vassilopoulos AE and Carrefour Marinopoulos AE v Elliniko Dimosio and Nomarchiaki Aftodioikisi Ioanninon* [2006] ECR I-8137, Opinion of AG Poiares Maduro, para 37.

[35] The dynamics of the social embedding and disembedding of the market are theorized in Karl Polanyi, *The Great Transformation. The Political and Economic Origins of our Time* (first published 1944, Beacon Press 2001). For a masterful commentary, see Fred Block and Margaret R Somers, "Beyond the Economistic Fallacy. The Holistic Social Science of Karl Polanyi" in Theda Skocpol (ed), *Vision and Method in Historical Sociology* (Cambridge University Press 1984). For an application of this dynamic to the EU context, see James A Caporaso and Sidney Tarrow, "Polanyi in Brussels: Supranational Institutions and the Transnational Embedding of Markets" (1993) 63 *International Organization* 593.

[36] Caporaso and Tarrow, "Polanyi in Brussels" 608-11.

right conferred by the Treaty and [one that] must be seen as a basic ingredient of Union citizenship."[37] The Court has interpreted the non-discrimination principle in the broad terms in order to protect EU citizens against disadvantages and burdens that they may experience as a consequence of mobility associated with work, study, tourism, or family relations, whether in the host state or in their member state of origin.[38] In the Court's jurisprudence, treaty prohibitions against discrimination extend to member state policies that are likely to disadvantage nationals of another member state even if they are applicable regardless of nationality.[39] Insofar as it entitles EU citizens to a wide range of rights in states other than their own, it amounts to a quintessential "right to have rights":[40] mobile Europeans may claim moral consideration and legal protection in their host states as a matter of right rather than charity, a rare accomplishment in a world where legal protection is still strongly attached to political membership.[41]

As I discussed at greater length in the previous chapter, the Court of Justice has interpreted the principle of non-discrimination, in conjunction with the citizenship provisions of the treaty, as requiring host states to extend their social assistance schemes to residents from other member

[37] Case C-274/96 *Bickel and Franz* [1998] ECR I-7650, Opinion of AG Jacobs, para 24.

[38] Bell, *Anti-Discrimination Law and the European Union* 33–40. EU law allows certain tightly patrolled exceptions to the non-discrimination principle, such as public sector employment and certain national benefits. For instance, in its *Even* decision, the ECJ allowed Belgium to restrict a military benefit granted to veterans of World War II to Belgian citizens and to exclude veterans from other member states who happened to reside in Belgium. Case 207/78 *Ministère Public contre Gilbert Even et Office National des Pensions pour Travailleurs Salariés* [1979] ECR 2019, paras 23–5.

[39] In a typical indirect discrimination case (Case C-278/94 *Commission v Belgium* [1996] ECR I-04307) the court held: "a provision of national law must be regarded as indirectly discriminatory if it is intrinsically liable to affect migrant workers more than national workers and if there is a consequent risk that it will place the former at a particular disadvantage. *It is not necessary to find that the provision in question does in practice affect a substantially higher proportion of migrant workers. It is sufficient that it is liable to have such an effect*" (para 20, emphasis added). Also see Case 237/94 *John O'Flynn v Adjudication Officer* [1996] ECR I-02617, para 20: "unless objectively justified and proportionate to its aim, a provision of national law must be regarded as indirectly discriminatory if it is intrinsically liable to affect migrant workers more than national workers and if there is a consequent risk that it will place the former at a particular disadvantage."

[40] Hannah Arendt, *The Origins of Totalitarianism* (first published 1951, Harcourt Inc 1967) 296, 298. Arendt writes that the stripping of a default "right to belong to some kind of organized community" not only brings about a "fundamental situation of rightlessness" but also amounts to a "deprivation of a place in the world" (296). For expositions of Arendt's enigmatic argument regarding membership, see Benhabib, *The Rights of Others*; cf Margaret Somers, *Genealogies of Citizenship. Markets, Statelessness, and the Right to Have Rights* (Cambridge University Press 2008). In the EU context, see Richard Bellamy, "The "Right to Have Rights": Citizenship Practice and the Political Constitution of the EU" in Richard Bellamy and Alex Warleigh (eds), *Citizenship and Governance in the European Union* (Continuum 2001).

[41] Frank I Michelman, "Parsing a Right to Have Rights" (1996) 3 *Constellations* 200, 205.

states.[42] Emblematically, in its *Martinez Sala* decision, the Court held that an EU citizen who became unemployed while exercising her right to free movement in another member state was entitled to childcare benefits on the same basis as nationals of the host state.[43] In *Grzelczyk*, it decided that the Belgian authorities had discriminated against a French national by denying him a minimum welfare allowance.[44] Anticipating objections that an extension of welfare benefits would expand the pool of recipients without expanding that of contributors, the Court argued that "a certain degree of financial solidarity" exists in the member states, which obligated them to extend certain social assistance schemes to Union citizens.[45]

The right of non-discrimination is also at the core of EU citizenship, which has been fashioned essentially as a right to equal treatment on the basis of nationality rather than as a freestanding supranational civic platform. Although EU citizenship is often treated as a democratizing innovation, it does little to empower member state citizens as *supranational* political agents. Article 20(2)(b) TFEU gives EU citizens "the right to vote and to stand as candidates in elections to the European Parliament and in municipal elections in their Member State of residence, *under the same conditions as nationals of that State*."[46] Member states get to decide how capacious electoral participation will be, as long as it is made available on the same terms to resident EU citizens.[47] The 1993 Directive that codifies the electoral rights associated with EU citizenship affirms this interpretation by describing these rights as "an instance of the application of the principle of non-discrimination between nationals and non-nationals."[48]

Although it entails a remarkable attempt to mitigate the national limits of political participation, the non-discrimination approach to EU citizenship

[42] Art 45(3) (ex-art 39 TEC) of TFEU makes the free movement of workers "subject to limitations justified on grounds of public policy, public security or public health," and 45(4) enables member states to limit access to employment in the public sector. The Court has construed these derogations narrowly, requiring that the member state's response (e.g. deportation, refusal of admission) be proportionate to the public policy end being pursued, and that its response respect the fundamental rights of the migrant. Second, free movement rights are subject to the migrant not becoming an "unreasonable burden" on the host member state, which means that member states may require non-economically active migrants to have adequate sickness insurance and financial resources. See arts 7(1)(b) and 8(4) of Directive 2004/38 respectively. For a detailed analysis, see Barnard, *Substantive Law of the EU*, ch 16.

[43] Case C-85/96 *Martinez Sala v Freistaat Bayern* [1998] ECR I-2691.

[44] Case C-184/99 *Rudy Grzelczyk v Centre Public d'Aide Sociale d'Ottignies-Louvain-la-Neuve* [2001] ECR I-6193.

[45] ibid para 44.

[46] Emphasis added. Also art 22(1) and (2) TFEU.

[47] Case C-300/04 *MG Eman and OB Sevinger v College van Burgemeester en Wethouders van Den Haag* [2006] ECR I-8060, para 45.

[48] Council Directive 93/109/EC of 6 December 1993 laying down detailed arrangements for the exercise of the right to vote and stand as a candidate in elections to the European Parliament for citizens of the Union residing in a Member State of which they are not nationals [1993] OJ L329.

is thin on civic substance. It leaves national citizenship rights untouched, regardless of how well or poorly they approximate principles of civic inclusion. Lacking so much as a basic guarantee of the right to vote, EU citizenship offers little recourse against member states with restrictive voting regimes. For instance, UK law prevents British citizens residing abroad from voting in European Parliament elections in the UK unless they have been registered at a UK address some time in the past fifteen years. More drastically, Cypriot citizens who have stayed outside Cyprus for longer than six months leading up to an election are disenfranchized in Cypriot elections.[49] EU law entitles mobile EU citizens to whatever restrictive or inclusive principles happen to govern the civic relationship between each member state and its citizens. Arguably, however, the location of this baseline matters as much as its equal application: being derivative of national conditions of citizenship, EU citizenship provides few legal or political resources that could help raise the all-important domestic threshold of democratic inclusion.[50] In sum, by extrapolating market-based rules against discriminatory treatment to govern other, more complex and capacious human relations, such as citizenship, the EU has opted for a negative norm of equality over a more generous conception that would enhance democracy and civic solidarity within and among member states.

Framed as a right of non-discrimination, moreover, EU citizenship offers little to citizens who have not exercised their mobility rights. By contrast, if it were framed as a freestanding set of supranational entitlements rather than as a reciprocal commitment by member states to extend national treatment to one another's citizens, it would benefit *all* citizens rather than simply those who reside in another state. For instance, a supranational right to participate in the political process could be marshaled by citizens to contest a broader range of domestic failures of democratic representation, accountability, or social inclusion, and might encourage member states to level up their democratic credentials. This would be a far more meaningful way to expand the horizons of democracy beyond the nation-state than transplanting the market-based principle of non-discrimination into the civic sphere.

[49] In January 2014, the Commission urged member states to discontinue practices that disenfranchize their own citizens when they exercise their rights of intra-EU mobility. It pointed out that Union citizenship "is additional to national citizenship and is designed to give additional rights to EU citizens, whereas in this case the exercise of the right of free movement may lead to losing a right of political participation." It singled out Denmark, Ireland, Cyprus, Malta, and the UK as imposing the strictest restrictions on the right to vote for nationals residing abroad. See European Commission, *Communication addressing the consequences of the disenfranchisement of Union citizens exercising their right to free movement* COM/2014/033 final.

[50] Dimitry Kochenov, "*Ius Tractum* of Many Faces: European Citizenship and the Difficult Relationship Between Status and Rights" 2008–9 15 *Columbia Journal of European Law* 169.

(III) THE DISCRIMINATORY EFFECTS OF THE NON-DISCRIMINATION PRINCIPLE

The close association between the principle of non-discrimination and the status of EU citizenship should be enough to dispel the misguided claim that this principle gives the EU a cosmopolitan character. As a political and legal project, contemporary cosmopolitanism aspires to overcome the moral and legal salience of political membership in determining a person's chances of accessing the basic social and institutional conditions necessary for human flourishing. While it is remarkable that nation-states riven by what Robert Schuman called "sanguinary divisions" have accepted wide-ranging commitments to non-discrimination on the basis of nationality,[51] the EU's legal system nonetheless draws fresh lines of distinction between members and non-members. Although recent supranational legislation has created important protections for third country nationals,[52] the right to equal treatment on the basis of nationality is reserved for EU citizens and does not extend in the same manner to those who lack a member state passport.[53] Paradoxically, the prohibition on discrimination based on citizenship has been configured to discriminate based on citizenship.

This is hardly surprising, since the right to equal treatment on the basis of nationality is a product of the exclusive bonds of reciprocity established between EU member states by the treaties, not duties that member states have assumed towards all of humanity. In other words, it is a "club good" made available to members and denied to outsiders rather than a universal entitlement. For this reason, the supranational prohibition on nationality-based discrimination lacks the universal scope that cosmopolitan inclusion demands, and instead delineates a supranational juridical space that preserves the salience of political membership.

But perhaps it is unfair to expect the EU, an entity of geographically delimited scope, to approximate a standard of inclusion that could only be

[51] Robert Schuman, *Declaration of May 9th 1950*. Available at http://www.cvce.eu/obj/the_schuman_declaration_paris_9_may_1950-en-9cc6ac38-32f5-4c0a-a337- 9a8ae4d5740f.html accessed March 17, 2016.

[52] For a list of the relevant legislation, see Chapter 5. Most notably, Directive 109 entitles third country nationals to "long-term resident" status in every member state after a period of lawful residence of five years, provided that they can show a stable income and sickness insurance. The status of long-term residency entitles third country nationals (TCNs) to be treated on the same basis as nationals of the member state as regards access to employment, minimum social assistance schemes, vocational training, tax benefits, as well as in regard to freedom of association and the recognition of professional qualifications. However, the Directive grants only limited rights of intra-Community free movement to TCNs. See Council Directive concerning the status of third-country nationals who are long-term residents, 2003/109/EC, 25 November 2003.

[53] In *Awoyemi*, the Court refused to allow a TCN to avail himself of a courtesy accorded to member state nationals (in this case, the right to use a driver's license issued by another member state beyond a certain period of residence in the host state). See Case C-230/97 *Ibinka Awoyemi* [1998] ECR I-6795. On the exclusion of TCNs from treaty rules on non-discrimination, see Kochenov, "*Ius Tractum* of Many Faces" 207–9.

met by a global polity. Perhaps it is fairer to regard it instead as a postnational order that governs a particular region of the world in line with cosmopolitan principles. Even setting aside the unequal status of TCNs, however, the EU does not create a cosmopolitan constitutional space cleared of all nationality-based distinctions and disadvantages. In certain instances, known as "purely internal situations," the application of the non-discrimination principle paradoxically hinders equal treatment between mobile and non-mobile EU citizens. The dispute over the so-called German beer purity laws is a famous case in point. In the mid-1980s, the *Reinheitsgebot* subjecting all beer sold in Germany to strict product requirements was challenged by the European Commission as hindering access into the German market by beer producers from other member states.[54] The Court of Justice forbade Germany from imposing these restrictions on imported beer, but left it up to the German authorities to decide whether or not to continue imposing them on *domestic* producers, thereby exposing the latter to competitive disadvantage.[55]

In such instances of "reverse discrimination," the citizens of the member state imposing the rules may not avail themselves of protections granted to other EU citizens under EU law since their situation is considered "purely internal."[56] Such disparate treatment may be justified with reference to regulatory imperatives in the sphere of market activity, but it is more troubling in cases concerning personal mobility. In the *Morson and Jhanjan* case, two plaintiffs of Dutch nationality invoked EU rules on family reunification to obtain a right of residence for their Surinamese parents.[57] However, the Court of Justice held that because the plaintiffs had never lived or worked in another member state, their situation fell exclusively in the member state's jurisdiction. Consequently, they could not avail themselves of EU rights to family reunification. If the plaintiffs had been residents of the Netherlands holding the nationality of any other member state (or Dutch nationals resident in any member state other than the Netherlands), they would have been entitled to the EU's family reunification rights on account of protections accorded to mobile EU citizens.[58]

[54] Case 178/84 *Commission v Germany* [1987] ECR 1227. [55] ibid para 63.

[56] The Court first used this logic in Case 86/78 *SA des Grandes Distilleries Peureux v Directeur des Services Fiscaux de la Haute-Saône et du Territoire de Belfort* [1979] ECR 897; and systematized it in Case 179/78 *R v Saunders* [1979] ECR 1129.

[57] Joined Cases 35 and 36/82 *Morson and Jhanjan v State of the Netherlands* [1982] ECR 3723. In para 16, the Court held that "the Treaty provisions on freedom of movement for workers and the rules adopted to implement them [i.e., family reunification] cannot be applied to cases which have no factor linking them with any of the situations governed by Community law."

[58] In *Uecker and Jacquet*, the ECJ held that "citizenship of the Union, established by Article 8 of the EC Treaty, is not intended to extend the scope ratione materiae of the Treaty also to internal situations which have no link with Community law." Joined cases C-64/96 and C-65/96 *Land Nordrhein-Westfalen v Kari Uecker and Vera Jacquet v Land Nordrhein-Westfalen* [1997] ECR I-3171, para 23.

The *Morson and Jhanjan* case sparked a debate about whether EU law betrays the principle of equality before the law by permitting instances of reverse discrimination that leave domestic claimants at a disadvantage. According to some observers, the onus for doing away with reverse discrimination rests with the member states themselves, since it is they, rather than the EU, who govern the burdens imposed on their own citizens. On this view, EU law demands only that member states refrain from burdening cross-border economic actors. Others, by contrast, argue that disparate treatment such as that at issue in the *Morson and Jhanjan* case is orthogonal to equality, fairness, and the promise of EU citizenship.[59] On this view, reverse discrimination should be eliminated by reinterpreting EU citizenship as a bundle of freestanding entitlements that all member state nationals can claim regardless of mobility.[60] This interpretive move would make Union citizenship a "fundamental" status of all member state citizens,[61] and eliminate the favorable treatment of mobile EU citizens relative to non-mobile ones.[62] In fact, the Court of Justice took a step in this direction in its *Ruiz Zambrano* decision, where it allowed a Colombian

[59] Alina Tryfonidou, "Reverse Discrimination in Purely Internal Situations: An Incongruity in a Citizens' Europe" (2008) 35 *Legal Issues of Economic Integration* 43; Niamh Nic Shuibhne, "Free Movement of Persons and the Wholly Internal Rule: Time to Move on?" (2002) 39 *CMLR* 731; Kochenov, "*Ius Tractum* of Many Faces" 213.

[60] Jacqueline Bhabha, "Enforcing the Human Rights of Citizens and Non-Citizens in the Era of Maastricht" in Birgit Meyer and Peter Geschiere (eds), *Globalization and Identity* (Blackwell Publishing 1999) 110–12.

[61] In *Grzelczyk*, the Court prophesied that "Union citizenship is destined to be *the fundamental status* of nationals of the Member States, enabling those who find themselves in the same situation to enjoy the same treatment in law irrespective of their nationality." (para 31, emphasis added. Also see Case C-413/99 *Baumbast and R v Secretary of State for the Home Department*, para 82; Case C-148/02 *Garcia Avello v Etat Belge* [2003] ECR I-11635, para 22; Case C-200/02 *Zhu and Chen v Secretary of State for the Home Department* [2004] ECR I-9925, para 25). This statement invokes the Court's favorite cipher, "fundamental," whose ambivalent meaning within the discursive universe of EU law was discussed at length in Chapter 3. What does it mean for Union citizenship to be "destined to be the *fundamental* status of nationals of the Member States"? To further complicate matters, the ECJ's later decisions express this formulation in slightly modified terms: "citizenship of the Union is *intended* to be the fundamental status of nationals of the Member States." (See Case C-291/05 *Minister voor Vreemdelingenzaken en Integratie v RNG Eind* [2007] ECR I-10719, para 32; Case C-185/08 *Janko Rottmann v Freistaat Bayern* [2010] ECR I-1449, para 43; Case C-34/09 *Ruiz Zambrano v Office National de l'Emploi* [2011] ECR I-01177, para 41). This later iteration shifts the meaning of the statement from a *predictive* claim to an argument about the *original intent* behind the status of Union citizenship. Either way, it seems to impart an as-yet unrealized, aspirational quality to Union citizenship. Furthermore, since art 9 TEU clearly states that "Union citizenship shall be additional to and not replace national citizenship," EU citizenship cannot become *the* fundamental status of member state nationals, but only *one* of several "fundamental" statuses of membership. In light of art 9 TEU, the most plausible interpretation of this statement is that the Court would like Union citizenship to become a fundamental status rather than one whose benefits are *contingent* on mobility and market participation. As noted in the main text (as well as in Chapter 5), although the *Ruiz Zambrano* decision came closest to such an interpretation of EU citizenship, other recent decisions have preserved the mobility nexus.

[62] Tryfonidou, "Reverse Discrimination in Purely Internal Situations" 46.

couple to rely on the Union citizenship rights of their young, Belgian-born children to obtain a right to reside and work in Belgium, even though the family had never exercised intra-EU mobility.[63] The Court did not, however, continue this generous line of interpretation in subsequent decisions.[64]

Fairness and equal treatment are not the only normative issues raised by situations where member states place their own citizens under greater burdens than those of other EU states. Also at stake are equally important questions regarding the allocation of constitutional authority between the EU and its member states. The distinction between purely internal situations and those that fall within the scope of EU law is a consequence of the pluralistic constitutional accommodation between the EU's functionally delineated sphere of competence and the constitutional autonomy retained by member states.[65] Any attempt to eliminate reverse discrimination is likely to destabilize this delicate accommodation. Furthermore, eradicating purely internal situations might have further deregulatory effects, since it might enable all member state citizens—as opposed to only those who have exercised their mobility rights—to marshal EU law against any national measure that adversely affects commercial activity. Under this scenario, national regulatory autonomy is likely to shrink further under the unforgiving gaze of the Court of Justice.[66] For these reasons, even though the asymmetry of entitlements occasioned by the EU's non-discrimination and mobility rules militates against any strong principle of equal treatment, eliminating the asymmetry would upend the EU's composite constitutional structure.

In sum, the EU's principle of non-discrimination on the basis of nationality creates some discriminatory effects of its own, first with regard to third country nationals, and second with regard to EU citizens who have not exercised their mobility rights. Both instances show that this principle does not necessarily tend towards universal inclusion, but can instead exclude and further differentiate in ways that raise fairness considerations of their own. This is not to say that the differential treatment arising from the EU's functionally delimited scope of authority should be eliminated no matter the costs, but to emphasize the peculiar trade-offs occasioned by the EU's system of functional constitutionalism.

[63] Case C-34/09 *Ruiz Zambrano*.

[64] See especially, Case C-434/09 *Shirley McCarthy v Secretary of State for the Home Department* [2011] ECR I-03375, para 49; Case C-256/11 *Murat Dereci and Others v Bundesministerium für Inneres* [2011] ECR I-11315, para 66.

[65] Cyril Ritter, "Purely Internal Situations, Reverse Discrimination, *Guimont, Dzodzi* and Article 234" (2006) 31 *European Law Review* 690.

[66] ibid 701–2.

(IV) NON-DISCRIMINATION RULES BEYOND THE MARKET: EU LAW AND DEMOCRATIC INCLUSION

As I emphasized in Chapter 3, the EU lacks the mandate to ensure human rights compliance by its member states so long as their actions fall outside the substantive scope of the treaties. In turn, that scope largely follows the functional contours of Europe's economic union, understood as a policy space that includes a single market, monetary union, exhaustive fiscal coordination, and market regulation. However, the EU's expanding mandate to eliminate discrimination on the basis of sex, sexual orientation, racial and ethnic origin, religion, and age is an exception to its otherwise limited scope of its human rights competence.[67] Although this broader equal treatment framework follows the template originally developed to protect market actors from nationality-based discrimination, its scope and significance extends beyond the imperatives of the market. Starting in the 1970s, the EU has progressively taken on the task of fighting discriminatory laws and practices in member states and supranational institutions on grounds other than nationality. In 1976, the Court of Justice became the unlikely venue for women to contest discriminatory policies in the workplace.[68] Article 119 of the Treaty of Rome (art 157 TFEU) provided simply that men and women should receive equal pay for equal work.[69] The provision had been intended to discourage "social dumping."[70] France was particularly concerned that intra-Community competition would disadvantage French businesses bound by more demanding labor standards than their counterparts in other member states. Article 119 embodied a compromise response to France's demand for more comprehensive harmonization of domestic social regulations.[71]

Between 1970 and 1978, Gabrielle Defrenne, a flight attendant with the Belgian flag carrier Sabena, represented by the women's rights attorney Eliane Vogel-Polsky, challenged Sabena's practice of compensating male flight attendants more generously. This practice allowed male attendants to retire later and enjoy a more advantageous pension plan.[72] The parties agreed that male flight attendants did identical work to female colleagues. In its decision,

[67] Art 3 TEU; arts 10 and 19 TFEU.

[68] Stone Sweet, *Judicial Construction of Europe* ch 4; Rachel Cichowski, *The European Court and Civil Society: Litigation, Mobilization, and Governance* (Cambridge University Press 2007); Catherine Hoskyns, *Integrating Gender. Women, Law and Politics in the European Union* (Verso 1996).

[69] After the Amsterdam renumbering, ex-art 119 became art 141 TEC, and is now art 157 TFEU following the entry into force of the Lisbon Treaty in 2009. Since much of my discussion here is historical, I will refer to art 119 in the remainder of the chapter to avoid anachronism.

[70] Bell, *Anti-Discrimination Law and the European Union* 9–10.

[71] Evelyn Ellis and Philippa Watson, *EU Anti-Discrimination Law* (Oxford University Press, 2013) 23.

[72] Case 43/75 *Defrenne v SABENA (II)* [1976] ECR 455.

the Court gave article 119 a far-reaching and unanticipated interpretation. Although this provision had been intended as a policy objective to be achieved in the long run rather than as a subjective right that could be invoked by individuals against states falling behind on their equality legislation, the Court nevertheless chose the latter interpretation.[73] It argued that article 119 had a "double aim," the first of which related to eliminating "competitive disadvantage" that might punish member states with higher standards of equality between the sexes, but the second of which concerned "the social objectives of the Community" beyond its being "merely an economic union."[74] Two years later, the ECJ went further in response to Ms. Defrenne's continued efforts to recover compensation for the early termination of her service. It described "the elimination of discrimination based on sex" as among the "fundamental rights" protected by the Court.[75] Finally, it held that "the economic aim pursued by Article 119 of the Treaty, namely the elimination of distortions of competition between undertakings established in different Member States, is secondary to the social aim pursued by the same provision, which constitutes the expression of a fundamental human right."[76]

By construing article 119 as an individual right against discrimination, the Court created new possibilities for private litigants and lobbying groups to challenge domestic employment policies that disadvantaged women.[77] In a long line of subsequent decisions, the ECJ included not only remuneration but also other job-related entitlements including vocational training, sick leave, and pensions within the scope of the term "pay" as used in the treaty.[78] Although the Equal Pay Directive of 1975 aimed at the "elimination of all discrimination on grounds of sex with regard to all aspects and conditions of remuneration,"[79] the ECJ's decisions preempted much of its content.[80]

The most important constitutional implication of the early sex equality litigation was to make supranational law relevant in matters that were

[73] In doing so, the Court relaxed the criteria it had set earlier concerning which treaty provisions were capable of generating direct effects: In *Van Gend en Loos*, it had held that in order to create rights for individuals, a treaty provision had to be "clear," "unconditional," and had to create "a negative obligation" on the part of states without being dependent on implementing measures. In *Defrenne II*, the Court chose to give direct effect to the "principle" of equal pay for equal work contained in art 119 EC, which was rather a general, imprecise, and not necessarily "negative" obligation.

[74] Case 43/75 *Defrenne II*, paras 8–10.

[75] Case 149/77 *Defrenne v SABENA (III)* [1978] ECR 1365, at paras 26–27.

[76] Case C-50/96 *Deutsche Telekom v Schröder* [2000] ECR I-743, para 57.

[77] Cichowski, *The European Court and Civil Society*.

[78] Stone Sweet, *Judicial Construction of Europe* 150–7.

[79] Council Directive 75/117/EEC of 10 February 1975 on the approximation of the laws of the Member States relating to the application of the principle of equal pay for men and women [1975] OJ L45/19, art 1.

[80] Stone Sweet, *The Judicial Construction of Europe* 158–9.

otherwise purely domestic. The women (and sometimes men) who sued their employers or state authorities in equal pay cases were not, for the most part, cross-border economic actors. Rather, the original market justification of article 119 gave the ECJ the warrant it needed to pierce through member state autonomy in matters of employment regulation. In subsequent cases, the Court expanded article 119 to combat indirect discrimination in areas such as the conditions of part-time employment, since the vast majority of part-time workers tended to be women.[81] In cases related to pregnancy and maternity discrimination, it ruled that employment practices discriminating against pregnant women amounted to direct discrimination on the basis of sex,[82] thereby taking European law deep into the territory of social policy competences reserved to member states.[83]

During this period, secondary legislation further enriched the legal resources available to women and women's groups in challenging an ever-wider array of domestic discriminatory practices. The 1976 Equal Treatment Directive established a much broader mandate on combating sex discrimination, providing that:

> there shall be no discrimination whatsoever on grounds of sex in the conditions, including selection criteria, for access to all jobs or posts, whatever the sector or branch of activity, and to all levels of the occupational hierarchy.[84]

Because the two directives focused on conditions of employment and remuneration, the Council adopted the Social Security Directive to combat sex discrimination in the administration of state social security schemes.[85] Even though there was a lull in EC sex equality legislation during the 1980s, perhaps in keeping with the deregulatory policies of that decade,[86] the Council caught up in the 1990s by extending the principle of equal treatment to pregnancy and maternity,[87] part-time

[81] Case 170/84 *Bilka-Kaufhaus GmbH v Weber von Hartz* [1986] ECR 1607.

[82] Case 177/88 *Dekker* [1990] ECR I-3941; Case C-32/93 *Webb v EMO Air Cargo Ltd* [1994] ECR I-3567.

[83] Rachel Cichowski, "Women's Rights, the European Court, and Supranational Constitutionalism" (2004) 38 *Law & Society Review* 489, 507.

[84] Council Directive 76/207/EEC of 9 February 1976 on the implementation of the principle of equal treatment for men and women as regards access to employment, vocational training and promotion, and working conditions [1976] OJ L39/40, art 3.

[85] Council Directive 79/7/EEC of 19 December 1978 on the progressive implementation of the principle of equal treatment for men and women in matters of social security [1979] OJ L6/24.

[86] Chrystalla Ellina, *Promoting Women's Rights. The Politics of Gender in the European Union* (Routledge 2003) 44–5.

[87] The Pregnancy Directive is technically part of the Council's workplace health and safety mandate rather than sex equality. See Council Directive 92/85/EEC of 19 October 1992 on the introduction of measures to encourage improvements in the safety and health at work of pregnant workers and workers who have recently given birth or are breastfeeding [1992] OJ L348/8.

work, and occupational social security schemes.[88] The Amsterdam Treaty widened the scope of the equal pay provision to "ensure the application of the principle of equal opportunities and equal treatment of men and women in matters of employment and occupation,"[89] and thereby also upgraded the supranational objective to that of ensuring *equal treatment* rather than merely preventing discrimination.[90] Finally, article 8 TFEU obligates the EU in all of its activities to "aim to eliminate inequalities, and to promote equality, between men and women." According to some observers, this signals a change in the EU's focus in the area of sex equality to a proactive one of "mainstreaming," understood as "the systematic incorporation of gender issues throughout all governmental institutions and policies."[91]

The impact of private litigation under supranational law to advance women's equality in the workplace clearly parallels the enthusiastic use of supranational mobility rights by market citizens to compel member states to remove hindrances to cross-border economic activity, discussed in Chapter 4.[92] However, whereas the normative significance of the principle of equal treatment on the basis of nationality can be understood exclusively with reference to market integration, the EU's championship of sex equality has given the supranational legal system a clear social dimension. It is one of the few domains in which European integration has pushed member states to raise the standards of domestic legal protection they afford their own citizens. In addition to providing a new avenue of appeal against unfair employment and remuneration practices, supranational benchmarks pushed member states to be more aggressive on sex equality than most of them were prepared to be at the time. Rachel Cichowski has described this transformation as one by which "the text of an international treaty that was mainly concerned with protecting businesses from unfair competition [evolved] into an elaborate set of policy arenas and procedures that today govern women's rights throughout Europe."[93]

For groups looking for creative legal strategies in the fight for equality, the Rome Treaty's equal pay rule was a "foot-in-the-door" for a future, more expansive social policy mandate for the EU.[94] For instance, the Court's expansive interpretation of sex equality norms encouraged challenges against

[88] For a full review of this legislation, see Ellis and Watson *EU Anti-Discrimination Law* chs 5–7.

[89] Ex-art 141(3) TEC, now art 157(3) TFEU.

[90] Ellis and Watson, *EU Anti-Discrimination Law* 15.

[91] Mark A Pollack and Emilie Hafner-Burton, "Mainstreaming Gender in the European Union" (2000) 7 *Journal of European Public Policy* 432, 434.

[92] This parallel is systematically mapped by Stone Sweet, *Judicial Construction of Europe* chs 3–4.

[93] Cichowski, "Women's Rights, the European Court, and Supranational Constitutionalism."

[94] Evelyn Ellis, *EU Anti-Discrimination Law* (Oxford University Press 2005) 24.

discrimination based on sexual orientation. In *P v S*,[95] the Court was asked to consider a British employer's decision to dismiss an employee because of his plans to undergo gender reassignment. Applying the 1976 Equal Treatment Directive to P's case, the Court held that such a dismissal amounted to discrimination on the basis of sex, and reiterated its position that "the right not to be discriminated against on grounds of sex constitutes a fundamental human right."[96]

In the absence of explicit legislation, however, this effort to stretch sex equality legislation to protect individuals against discrimination on the basis of sexual orientation revealed its limits.[97] In its 1998 *Grant* decision, the Court of Justice justified its reticence to oppose member state laws refusing marriage benefits to same-sex couples by observing that:

> in the present state of the law within the Community, stable relationships between two persons of the same sex are not regarded as equivalent to marriages or stable relationships outside marriage between persons of opposite sex.[98]

The Court's refusal to consider stable, long-term same-sex and opposite-sex relationships as equivalent forms of partnership was disappointing to marriage equality advocates. Some critics argued that this was inconsistent with its courageous decision in *P v S*, while others blamed the narrow grounds of protection provided under EU law for LGBT individuals. Although the EU's equality mandate has since been extended, the *Grant* decision illustrates the limitations of using a non-discrimination paradigm rather than a substantive standard of equality before the law. In refusing to draw moral and legal equivalence between civil union and marriage as partnerships, the Court cited the "great diversity of laws and the absence of any general assimilation of marriage and other forms of statutory union" among the member states on this matter.[99] Without a substantive EU baseline requiring marriage equality (or equal benefits for non-marital unions among couples unable to marry), the non-discrimination principle offered some protection, but not full equality.[100]

[95] Case C-13/94 *P v S and Cornwall County Council* [1996] ECR I-2143.

[96] ibid.

[97] Paul Craig and Gráinne de Búrca, *EU Law. Text, Cases, and Materials* (4th edn, Oxford University Press 2007) 412.

[98] Case C-249/96 *Lisa Jacqueline Grant v South-West Trains Ltd.* [1998] ECR I-00621; also, Case T-263/97 *D v Council* [1999] ECR II-1.

[99] Case T-263/97 *D v Council* [1999] ECR II-1, paras 35–6, 50.

[100] The Court has since ruled that member states that refuse to allow same sex couples to marry must ensure that legal benefits of marriage are extended to civil partnerships between same-sex couples. Case C-267/12 *Frédéric Hay v Crédit Agricole Mutuel de Charente-Maritime et des Deux-Sèvres* ECLI:EU:C:2013:823. Also see the discussion of *Maruko* below.

Subsequent treaty amendments expanded the EU's equal treatment mandate by designating additional protected groups and establishing legislative competences. The Amsterdam Treaty required the EU to "combat discrimination based on sex, racial or ethnic origin, religion or belief, disability, age or sexual orientation" in its own activities.[101] In addition, the EU's Charter of Fundamental Rights has concretized the principle of equality before the law with explicit prohibitions on a variety of grounds of discrimination.[102] The Treaty on European Union lists non-discrimination among the Union's constitutional values and includes "combat[ing] social exclusion and discrimination" among its aims.[103] Finally, article 19 TFEU empowers the EU legislator to "take appropriate action to combat discrimination based on sex, racial or ethnic origin, religion or belief, disability, age or sexual orientation" within the limits of the powers conferred by the treaties.[104] Relative to the earlier prohibition on gender-based pay discrimination, article 19's relationship to market integration is even more tenuous.[105] That is to say, its normative force extends beyond what I have argued is the predominant functionalist logic of the EU's legal order, and deserves closer analysis for that reason.

The extension of the treaty mandate regarding equal treatment has been followed by a flurry of legislative activity and has energized civil society groups engaged in domestic contests for inclusion. The EU's gender equality legislation was revised in accordance with the more demanding standard of ensuring equal opportunities and equal treatment in employment, and policies of gender mainstreaming were put into place.[106] In 2000, the Council adopted a framework directive to secure equal treatment in employment and occupation, which protects individuals from discrimination on the grounds of religion or belief, disability, age, and sexual orientation,[107] and a separate directive devoted to eradicating discrimination on the basis of racial and ethnic origin in matters related to employment conditions, remuneration, education and vocational training, public goods and services such as housing, and social benefits such as healthcare.[108]

[101] Art 10 TFEU.

[102] Ch III, arts 20–6. As discussed in Chapter 3, however, rights enshrined in the Charter are not meant to give the EU an additional mandate to exercise human rights review over member states.

[103] Arts 2 and 3(3) TEU respectively.

[104] Ex-art 13 TEC, now art 19 TFEU.

[105] Bell, *Anti-Discrimination Law and the European Union* 121.

[106] Directive 2006/54/EC of the European Parliament and of the Council of 5 July 2006 on the implementation of the principle of equal opportunities and equal treatment of men and women in matters of employment and occupation ('Recast' Directive) [2006] OJ L204/23.

[107] Council Directive 2000/78/EC of 27 November 2000 establishing a general framework for equal treatment in employment and occupation [2000] OJ L303/16.

[108] Directive 2000/43 has been drafted so as to avoid extending the rights of third country nationals or altering member state policies on the admission and residence conditions of migrants. Thus this

These laws build on the EC's earlier, rather unlikely victories in championing sex equality.[109]

Taken together, the new article 19 mandate, the Charter's chapter on equality rights, and the new secondary legislation in the area of non-discrimination strengthen the EU's claim to offer constitutional protections to citizens outside of the market framework. The progressive momentum of supranational law is particularly clear in the area of LGBT equality. In the 2008 *Maruko* case,[110] the Court of Justice refrained from decreeing a blanket right of same sex couples to marry, but argued that member states needed to ensure that domestic laws on marriage and civil status conformed to supranational prohibitions against discrimination based on sexual orientation.[111] In practice, this means that although civil status and the benefits flowing from it are reserved areas of member state competence, civil unions short of marriage may be challenged under every condition enumerated in the Framework Directive, including employment conditions and pay. Just as women's rights activists leveraged supranational law to challenge gendered employment practices in the domestic context, the new norms create opportunities for litigants to chip away at heteronormative marriage regimes that many member states continue to uphold.

In other categories of discriminatory practice outlawed by the treaty and relevant directives, including race, ethnicity, religion, belief, and disability, the gaps, evasions, and ellipses are once again likely to be filled by the CJEU in a way that expands the scope of supranational law.[112] In a pioneering case relating to racial discrimination, a Belgian anti-racism NGO was allowed to sue a home contractor who had stated in the press that he could

directive "does not cover difference of treatment based on nationality and is without prejudice to provisions and conditions relating to the entry into and residence of third-country nationals and stateless persons on the territory of Member States, and to any treatment which arises from the legal status of the third-country nationals and stateless persons concerned." See Council Directive 2000/43/EC of 29 June 2000 implementing the principle of equal treatment between persons irrespective of racial or ethnic origin [2000] OJ L180/22, art 2. Some of these conditions are regulated by Directive 2003/109, discussed in Chapter 5.

[109] The 2000 Framework Directive is prefaced by references to the EU's achievements in this area. See Council Directive 2000/78, Preamble at Recital 2.

[110] Case C-267/06 *Tadao Maruko v Versorgungsanstalt der deutschen Bühnen* [2008] ECR I-1757.

[111] The Court of Justice held:

> "Admittedly, civil status and the benefits flowing therefrom are matters which fall within the competence of the Member States and Community law does not detract from that competence. However, it must be recalled that in the exercise of that competence the Member States must comply with Community law and, in particular, with the provisions relating to the principle of non-discrimination." *Maruko*, para 59.

[112] Andrea Eriksson, "European Court of Justice: Broadening the Scope of European Nondiscrimination Law" (2009) 7 *International Journal of Constitutional Law* 731.

not hire immigrant workers due to customers' reservations about allowing "Moroccans" into their homes. In its judgment, the ECJ found the public statement to be evidence of a directly discriminatory hiring practice even in the absence of an actual victim.[113] In the controversial *Mangold* decision, the Court enforced the prohibition against discrimination on the basis of age against Germany, even though the deadline for member state compliance with the relevant directive had not elapsed.[114] Germany's procedural objection was irrelevant, the Court held, because the prohibition on age discrimination concretized a general principle of equal treatment binding on member states regardless of implementing legislation.[115] Similarly, the plaintiff's complaint of age discrimination against her employer in the subsequent *Küçükdeveci* case should have been inadmissible, since the Court does not normally grant direct effect to directives in disputes between private parties.[116] To circumvent this difficulty, the Court recalled its *Mangold* decision and invoked article 21(1) of the EU Charter of Fundamental Rights prohibiting age discrimination, elevating the principle of non-discrimination to the rank of a constitutional norm that generates obligations on the part of private as well as public actors.[117] In sum, although article 19 was intended more as a framework for further legislative action at the EU level, these decisions have carved out "an independently applicable principle of equality" that originates in supranational law.[118]

What connection is there, if any, between the principle of non-discrimination on the basis of nationality and the new substantive grounds of discrimination covered under EU law? Some scholars refuse to treat the two areas of European law under the same rubric.[119] After all, the prohibition of nationality-based discrimination is the logical requirement of an internal market in goods, services, labor, and capital, whereas prohibiting discrimination on the basis of sex, race, or age is neither a uniquely supranational objective nor a strict logical requirement of economic union. In moving beyond nationality-based discrimination to target other forms

[113] The Court held that such statements were "clearly likely to strongly dissuade certain candidates from submitting their candidature and, accordingly, to hinder their access to the labour market." Case C-54/07 *Centrum voor Gelijkheid van Kansen en voor Racismebestrijding v Firma Feryn* [2008] ECR I-5187, para 25.

[114] Case C-144/04 *Werner Mangold v Rüdiger Helm* [2005] ECR I-9981.

[115] ibid para 75. The Court referred to equal treatment as a "general principle of EC law," invoking an amorphous category of highest-rung constitutional norms that originates in the Court's jurisprudence. The Court claims to derive "general principles of EU law" from the constitutional traditions of the member states as well as the international treaties to which they are signatories (most notably, the ECHR).

[116] Case C-555/07 *Seda Kücükdeveci v Swedex GmbH & Co. KG* [2010] ECR I-365.

[117] ibid para 51.

[118] More, "The Principle of Equal Treatment" 545.

[119] E.g. Ellis, *EU Anti-Discrimination Law*.

of discriminatory treatment, therefore, the EU has broadened the prohibition against protectionism into a constitutional principle of equality before the law. On the one hand, this suggests that the EU's legal order has in important respects advanced beyond functional constitutionalism. In this respect, the EU reproduces the standards of equality enshrined in domestic constitutions at the supranational level and remedies failures by member state institutions to live up to those standards. It also complements a wider, composite system of human rights protection that includes not only member state constitutions but also the European Convention on Human Rights (ECHR), including Protocol 12 prohibiting discrimination, the European Social Charter, and the Community Charter of the Fundamental Social Rights of Workers.[120]

On the other hand, despite having extended into the social domain, EU non-discrimination law still bears the imprint of the market liberalization logic that inspired it. For instance, the scope of the Framework Directive, which prohibits discrimination based on religion or belief, disability, age, or sexual orientation is limited to employment and occupation. Discriminatory practices by member states that fall outside the domain of employment and occupation, such as bans on wearing religious dress in public, may not be remedied by EU law. Although the race directive has been framed relatively more broadly to apply in the domains of social protection, education, and public goods provision in addition to employment and occupation, it may still exclude some egregious forms of racial or ethnic discrimination.[121]

Furthermore, like most areas of social policy, preventing discriminatory treatment is still relevant to the EU's aim of harmonizing the rules of the market. As the European Commission argued in its White Paper on European Social Policy, vesting the EU with a mandate to "combat discrimination on the grounds of race, religion, age and disability" had become imperative in order to "make a reality of free movement within the single market."[122] Even though the EU has been quite successful in combating discrimination on the basis of nationality, the Commission argued, other types of discrimination might also discourage labor mobility.[123] Ensuring equal treatment and combating social marginalization would not only help to achieve "a more flexible and efficient European labor market" but would also give "a

[120] Ellis and Watson, *EU Anti-Discrimination Law* 104–17.

[121] Paul Craig and Gráinne de Búrca, *EU Law: Text, Cases, and Materials* (6th edn, Oxford University Press 2015) 906–7.

[122] European Commission, "White Paper on European Social Policy. A Way Forward for the Union" COM (94) 333 final, 42.

[123] Bell, *Anti-Discrimination Law* 42.

concrete and practical expression of European citizenship."[124] The Framework Directive confirms a similar link, reasoning that:

> [d]iscrimination based on religion or belief, disability, age or sexual orientation may undermine the achievement of the objectives of the EC Treaty, in particular the attainment of a high level of employment and social protection, raising the standard of living and the quality of life, economic and social cohesion and solidarity, and the free movement of persons.[125]

The same document also underlines the importance of "[promoting] coordination between employment policies of the Member States" and states that creating "a labor market favorable to social integration" is instrumental to that end. The harms of discrimination on the basis of age and disability are also explained, inter alia, on those grounds.[126]

Furthermore, by applying market-oriented norms of non-discrimination to other, more complex and capacious human relations, the EU has opted for a negative norm of equality over richer conceptions that might include civic reciprocity, solidarity, and fair equality of opportunity. While the normative framework prohibiting direct and indirect discrimination has been effective at dismantling barriers to commercial mobility, it is a superficial strategy for fighting entrenched, institutionalized patterns of social domination and marginalization. Often, such patterns result from underlying institutions and social structures rather than overt discrimination, such as the chronic undervaluation of professions traditionally considered as "women's work."[127] Egalitarian enforcement of an inherently patriarchal, heteronormative, ethnocentric, or ableist baseline will simply perpetuate gendered, social, and cultural forms of domination.[128] Such patterns can only be broken through more capacious and creative policies that respond to the specific needs and circumstances of the dominated group, including

[124] European Commission, "White Paper on European Social Policy" 28.

[125] Council Directive 2000/78 establishing a general framework for equal treatment in employment and occupation, Preamble, recital 11.

[126] Directive 2000/43 on discrimination on the basis of racial origin or ethnicity contains a similar statement on the likely effects of such discrimination on attaining the economic objectives of the treaty, but also makes clear that such discrimination is above all contrary to the values of democracy, basic rights, and the rule of law observed by member states. Council Directive 2000/43/EC, Preamble, recitals 9, 2–3 respectively.

[127] The Court considered this problem, inter alia, in Case C-127/92 *Enderby v Frenchay Health Authority and Secretary of State for Health* [1993] ECR I-05535. That case was brought by a speech therapist who claimed indirect discrimination on the grounds that speech therapists, who were predominantly women, were remunerated at far lower rates than comparable professions, e.g. pharmacists, who were predominantly men. The Court accepted the claim that such a situation constitutes indirect discrimination provided that the work is of equal value and the difference in pay cannot be attributed to market forces.

[128] Iris Marion Young, *Justice and the Politics of Difference* (Princeton University Press 1990) ch 4.

tailored social assistance programs, opportunities for political participation, mobilization, and advocacy, educational initiatives, public awareness and outreach campaigns, positive discrimination, and the affirmation and accommodation of difference.[129]

Furthermore, marginalized groups often lack the resources, opportunities, and coordination required to marshal available supranational legal remedies against the domestic practices that disadvantage them. As Conant writes, "[t]he formal institutionalization of law, without a corresponding development of organizational support, creates nothing but hollow rights that are meaningless in practice."[130] Her research reveals that the progressive effects of supranational rights have tended to depend on the organizational infrastructure of the groups willing to pursue them.[131] In the case of women's rights, for instance, victims of discrimination such as Ms. Defrenne were aided by lawyers and organizations willing and able to push the boundaries of European law in order to effect domestic change.[132] Over the 1990s, scores of domestic and transnational women's groups have set up shop in Brussels, creating policy and information networks that are highly successful in advancing women's causes throughout the Union.[133]

Other causes have not been as fortunate. The EU's broad failure to combat injustices against Roma citizens in several member states, including discriminatory treatment, lack of basic educational opportunities and social protections, and occasional instances of mass expulsion, furnishes a poignant example of the inequality of access to supranational guarantees of equality.[134] Documentary rights guarantees mean little for chronically disenfranchized groups who confront deep-seated failures of recognition. Litigation provides remedies for individuals and organized groups, but cannot eliminate entrenched practices of social and political exclusion. Marginalized groups such as the Roma require systemic remedies, political

[129] ibid ch 7.

[130] Lisa Conant, "Europe's No Fly Zone? Rights, Obligations, and Liberalization in Practice" in Tanja Börzel and Rachel A Cichowski (eds), *The State of the European Union, vol.6: Law, Politics, and Society* (Oxford University Press 2003) 250.

[131] Lisa Conant, *Justice Contained. Law and Politics in the European Union* (Cornell University Press 2002).

[132] Rachel Cichowski suggests that Germany, the Netherlands, and the UK have been the target of many sex equality suits under European law, not because their standards in this area are particularly low (quite the contrary) but because they "possess a greater number of equality law experts who systematically test the scope of both EU law and their own national laws by providing real situations for previously vague EU equality laws." Cichowski, "Women's Rights, the European Court, and Supranational Constitutionalism" 497–8; also, Stone Sweet, *Judicial Construction* 185–6.

[133] See especially, Cichowski, *The European Court and Civil Society*, ch 5.

[134] Amnesty International, *Left Out: Violations of the Rights of Roma in Europe* (Amnesty International Publications 2010). Available at: https://www.amnesty.org/download/Documents/36000/eur010212010en.pdf accessed October 5, 2015.

inclusion, and affirmative cultural revaluation in order to overcome the ossified structures of racism and malign neglect arrayed against them in many member states.[135] The EU can continue to play a supporting role in these struggles by establishing benchmarks, enumerating shared norms, and naming and shaming the laggards. Its capacity to induce member states and their societies as a whole to become more democratic, inclusive, and pluralistic is perhaps more extensive than that of a conventional international organization, but the scope of its power in this area is nowhere near as transformative as it is in the sphere of the market. This contrast suggests that the paradigm of functional constitutionalism, which highlights the centrality of economic union to the EU's mission remains the most apposite interpretive category, and that other models of supranational constitutional authority are more aspirational than actual.

[135] For a classic articulation of the value of affirmative and transformative remedies against chronic exclusion, see Nancy Fraser, *Justice Interruptus: Critical Reflections on the "Postsocialist" Condition* (Routledge 1997).

Conclusion: Waking from the European Dream

Allured by the prospect of a postnational future, its admirers have draped the European Union (EU) in the vivid hues of cosmopolitan, civic republican, and liberal democratic theories. Sadly, none of these fetching garments quite fits the model. Peeling back the gossamer of aspiration, we find the brute structure of *functional constitutionalism*: the sturdy bulk of rules, principles, and procedures that sustain an economic union among states. Although the EU has been remarkably successful at "establishing [and] ensuring the functioning of the internal market," understood as "an area without internal frontiers in which the free movement of goods, persons, services and capital is ensured,"[1] it hardly adds up to a supranational democracy, a nascent cosmopolitan order, or a solidary civic community. Member states have entrusted the EU with a constellation of policy objectives, mostly in the economic sphere, that they cannot achieve singly, and have furnished it with the measure of power necessary for discharging this mandate. In return, the EU provides the coordination, rule-making, monitoring, and enforcement necessary to guide states toward their shared goals. It has been designed to prioritize the tasks of effective economic governance over many other political values and ends, however prized they may be outside the EU's self-contained normative universe.

This is not to say that the EU's actions are not highly politically salient. As celebrated economist Lionel Robbins emphasized in his wartime plea for a commercial federation of European nations, "the economic problem is essentially political."[2] So far, however, the elusive pledge of "ever closer union" has delivered a regime of commercial mobility, market liberalization, unfettered competition, monetary union, and unforgiving fiscal discipline. This *finalité economique* hardly resembles the loftier hopes fastened to the European integration project. The aim of this concluding chapter is to take stock of how well the EU's current constitutional structure is equipped to meet some of the political desiderata that have been ascribed to it.

[1] Art 26(1–2) TFEU.

[2] Lionel Robbins, "Federal Union Examined III" *The Spectator* (London, March 28, 1940).

(I) BRIDLING THE SOVEREIGN STATE

Demystified, the EU rests on a web of generative commitments that states have made to one another. Over time, these commitments have transformed the states that created them. Their complexity, adaptability, and substantive range, together with the wide array of institutions tasked with elaborating and enforcing them make the EU a formidable feat of statecraft.

Contemporary political thought finds much to celebrate in a resilient institutional structure that effectively bridles the sovereign prerogatives of states. In his seventeenth-century anti-tyrannical manifesto, John Locke famously depicted the sovereign as a fearsome lion, far more powerful than the petty varmints it was meant to control, and therefore ever-ready to devour them. Playing on the liberals' worst fears, authoritarian thinkers from Thomas Hobbes to Carl Schmitt have stressed the logical impossibility of constraining the sovereign's power through laws. Ever-alert to the "the encroaching spirit of power,"[3] liberals find reason to rejoice whenever political systems successfully conquer that spirit and ensure that the sovereign is "effectually restrained from passing the limits assigned to it."[4]

Liberals often greet international law with similar enthusiasm, since it, too, represents an attempt to constrain the power of states and regulate their behavior.[5] Institutions established under international law have historically been far more likely to succumb to centrifugal forces than to engender oppressive ones of their own. Given the enduring significance of states and the relatively low survival rate of institutions designed to constrain them, liberal observers may be forgiven for lionizing any international body that successfully resists the machinations of sovereignty as a "further stage in civilizing state power."[6] The EU's signal success in corralling its member states into an extensive pattern of cooperation has also been a cause for celebration. Well into its seventh decade, European integration has engendered supranational mechanisms of deliberation, negotiation, concerted decision-making, and compliance. The agreements out of which the European Communities germinated could easily have wilted into oblivion. Instead, they have nourished a verdant, sprawling union whose twenty-eight member states make up the world's largest economy,[7] with its own

[3] James Madison, "Federalist No. 48" in Alexander Hamilton, James Madison, and John Jay eds, *The Federalist Papers* (Ian Shapiro ed, Yale University Press 2009).

[4] Madison, "Federalist No. 48."

[5] Martti Koskenniemi, *Gentle Civilizer of Nations: The Rise and Fall of International Law 1870–1960* (Cambridge University Press 2002).

[6] Jürgen Habermas, *The Crisis of the European Union: A Response* (Polity Press 2012) 45.

[7] In 2014, Eurostat reported that the EU was the largest economy in the world by GDP and the world's largest trading block, and held the largest share of world trade in goods and services. See Eurostat, *The*

judiciary, legislature, currency, and foreign policy outfit. The EU has not only kept Robert Schuman's promise of making war unthinkable among the original six member states, but has also expanded it eastward, underwriting democratic transitions in East Central Europe following the fall of communist regimes.

Perhaps the most impressive achievement of European integration is how effective it has been at establishing "a new legal order of international law for the benefit of which the states have limited their sovereign rights, albeit within limited fields, and the subjects of which comprise not only the member states but also their nationals."[8] Whatever the causal factors explaining its development and resilience, the EU's legal system represents a signal triumph for law in the face of the unforgiving calculus of power politics. Much like constitutionalism in the domestic context, European integration embodies the logic of "*garantisme*," a term Giovanni Sartori used to describe adherence to a "fundamental law, or a fundamental set of principles, and a correlative institutional arrangement, which would restrict arbitrary power and ensure a 'limited government.'"[9] Modern European history records an uneasy coexistence between the constitutional ideal and the nation-state as the political unit within which it has been instantiated. Although constitutionalism seeks to discipline sovereign power, it largely leaves the state's external relations and its treatment of foreigners unfettered. According to many observers, the EU complements domestic constitutionalism by constraining the arbitrary exercise of state power in the international sphere, expanding its scope of moral concern,[10] and establishing a deliberative community among its member states.[11] As Kant put it, "The problem of establishing a perfect civil constitution is subordinate to the problem of a law-governed external relationship with other states, and cannot be solved unless the latter is also solved."[12]

EU in the World 2014. A Statistical Portrait (Publications Office of the European Union 2014). Available at <dx.doi.org/10.2785/48181> accessed October 6, 2015.

[8] Case 26/62 *Van Gend en Loos v Nederlandse Administratie der Belastingen* [1963] ECR 1.

[9] Giovanni Sartori, "Constitutionalism: A Preliminary Discussion" (1962) 56 *American Political Science Review* 853, 855.

[10] E.g. Miguel Poiares Maduro, "Sovereignty in Europe: The European Court of Justice and the Creation of a European Political Community" in Mary L Volcansek and John F Stack Jr. (eds), *Courts Crossing Borders: Blurring the Lines of Sovereignty* (Carolina Academic Press 2005).

[11] Christian Joerges and Jurgen Neyer, "From Intergovernmental Bargaining to Deliberative Political Processes: The Constitutionalisation of Comitology" (1997) 3 *ELJ* 273, 294.

[12] Immanuel Kant, "Idea for a Universal History with a Cosmopolitan Purpose" [1784] in *Political Writings* (H Reiss ed, HB Nisbet tr, 2nd edn, Cambridge University Press 1997) 47. Updating this argument, Kumm writes, "The cosmopolitan paradigm repositions national constitutional practice as an integral part of a global practice of law and reconceives public international law in light of constitutional principles." Mattias Kumm, "The Cosmopolitan Turn in Constitutionalism: On the Relationship between Constitutionalism in and beyond the State" in Jeffrey L Dunoff and

The same conviction that constitutional regimes require the buttress of a law-governed international order also lies at the foundations of the European integration process. As future European Commissioner Altiero Spinelli and Ernesto Rossi put it in the 1941 Ventotene Manifesto, "[t]he absolute sovereignty of national states has given each the desire to dominate, since each one feels threatened by the strength of the others."[13] In a geopolitically congested continent, even stable constitutional democracies were forced into military mobilization by the imperative of protecting themselves from their neighbors. The mistrust fostered by an anarchic international environment gave an edge to repressive and belligerent regimes. Likewise, the postwar generation viewed the experience of fascism and totalitarianism as tragic proof of how easily the sovereign state could morph "from [the] guardian of civil liberty … into the master of vassals bound into servitude."[14] Even constitutional democracies were not immune to the solipsistic ethic of nationalism. For Monnet, the tendency to economic protectionism was symptomatic of this problem. As he wrote in 1943:

> There will be no peace in Europe if states rebuild themselves on the basis of national sovereignty, which brings with it the politics of prestige and economic protectionism. If the countries of Europe protect themselves against one another again, the constitution of vast armies will again be necessary … European states are too constrained [*étroits*] to guarantee their peoples the prosperity that modern conditions make possible and consequently necessary.[15]

The problem with protectionism, according to Monnet, is not primarily one of economic inefficiency but of a hostile delineation of the national "self" from the foreign "other." The sovereign state's lawless external behavior poses a standing threat to its commitment to constitutional principles and the rule of law in the domestic sphere. In other words, supranationalism was conceived not only as an extension of domestic constitutionalism but also, crucially, as its *conditio sine qua non*.

Viewed against this background, the European Coal and Steel Community (ECSC) represents a pilot attempt at securing domestic liberal institutions by means of supranational constitutional discipline. Its immediate tasks included

Joel P Trachtman (eds), *Ruling the World? Constitutionalism, International Law, and Global Governance* (Cambridge University Press 2009) 271.

[13] Altiero Spinelli and Ernesto Rossi, "The Manifesto of Ventotene for a Free and United Europe" (1941). Available http://www.cvce.eu/obj/the_manifesto_of_ventotene_1941-en-316aa96c-e7ff-4b9e-b43a-958e96afbecc.html accessed October 6, 2015.

[14] Spinelli and Rossi, "The Manifesto of Ventotene."

[15] Jean Monnet, *Note de Réflexion de 5 août 1943*. Available at http://www.cvce.eu/obj/note_de_reflexion_de_jean_monnet_alger_5_aout_1943-fr-b61a8924-57bf-4890-9e4b-73bf4d882549.html accessed October 5, 2015.

building and maintaining a common market in coal and steel by policing interference by governments, breaking up monopolies, managing crises, levying a direct tax on firms under its jurisdiction, and requiring firms and governments to correct "abnormally low wages."[16] However, this narrow substantive scope was the result of a strategic choice: the ECSC removed key industries of warfare from national control and pioneered genuinely supranational mechanisms of governance, but did not induce the political anxieties that full-blown federalist projects did. The ECSC High Authority, which became the precursor to the European Commission, was "the first time an executive body with its own leadership had been established outside" national ministries and stood as a viable complement to national administration.[17] Similarly, the ECSC's judicial arm, the Court of Justice, was assigned functions tantamount to judicial review over member states within the scope of the Treaty of Paris.[18]

As its founders understood it, the value of institutions such as the ECSC lay not primarily in the immediate policy gains they brought but in their capacity to reconfigure the beliefs, loyalties, and behavior of the actors who participated in them. A believer in—what we would today call—institutional design, Jean Monnet contended that "[r]ules and institutions do not change men's natures but they do bring about a change in their behaviour towards one another."[19] To avoid the pernicious lure of populism, protectionism, and belligerence, states did not need to be cured of their inherent selfishness but presented with strong incentives for cooperation. Inspired by nineteenth-century Swiss philosopher Henri Frédéric Amiel, Monnet held that institutions could change the behavior (if not the nature) of political actors by subjecting them to the discipline of rules. Just as nation-states had enveloped their peoples within cocoons of mutual fear, animosity, and protectionism, "[t]he pooling of their resources [would] eliminate suspicion and distrust" between them.[20] Over time, he hoped,

[16] As Ernst Haas observed, even the term "supranationalism" is itself a symptom of this strategy: the ECSC and EC's founders wanted to set these institutions "apart from the full federation which many of them hoped to achieve by way of supranationality." Ernst B Haas, *The Uniting of Europe* (first published 1958, Stanford University Press 1968) 40.

[17] Deirdre Curtin and Morten Egeberg, "Tradition and Innovation: Europe's Accumulated Executive Order" (2008) 31 *West European Politics* 639, 642.

[18] Haas, *The Uniting of Europe* 57–8.

[19] Jean Monnet, speech to the Joint Meeting of the Members of the Consultative Assembly of the Council of Europe and the Members of the Common Assembly of the European Community of Coal and Steel, in *Official Report of the Debate* (Strasbourg, June 22, 1953) 11. Available at <http://aei.pitt.edu/34049/4/A601.pdf> accessed December 7, 2015.

[20] Jean Monnet, speech to the Common Assembly of the ECSC, Strasbourg, January 12, 1953 in Jean Monnet, *The United States of Europe Has Begun. The European Coal and Steel Community Speeches and Addresses 1952–1954* (University of Pittsburgh Archive of European Integration 1955) microfiche, 16.

the practice of supranational decision-making would transform parochial definitions of the national interest into what Tocqueville called "self-interest well understood,"[21] and forge a wider community of interests that would transcend "sanguinary divisions."[22] For these reasons, Monnet described institutions as repositories of humanity's collective experience[23] and, elsewhere, as "the true cornerstones of civilization."[24]

Although Monnet disagreed with the subsequent shift from sectoral to market integration and was absent from the Treaty of Rome negotiations,[25] the European Economic Community followed the technocratic example of the ECSC rather than the politicized option of grand integration schemes such as the Council of Europe or the European Defense and Political Communities. Despite their functionally tailored mandates, however, the Treaties of Paris and Rome were both constitutional in ambition. Shortly after its inception, the Court of Justice interpreted the certain provisions of the Treaty of Rome as internally enforceable obligations that citizens could invoke against member states in their domestic courts.[26] As David Edward, a former judge of the Court of Justice of the European Union (CJEU), observes, the treaties created "legally enforceable guarantees that [member state citizens] will be treated equally and without discrimination, and that they will not be subjected to arbitrary decisions."[27] Although these guarantees mostly relate to commercial activity, Edward argues, they enable individuals working and residing in other member states to count on standards of legality, fairness, and equality whose application to foreign nationals had once been discretionary. For this reason:

> the freedoms guaranteed by the Treaties are *not* just secondary "economic" rights to be relegated to an annexe ... They are rights that are in every sense as fundamental and important for the average citizen as those enshrined in the European Convention on Human Rights.[28]

[21] See, especially, Alexis de Tocqueville, *Democracy in America* (first published 1840, Harvey C Mansfield and Delba Winthrop tr and ed, University of Chicago Press 2000) 501, where Tocqueville defines self-interest well understood as the belief that "man, in serving those like him, serves himself, and that his particular interest is to do good."

[22] Robert Schuman, *Declaration of 9 May 1950*. Available at http://www.cvce.eu/obj/the_schuman_declaration_paris_9_may_1950-en-9cc6ac38-32f5-4c0a-a337- 9a8ae4d5740f.html accessed March 17, 2016.

[23] Monnet, speech to the Joint Meeting of the Council of Europe and the ECSC, 122.

[24] Jean Monnet, speech to the Common Assembly of the ECSC, Strasbourg, January 12, 1953 in Jean Monnet, *The United States of Europe Has Begun. The European Coal and Steel Community Speeches and Addresses 1952–1954* (University of Pittsburgh Archive of European Integration 1955) microfiche, 16.

[25] Andrew Moravcsik, *The Choice for Europe. Social Purpose and State Power from Messina to Maastricht* (Cornell University Press 1998) 139–42.

[26] Case 26/62 *Van Gend en Loos*.

[27] Sir David Edward, acceptance speech for the UACES Award for Lifetime Achievement by a Practitioner delivered at the University Association for Contemporary European Studies Annual Conference, Edinburgh, UK, September 2, 2008. On file with the author.

[28] ibid.

For similar reasons, EU scholars have hailed the EU's constitutional system as an attempt to "[correct] the constitutional limits of national political communities" in favor of expanding the sphere of autonomy enjoyed by individuals.[29] Viewed through this lens, the EU appears as a constitutional project par excellence.

In cheering the unlikely success of European integration, however, many observers have been tempted to overlook or forgive its shortcomings, not simply as measured against the benchmark of parliamentary democracy, but by more open-ended standards of democratic participation, equal inclusion, individual rights, distributive justice, administrative accountability, and cosmopolitan right. Since its fledgling beginnings, the EU has gone from a critical project designed to bridle sovereign power into an increasingly hegemonic institution in its own right. In particular, it has come to represent a stifling discipline of technocratic rule that citizens increasingly find harsh, alienating, and heteronomous. Although the EU's system of functional constitutionalism has succeeded in constraining sovereign states, it is not clear that it furthers the principles associated with the modern tradition of constitutional democracy.

Part of the lesson, long known to constitutional theorists, is that constitutional constraints, as such, are substantively underdetermined.[30] The normative value of any framework of sovereign commitment hinges as much on the principles, standards, and rules by which it guides political actors. As the historical experience of constitutionalism shows, constitutional commitment is not necessarily emancipatory; in fact, it can entrench hegemonic power, ossify injustice, perpetuate exclusion, stand in the way of democratic rejuvenation, and hamstring government in the face of social change.[31] A political system that practices constitutional discipline might still be authoritarian, racist, or exploitative.[32] Likewise, a supranational system of sovereign commitment deserves critical scrutiny in terms of its guiding principles, substantive norms, and procedural mechanisms. Although the EU constrains sovereign states, attending to the substantive content of these constraints, as the foregoing chapters have done, leads to a far more

[29] Maduro, "Sovereignty in Europe" 57.

[30] Neil MacCormick, *Questioning Sovereignty: Law, State, and Nation in the European Commonwealth* (Oxford University Press 1999) 103.

[31] James Tully, *Strange Multiplicity: Constitutionalism in an Age of Diversity* (Cambridge University Press 1995); Ran Hirschl, *Towards Juristocracy: The Origins and Consequences of the New Constitutionalism* (Harvard University Press 2004); Melissa Schwartzberg, *Democracy and Legal Change* (Cambridge University Press 2007); Richard Bellamy, *Political Constitutionalism: A Republican Defence of the Constitutionality of Democracy* (Cambridge University Press 2007).

[32] Turkuler Isiksel, "Between Text and Context: Turkey's Tradition of Authoritarian Constitutionalism" (2013) 11 *International Journal of Constitutional Law* 702.

qualified assessment of its constitutional promise. In the remainder of this chapter, I will reiterate some perils and pitfalls of what I have called the EU's system of *functional constitutionalism.*

(II) THE TROUBLE WITH EPISTOCRACY

However open-ended its terms, no constitution is devoid of some purposive direction. Statements of principles and values, shared identity, cultural and religious heritage, and historic mission define a particular political community and chart courses for it to follow. The metaphor that Hobbes used to represent the relationship between individual liberty and the law is equally descriptive of constitutions: the effect of constitutional norms "is not to bind the People from all Voluntary actions; but to direct and keep them in such a motion, as not to hurt themselves by their own impetuous desires, rashnesse, or indiscretion; as Hedges are set, not to stop Travellers, but to keep them in the way."[33] A constitution is meant to enable a political community to pursue its aims even as it steers it towards certain directions and forecloses others. The distinguishing characteristic of a constitutional regime is that however strong the groundswell behind it, political will can only find legitimate expression within the parameters of the constitution.

In committing its member states to the enterprise of economic union, the legal system of the EU similarly charts a course that they must follow at the expense of others. Compared to most constitutional systems, however, it is far more extensive in its prescriptive detail. It elevates minutely specified aims above the fray of majoritarian contestation.[34] It ensures their effective and uniform application by vesting individuals with the power to invoke them against errant member states. Finally, it equips supranational institutions with the power to advance, but not to retard or revise the aims stipulated in the treaties. Having curtailed opportunities for democratic revision, the EU's very claim to exercise legitimate authority is premised on the desirability and successful realization of these aims, foremost among them the establishment of an economic union that yields prosperity and affluence for its member states and their citizens.

The market-related, fiscal, and monetary policies enshrined in the treaties and the highly technocratic means employed to realize these objectives are each contestable in their own right. The point of the present inquiry is

[33] Thomas Hobbes, *Leviathan* (first published 1651, Richard Tuck ed, Cambridge University Press 1996) 239–40.

[34] Dieter Grimm, "The Democratic Costs of Constitutionalisation: The European Case" (2015) 21 *ELJ* 460, 464.

not so much to wade into those controversies as to critically assess the system of functional constitutionalism that gives them expression. Most notably, this system is fundamentally at odds with the democratic hopes pegged to the European integration project. To the extent that it views public policy as a matter of competence, impartial judgment, and expert knowledge rather than political conflict and accommodation, the EU espouses an epistocratic mode of power. According to David Estlund, an epistocracy is a political regime that asks citizens to "surrender" their own standards of judgment in favor of experts who are better placed than they to address the policy questions that affect their lives.[35] Since their founding, supranational institutions have been portrayed as necessary for administering questions of policy that are either too complex or too vulnerable to distortion to be left to democratically accountable institutions. As I argued in the introductory chapter, the EU's democratic attenuation is not a "deficit" but a deliberate, systemic feature rooted in a profound postwar mistrust towards popular power.[36] To the founding generation, entrusting decisions to competent, stable, impartial, and rational decision-makers at the supranational level represented a way to counteract the vicissitudes of majoritarian politics.[37] The transfer of legislative and judicial authority to the EU is still framed predominantly "as a technical necessity: it is a way of binding the hands of national governments in order to insulate policymaking from partisanship and short-term electioneering."[38]

The EU's current institutional configuration continues to reflect this epistocratic logic. Most of its competences are exercised by democratically attenuated institutions, including the Commission, the Court of Justice, and the European Central Bank (ECB). Since its main legislative organ, the Council, is composed of members of national executives, nearly every expansion of the EU's mandate diminishes democratic control over decision-making. Although individual members of the Council are elected or democratically accountable officials in their respective domestic systems, the institution as a whole is removed from democratic control. Furthermore, the direct applicability of many of the decisions issued by the EU's organs short-circuits the power of national parliaments to contest, revise, and adapt supranational norms. Legislation that requires transposition

[35] David Estlund, "Beyond Fairness and Deliberation: The Epistemic Dimension of Democratic Authority" in James Bohman and William Rehg eds, *Deliberative Democracy. Essays on Reason and Politics* (MIT Press 1997) 181–3.

[36] Jan-Werner Müller, *Contesting Democracy: Political Ideas in Twentieth-Century Europe* (Yale University Press 2011) 149.

[37] ibid.

[38] Christopher J Bickerton, *European Integration: From Nation-States to Member States* (Oxford University Press 2012) 14.

into statute by national parliaments allows these assemblies very limited room for adjustment in light of their constituencies' preferences, on pain of an infringement action.[39] Even in purely domestic matters, national legislatures are constrained in their decisions by the existing *acquis communautaire* and the duty of sincere cooperation enumerated in article 4(3) of the Treaty on European Union (TEU), which enjoins member states from jeopardizing the attainment of the EU's objectives in *any* area of domestic policy.[40] On many important matters, national parliaments are either treated as mere stenographers of EU law or are regarded as unreliable. A 2012 joint statement by the four presidents (of the Council, Commission, Eurogroup, and ECB) recommending deeper fiscal integration affirmed as much when it stated derisively that national parliaments were "not in the best position to take [the common interest of the union] into account fully."[41]

The technocratic basis of supranational authority is deeply at odds with the democratic presumption that citizens are competent judges of matters of public interest. For this reason, the hope expressed by Habermas and others that supranational governance can re-establish democratic control over global forces that individual member states cannot govern appears overly sanguine.[42] Rather than reconstituting and mobilizing democratic mechanisms at the supranational level to tackle the challenges of an interdependent world, the EU is itself complicit in member states' loss of democratic autonomy. This is not to say that the EU has robbed member states of their democratic autonomy like a burglar in the dead of night; to the contrary, generations of elected representatives have voluntarily transferred extensive decision-making powers to the EU. However, the rationale behind these transfers was a desire to reap the policy benefits of cooperation rather than a concern for expanding the scope of democratic self-rule. The democratic enhancements introduced into EU decision-making by consecutive treaties from Maastricht to Lisbon have merely papered over its

[39] D Kochenov, *EU Enlargement and the Failure of Conditionality* (Kluwer Law 2007) 127.

[40] ibid 127.

[41] Herman Van Rompuy, in cooperation with José Manuel Barroso, Jean-Claude Juncker, and Mario Draghi, *Towards A Genuine Economic and Monetary Union*, December 5, 2012, 16. Available at <http://www.consilium.europa.eu/uedocs/cms_Data/docs/pressdata/en/ec/134069.pdf> accessed December 7, 2015.

[42] This is a major motivating force behind Jurgen Habermas's indefatigable advocacy of European integration. He writes: "We will only be able to meet the challenges of globalization in a reasonable manner if the postnational constellation can successfully develop new forms for the democratic self-steering of society. Therefore I would like to test the conditions for a democratic politics beyond the nation-state through the exemplary case of the European Union." However, Habermas acknowledges that "There are additional reasons in favor of European unification that have nothing to do with the question of how democracy can survive the nation-state as the form of its realization." Jürgen Habermas, *The Postnational Constellation: Political Essays* (Max Pensky tr and ed, MIT Press 1998) 88.

functionalist configuration. Since the EU's authority rests on a deliberate trade-off between democratic and technocratic legitimacy, its mechanisms of democratic participation serve merely as palliatives.

Finally, the functionalist basis of the EU's authority frustrates expectations that the EU might ensure member states' observance of principles of constitutional democracy in their domestic affairs. Although article 2 TEU enjoins the EU to uphold "the values of respect for human dignity, freedom, democracy, equality, the rule of law and respect for human rights, including the rights of persons belonging to minorities," the EU's institutional configuration is at odds with this aspiration. Not only does the EU lack the competences to fully realize the commitments to principles such as democracy and human rights, but it also detracts in important ways from the ability of member states to realize these values in the domestic sphere. Having configured the EU's authority in line with a technocratic, problem-solving model of legitimation, member states do not expect normative backtalk, let alone disciplinary action, concerning the basic structure of their domestic political systems. Although the EU exercises great power over member states in the economic sphere, this influence barely extends to the constitutional values enumerated in article 2. Whatever its lofty aspirations, the EU is still seen by its member states and citizens as a source of goods rather than values.

To be sure, providing public goods, preventing public harms, and otherwise fulfilling the tasks entrusted to them are key to the legitimacy of all political institutions, not just of the EU. Failure to meet these expectations is likely to undermine any political order, however admirable its values. In the case of international institutions, however, other sources of political legitimacy, such as democratic accountability, patriotic allegiance, and social justice tend to be shallow compared to states. As Curtin writes, "In contradistinction to the open-ended and general public tasks of states, international organizations are created to perform specific functional tasks."[43] This makes them beholden to legitimation by results. After all, the anticipated benefits of cooperation are the main reason why many states "have traded the people's sovereign self-rule in areas previously defined as domestic."[44] However, the extraordinary breadth of the EU's powers raises important questions about the adequacy of functional legitimation, and the compatibility of different sources of political legitimacy. How far (if at all) can gains in policy effectiveness make up for losses in democratic control? If citizens cannot regard the decisions that govern them as having been

[43] Deirdre Curtin, *Accumulated Executive Power in Europe: The "Most Dangerous" Branch of Government in the European Union* (KNAW Press 2009) 8.

[44] Beth Simmons, "Globalization, Sovereignty, and Democracy" in PF Nardulli (ed), *International Perspectives on Contemporary Democracy* (University of Illinois Press 2008) 173.

authorized by them or by their elected representatives, does it matter that these are, by whatever other measure, the *best* decisions available in the circumstances? Is an objective measure of the public interest available outside of what citizens and their representatives decide as being desirable for their polity?

Clearly, there is no abstract formula for calibrating the trade-off between democratic and effective rule as alternative grounds on which the legitimacy claim of a political entity can be built. However, the EU's current predicament suggests that competent rule is, by itself, a treacherous basis on which to rest its extensive powers. Since foundering against the rocky shores of the global recession,[45] the EU's promise of ever-increasing prosperity has come under intense strain. Given the extensive imbrication between domestic and supranational institutions, such failures of competence do not only expose the EU to existential crisis, but also sap popular confidence in domestic democratic structures. The next section reviews the sustainability of the EU's purposive mode of legitimation in light of its latest and arguably most perilous crisis to date.

(III) THE INTERNAL TENSIONS OF FUNCTIONAL CONSTITUTIONALISM

If the EU has so far relied on a trade-off between democratic and technocratic modes of authority, the recent financial and sovereign debt crisis has tipped the scales even further toward the latter. From the beginning, the lopsided design of the Economic and Monetary Union (EMU) has meant that while monetary policy was a supranational matter, fiscal policy rested with member states, who pledged to observe the targets enumerated in the Stability and Growth Pact in lieu of endowing the EU with greater fiscal capacity. The escalation of the global financial crisis into a sovereign debt crisis in many euro area states was attributed partly to a failure of this regime of fiscal discipline. In response, the member states scrambled to adopt new assistance and oversight facilities. The Treaty on Stability, Coordination, and Governance (TSCG), together with a series of secondary legislation known as the "six-pack" and the "two-pack," are intended to consolidate fiscal coordination and monitoring, and further tighten existing constraints on domestic budgets and macroeconomic policy. When member states exceed the deficit and public debt thresholds specified by the rules of the EMU, they are subjected to the rigorous corrective diet of the excessive

[45] International Monetary Fund, *Global Economic Outlook 2009* (International Monetary Fund 2009). Available at http://www.imf.org/external/pubs/ft/weo/2009/01/pdf/text.pdf accessed October 6, 2015.

deficit procedure. Finally, member states must coordinate their economic policy cycles and ensure the conformity of their economic priorities, budgetary choices, and structural reforms with EU rules by participating in the European Semester. These supervisory measures have corralled member states into a protracted austerity zone, forcing them to pare down public spending, and with it, the social protections they afford their citizens.[46] In a particularly audacious instance of flouting national constitutional autonomy, the TSCG obligates member states to implement balanced budget rules "through provisions of binding force and permanent character, *preferably constitutional*,"[47] demanding not only tighter fiscal discipline but its constitutional entrenchment.[48]

Taken together, these measures have whittled down national budgetary discretion to a vanishing point. Such drastic curtailment of "the power of the purse" divests representative democracy of one of its defining features, namely parliamentary control of public expenditure.[49] Greece's turbulent political trajectory sadly bears out this phenomenon: having careened between center-left, center-right, and radical left governments since 2011 and resoundingly rejected a bailout package in 2015, the Greek electorate has so far failed to effect even the slightest course correction regarding their country's economic policies.[50] Furthermore, EMU rules have been more forgivingly applied to larger states such as France and Germany, exacerbating the power asymmetries between larger and/or creditor states and smaller and/or debtor states.[51] While Greece is an admittedly extreme case, its situation is not asymptomatic. Arguably, only a select few states in the eurozone retain the luxury of being able to generate change in domestic economic policy through electoral alternation.

[46] Dorte Sindbjerg Martinsen and Hans Vollaard, "Implementing Social Europe in Times of Crises: Re-established Boundaries of Welfare?" (2014) 37 *West European Politics* 677; Caroline de la Porte and David Natali, "Altered Europeanisation of Pension Reform in the Context of the Great Recession: Denmark and Italy Compared" (2014) 37 *West European Politics* 732; OECD Directorate for Employment, Labour, and Social Affairs, "Social Expenditure Update" (November 2014). Available at <http://www.oecd.org/els/soc/OECD2014-Social-Expenditure-Update-Nov2014-8pages.pdf> accessed December 5, 2015.

[47] Treaty on Stability, Coordination, and Governance, art 3(2).

[48] Kenneth Armstrong, "The New Governance of EU Fiscal Discipline" (2013) 38 *European Law Review* 601.

[49] "[The] power over the purse may, in fact, be regarded as the most complete and effectual weapon with which any constitution can arm the immediate representatives of the people, for obtaining a redress of every grievance, and for carrying into effect every just and salutary measure" Madison, "Federalist No. 58."

[50] Paul Craig, "Economic Governance and the Euro Crisis: Constitutional Architecture and Constitutional Implications" in Maurice Adams, Federico Fabbrini, and Pierre Larouche (eds), *The Constitutionalization of European Budgetary Constraints* (Hart Publishing 2014) 39.

[51] Wolfgang Streeck, *Buying Time. The Delayed Crisis of Democratic Capitalism* (P Camiller tr, Verso 2014), 106.

Racing against time, capital flight, mounting debts, and a credit crunch, some of the pragmatic fixes to which the member state governments have resorted to address the euro crisis skirt the niceties of the EU's own legislative and constitutional procedures. For instance, the TSCG was adopted as an international agreement rather than as EU legislation in part because this was "a less contestable route" by which to mandate the adoption of balanced budget rules in domestic law that "would at the very least run counter to the very discretion which directives are supposed to afford Member States."[52] In another creative move, euro area member states chose to route emergency funds destined for Ireland, Greece, and Portugal through a private corporation created for the purpose, namely the European Financial Stability Facility (EFSF). This ad hoc remedy has since been subsumed under the European Stability Mechanism (ESM), which has far greater capacity to provide financial assistance to states but has itself had to be established outside the EU's formal legal framework, since "the EU itself was not empowered to establish such a stability mechanism."[53] When called upon to rule on the compatibility of these measures with the EU treaties, including constitutional limits on the powers of EU institutions, the Court of Justice soft-pedaled its judicial review duties, presumably so as not to trip up the concerted crisis response.[54]

Meanwhile, the crisis has intensified the EU's chronic reliance on executive decision-making. "What has emerged from the euro crisis," writes Sergio Fabbrini, "is a sort of federation of domestic governments which is highly centralized and intrusive in member states' economic policies,"[55] awarding greater independence to member state executives and further attenuating parliamentary oversight. Decisions that concern domestic revenue and expenditure, emergency funding, and banking regulation are increasingly made on an ad hoc basis by independent bodies, clusters of bureaucrats, government ministers, and international institutions that sideline the Union's constitutionally mandated decision-making mechanisms. The fate of member state economies is increasingly yoked to declarations by ECOFIN, the

[52] Kenneth A Armstrong, "Differentiated Economic Governance and the Reshaping of Dominium Law" in *The Constitutionalization of European Budgetary Constraints* 70.

[53] Paul Craig, "Economic Governance and the Euro Crisis: Constitutional Architecture and Constitutional Implications" 25.

[54] Case C-370/12 *Thomas Pringle v the Government of Ireland, Ireland, and the Attorney General* [2012] ECLI:EU:C:2012:756. For an analysis of the Court's "teleological" reasoning and its predictable outcome, see Paul Craig, "*Pringle*: Legal Reasoning, Text, Purpose, and Teleology" (2013) 20 *Maastricht Journal of European and Comparative Law* 3.

[55] Sergio Fabbrini, "Executive Power in the European Union: The Implications of the Euro Crisis." Paper presented at the EU Studies Association 14th Biennial Conference, Boston, March 5–7, 2015, 3. On file with the author.

ECB, International Monetary Fund, and the European Commission. Acting under the ominous epithet of "the Troika," the latter three institutions conclude memorandums of understanding that codify, down to the minute detail, structural reforms that cash-strapped member states must adopt in exchange for much-needed financial assistance. Since these fiscal roadmaps are adopted pursuant to the ESM, which formally falls outside the EU's constitutional framework, they are not subject to the procedural constraints and accountability mechanisms afforded by the latter.[56] Lastly, ECOFIN and the Eurogroup have emerged from the crisis with a remarkable degree of autonomy within the EU's decision-making structure, acting in the manner of an *imperium-in-imperio* within the Council. These new configurations of power tend also to sideline the European Parliament in its hard-won status as co-legislator and undermine its effectiveness as an institutional actor.[57]

Paring away the democratic accoutrements that supranational decision-making has acquired over the past few decades, the crisis has exposed the functionalist logic animating it. The viability of EMU has been pursued at the cost of other constitutional values that member states affirm and to which the EU, too, pays lip service. The measures taken in response to the crisis reflect the priority given to the imperative of keeping monetary union afloat at the cost of stretching or circumventing the norms and procedures codified by the treaties. In other words, the problem goes beyond the mere lack of democratic authorization or oversight; more fundamentally, the measures sometimes fail to conform even to the EU's own criteria of legal validity. According to Christian Joerges, "[t]he practice of European crisis policy, which is seeking refuge in a [*sic*] technocratic expertise and political bargaining, disregards Europe's commitments to democracy and the rule of law."[58] Others have argued that the EU's crisis response inaugurates "a foundational period of a new mode of European integration."[59] In Müller's view, the EU's dramatic intervention in member states' social and political systems (such as forcing Greece to "renegotiate [its] basic social contract") represents not just a quantitative but a "qualitative" break from its limited constitutional role of "constraining democracy" within member states and securing their "liberal-democratic arrangements."[60]

56 Craig, "Economic Governance and the Euro Crisis" 26.

57 Fabbrini, "Executive Power in the European Union" 12.

58 Christian Joerges, "Law and Politics in Europe's Crisis: On the History of the Impact of an Unfortunate Configuration" (2014) 21 *Constellations* 249, 255.

59 Edoardo Chiti, Agustín José Menéndez, and Pedro Gustavo Teixeira, "The European Rescue of the European Union" in Edoardo Chiti, Agustín José Menéndez, and Pedro Gustavo Teixeira (eds), *The European Rescue of the European Union? The Existential Crisis of the European Political Project* (ARENA Report No03/12; RECON Report No. 19, 2012) 392.

60 Jan-Werner Müller, "Beyond Militant Democracy?" (2012) *New Left Review* 39, 44.

Others have gone further, glimpsing the specter of authoritarian thinkers such as Carl Schmitt in the EU's crisis response,[61] and describing the outcome as a form of "post-democratic executive federalism,"[62] "authoritarian liberalism,"[63] or "executive emergency constitutionalism" designed to "minimize public debate and to avoid the ordinary filters of the democratic constitutional state."[64]

Although these observers are right to be alarmed, I contend that the crisis does not so much represent a radical break with the EU's *modus operandi* as it throws into high relief the profound functionalist reflex already built into its constitutional structure. As I have argued throughout the book, the EU has been designed and operates primarily as an institutional framework for economic union. Whereas a political union acquires legitimacy to the extent that it can be understood by citizens as representative of and responsive to their will, a functionalist scheme acquires its legitimacy from a cardinal objective that it pursues at the expense of other values and principles. This order of priority need not become pathological until the cardinal objective comes into conflict with other important and deeply held values. The euro crisis has generated precisely such a conflict. It is entirely in keeping with its teleological configuration that the EU has responded to the imperative of saving the euro by compromising on other principles such as the rule of law, democracy, and egalitarian reciprocity between member states. In a stark acknowledgment of this ordering of values, a 2012 report on the Future of Europe, signed by the foreign ministers of eleven eurozone countries, held that "[s]trengthening the Economic and Monetary Union has absolute priority"[65] and called for a dramatically strengthened framework of economic union among member states, including supranational oversight of member states' budgets, banking supervision, and the mutualization of sovereign risk. The declaration also proclaimed that "[t]he Euro has profound economic advantages and is the most powerful symbol of European integration," confirming not only the pragmatic importance of the single currency but giving it pride of place among the EU's constitutional values.

From its inception, the project of monetary union ratcheted up the functionalist logic of the EU not only by ensconcing member states in an

[61] For an overview of recent commentary summoning Schmitt's ghost, see Joerges, "Law and Politics in Europe's Crisis" 253–5.

[62] Habermas, *The Crisis of the European Union* 12.

[63] Michael A Wilkinson, "The Specter of Authoritarian Liberalism: Reflections on the Constitutional Crisis of the European Union" (2013) 14 *German Law Journal* 527.

[64] Chiti, Menendez, and Teixeira, "The European Rescue of the European Union" 417.

[65] Future of Europe Group comprising the Foreign Ministers of Austria, Belgium, Denmark, France, Italy, Germany, Luxembourg, the Netherlands, Poland, Portugal, and Spain, *Final Report of the Future of Europe Group* (September 17, 2012) 1.

entrenched system of fiscal discipline, but also by intensifying their interdependence on nearly every economic and social vector. Prior to monetary union, even persistent failures by member states to observe the rules of the single market did not seriously endanger the stability of the errant member state, much less threaten the viability of the Union as a whole. By contrast, delegating control over monetary policy has made the health and stability of the euro an existential matter for all. In other words, EMU created an extensive community of fate, without, however, establishing the fiscal, social, and political infrastructure necessary for fairly allocating its risks, burdens, and benefits. Under intense strain, singular regard for the survival of economic and monetary union has led the EU and its member states to abandon some of the constitutional means by which they have pursued that aim.

During one of the frantic moments of the crisis, ECB President Mario Draghi encapsulated this contradiction in a single sentence by declaring: "Within our mandate, the ECB is ready to do whatever it takes to preserve the euro." With Machiavellian bravado, he added, "And believe me, it will be enough."[66] Could the ECB stay within its constitutional mandate *and* do whatever was necessary? Or would the adage—*necessitas non habet legem*—prevail? Shortly after Draghi's statement, the ECB unveiled the controversial Outright Monetary Transactions (OMT) program, which would enable it to purchase sovereign bonds issued by eurozone states on secondary markets.[67] The program was meant primarily to reassure lenders, and has not been used to date. However, critics, among them the German Federal Constitutional Court, have charged that the program exceeds the ECB's mandate by enabling it to act as a de facto lender of last resort.[68] Guided by its concern for the successful realization of the EU's *telos*, the CJEU affirmed the legality of OMT.[69] However, the CJEU's own status as an institutional agent of purposive integration serves only to heighten the tension between respect for constitutional constraints on public power and the EU's fealty to the substantive goals entrusted to it.

The conflict over the constitutional validity of OMT illustrates the way in which the euro crisis has exacerbated the tension endemic to *functional constitutionalism*, bringing purpose into conflict with the legal means for its pursuit. To recall Neil MacCormick's astute formulation, "Constitutionalism as

[66] Mario Draghi, speech at the Global Investment Conference in London, July 26, 2012. Available at https://www.ecb.europa.eu/press/key/date/2012/html/sp120726.en.html accessed October 6, 2015.

[67] Samuel Dahan, Olivier Fuchs, and Marie-Laure Layus, "*Whatever It Takes?* Regarding the *OMT* Ruling of the German Federal Constitutional Court" (2015) 18 *Journal of International Economic Law* 137.

[68] Bundesverfassungsgericht Case No 2 BvR 2728/13 *OMT Judgment* 14 January 2014.

[69] Case C-62/14 *Gauweiler and Others v Deutscher Bundestag* ECLI:EU:C:2015:400.

a *minimal* virtue involves duly respecting the conditional quality of powers conferred ... and involves observing faithfully the (interpreted) conditions of the respective agencies' empowerment."[70] Arguably, the functional imperative of keeping the euro afloat has so far been achieved at the cost of circumventing the grant of powers in the EU's constitutional settlement and disregarding their conditional quality.

(IV) BEYOND ECONOMISM

The serpentine course of European integration has been shaped by many competing, contingent, and historically embedded forces, and it would be simplistic—not to mention inaccurate—to reduce it to any single logic. The transition from the European Community to the EU in the early 1990s marks a watershed moment, not least because it represents an attempt to expand the political scope of the European project beyond its original focus on market integration. Notwithstanding these transformations, however, the category of functional constitutionalism remains central to understanding the EU.

Functional constitutionalism originates from the strategy, espoused by many of the founders of European integration, to delegate the *finalité politique* of integration to the force of economic necessity. Integration would work with the grain of national ambition rather than against it, using material incentives to gradually envelop states in a political union. However, in laboring under the guise of non-ideological and value-neutral governance, European integration has thwarted the possibility of building a European civic sphere by denying the need for it. To the extent that its democratic potential has been stunted by a focus on generating wealth, the EU illustrates a more generic predicament of political life in advanced capitalist democracies.[71] As the eminent European historian Tony Judt pointed out in a 2009 essay, many western societies exhibit a pathology of public discourse that reduces just about any question of public policy to one of wealth maximization. Judt calls this monomaniacal value system "economism":[72]

> For the last thirty years, in much of the English-speaking world (though less so in continental Europe and elsewhere), when asking ourselves whether we support a proposal or initiative, we have not asked, is it good or bad? Instead we inquire: Is it efficient? Is it productive? Would it benefit gross domestic

[70] MacCormick, *Questioning Sovereignty* 103.

[71] The following passages build on Turkuler Isiksel, "The Dream of a Commercial Peace," in Luuk van Middelaar and Philippe van Parijs (eds), *After the Storm. How to Save Democracy in Europe* (Lannoo 2015).

[72] Tony Judt, "What is Living and what is Dead in Social Democracy?" *The New York Review of Books* (New York, December 17, 2009). Available at: http://www.nybooks.com/articles/archives/2009/dec/17/what-is-living-and-what-is-dead-in-social-democrac/?pagination=false accessed October 7, 2015.

> product? Will it contribute to growth? This propensity to avoid moral considerations, to restrict ourselves to issues of profit and loss—economic questions in the narrowest sense—is not an instinctive human condition. It is an acquired taste.

Judt fears, rightly, that we are fast losing our ability to evaluate political ideals, institutions, and policies except in terms of their economic value. Quanta such as revenue, growth, employment, or private wealth are not treated as one vector of the public interest, but increasingly as the only indicators that citizens and leaders are willing to consider. This narrowing of public debate comes at the expense of principles such as popular self-rule, individual liberty, social justice, and equality. Like wealthy corporations who nickel and dime their lowest earning employees, the most affluent societies on the planet can be ruthlessly frugal in tackling serious social problems, in part because they have come to prioritize cost-effectiveness over ideals of fairness, equality of opportunity, civic cohesion, and individual self-respect. Throughout the euro crisis, creditor states and institutions illustrated this tendency with their unyielding insistence on strict austerity policies and the timely repayment of loans, even at the cost of wearing away the social safety net on which millions of their citizens depend. Once the hallmark of postwar European civilization, the welfare state has come to be regarded as an obstacle to the efficient operation of the market.

The EU's functional constitutionalism exemplifies the ascent of economic logic as a privileged measure of legitimacy and the corresponding decline of other ideals once considered central to constitutionalism. However, the EU's double-barreled crisis of democratic legitimacy and technocratic competence illustrates the fallacy of trying to replace political debate with the false certainty of economic prescription. What contemporary polity is capable of delivering uninterrupted economic prosperity, particularly in the turbulent world of casino capitalism? As long as the EU represents little more to its citizens than a marriage of convenience, a union for richer, but not for poorer, every economic crisis is bound to threaten its continued existence. The most urgent order of business for EU member states and citizens, therefore, is to find ways of articulating the value of European integration in terms other than the economic. If they are unable to do so, no grand gesture of political unity, no display of symbols, flags, flashy buildings, crisp banknotes, or self-congratulatory holidays can make up for the absence of a prolific, passionate, diverse, and even cacophonous European public that takes confidence in the political, and not merely commercial, bonds of its union.

It would be unfair not to admire the triumph of a system of commercial peace in Europe. It would also be reckless not to acknowledge its limitations. Representing supranational governance to citizens as a get-rich-quick scheme may have insulated the fledgling European Communities from damaging political opposition in the initial decades, but it has also prevented civic engagement with the integration project from taking root. The strategy of elevating economic union above the messiness of democratic politics has managed only to postpone the inevitable reintrusion of politics onto the supranational scene in embittered and disaffected form. Having been excluded from the decisions that shaped ever-closer union, European publics are now contesting the arrogance of technocracy by professing dismissive euroskepticism, resentful populism, and virulent xenophobia. The lesson here is that democratic politics can only ever be circumvented at the cost of anti-democratic politics. Ultimately, however, "politics cannot be taken out of politics."[73] If anything, the intensification of interdependence among member states has made the question of the Union's *finalité politique* even more contentious, and has shown that it cannot be resolved by the immanent logic of economic union. The lesson of the crisis should be a frank acknowledgment of the fragility and contingency of the European project and the indispensability of civic commitment for ensuring its resilience. Economic union does not exhaust the horizons of the European project, but the challenge remains that of bringing those horizons into focus.

[73] Sartori, "Constitutionalism" 864.

Bibliography

Abbott KW, Keohane RO, Moravcsik A, Slaughter A-M, and Snidal D, 'The Concept of Legalization' (2000) 54 International Organization 400

Acemoglu D and Robinson J, *Why Nations Fail: The Origins of Power, Prosperity, and Poverty* (Crown Publishers 2012)

Ackerman B, *We the People. Foundations* (Belknap 1991)

Ackerman B, 'The New Separation of Powers' (2000) 113 Harvard Law Review 633

Afilalo A, 'Constitutionalization Through the Back Door: A European Perspective on NAFTA's Investment Chapter' (2001) 34 NYU Journal of International Law and Politics 1

Almqvist J, 'A Human Rights Critique of European Judicial Review. Counter-Terrorism Sanctions' (2008) 57 International and Comparative Law Quarterly 303

Alston P, 'Conjuring up New Human Rights: A Proposal for Quality Control' (1984) 78 American Journal of International Law 607

Alston P (ed), *The EU and Human Rights* (Oxford University Press 1999)

Alston P, 'Resisting the Merger and Acquisition of Human Rights by Trade Law: A Reply to Petersmann' (2002) 13 European Journal of International Law 815

Alter K, *Establishing the Supremacy of European Law. The Making of an International Rule of Law in Europe* (Oxford University Press 2001)

Amar A, *America's Constitution: A Biography* (Random House 2006)

Amnesty International, 'Left Out: Violations of the Rights of Roma in Europe' (Amnesty International Publications 2010) <https://www.amnesty.org/download/Documents/36000/eur010212010en.pdf> accessed 5 October 2015

Anderson B, *Imagined Communities: Reflections on the Origin and Spread of Nationalism* (Verso 1983)

Archibugi D and Held D (eds), *Cosmopolitan Democracy: An Agenda for a New World Order* (Polity Press 1995)

Arendt H, *The Origins of Totalitarianism* (first published 1951, Harcourt Inc. 1967)

Arendt H, *On Revolution* (first published 1962, Penguin Books 1977)

Aristotle, *Politics* (Lord C tr and ed, The University of Chicago Press 1984)

Armstrong K, 'The New Governance of EU Fiscal Discipline' (2013) 38 European Law Review 601

Armstrong K, 'Differentiated Economic Governance and the Reshaping of Dominium Law' in Adams M, Fabbrini F, and Larouche P (eds), *The Constitutionalization of European Budgetary Constraints* (Hart Publishing 2014)

Auel K and Raunio T, 'Debating the State of the Union? Comparing Parliamentary Debates on EU Issues in Finland, France, Germany and the UK' (2014) 20 The Journal of Legislative Studies 13

Avbelj M and Komárek J, 'Four Visions of Constitutional Pluralism' (2008) 2 European Journal of Legal Studies. <http://www.ejls.eu/4/61UK.pdf> accessed 8 October 2015

Axelrod R, *The Evolution of Cooperation* (Basic Books 1984)

Axelrod R and Keohane RO, 'Achieving Cooperation Under Anarchy: Strategies and Institutions' (1985) 38 World Politics 226

Ball T and Pocock JGA (eds), *Conceptual Change and the Constitution* (University Press of Kansas 1988)

Barav A, 'The Judicial Power of the European Economic Community' (1980) 53 Southern California Law Review 461

Barnard C, *The Substantive Law of the EU. The Four Freedoms* (2nd edn, Oxford University Press 2007)

Barnard C, *The Substantive Law of the EU. The Four Freedoms* (3rd edn, Oxford University Press 2010)

Barroso JMD, 'The State of the European Union' Public address delivered at Princeton University Woodrow Wilson School of Public and International Affairs (8 April 2015). Text on file with the author

Bartolini S, *Restructuring Europe. Center Formation, System Building, and Political Structuring Between the Nation-State and the European Union* (Oxford University Press 2005)

Beard CA, *An Economic Interpretation of the Constitution of the United States* (first published 1913, Macmillan Company 1921)

Beetham D and Lord C, *Legitimacy and the European Union* (Longman 1998)

Beitz CR, *Political Theory and International Relations* (Princeton University Press 1979)

Beitz CR, *The Idea of Human Rights* (Oxford University Press 2009)

Bell M, *Anti-Discrimination Law and the European Union* (Oxford University Press 2002)

Bellamy R, 'The "Right to Have Rights": Citizenship Practice and the Political Constitution of the EU' in Bellamy R and Warleigh A (eds), *Citizenship and Governance in the European Union* (Continuum 2001)

Bellamy R, *Political Constitutionalism: A Republican Defense of the Constitutionality of Democracy* (Cambridge University Press 2007)

Bellamy R, 'Democracy Without Democracy: Can the EU's Democratic "Outputs" be Separated from the Democratic "Inputs" Provided by Competitive Parties and Majority Rule?' (2010) 17 Journal of European Public Policy 2

Bellamy R and Castiglione D, 'Building the Union: The Nature of Sovereignty in the Political Architecture of Europe' (1997) 16 Law & Philosophy 422

Bellamy R and Warleigh A (eds), *Citizenship and Governance in the European Union* (Continuum 2001)

Benhabib S, *The Rights of Others. Aliens, Citizens, and Residents* (Cambridge University Press 2004)

Benhabib S, *Another Cosmopolitanism. The Berkeley Tanner Lectures* (Oxford University Press 2006)

Benton L, *A Search for Sovereignty: Law and Geography in European Empires, 1400–1900* (Cambridge University Press 2010)

Benton M and Petrovic M, *How Free is Free Movement? Dynamics and Drivers of Mobility within the European Union* (Migration Policy Institute Europe 2013)

Bergman T, Müller WC, Strøm K, and Blomgren M, 'Democratic Delegation and Accountability' in Strøm K, Müller WC, and Bergman T (eds), *Delegation and Accountability in Parliamentary Democracies* (Oxford University Press 2003)

Besselink L, 'Entrapped by the Maximum Standard: On Fundamental Rights, Pluralism, and Subsidiarity in the European Union' (1998) 35 Common Market Law Review 629

Besson S, 'The European Union and Human Rights: Towards a Post-National Human Rights Institution?' (2006) 6 Human Rights Law Review 323

Bhabha J, 'Enforcing the Human Rights of Citizens and Non-Citizens in the Era of Maastricht' in Meyer B and Geschiere P (eds), *Globalization and Identity* (Blackwell Publishing 1999)

Bickel A, *The Least Dangerous Branch? The Supreme Court at the Bar of Politics* (Yale University Press 1986)

Bickerton CJ, *European Integration: From Nation-States to Member States* (Oxford University Press 2012)

Blackstone W, *Commentaries on the Laws of England* (Jones WC ed, Bancroft-Whitney Company 1915)

Block F and Somers MR, 'Beyond the Economistic Fallacy. The Holistic Social Science of Karl Polanyi' in Skocpol T (ed), *Vision and Method in Historical Sociology* (Cambridge University Press 1984)

von Bogdandy A, 'The European Union as a Human Rights Organisation? Human Rights and the Core of the European Union' (2000) 37 Common Market Law Review 1307

von Bogdandy A, 'A Disputed Idea Becomes Law: Remarks on European Democracy as a Legal Principle' in Kohler-Koch B and Rittberger B (eds), *Debating the Democratic Legitimacy of the European Union* (Rowman & Littlefield 2007)

von Bogdandy A, Kottmann M, Antpöhler C, Dickschen J, Hentrei S, and Smrkolj M, 'Reverse Solange—Protecting the Essence of Fundamental Rights against EU Member States' [2012] 49 Common Market Law Review 489

Bosniak L, 'The Citizenship of Aliens' (1998) 56 Social Text 29

de Bracton H, *On the Laws and Customs of England* (Thorne SE tr and ed, Belknap 1968)

Brandsma GJ and Blom-Hansen J, 'Negotiating the Post-Lisbon Comitology System: Institutional Battles over Delegated Decision-making' (2012) 50 Journal of Common Market Studies 939

Brennan G and Buchanan JM, *The Reason of Rules. Constitutional Political Economy* (Cambridge University Press 1985)

Brown W, *Walled States, Waning Sovereignty* (MIT Press 2010)

Brunkhorst H, 'The Legitimation Crisis of the European Union' (2006) 13 Constellations 165

Buchanan JM, 'Constitutional Restrictions on the Power of Government' in Buchanan JM (ed), *Choice, Contract, and Constitutions* (Liberty Fund 2001)

Buchanan JM and Tullock G, *The Calculus of Consent* (University of Michigan Press 1962)

Bulterman M, 'Fundamental Rights and the United Nations Financial Sanction Regime: The *Kadi* and *Yusuf* Judgments of the Court of First Instance of the European Communities' (2006) 19 Leiden Journal of International Law 753

de Búrca G, 'The Language of Rights and European Integration' in Shaw J and More G (eds), *New Legal Dynamics of European Union* (Clarendon Press 1995)

de Búrca G, 'The European Court of Justice and the International Legal Order after *Kadis'* (2010) 51 Harvard International Law Journal 1

de Búrca G, 'The Road Not Taken: The European Union as a Global Human Rights Actor' (2011) 105 American Journal of International Law 649

de Búrca G, 'After the EU Charter of Fundamental Rights: The Court of Justice as a Human Rights Adjudicator?" (2013) 20 Maastricht Journal of European and Comparative Law 168

Burley A-M and Mattli W, 'Europe before the Court' (1993) 47 International Organization 41

Byrne A, 'Free Flow of Labour Stemmed as Belgium Cracks down on Migrants' *Financial Times* (London, 16 March 2014)

Caporaso J, Marks G, Moravcsik A, and Pollack M, 'Does the European Union Represent an *n* of 1?' (1997) X ECSA Review 1

Caporaso JA and Tarrow S, 'Polanyi in Brussels: Supranational Institutions and the Transnational Embedding of Markets' (1993) 63 International Organization 593

Carens J, 'Aliens and Citizens: The Case for Open Borders' (1987) 49 Review of Politics 251

Cass DZ, *The Constitutionalization of the World Trade Organization. Legitimacy, Democracy, and Community in the International Trading System* (Oxford University Press 2005)

Cederman L-E, 'Nationalism and Bounded Integration: What it Would Take to Construct a European Demos' (2001) 7 European Journal of International Relations 139

Cheneval F and Schimmelfennig F, 'The Case for Democracy in the European Union' (2012) 51 Journal of Common Market Studies 334

Chiti E, Menéndez AJ, and Teixeira PG, 'The European Rescue of the European Union' in Chiti E, Menéndez AJ, and Teixeira PG (eds), *The European Rescue of the European Union? The Existential Crisis of the European Political Project* (ARENA Report No 3/12; RECON Report No 19 2012)

Choudhry S (ed), *The Migration of Constitutional Ideas* (Cambridge University Press 2007)

Cichowski R, 'Women's Rights, the European Court, and Supranational Constitutionalism' (2004) 38 Law & Society Review 489

Cichowski RA, *The European Court and Civil Society: Litigation, Mobilization, and Governance* (Cambridge University Press 2007)

Cohen J, 'An Epistemic Conception of Democracy' (1986) 97 Ethics 26

Cohen J, 'Minimalism about Human Rights: The Most we Can Hope for?' (2004) 12 Journal of Political Philosophy 190

Cohen JL, 'Sovereignty in the Context of Globalization: A Constitutional Pluralist Perspective' in Besson S and Tasioulas J (eds), *The Philosophy of International Law* (Oxford University Press 2010)

Cohen JL *Globalization and Sovereignty. Rethinking Legality, Legitimacy and Constitutionalism* (Oxford University Press 2012)

Cohen J and Sabel C, 'Directly-Deliberative Polyarchy' (1997) 3 European Law Journal 313

Cohen J and Sabel CF, 'Sovereignty and Solidarity: EU and US' in Zeitlin J and Trubek DM (eds), *Governing Work and Welfare in a New Economy* (Oxford University Press 2003)

Cohen J and Sabel C 'Global Democracy?' (2005) 37 International Law and Politics 763

Comité Intergouvernemental Créé par la Conférence de Messine, 'Rapport des Chefs de Délégation aux Ministres des Affaires Etrangères' (Secrétariat 1956)

Committee of Experts on the Application of ILO Conventions and Recommendations, Report of the Committee of Experts (International Labour Office 2010) <http://www.ilo.org/wcmsp5/groups/public/@ed_norm/@relconf/documents/meetingdocument/wcms_123424.pdf> accessed 28 November 2015

Conant L, *Justice Contained. Law and Politics in the European Union* (Cornell University Press 2002)

Conant L, 'Europe's No Fly Zone? Rights, Obligations, and Liberalization in Practice' in Börzel T and Cichowski RA (eds), *The State of the European Union, vol 6: Law, Politics, and Society* (Oxford University Press 2003)

Conant L, 'Rights and the Limits of Transnational Solidarity in Europe' in Jackson DW, Tolley MC, and Volcansek ML (eds), *Globalizing Justice: Critical Perspectives on Transnational Law and the Cross-border Migration of Legal Norms* (SUNY Press 2010)

Constant B, *Political Writings* (Fontana B tr and ed, Cambridge University Press 1988)

Coppel J and O'Neill A, 'The European Court of Justice: Taking Rights Seriously?' (1992) 12 Legal Studies 227

Corwin ES, 'The "Higher Law" Background of American Constitutional Law' (1928) 42 Harvard Law Review 149

Craig P, 'Constitutions, Constitutionalism, and the European Union' (2001) 7 European Law Journal 125

Craig P, '*Pringle*: Legal Reasoning, Text, Purpose, and Teleology' (2013) 20 Maastricht Journal of European and Comparative Law 3

Craig P, 'EU Accession to the ECHR Competence, Procedure, and Substance' (2013) 36 Fordham International Law Journal 1114

Craig P and de Búrca G, *EU Law: Text, Cases, and Materials* (4th edn, Oxford University Press 2007)

Craig P and de Búrca G, *EU Law: Text, Cases, and Materials* (6th edn, Oxford University Press 2015)

Cranston M, 'Human Rights, Real and Supposed' in Hayden P (ed), *The Philosophy of Human Rights* (Paragon House 2001)

Curtin D, *Accumulated Executive Power in Europe: The 'Most Dangerous' Branch of Government in the European Union* (KNAW Press 2009)

Curtin D, *Executive Power of the European Union. Law, Practices, and the Living Constitution* (Oxford University Press 2009)

Curtin D and Egeberg M, 'Tradition and Innovation: Europe's Accumulated Executive Order' (2008) 31 West European Politics 639

Dahan S, Fuchs O, and Layus M-L, '*Whatever It Takes?* Regarding the *OMT* Ruling of the German Federal Constitutional Court' (2015) 18 Journal of International Economic Law 137

Dahl RA, 'Can International Organizations Be Democratic? A Skeptic's View' in Shapiro I and Hacker-Cordón C (eds), *Democracy's Edges* (Cambridge University Press 1999)

Dam KW, 'The American Fiscal Constitution' (1977) 44 The University of Chicago Law Review 271

Davenport CA, ' "Constitutional Promises" and Repressive Reality: A Cross-national Time-series Investigation of Why Political and Civil Liberties Are Suppressed' (1996) 58 Journal of Politics 627

Dawson M and de Witte B, 'The EU Legal Framework of Social Inclusion and Social Protection: Between the Lisbon Strategy and the Lisbon Treaty' in Cantillon B, Verschueren H, and Ploscar P (eds), *Social Inclusion and Social Protection in the EU: Interactions Between Law and Policy* (Intersentia 2012)

Dehousse R, *The European Court of Justice: The Politics of Judicial Integration* (St. Martin's Press 1998)

Dehousse R, 'Towards a Regulation of Transnational Governance? Citizen's Rights and the Reform of Comitology Procedures' in Joerges C and Vos E (eds), *EU Committees: Social Regulation, Law and Politics* (Hart Publishing 1999)

Dehousse R, 'Rediscovering Functionalism' (2000) Harvard Jean Monnet Working Paper No 7/00

Dehousse R, 'Comitology: Who Watches the Watchmen?' (2003) 10 Journal of European Public Policy 798

Deighton A, 'Introduction' in Deighton A (ed), *Building Postwar Europe. National Decision-makers and European Institutions 1948–63* (St. Martin's Press 1995)

Diebold W, 'A Personal Note' in Schwabe K (ed), *Die Anfänge des Schuman-Plans 1950/51* (Nomos 1988)

Donnelly J, *The Concept of Human Rights* (Oxford University Press 1985)

Douglass F, 'What to the Slave is the Fourth of July?' [1852] reproduced in *Frederick Douglass: Oratory from Slavery* (Chesebrough D ed, Greenwood Press 1998)

Downes T, 'Market Citizenship: Functionalism and Fig-leaves' in Bellamy R and Warleigh A (eds), *Citizenship and Governance in the European Union* (Continuum 2001)

Doyle M, 'The UN Charter—A Global Constitution?' in Dunoff JL and Trachtman JP (eds), *Ruling the World? Constitutionalism, International Law, and Global Governance* (Cambridge University Press 2009)

Draghi M, Speech at the Global Investment Conference in London (26 July 2012) <https://www.ecb.europa.eu/press/key/date/2012/html/sp120726.en.html> accessed 6 October 2015

Duff A, 'Building a Parliamentary Europe' (1994) 29 Government and Opposition 147

Dunoff JL and Trachtman JP, 'A Functional Approach to International Constitutionalization' in Dunoff JL and Trachtman JP (eds), *Ruling the World? Constitutionalism, International Law, and Global Governance* (Cambridge University Press 2009)

Dupuy P-M, Petersmann E-U, and Francioni F (eds), *Human Rights in International Investment Law and Arbitration* (Oxford University Press 2009)

Dworkin R, *Taking Rights Seriously* (Harvard University Press 1977)

Dworkin R, *Freedom's Law: The Moral Reading of the American Constitution* (Harvard University Press 1996)

Eckes C, 'Judicial Review of European Anti-Terrorism Measures—The *Yusuf* and *Kadi* Judgments of the Court of First Instance' (2008) 14 European Law Journal 74

Edward D, 'Nations, States, People and Commerce' in Prince G (ed), *A Window on Europe* (Canongate 1993)

Edward D, Acceptance Speech for the UACES Award for Lifetime Achievement by a Practitioner. Delivered at the University Association for Contemporary European Studies Annual Conference (Edinburgh, UK, 2 September 2008). On file with the author

Eeckhout P, 'The EU Charter of Fundamental Rights and the Federal Question' [2002] 39 Common Market Law Review 945

Eeckhout P, 'Community Terrorism Listing, Fundamental Rights, and UN Security Council Resolution. In Search of the Right Fit' (2007) 3 European Constitutional Law Review 183

Eijsbouts WT and Besselink L, ' "The Law of Laws"—Overcoming Pluralism' (2008) 4 European Constitutional Law Review 395

Eising R, 'The Access of Business Interests to EU Institutions: Towards Elite Pluralism?' (2007) 14 Journal of European Public Policy 384

Elazar DJ, 'The Role of Federalism in Political Integration' in Elazar DJ (ed), *Federalism and Political Integration* (Turtledove Publishing 1979)

Ellina C, *Promoting Women's Rights. The Politics of Gender in the European Union* (Routledge 2003)

Ellis E, *EU Anti-Discrimination Law* (Oxford University Press 2005)

Ellis E and Watson P, *EU Anti-Discrimination Law* (Oxford University Press 2013)

Elster J, *Ulysses and the Sirens. Studies in Rationality and Irrationality* (Cambridge University Press 1984)

Elster J, 'Introduction' in Elster J and Slagstad R (eds), *Constitutionalism and Democracy* (Cambridge University Press 1988)

Elster J, *Ulysses Unbound. Studies in Rationality, Precommitment, and Constraints* (Cambridge University Press 2000)

Elster J, 'Don't Burn Your Bridge before You Come to it: Some Ambiguities and Complexities of Precommitment' (2003) 81 Texas Law Review 1751

Elster J and Slagstad R (eds), *Constitutionalism and Democracy* (Cambridge University Press 1988)

Ely JH, *Democracy and Distrust. A Theory of Judicial Review* (Harvard University Press 1980)

Eriksen EO and Fossum JE (eds), *Democracy in the European Union: Democracy Through Deliberation?* (Routledge 2000)

Eriksson A, 'European Court of Justice: Broadening the Scope of European Nondiscrimination Law' (2009) 7 International Journal of Constitutional Law 731

EskridgeJr WN and Ferejohn J, *A Republic of Statutes. The New American Constitution* (Yale University Press 2010)

Estlund D, 'Beyond Fairness and Deliberation: The Epistemic Dimension of Democratic Authority' in Bohman J and Rehg W (eds), *Deliberative Democracy. Essays on Reason and Politics* (MIT Press 1997)

Estlund D, *Democratic Authority: A Philosophical Framework* (Princeton University Press 2008)

European Coal and Steel Community High Authority Information Service, *The European Community for Coal and Steel* (High Authority 1955)

European Commission Directorate General for Internal Policies, 'The Impact of the ECJ Judgments on *Viking, Laval, Rüffert*, and *Luxembourg* on the Practice of Collective Bargaining and the Effectiveness of Social Action' IP/A/EMPL/ST/2009-11 (May 2010)

European Commission, 'Expert Groups Explained' <http://ec.europa.eu/transparency/regexpert/index.cfm?do=faq.faq&aide=2 accessed November 28, 2015>

Eurostat, 'The EU in the World 2014. A Statistical Portrait' (Publications Office of the European Union 2014) <dx.doi.org/10.2785/48181> accessed 6 October 2015

Eurostat, 'Migrant Integration Statistics—Employment, April 2015' <http://ec.europa.eu/eurostat/statistics-explained/index.php/Migrant_integration_statistics_-_employment#Unemployment> accessed November 28, 2015

Everson M, 'The Legacy of the Market Citizen' in Shaw J and More G (eds), *New Legal Dynamics of European Union* (Clarendon Press 1995)

Everson M, 'The Constitutionalization of European Administrative Law: Legal Oversight of a Stateless Internal Market' in Joerges C and Vos E (eds), *EU Committees: Social Regulation, Law and Politics* (Hart Publishing 1999)

Fabbrini S, 'Executive Power in the European Union: The Implications of the Euro Crisis.' (Paper presented at the EU Studies Association 14th Biennial Conference, Boston, 5–7 March 2015) (not yet published). On file with the author

di Fabio U, 'A European Charter: Towards a Constitution for the Union' (2001) 7 Columbia Journal of European Law 159

Fabre C, 'A Philosophical Argument for a Bill of Rights' (2000) 30 British Journal of Political Science 77

Falk RA, Johansen RC, and Kim SS, 'Global Constitutionalism and World Order' in Falk RA, Johansen RC, Kim SS (eds), *The Constitutional Foundations of World Peace* (SUNY Press 1993)

Falkner G, Treib O, Hartlapp M, and Leiber S, *Complying with Europe: EU Harmonisation and Soft Law in the Member States* (Cambridge University Press 2005)

Fassbender B, 'The United Nations Charter as Constitution of the International Community' (1998) 36 Columbia Journal of Transnational Law 529

Fassbender B, 'Rediscovering a Forgotten Constitution: Notes on the Place of the UN Charter in the International Legal Order' in Dunoff JL and Trachtman JP (eds), *Ruling the World? Constitutionalism, International Law, and Global Governance* (Cambridge University Press 2009)

Feldstein M, 'EMU and International Conflict' (1997) 76 Foreign Affairs 60

Ferejohn J and Sager L, 'Commitment and Constitutionalism' (2003) 81 Texas Law Review 1929

Ferrara M, 'Modest Beginnings, Timid Progresses: What's Next for Social Europe?' in Cantillon B, Verschueren H, and Ploscar P (eds), *Social Inclusion and Social Protection in the EU: Interactions Between Law and Policy* (Intersentia 2012)

Ferrara M, 'Social Europe and its Components in the Midst of the Crisis: A Conclusion' (2014) 37 West European Politics 825

Finnis J, *Natural Law and Natural Rights* (Oxford University Press 1980)

Fischer J, 'From Confederacy to Federation: Thoughts on the Finality of European Integration.' Speech delivered at Humboldt University in Berlin (12 May 2000)

Fligstein N, *Euroclash: The EU, European Identity, and the Future of Europe* (Oxford University Press 2008)

Fligstein N and Stone Sweet A, 'Constructing Polities and Markets: An Institutionalist Account of European Integration' (2002) 107 American Journal of Sociology 1206

Føllesdal A and Hix S, 'Why there Is a Democratic Deficit in the EU: A Response to Majone and Moravcsik' (2006) 44 Journal of Common Market Studies 533

Fontanella-Khan J, Wiesmann G, and Warrell H, 'UK Seeks EU Support over "Benefits Tourism"' *Financial Times* (London, 7 March 2013)

Forsyth M, *Unions of States. The Theory and Practice of Confederation* (Holmes & Meier Publishers 1981)

Forsyth M, 'The Political Theory of Federalism and the Relevance of Classical Approaches' in Hesse JJ and Wright V (eds), *Federalizing Europe? The Costs, Benefits, and Preconditions of Federal Political Systems* (Oxford University Press 1996)

Fraser N, *Justice Interruptus: Critical Reflections on the 'Postsocialist' Condition* (Routledge 1997)

Friedrich CJ, 'Constitutions and Constitutionalism' in Sills DL (ed), *International Encyclopedia of the Social Sciences* (Macmillan 1968)

Future of Europe Group Comprising the Foreign Ministers of Austria, Belgium, Denmark, France, Italy, Germany, Luxembourg, the Netherlands, Poland, Portugal, and Spain, 'Final Report of the Future of Europe Group' (17 September 2012)

Gallie WB, 'Essentially Contested Concepts' (1956) 56 Proceedings of the Aristotelian Society 167

Garrett G and Weingast BR, *Ideas, Interests and Institutions: Constructing the EC's Internal Market* (University of California Center for German and European Studies 1991)

van Gelderen M and Skinner Q (eds), *Republicanism. A Shared European Heritage*, vol I (Cambridge University Press 2002)

Gellner E, *Nations and Nationalism* (Cornell University Press 1983)

Gerber DJ, 'Constitutionalizing the Economy: German Neo-Liberalism, Competition Law, and the "New Europe"' (1994) 42 American Journal of Comparative Law 25

Gewirth A, *Human Rights. Essays on Justification and Applications* (University of Chicago Press 1982)

Gilpin R, *The Political Economy of International Relations* (Princeton University Press 1987)

Ginsburg T and Simpser A (eds), *Constitutions in Authoritarian Regimes* (Cambridge University Press 2013)

Giubboni S, *Social Rights and Market Freedom in the European Constitution: A Labour Law Perspective* (Inston R tr, Cambridge University Press 2006)

Godrand F, *Eurospeak: The User's Guide. Dictionary of the Single Market* (Nicholas Brealy Publishing 1992)

Goldsmith JL and Posner EA, *The Limits of International Law* (Oxford University Press 2006)

Goodale M and Merry SE (eds), *The Practice of Human Rights: Tracking Law Between the Global and the Local* (Cambridge University Press 2007)

Goodin RE, 'If People Were Money…' in Barry B and Goodin RE (eds), *Free Movement. Ethical Issues in the Transnational Migration of People and of Money* (The Pennsylvania State University Press 1992)

Goodman R and Pegram T (eds), *Human Rights, State Compliance, and Social Change: Assessing National Human Rights Institutions* (Cambridge University Press 2011)

Gragl P, 'The Shortcomings of Dublin II: Strasbourg's *M.S.S.* Judgment and its Implications for the European Legal Order' (2012) European Yearbook on Human Rights 123

Griffin J, *On Human Rights* (Oxford University Press 2008)

Griller S, 'International Law, Human Rights and the European Community's Autonomous Legal Order: Notes on the European Court of Justice Decision in *Kadi*' (2008) 4 European Constitutional Law Review 528

Grimm D, 'Does Europe Need a Constitution?' (1995) 1 European Law Journal 282

Grimm D, 'Treaty or Constitution? The Legal Basis of the European Union after Maastricht' in Eriksen EO, Fossum JE, and Menendez AJ (eds), *Developing a Constitution for Europe* (Routledge 2004)

Grimm D, 'The Democratic Costs of Constitutionalisation: The European Case' (2015) 21 European Law Journal 460

Guild E, 'The Europeanisation of Europe's Asylum Policy' (2006) 18 International Journal of Refugee Law 630

Gutmann A, 'Democracy' in Goodin RE and Pettit P (eds), *A Companion to Contemporary Political Philosophy* (Blackwell Reference Online 1995)

Haas EB, *The Uniting of Europe. Political, Social, and Economic Forces 1950–1957* (first published 1958, University of Notre Dame Press 2004)

Haas EB, *The Obsolescence of Regional Integration Theory* (University of California Press 1975)

Habermas J, 'On the Internal Relation Between the Rule of Law and Democracy' (1995) 3 European Journal of Philosophy 12

Habermas J, 'Remarks on Dieter Grimm's "Does Europe Need a Constitution?"' (1995) 1 European Law Journal 303

Habermas J, *Between Facts and Norms: Contributions to a Discourse Theory of Law and Democracy* (Rehg W tr, MIT Press 1996)

Habermas J, *The Postnational Constellation: Political Essays* (Pensky M tr and ed, MIT Press 1998)

Habermas J, *The Inclusion of the Other* (Cronin C and de Grieff P eds, MIT Press 1998)

Habermas J, 'Why Europe Needs a Constitution' (2001) 11 New Left Review 5

Habermas J, *Europe. The Faltering Project* (Cronin C tr, Polity 2009)

Habermas J, *The Crisis of the European Union: A Response* (Cronin C tr, Polity 2012)

Halberstam D and Stein E, 'The United Nations, the European Union, and the King of Sweden: Economic Sanctions and Individual Rights in a Plural World Order' (2009) 46 Common Market Law Review 13

Hallstein W, 'Some of Our "Faux Problèmes" in the European Economic Community' (1965) 21 The World Today 10

Hamilton A, 'Letter to James Duane dated 3 September 1780' <http://press-pubs.uchicago.edu/founders/documents/v1ch5s2.html> accessed 8 October 2015

Hamilton A, Madison J, and Jay J, *The Federalist Papers* (Shapiro I ed, Yale University Press 2009)

Hanssen P and Jonsson S, *Eurafrica. The Untold History of European Integration and Colonialism* (Bloomsbury 2014)

Hardin R, 'Why a Constitution?' in Grofman B and Wittman D (eds), *The Federalist Papers and the New Institutionalism* (Agathon Press 1989)

Held D, *Political Theory and the Modern State. Essays on State, Power, and Democracy* (Polity Press 1989)

Held D, *Democracy and the Global Order: From the Modern State to Cosmopolitan Governance* (Stanford University Press 1995)

Held D, 'Principles of Cosmopolitan Order' in Brock G and Brighouse H (eds), *The Political Philosophy of Cosmopolitanism* (Cambridge University Press 2005)

Held D, McGrew A, Goldblatt D, and Perraton J, *Global Transformations. Politics, Economics, and Culture* (Polity Press 1999)

Helfer LR, 'Constitutional Analogies in the International Legal System' (2003) 37 Loyola of Los Angeles Law Review 193

Hendrickson DC, *Peace Pact: The Lost World of the American Founding* (University of Kansas Press 2003)

Henry P, 'Shall Liberty or Empire Be Sought?' Speech to the Virginia Convention (5 June 1788) <https://en.wikisource.org/wiki/Henry%27s_speech_in_the_Virginia_Ratifying_Convention> accessed 8 October 2015

Hervey TK, 'Migrant Workers and Their Families in the European Union: The Pervasive Market Ideology of Community Law' in Shaw J and More G (eds), *New Legal Dynamics of European Union* (Clarendon Press 1995)

Hinarejos A, '*Laval* and *Viking*: The Right to Collective Action versus EU Fundamental Freedoms' (2008) 8 Human Rights Law Review 714

Hirschl R, 'The Political Origins of the New Constitutionalism' (2004) 11 Indiana Journal of Global Legal Studies 71

Hirschl R, *Towards Juristocracy: The Origins and Consequences of the New Constitutionalism* (Harvard University Press 2004)

Hix S, *What's Wrong with the European Union and How to Fix It* (Polity 2008)

Hobbes T, *Leviathan* (first published 1651, Tuck R ed, Cambridge University Press 1996)

Hoffman S, 'Obstinate or Obsolete: The Fate of the Nation State and the Case of Western Europe' (1966) 95 Daedalus 862

Hoffman J, 'Terrorism Blacklisting: Putting European Human Rights Guarantees to the Test' (2008) 15 Constellations 543

Holmes P, 'The WTO and the EU: Some Constitutional Comparisons' in de Burca G and Scott J (eds), *The EU and the WTO: Legal and Constitutional Issues* (Hart Publishing 2001)

Holmes S, *Passions and Constraint* (University of Chicago Press 1995)

Holmes S, 'To "Facilitate Future Invasions of the Remainder": Westward Expansion and its Natural Enemies in the *Federalist Papers*' (forthcoming). Draft paper on file with the author

Holmes S and Sunstein CR, 'The Politics of Constitutional Revision in Eastern Europe' in Levinson S (ed), *Responding to Imperfection. The Theory and Practice of Constitutional Amendment* (Princeton University Press 1995)

Honig B, *Political Theory and the Displacement of Politics* (Cornell University Press 1993)

Hoogenboom A, 'In Search of a Rationale for the EU Citizenship Jurisprudence' (2015) 35 Oxford Journal of Legal Studies 301

Hooghe L and Marks G, 'The Making of a Polity: The Struggle over European Integration' (1997) 1 European Integration Online Papers <http://eiop.or.at/eiop/pdf/1997-004.pdf> accessed 6 October 2015

Hooghe L and Marks G, *Multi-level Governance and European Integration* (Rowman & Littlefield 2001)

Hooghe L and Marks G, 'Unraveling the Central State, but how? Types of Multi-level Governance' (2003) 97 American Political Science Review 233

Höpner M and Schäfer A, 'Embeddedness and Regional Integration: Waiting for Polanyi in a Hayekian Setting' (2012) 66 International Organization 429

Hoskyns C, *Integrating Gender. Women, Law and Politics in the European Union* (Verso 1996)

Howse R, 'From Politics to Technocracy—and Back Again: The Fate of the Multilateral Trading Regime' (2002) 96 American Journal of International Law 94

Howse R and Nicolaïdis K, 'Legitimacy through "Higher Law"? Why Constitutionalizing the WTO is a Step Too Far' in Cottier T and Mavroidis PC (eds), *The Role of the Judge in International Trade Regulation: Experience and lessons for the WTO* (University of Michigan Press 2003)

Hoyt RS, 'The Coronation Oath of 1308' (1956) 71 The English Historical Review 353

Ignatieff M, *Human Rights as Politics and Idolatry* (Princeton University Press 2001)

International Monetary Fund, *Global Economic Outlook 2009* (International Monetary Fund 2009) <http://www.imf.org/external/pubs/ft/weo/2009/01/pdf/text.pdf> accessed 6 October 2015

Ipsen HP, *Verfassungsperspektiven der Europäischen Gemeinschaften* (Walter de Gruyter & Co 1970)

Ipsen HP, *Europäisches Gemeinschaftsrecht* (J.C.B. Mohr 1972)

Ipsen HP, 'Die Verfassungsrolle des Europäischen Gerichtshofs für die Integration' in Schwarze J (ed), *Der Europäische Gerichtshof als Verfassungsgericht und Rechtsschutzinstanz* (Nomos 1983)

Ipsen HP, *Europäisches Gemeinschaftsrecht in Einzelstudien* (Nomos 1984)

Ipsen HP, 'Die Bundesrepublik Deutschland in den Europäischen Gemeinschaften' in Isensee J and Kirchhof P (eds), *Handbuch des Staatsrechts der Bundesrepublik Deutschland*, vol VII (Müller 1992)

Isiksel T, 'Fundamental Rights in the EU after *Kadi and Al Barakaat*' (2010) 15 European Law Journal 551

Isiksel T, 'Peter L. Lindseth, *Power and Legitimacy. Reconciling Europe and the Nation-State* (Oxford University Press) 2010. 364 p' (2012) 8 European Constitutional Law Review 128

Isiksel T, 'Between Text and Context: Turkey's Tradition of Authoritarian Constitutionalism' (2013) 11 International Journal of Constitutional Law 702

Isiksel T, 'The Dream of a Commercial Peace' in van Middelaar L and van Parijs P (eds), *After the Storm. How to Save Democracy in Europe* (Lannoo 2015)

Jacobs FG, 'Introduction' in Guild E (ed), *The Legal Framework and Social Consequences of Free Movement of Persons in the European Union* (Kluwer Law International 1998)

Jacobsohn GJ, *Apple of Gold* (Princeton University Press 1993)

Jervis R, 'Cooperation Under the Security Dilemma' (1978) 30 World Politics 167

Joerges C, 'Taking the Law Seriously: On Political Science and the Role of Law in the Process of European Integration' (1996) 2 European Law Journal 105

Joerges C, 'Bureaucratic Nightmare, Technocratic Regime and the Dream of Good Transnational Governance' in Joerges C and Vos E (eds), *EU Committees: Social Regulation, Law and Politics* (Hart Publishing 1999)

Joerges C, 'The Law in the Process of Constitutionalizing Europe' (2002/04) EUI Working Paper

Joerges C, 'Europe a *Großraum*? Shifting Legal Conceptualisations of the Integration Project' in Joerges C and Ghaleigh NS (eds), *Darker Legacies of Law in Europe* (Hart 2003)

Joerges C, 'Law and Politics in Europe's Crisis: On the History of the Impact of an Unfortunate Configuration' (2014) 21 Constellations 249

Joerges C and Everson M, 'Law, Economics and Politics in the Constitutionalization of Europe' in Eriksen EO, Fossum JE, and Menendez AJ (eds), *Developing a Constitution for Europe* (Routledge 2004)

Joerges C and Neyer J, 'From Intergovernmental Bargaining to Deliberative Political Processes: The Constitutionalisation of Comitology' (1997) 3 European Law Journal 273

Joerges C and Neyer J, 'Transforming Strategic Interaction into Deliberative Problem-solving: European Comitology in the Foodstuffs Sector' (1997) 4 Journal of European Public Policy 609

Joerges C and Rödl F, 'Informal Politics and Formalised Law: Reflections after the Judgments of the ECJ in *Viking* and *Laval*' (2009) 15 European Law Journal 1

Judt T, 'What Is Living and what Is Dead in Social Democracy?' *The New York Review of Books* (New York, 17 December 2009) <http://www.nybooks.com/

articles/archives/2009/dec/17/what-is-living-and-what-is-dead-in-social-democrac/?pagination=false> accessed 7 October 2015

Jung C, Lust-Okar E, and Shapiro I, 'Problems and Prospects for Democratic Settlements: South Africa as a Model for the Middle East and Northern Ireland?' (2005) 33 Politics & Society 277

Kalmo H and Skinner Q (eds), *Sovereignty in Fragments. The Past, Present and Future of a Contested Concept* (Cambridge University Press 2010)

Kant I, *Political Writings* (Reiss H ed, Nisbet HB tr, 2nd edn, Cambridge University Press 1997)

Keck ME and Sikkink K, *Activists Beyond Borders* (Cornell University Press 1998)

Keith LC, 'Constitutional Provisions for Individual Human Rights (1977–1996): Are They Mere "Window Dressing"?' (2002) 55 Political Research Quarterly 111

Kelemen RD, 'The EU Rights Revolution: Adversarial Legalism and European Integration' in Börzel T and Cichowski RA (eds), *The State of the European Union, vol 6: Law, Politics, and Society* (Oxford University Press 2003)

Kelemen RD, *Eurolegalism: The Transformation of Law and Regulation in the European Union* (Harvard University Press 2011)

Kennedy D, 'New Approaches to Comparative Law: Comparativism and International Governance' (1997) Utah Law Review 545

Keohane RO, *After Hegemony. Cooperation and Discord in the World Political Economy* (Princeton University Press 1984)

Keohane RO, 'International Institutions: Two Approaches' (1988) 32 International Studies Quarterly 379

Keohane RO, Macedo S, and Moravcsik A, 'Democracy-Enhancing Multilateralism' (2009) 63 International Organization 1

Klabbers J, '*EJIL* Foreword: The Transformation of International Organizations Law' (2015) 26 European Journal of International Law 9

Kochenov D, *EU Enlargement and the Failure of Conditionality* (Kluwer Law 2007)

Kochenov D, '*Ius Tractum* of Many Faces: European Citizenship and the Difficult Relationship Between Status and Rights' (2008–2009) 15 Columbia Journal of European Law 169

Kochenov D, 'The Right to Have *What* Rights? EU Citizenship in Need of Clarification' (2013) 19 European Law Journal 502

Kohler-Koch B and Rittberger B (eds), *Debating the Democratic Legitimacy of the European Union* (Rowman & Littlefield 2007)

Koskenniemi M, 'The Effect of Rights on Political Culture' in Alston P, Bustelo M, and Heenan J (eds), *The EU and Human Rights* (Oxford University Press 1999)

Koskenniemi M, *Gentle Civilizer of Nations: The Rise and Fall of International Law 1870–1960* (Cambridge University Press 2002)

Kostakopoulou D, 'Invisible Citizens? Long-term Resident Third-country Nationals in the EU and Their Struggle for Recognition' in Bellamy R and Warleigh A (eds), *Citizenship and Governance in the European Union* (Continuum 2001)

Kostakopoulou D, 'Ideas, Norms, and European Citizenship: Explaining Institutional Change' (2005) 68 Modern Law Review 233

Krasner S, *Sovereignty. Organized Hypocrisy* (Princeton University Press 1999)

Krisch N, 'The Open Architecture of European Human Rights Law' (2008) 71 Modern Law Review 183

Krisch N and Kingsbury B, 'Global Governance and Global Administrative Law in the International Legal Order' (2006) 17 European Journal of International Law 1

Kumm M, 'The Cosmopolitan Turn in Constitutionalism: On the Relationship Between Constitutionalism in and Beyond the State' in Dunoff JL and Trachtman JP (eds), *Ruling the World? Constitutionalism, International Law, and Global Governance* (Cambridge University Press 2009)

Kunoy B and Dawes A, 'Plate Tectonics in Luxembourg: The *Ménage à Trois* Between EC Law, International Law and the European Convention on Human Rights Following the UN Sanctions Cases' (2009) 46 Common Market Law Review 73

Kuper A, 'Rawlsian Global Justice: Beyond the Law of Peoples to a Cosmopolitan Law of Persons' (2000) 28 Political Theory 640

Laderchi FPR, 'Report on Italy' in Slaughter A-M, Stone Sweet A, and Weiler J (eds), *The European Courts and National Courts* (Hart Publishing 1998)

Landemore H, *Democratic Reason: Politics, Collective Intelligence, and the Rule of the Many* (Princeton University Press 2012)

Lasser M, *Judicial Deliberations: A Comparative Analysis of Transparency and Legitimacy* (Oxford University Press 2004)

Lauterpacht H, *International Law and Human Rights* (first published 1950, Archon Books 1968)

Law DS, 'The Paradox of Omnipotence: Courts, Constitutions, and Commitments' (2006) 40 Georgia Law Review 407

Law DS, 'Constitutions' in Kane P and Kritzer H (eds), *Oxford Handbook of Empirical Legal Research* (Oxford University Press 2010)

Law DS and Versteeg M, 'Sham Constitutions' (2013) 101 California Law Review 863

Lecourt R, *L'Europe des Juges* (Bruylant 1976)

Lehndorff S (ed), *A Triumph of Failed Ideas. European Models of Capitalism in the Crisis* (European Trade Union Institute 2012)

Leibfried S, 'Social Policy: Left to the Judges and the Markets?' in Wallace H, Pollack MA, and Young AR (eds), *Policy-making in the European Union* (7th edn, Oxford University Press 2015)

Lenart J, ' "Fortress Europe": Compliance of the Dublin II Regulation with the European Convention for the Protection of Human Rights and Fundamental Freedoms' (2012) 28 Merkourios: Utrecht Journal of International and European Law 4

Lindberg LN, *The Political Dynamics of European Economic Integration* (Stanford University Press 1963)

Lindseth PL, 'The Contradictions of Supranationalism: Administrative Governance and Constitutionalization in European Integration since the 1950s' (2003) 37 Loyola of Los Angeles Law Review 363

Lindseth PL, *Power and Legitimacy. Reconciling Europe and the Nation-State* (Oxford University Press 2010)

Lindseth PL, 'Author's Reply: "Outstripping", or the Question of "Legitimate for What?" in EU Governance' (2012) 8 European Constitutional Law Review 153

Linklater A, 'Citizenship and Sovereignty in the Post-Westphalian European State' in Archibugi D, Held D, and Köhler M (eds), *Re-imagining Political Community. Studies in Cosmopolitan Democracy* (Stanford University Press 1998)

List C and Goodin RE, 'Epistemic Democracy: Generalizing the Condorcet Jury Theorem' (2001) 9 Journal of Political Philosophy 277

Locke J, *Second Treatise of Government* (Macpherson CB ed, Hackett 1980)

Lutz D, *Principles of Constitutional Design* (Cambridge University Press 2006)

Lynskey O, 'The Data Retention Directive Is Incompatible with the Rights to Privacy and Data Protection and Is Invalid in its Entirety: *Digital Rights Ireland*' (2014) 51 Common Market Law Review 1789

Maas W, 'The Genesis of European Rights' (2005) 43 Journal of Common Market Studies 1009

Maas W, *Creating European Citizens* (Rowman & Littlefield Publishers 2007)

MacCormick N, *Questioning Sovereignty: Law, State, and Nation in the European Commonwealth* (Oxford University Press 1999)

Maduro MP, *We the Court: The European Court of Justice and the European Economic Constitution* (Hart Publishing 1998)

Maduro MP, 'Contrapunctual Law: Europe's Constitutional Pluralism in Action' in Walker N (ed), *Sovereignty in Transition* (Hart Publishing 2003)

Maduro MP, 'The Double Constitutional Life of the Charter of Fundamental Rights of the European Union' in Hervey TK and Kenner J (eds), *Economic and Social Rights under the EU Charter of Fundamental Rights—A Legal Perspective* (Hart Publishing 2003)

Maduro MP, 'Europe and the Constitution: What if this Is as Good as it Gets?' in Weiler JHH and Wind M (eds), *European Constitutionalism Beyond the State* (Cambridge University Press 2003)

Maduro MP, 'The Importance of Being Called a Constitution: Constitutional Authority and the Authority of Constitutionalism' (2005) 3 International Journal of Constitutional Law 332

Maduro MP, 'Sovereignty in Europe: The European Court of Justice and the Creation of a European Political Community' in Volcansek ML and Stack Jr JFF (eds), *Courts Crossing Borders: Blurring the Lines of Sovereignty* (Carolina Academic Press 2005)

Maduro MP, 'Courts and Pluralism: Essay on a Theory of Judicial Adjudication in the Context of Legal and Constitutional Pluralism' in Dunoff JL and Trachtman

JP (eds), *Ruling the World? Constitutionalism, International Law, and Global Governance* (Cambridge University Press 2009)

Majone G, 'The European Community: An "Independent Fourth Branch of Government"?' (1993) EUI Working Paper SPS No 93/9

Majone G, 'The Rise of the Regulatory State in Europe' (1994) 17 Journal of Public Policy 77

Majone G, 'From the Positive to the Regulatory State: Causes and Consequences of Changes in the Mode of Governance' (1997) 17 Journal of Public Policy 139

Majone G, 'Europe's "Democratic Deficit": The Question of Standards' (1998) 4 European Law Journal 5

Majone G, *Dilemmas of European Integration. The Ambiguities and Pitfalls of Integration by Stealth* (Oxford University Press 2005)

Mancini F and Keeling DT, 'Democracy and the European Court of Justice' (1994) 57 Modern Law Review 175

Marks G, Hooghe L, and Blank K, 'European Integration from the 1980s: State-Centric v. Multi-level Governance' (1996) 34 Journal of Common Market Studies 341

Marshall TH and Bottomore T, *Citizenship and Social Class* (first published 1950, Pluto Press 1992)

Martiniello M, 'Citizenship of the European Union: A Critical View' in Bauböck R (ed), *From Aliens to Citizens* (Avebury 1994)

Mattli W and Slaughter A-M, 'Constructing the European Community Legal System from the Ground up' (1996) EUI Working Papers

Mazey S and Richardson J, 'The Logic of Organization: Interest Groups' in Richardson J (ed), *European Union: Power and Policy-Making* (Routledge 1996)

Mazey S and Richardson J, 'Institutionalizing Promiscuity: Commission-Interest Group Relations in the European Union' in Stone Sweet A, Sandholtz W, and Fligstein N, *The Institutionalization of Europe* (Oxford University Press 2001)

McIlwain CH, *Constitutionalism Ancient and Modern* (Cornell University Press 1940)

McCormick JP, *Weber, Habermas, and Transformations of the European State. Constitutional, Social, and Supranational Democracy* (Cambridge University Press 2007)

Menon A and Weatherill S, 'Transnational Legitimacy in a Globalising World: How the European Union Rescues its States' (2008) 31 West European Politics 397

Mestmäcker E-J, 'On the Legitimacy of European Law' (1994) 58 Rabels Zeitschrift für ausländisches und internationals Privatrecht 615

Michelman F, 'Law's Republic' (1989) 97 Yale Law Journal 1493

Michelman FI, 'Parsing a Right to Have Rights' (1996) 3 Constellations 200

Michelman FI, 'What Do Constitutions Do that Statutes Don't (Legally Speaking)?' in Bauman RW and Kahana T (eds), *The Least Examined Branch: The Role of Legislatures in the Constitutional State* (Cambridge University Press 2006)

Miller AS, 'Toward a Definition of "the" Constitution' (1983) 8 University of Dayton Law Review 633

Miller D, *Citizenship and National Identity* (Polity Press 2000)

Miller D, *National Responsibility and Global Justice* (Oxford University Press 2007)

Milward A, *European Rescue of the Nation-state* (2nd edn, Routledge 2000)

Mitrany D, 'The Prospect of Integration: Federal or Functional' (1965) 4 Journal of Common Market Studies 119

Mitrany D, *The Functional Theory of Politics* (LSE / Martin Robertson 1975)

Monnet J, 'Note de Réflexion de 5 août 1943' <http://www.cvce.eu/obj/note_de_reflexion_de_jean_monnet_alger_5_aout_1943-fr-b61a8924-57bf-4890-9e4b-73bf4d882549.html> accessed 5 October 2015

Monnet J, Speech to the Joint Meeting of the Members of the Consultative Assembly of the Council of Europe and the Members of the Common Assembly of the European Community of Coal and Steel, in *Official Report of the Debate* (Strasbourg, 22 June 1953) 122 <http://aei.pitt.edu/34049/4/A601.pdf> accessed 7 December 2015

Monnet J, *The United States of Europe Has Begun. The European Coal and Steel Community Speeches and Addresses 1952–1954* (University of Pittsburgh Archive of European Integration, microfiche, Paris 1955)

Moore C, 'A Maastricht Phrasebook' *The Spectator* (London, 23 November 1991)

Moravcsik A, 'Preferences and Power in the European Community: A Liberal Intergovernmentalist Approach' (1993) 31 Journal of Common Market Studies 473

Moravcsik A, *The Choice for Europe. Social Purpose and State Power from Messina to Maastricht* (Cornell University Press 1998)

Moravcsik A, 'The Origins of Human Rights Regimes: Democratic Delegation in Postwar Europe' (2000) 54 International Organization 217

Moravcsik A, 'In Defence of the "Democratic Deficit": Reassessing Legitimacy in the European Union' (2002) 40 Journal of Common Market Studies 603

Moravcsik A, 'The European Constitutional Compromise and the Neofunctionalist Legacy' (2005) 12 Journal of European Public Policy 349

Moravcsik A and Sangiovanni A, 'On Democracy and "Public Interest" in the European Union' in Streeck W and Mayntz R (eds), *Die Reformierbarkeit der Demokratie. Innovationen und Blockaden* (Campus 2002)

More G, 'The Principle of Equal Treatment: From Market Unifier to Fundamental Right?' in Craig P and de Búrca G (eds), *The Evolution of EU Law* (Oxford University Press 1999)

Moury C and Héritier A, 'Shifting Competences and Changing Preferences: The Case of Delegation to Comitology' (2012) 19 Journal of European Public Policy 1316

Mouzourakis M, ' "We Need to Talk About Dublin": Responsibility under the Dublin System as a Blockage to Asylum Burden-Sharing in the European Union' (2014) Oxford Refugee Studies Centre Working Paper Series No. 105

Moyn S, *The Last Utopia: Human Rights in History* (Belknap 2012)

Mueller DC, *Constitutional Democracy* (Oxford University Press 1996)

Müller J-W, *Contesting Democracy: Political Ideas in Twentieth-Century Europe* (Yale University Press 2011)

Müller J-W, 'Beyond Militant Democracy?' (2012) New Left Review 39

Nagel T, 'The Problem of Global Justice' (2005) 33 Philosophy & Public Affairs 113

Neyer J, *The Justification of Europe: A Political Theory of Supranational Integration* (Oxford University Press 2012)

Nic Shuibhne N, 'Free Movement of Persons and the Wholly Internal Rule: Time to Move on?' (2002) 39 Common Market Law Review 731

Nic Shuibhne N, 'The Resilience of EU Market Citizenship' (2010) 47 Common Market Law Review 1597

Nic Shuibhne N, *The Coherence of EU Free Movement Law: Constitutional Responsibility and the Court of Justice* (Oxford University Press 2013)

Nicolaïdis K, 'European Demoïcracy and its Crisis' (2012) 51 Journal of Common Market Studies 351

Niessen J, *Five Years of EU Migration and Asylum Policymaking under the Amsterdam and Tampere Mandates* (Migration Policy Group 2004)

Nord HR, 'The Role of the Parliament of the European Communities' *Internationale Spectator* (The Hague, 8 April 1965) 685

North DC, 'Institutions and Credible Commitment' (1993) 149 Journal of Institutional and Theoretical Economics 11

North DC, 'The New Institutional Economics and Third World Development' in Harriss J, Hunter J, and Lewis CM (eds), *The New Institutional Economics and Third World Development* (Routledge 1997)

North DC and Weingast BR, 'Constitutions and Commitment: The Evolution of Institutions Governing Public Choice in Seventeenth-century England' (1989) 49 Journal of Economic History 803

Ober J, *Democracy and Knowledge: Innovation and Learning in Classical Athens* (Princeton University Press 2008)

OECD Directorate for Employment, Labour, and Social Affairs, 'Social Expenditure Update' (November 2014) <http://www.oecd.org/els/soc/OECD2014-Social-Expenditure-Update-Nov2014-8pages.pdf> accessed 5 December 2015

Offe C, *The Democratic Welfare State. A European Regime under the Strain of European Integration* (IHS Political Science Series no 68, Institute for Advanced Studies 2000)

Offe C, *Europe Entrapped* (Polity 2015)

Peers S, 'Fundamental Right or Political Whim? WTO Law and the European Court of Justice' in de Burca G and Scott J (eds), *The EU and WTO: Legal and Constitutional Issues* (Hart Publishing 2001)

Perju V, 'Reason and Authority in the European Court of Justice' (2009) 49 Virginia Journal of International Law 308

Persson T and Tabellini G, *The Economic Effects of Constitutions* (MIT Press 2003)

Pescatore P, 'The Doctrine of "Direct Effect": An Infant Disease of Community Law' (1983) 8 European Law Review 155

Peters A, 'Compensatory Constitutionalism: The Function and Potential of Fundamental International Norms and Structures' (2006) 19 Leiden Journal of International Law 579

Petersmann E-U, *Constitutional Functions and Constitutional Problems of International Economic Law* (University Press Fribourg Switzerland 1991)

Petersmann E-U, 'How to Constitutionalize International Law and Foreign Policy for the Benefit of Civil Society?' (1999) 20 Michigan Journal of International Law 1

Petersmann E-U, 'Time for a United Nations "Global Compact" for Integrating Human Rights into the Law of Worldwide Organizations: Lessons from European Integration' (2002) 13 European Journal of International Law 621

Pettit P, *Republicanism. A Theory of Freedom and Government* (Oxford University Press 1999)

Pettit P, 'Depoliticizing Democracy' (2004) 17 Ratio Juris 52

Plato, *Statesman* (Rowe CJ tr, Hackett 1999)

Pocock JGA, *The Ancient Constitution and the Feudal Law* (Cambridge University Press 1957)

Pocock JGA, *The Machiavellian Moment. Florentine Political Thought and the Atlantic Republican Tradition* (Princeton University Press 1975)

Pogge T, 'An Egalitarian Law of Peoples' (1994) 23 Philosophy and Public Affairs 195

Polanyi K, *The Great Transformation. The Political and Economic Origins of Our Time* (first published 1944, Beacon Press 2001)

Pollack MA, 'Deliberative Democracy? Two Images of Comitology' (2003) 36 Comparative Political Studies 125

Pollack MA and Hafner-Burton E, 'Mainstreaming Gender in the European Union' (2000) 7 Journal of European Public Policy 432

de la Porte C and Natali D, 'Altered Europeanisation of Pension Reform in the Context of the Great Recession: Denmark and Italy Compared' (2014) 37 West European Politics 732

Proceedings of Commissioners to Remedy Defects of the Federal Government, Annapolis, 11 September 1786 <http://avalon.law.yale.edu/18th_century/annapoli.asp> accessed 27 November 2015

Przeworski A, 'Minimalist Conception of Democracy: A Defense' in Shapiro I and Hacker-Cordon C (eds), *Democracy's Value* (Cambridge University Press 1999)

Rawls J, *A Theory of Justice* (first published 1971, revised edn, Harvard University Press 1999)

Rawls J, *The Law of Peoples* (Harvard University Press 1999)

Raz J, 'Human Rights without Foundations' in Besson S and Tasioulas J (eds), *The Philosophy of International Law* (Oxford University Press 2010)

Reh C, 'The Lisbon Treaty: De-constitutionalizing the European Union?' (2009) 47 Journal of Common Market Studies 625

Reif K and Schmitt H, 'Nine Second-Order Elections. A Conceptual Framework for the Analysis of European Election Results' (1980) 8 European Journal of Political Research 3

Rhinard M, 'The Democratic Legitimacy of the European Union Committee System' (2002) 15 Governance 185

Riker WH, *Liberalism Against Populism: A Confrontation Between the Theory of Democracy and the Theory of Social Choice* (first published 1982, Waveland Press 1988)

Ritter C, 'Purely Internal Situations, Reverse Discrimination, *Guimont, Dzodzi* and Article 234' (2006) 31 European Law Review 690

Robbins L, 'Federal Union Examined III' *The Spectator* (London, 28 March 1940)

Van Rompuy H, in cooperation with Barroso JM, Juncker J-C, and Draghi M, *Towards A Genuine Economic and Monetary Union* (5 December 2012) <http://www.consilium.europa.eu/uedocs/cms_Data/docs/pressdata/en/ec/134069.pdf> accessed 7 December 2015

Root H, 'Tying the King's Hands' (1989) 1 Rationality and Society 240

Rosanvallon P, *Democratic Legitimacy: Impartiality, Reflexivity, Proximity* (Princeton University Press 2011)

Rosenfeld M, 'Is Global Constitutionalism Meaningful or Desirable?' (2014) 25 European Journal of International Law 177

Ruggie JG, 'Collective Goods and Future International Collaboration' (1972) 66 American Political Science Review 874

Ruggie JG, 'International Regimes, Transactions, and Change: Embedded Liberalism in the Postwar Economic Order' (1982) 36 International Organization 379

Sajó A, *Limiting Government. An Introduction to Constitutionalism* (Central European University Press 1999)

Sajó A, 'Constitution without the Constitutional Moment: A View from the New Member States' (2005) 3 International Journal of Constitutional Law 243

Sandholtz W and Stone Sweet A (eds), *European Integration and Supranational Governance* (Oxford University Press 1998)

Sangiovanni A, 'Global Justice, Reciprocity, and the State' (2007) 35 Philosophy & Public Affairs 3

Sartori G, 'Constitutionalism: A Preliminary Discussion' (1962) 56 American Political Science Review 853

Sartori G, 'Concept Misformation in Comparative Politics' (1970) 64 American Political Science Review 1033

Sarugger S, 'Interest Groups and Democracy in the European Union' (2008) 31 West European Politics 1274

Sassen S, *Losing Control? Sovereignty in an Age of Globalization* (Columbia University Press 1996)

Sassen S, *Territory, Authority, and Rights. From Medieval to Global Assemblages* (Princeton University Press 2006)

Scharpf FW, 'Negative and Positive Integration in the Political Economy of European Welfare States' in Marks G, Scharpf FW, Schmitter PC, and Streeck W (eds), *Governance in the European Union* (Sage 1996)

Scharpf FW, 'Economic Integration, Democracy, and the Welfare State' (1997) 4 Journal of European Public Policy 18

Scharpf FW, *Governing in Europe: Effective or Democratic?* (Oxford University Press 1999)

Scharpf FW, 'Democratic Legitimacy under Conditions of Regulatory Competition: Why Europe Differs from the United States' in Nicolaïdis K and Howse R (eds), *The Federal Vision* (Oxford University Press 2001)

Scharpf FW, 'The European Social Model: Coping with the Challenges of Diversity' (2002) 40 Journal of Common Market Studies 645

Scharpf FW, *Problem Solving Effectiveness and Democratic Accountability in the EU* (IHS Political Science Series No 107, Vienna Institute for Advanced Studies 2006)

Scharpf FW, 'The Asymmetry of European Integration, or, why the EU Cannot Be a Social Market Economy' (2010) 8 Socio-Economic Review 211

Scharpf FW, 'No Exit from the Euro-Rescuing Trap?' (MPIfG Discussion Paper No 14/4, Max-Planck-Institut für Gesellschaftsforschung 2014)

Scheppele KL, 'The International Standardization of National Security Law' (2010) 4 Journal of National Security Law and Policy 437

Scheppele KL, 'Enforcing the Basic Principles of EU Law through Systemic Infringement Procedures' in Kochenov D and Closa C (eds), *Reinforcing the Rule of Law Oversight in the European Union* (Cambridge University Press 2016)

Schmitt H, 'The European Parliament Elections of June 2004: Still Second-Order?' (2005) 28 West European Politics 650

Schmitter PC, 'Three Neo-Functional Hypotheses about International Integration' (1969) 23 International Organization 161

Schmitter PC, *How to Democratize the EU—and Why Bother?* (Rowman & Littlefield 2000)

Schmitter PC, 'Ernst B. Haas and the Legacy of Neofunctionalism' (2005) 12 Journal of European Public Policy 255

Schmitter PC and Bauer MW, 'A (Modest) Proposal for Expanding Social Citizenship in the European Union' (2001) 11 Journal of European Social Policy 55

Schneiderman D, 'Constitution or Model Treaty? Struggling over the Interpretive Authority of NAFTA' in Choudhry S (ed), *The Migration of Constitutional Ideas* (Cambridge University Press 2007)

Schumpeter J, *Capitalism, Socialism, and Democracy* (George Allen & Unwin Ltd 1942)

Schwartzberg M, *Democracy and Legal Change* (Cambridge University Press 2007)

Searle JR, *Speech Acts: An Essay in the Philosophy of Language* (Cambridge University Press 1969)

Sedelmeier U, 'Anchoring Democracy from above? The European Union and Democratic Backsliding in Hungary and Romania after Accession' (2014) 52 Journal of Common Market Studies 105

Sejersted F, 'Democracy and the Rule of Law: Some Historical Experiences of Contradictions in the Striving for Good Government' in Elster J and Slagstad R (eds), *Constitutionalism and Democracy* (Cambridge University Press 1988)

Shapiro I, *Democratic Justice* (Yale University Press 1999)

Shapiro M, 'The European Court of Justice' in Craig P and de Búrca G (eds), *The Evolution of EU Law* (Oxford University Press 1999)

Shapiro M, 'The Institutionalization of European Administrative Space' in Stone Sweet A, Sandholtz W, and Fligstein N, *The Institutionalization of Europe* (Oxford University Press 2001)

Shaw J, 'Process, Responsibility and Inclusion in EU Constitutionalism' (2003) 9 European Law Journal 45

Shaw J, *The Transformation of Citizenship in the European Union. Electoral Rights and the Restructuring of Political Space* (Cambridge University Press 2007)

Shepsle KA, 'Discretion, Institutions and the Problem of Government Commitment' in Bourdieu P and Coleman J (eds), Social Theory for a Changing Society (Russell Sage 1991)

Shue H, *Basic Rights. Subsistence, Affluence, and US Foreign Policy* (2nd edn, Princeton University Press 1996)

Sièyes EJ, 'What is the Third Estate?' [1789] in *Political Writings* (Michael Sonenscher tr, Hackett Publishing Co. 2003)

Simmons B, 'Globalization, Sovereignty, and Democracy' in Nardulli PF (ed), *International Perspectives on Contemporary Democracy* (University of Illinois Press 2008)

Simmons BA, *Mobilizing for Human Rights: International Law and Domestic Politics* (Cambridge University Press 2009)

Sindbjerg MD and Vollaard H, 'Implementing Social Europe in Times of Crises: Re-established Boundaries of Welfare?' (2014) 37 West European Politics 677

Skowronek S, *Building a New American State: The Expansion of National Administrative Capacities 1877–1920* (Cambridge University Press 1982)

Somek A, 'Authoritarian Constitutionalism: Austrian Constitutional Doctrine 1933 to 1938 and its Legacy' in Joerges C and Ghaleigh NS (eds), *Darker Legacies of Law in Europe* (Hart 2003)

Somek A, *Individualism. An Essay on the Authority of the European Union* (Oxford University Press 2008)

Somek A, 'The Argument from Transnational Effects I: Representing Outsiders through Freedom of Movement' (2010) 16 European Law Journal 315

Somek A, 'The Argument from Transnational Effects II: Establishing Transnational Democracy' (2010) 16 European Law Journal 375

Somers MR, *Genealogies of Citizenship. Markets, Statelessness, and the Right to Have Rights* (Cambridge University Press 2008)

Spaak P-H, Address to the ECSC Common Assembly (Strasbourg, 13 March 1956) <http://www.cvce.eu/content/publication/1999/1/1/3d626775-5b70-49b8-b0ca-c4c9c22cb02b/publishable_en.pdf> accessed 6 October 2015

Spaventa E, 'From *Gebhard* to *Carpenter*. Towards a (Non-) Economic European Constitution' (2004) 41 Common Market Law Review 743

Spaventa E, 'Leaving *Keck* Behind? The Free Movement of Goods after the Rulings in *Commission v Italy* and *Mickelsson and Roos*' (2009) 34 European Law Review 914

Spinelli A, 'The American Constitutional Model and Attempts at European Unification' (first published 1957, 2005) 47 The Federalist 115 <http://www.thefederalist.eu/site/files/PDF/EN/2000/2005-2-EN.pdf> accessed 8 October 2015

Spinelli A and Rossi E, 'The Manifesto of Ventotene for a Free and United Europe' (1941) <http://www.cvce.eu/obj/the_manifesto_of_ventotene_1941-en-316aa96c-e7ff-4b9e-b43a-958e96afbecc.html> accessed 6 October 2015

Stanton EC and Mott L, 'The Seneca Falls Declaration of Sentiments' [1848] reproduced in *History of Woman Suffrage*, vol I (Fowler & Wells 1881)

Stein E, 'Lawyers, Judges, and the Making of a Transnational Constitution' (1981) 75 American Journal of International Law 1

Stepan A, 'Federalism and Democracy: Beyond the US Model' (1999) 1c Journal of Democracy 19

Stolleis M, *A History of Public Law in Germany 1914–1945* (Dunlap T tr, Oxford University Press 2004)

Stolleis M, *Geschichte des Öffentlichen Rechts in Deutschland 1945–1990* (C.H. Beck 2012)

Stone Sweet A, *Governing with Judges: Constitutional Politics in Europe* (Oxford University Press 2000)

Stone Sweet A, *The Judicial Construction of Europe* (Oxford University Press 2004)

Stone Sweet A, 'Constitutionalism, Legal Pluralism, and International Regimes' (2009) 16 Indiana Journal of Global Legal Studies 621

Stone Sweet A, 'Investor-State Arbitration: Proportionality's New Frontier' (2010) 4 Law and Ethics of Human Rights 48

Stone Sweet A and Keller H, *Assessing the Impact of the ECHR on National Legal Systems* (Oxford University Press 2008)

Stone Sweet A, Sandholtz W, and Fligstein N (eds), *The Institutionalization of Europe* (Oxford University Press 2001)

Stourzh G, '*Constitution*: Changing Meanings of the Term from the Early Seventeenth to the Late Eighteenth Century' in Ball T and Pocock JGA (eds), *Conceptual Change and the Constitution* (University Press of Kansas 1988)

Streeck W, 'Competitive Solidarity: Rethinking the "European Social Model"' in Hinrichs K, Kitschelt H, and Wiesenthal H (eds), *Kontingenz und Krise: Institutionenpolitik in kapitalistischen und postsozialistischen Gesellschaften. Claus Offe zu seinem 60. Geburstag* (Campus 2000)

Streeck W, 'Citizenship under Regime Competition' in Eder K and Giesen B (eds), *European Citizenship Between National Legacies and Postnational Projects* (Oxford University Press 2001)

Streeck W, *Buying Time. The Delayed Crisis of Democratic Capitalism* (Camiller P tr, Verso 2014)

Tamir Y, *Liberal Nationalism* (Princeton University Press 1995)

Teitel R, 'Comparative Constitutional Law in a Global Age' (2004) 117 Harvard Law Review 2570

Teubner G, *Constitutional Fragments: Societal Constitutionalism and Globalization* (Oxford University Press 2012)

de Tocqueville A, *Democracy in America* (first published 1840, Mansfield HC and Winthrop D trs and eds, University of Chicago Press 2000)

Tribe LH, 'The Puzzling Persistence of Process-based Constitutional Theories' (1980) 89 Yale Law Journal 1063

Tryfonidou A, 'Reverse Discrimination in Purely Internal Situations: An Incongruity in a Citizens' Europe' (2008) 35 Legal Issues of Economic Integration 43

Tryfonidou A, 'Case Note: (Further) Signs of a Turn of the Tide in the CJEU's Citizenship Jurisprudence' (2013) 14 Maastricht Journal 302

Tsakatika M, 'Governance vs Politics: The European Union's Constitutive "Democratic Deficit"' (2007) 14 Journal of European Public Policy 867

Tully J, *Strange Multiplicity: Constitutionalism in an Age of Diversity* (Cambridge University Press 1995)

Tully J, 'The Unfreedom of the Moderns in Comparison to their Ideals of Constitutional Democracy' (2002) 65 The Modern Law Review 204

Tully J, *On Global Citizenship: James Tully in Dialogue* (Bloomsbury 2014)

Tushnet M, 'The Possibilities of Comparative Constitutional Law' (1999) 108 Yale Law Journal 1125

Urbinati N, *Representative Democracy. Principles & Genealogy* (University of Chicago Press 2006)

Urbinati N, 'Competing for Liberty: The Republican Critique of Democracy' (2012) 106 American Political Science Review 607

Urbinati N, *Democracy Disfigured* (Harvard University Press 2014)

Vasileva K, 'Nearly Two-thirds of the Foreigners Living in EU Member States are Citizens of Countries Outside the EU-27' (2012) Eurostat Statistics in Focus No 31/2012, 2 <http://ec.europa.eu/eurostat/documents/3433488/5584984/KS-SF-12-031-EN.PDF/be48f08f-41c1-4748-a8a5-5d92ebe848f2> accessed 29 November 2015

Viroli M, *Republicanism* (Hill and Wang 2002)

Voigt S, 'Positive Constitutional Economics: A Survey' (1997) 90 Public Policy 205

Walker N, 'The Idea of Constitutional Pluralism' (2002) 65 Modern Law Review 317

Walker N, 'Postnational Constitutionalism and the Problem of Translation' in Weiler J and Wind M (eds), *European Constitutionalism Beyond the State* (Cambridge University Press 2003)

Walker N, 'The Legacy of Europe's Constitutional Moment' (2004) 11 Constellations 368

Walker N, 'Beyond Boundary Disputes and Basic Grids: Mapping the Global Disorder of Normative Orders' (2008) 6 International Journal of Constitutional Law 373

Walker N, 'Beyond the Holistic Constitution?' in Dobner P and Loughlin M (eds), *The Twilight of Constitutionalism* (Oxford University Press 2010)

Waltz K, *Theory of International Politics* (McGraw-Hill 1979)

Weiler JHH, 'The Community System: The Dual Character of Supranationalism' (1981) 1 Yearbook of European Law 268

Weiler JHH, 'Eurocracy and Distrust: Some Questions Concerning the Role of the European Court of Justice in the Protection of Fundamental Human Rights within the Legal Order of the European Communities' (1986) 61 Washington Law Review 1103

Weiler JHH, 'The Transformation of Europe' (1991) 100 Yale Law Journal 2403

Weiler JHH, 'European Neo-constitutionalism: In Search of Foundations for the European Constitutional Order' (1996) 44 Political Studies 517

Weiler JHH, 'The Reformation of European Constitutionalism' (1997) 35 Journal of Common Market Studies 97

Weiler JHH, *The Constitution of Europe* (Cambridge University Press 1999)

Weiler JHH, 'Epilogue: "Comitology" as Revolution—Infranationalism, Constitutionalism, and Democracy' in Joerges C and Vos E (eds), *EU Committees: Social Regulation, Law and Politics* (Hart Publishing 1999)

Weiler JHH, 'In Defence of the Status Quo: Europe's Constitutional *Sonderweg*' in Weiler JHH and Wind M (eds), *European Constitutionalism Beyond the State* (Cambridge University Press 2003)

Weiler JHH and Lockhart NJS, ' "Taking Rights Seriously" ' Seriously: The European Court and its Fundamental Rights Jurisprudence" Parts I & 2 (1995) 32 Common Market Law Review 61, 579

Weiler JHH, Haltern UR, and Mayer FC, 'European Democracy and its Critique' (1995) 18 West European Politics 4

Whelan FG, 'Democratic Theory and the Boundary Problem' in Pennock JR and Chapman JW (eds), *Nomos XXV: Liberal Democracy* (New York University Press 1983)

White J, 'Europe and the Common' (2010) 58 Political Studies 104

Wiener A, *'European' Citizenship Practice: Building Institutions of a Non-State* (Westview Press 1999)

Wiener A, Lang Jr AF, Tully J, Maduro MP, and Kumm M, 'Global Constitutionalism: Human Rights, Democracy, and the Rule of Law' (2012) 1 Global Constitutionalism 1

Wilkinson MA, 'The Specter of Authoritarian Liberalism: Reflections on the Constitutional Crisis of the European Union' (2013) 14 German Law Journal 527

Wind M, 'Post-National Citizenship in Europe: The EU as a "Welfare Rights Generator"?' (2009) 15 Columbia Journal of European Law 239

Winzen T, 'National Parliamentary Control of EU Affairs: A Cross-country and Longitudinal Comparison' (2012) 35 West European Politics 657

Young IM, *Justice and the Politics of Difference* (Princeton University Press 1990)

Zürn M, 'Globalizing Interests: An Introduction' in Zürn M and Walter G (eds), *Globalizing Interests. Pressure Groups and Denationalization* (SUNY Press 2005)

Index

The manufacturer's authorised representative in the EU for product safety is Oxford University Press España S.A. of El Parque Empresarial San Fernando de Henares, Avenida de Castilla, 2 - 28830 Madrid (www.oup.es/en or product.safety@oup.com). OUP España S.A. also acts as importer into Spain of products made by the manufacturer.
Printed and bound by CPI Group (UK) Ltd, Croydon, CR0 4YY
14/09/2026
02216305-0009